T0295905

Quantitative Finance and Economics

Quantitative Finance and Economics

Edited by Douglas Walsh

www.statesacademicpress.com

States Academic Press,
109 South 5th Street,
Brooklyn, NY 11249, USA

Visit us on the World Wide Web at:
www.statesacademicpress.com

ISBN: 978-1-63989-739-1

Cataloging-in-Publication Data

Quantitative finance and economics / edited by Douglas Walsh.
p. cm.
Includes bibliographical references and index.
ISBN 978-1-63989-739-1
1. Finance--Mathematical models. 2. Economics, Mathematical. 3. Investments--Mathematics.
3. Business mathematics. 4. Economics--Mathematical models. I. Walsh, Douglas.
HG106 .Q36 2023
332.015 195--dc23

Table of Contents

Preface... VII

Chapter 1   **LIBOR Fallback and Quantitative Finance**.. 1
Marc Pierre Henrard

Chapter 2   **Machine Learning for Quantitative Finance Applications: A Survey**........................ 16
Francesco Rundo, Francesca Trenta, Agatino Luigi di Stallo and Sebastiano Battiato

Chapter 3   **On the Relationship of Cryptocurrency Price with US Stock and
Gold Price using Copula Models**... 36
Jong-Min Kim, Seong-Tae Kim and Sangjin Kim

Chapter 4   **The Net Worth Trap: Investment and Output Dynamics in
the Presence of Financing Constraints**.. 51
Jukka Isohätälä, Alistair Milne and Donald Robertson

Chapter 5   **Some Notes on the Formation of a Pair in Pairs Trading**... 82
José Pedro Ramos-Requena, Juan Evangelista Trinidad-Segovia and
Miguel Ángel Sánchez-Granero

Chapter 6   **Detection of Near-Multicollinearity through Centered and
Noncentered Regression**.. 99
Román Salmerón Gómez, Catalina García García and José García Pérez

Chapter 7   **Do Trade and Investment Agreements Promote Foreign Direct
Investment within Latin America? Evidence from a Structural Gravity Model**....... 116
Marta Bengoa, Blanca Sanchez-Robles and Yochanan Shachmurove

Chapter 8   **The VIF and MSE in Raise Regression**... 148
Román Salmerón Gómez, Ainara Rodríguez Sánchez,
Catalina García García and José García Pérez

Chapter 9   **Deep Learning Methods for Modeling Bitcoin Price**... 176
Prosper Lamothe-Fernández, David Alaminos, Prosper Lamothe-López and
Manuel A. Fernández-Gámez

Chapter 10   **Market Volatility of the Three Most Powerful Military Countries during
their Intervention in the Syrian War**.. 189
Viviane Naimy, José-María Montero, Rim El Khoury and Nisrine Maalouf

Chapter 11   **Dispersion Trading Based on the Explanatory Power of S&P 500 Stock Returns**.................................. 210
Lucas Schneider and Johannes Stübinger

Permissions

List of Contributors

Index

Preface

Quantitative finance is the study of financial markets and securities by using mathematical models and very huge datasets. It draws concepts from mathematics, finance, statistics, and programming. Quantitative finance allows for the creation of financial models that can be utilized for pricing a variety of financial assets such as financial derivatives products. Quantitative economics is an area of study that involves the application of tools from computer science and mathematical sciences such as stochastic models, algorithms, statistics, numerical analysis, possibility theory, and optimization theory, for effectively modeling different economic situations. It involves the study of the use of resources for the manufacture, supply and consumption of goods and services. The study of quantitative economics focuses on the quantifiable features of financial systems. This book explores all the important aspects of quantitative finance and economics in the present day scenario. It elucidates new techniques and their applications in a multidisciplinary manner. This book will serve as a reference to a broad spectrum of readers.

The information contained in this book is the result of intensive hard work done by researchers in this field. All due efforts have been made to make this book serve as a complete guiding source for students and researchers. The topics in this book have been comprehensively explained to help readers understand the growing trends in the field.

I would like to thank the entire group of writers who made sincere efforts in this book and my family who supported me in my efforts of working on this book. I take this opportunity to thank all those who have been a guiding force throughout my life.

Editor

LIBOR Fallback and Quantitative Finance

Marc Pierre Henrard [1,2]

[1] muRisQ Advisory, 8B-1210 Brussels, Belgium; marc.henrard@murisq.com
[2] University College London, London WC1E 6BT, UK

Abstract: With the expected discontinuation of the LIBOR publication, a robust fallback for related financial instruments is paramount. In recent months, several consultations have taken place on the subject. The results of the first ISDA consultation have been published in November 2018 and a new one just finished at the time of writing. This note describes issues associated to the proposed approaches and potential alternative approaches in the framework and the context of quantitative finance. It evidences a clear *lack of details* and *lack of measurability* of the proposed approaches which would not be achievable in practice. It also describes the potential of asymmetrical information between market participants coming from the *adjustment spread* computation. In the opinion of this author, a fundamental revision of the fallback's foundations is required.

Keywords: LIBOR fallback; derivative pricing; multi-curve framework; collateral; pay-off measurability; value transfer; ISDA consultations

1. Introduction

Since their creation in 1986, LIBOR benchmarks[1] have grown in importance to the point of being called in finance newspapers *the most important number in the world*. This was the case up to July 2017, when Bailey (2017), the CEO of the U.K. Financial Conduct Authority (FCA), indicated in a speech that there is an increased expectation that some LIBOR benchmarks will be discontinued in a not too distant future. The discontinuation of such benchmarks is in large part related to the decrease of importance of unsecured interbank lending, on which LIBOR benchmarks are based, since the financial crisis and to a lesser extent to the scandals that have plagued them.

The discontinuation of such benchmarks, which have been at the centre of the derivative market for so long and which support derivatives with notional in the hundreds of trillions USD, is a major challenge for the market. The market participants have to find new ways to express their views on and hedge interest rates but also to devise a mechanism to transition the existing trades to a new world without LIBOR. The term *fallback* is associated to the latter issue. The fallback's challenge is first and foremost a legal challenge as LIBOR is engraved in many legal contracts. Unfortunately, the way LIBOR has been referenced in those contracts, some of them with a maturity beyond 50 years, is not robust in the case of discontinuation of the number's publication. That weakness is now widely recognised by those who wrote and signed those contracts.

The legal wording has to be updated in order not to rely on numbers that may stop to exist soon. This includes changes to the wording for new contracts to avoid problems in the future and repapering existing contracts that have a maturity beyond the expected LIBOR's discontinuation date. All that

---

[1] We use the term LIBOR to designate benchmarks related to interbank lending. Sensu stricto, the term LIBOR is restricted to the benchmarks administered by IBA and fixing in London. By abuse of language, we extend it in this note to other similar benchmarks such as EURIBOR, TIBOR, BBSW, etc.

must be realised within the constraints and a timeframe imposed by new regulations, in particular the European Benchmark Regulation.

This is certainly a legal challenge that has to be solved first by legal means. ISDA®, the association which publishes the *ISDA Master Agreement* used by most financial institutions, has issued two consultations on the subject: ISDA (2018b) and ISDA (2019). However, a legal challenge does not mean that it can be solved by pure rewording without taking the underlying reality of the derivative's market into consideration. There are constraints on the way the contracts can be drafted and amended imposed by the financial reality that those contracts represent.

In this note, we review those constraints in the framework and with the language of quantitative finance. Those constraints, imposed by the physical world, seem to have been neglected by people in charge of the legal aspects. Writing the constraints in term of quantitative finance is, to this author's point of view, the easiest way to express the requirements in a clear language. Even if it may require an understanding of that language, far from obfuscating the requirements, it makes them explicit and accessible to all. We do not use a specific model to quantify the impacts of the discontinuation. We use the language of quantitative finance and option pricing in a model-free way, based only on the foundations of option pricing. We found that the proposed solution lacks the basic requirement of achievability for some products and potentially introduces an asymmetry of information between market participants. In some sense, this note is late in the process; such a fundamental analysis should have been published together with the first version of the consultations.

Many documents cover the LIBOR transition and fallback from an overview perspective, e.g., Schrimpf and Sushko (2019) published in a recent BIS quarterly review. Most of them are from a management consulting perspective and review the organisational steps and are not directly relevant for this analysis. Others, such as Duffie (2018) and Zhu (2019), look at how to reduce the exposure to LIBOR before the fallback. In this author's opinion, this should be the goal of financial institutions. However, even if the exposure to LIBOR is eliminated before the discontinuation date, this technical note is still important as the details of the fallback are relevant to estimate the present value of the instruments to be terminated and to analyse the transfer of value created by the new rules. In a third direction of developments, specific models have been proposed to deal with the instruments resulting from the fallback, subject to the proposal being achievable, such as Lyashenko and Mercurio (2019). To our knowledge, no other document analyses the fallback options from a quantitative finance perspective, except preliminary notes by this author, e.g., Henrard (2019b).

This note contains facts and opinions. The facts have been described as precisely as possible. The opinions refer to what could have been done to obtain a more robust consultation process and the obstacle still existing to reach an achievable solution.

The main objective of this note is not to impose a specific solution but to review constraints on acceptable solutions. To obtain a realistic achievable solution, one has to accept to discuss the problem full complexity, its constraints and review all the potential solutions. If this note helps in clarifying the open questions before a practical solution can be reached, it will have achieved its main objective.

2. Fallback, Notations and Vanilla Products

The fallback associated to LIBOR derivatives is the wording in the financial contracts, typically master agreements, that indicates what happens if a LIBOR fixing is not published. The fallback is potentially specific to each contract and should not be confused with the waterfall approach used to determine the LIBOR fixing itself.

To understand the intricacies of a fallback process applied to LIBOR derivatives, we have to start with the detailed description of LIBOR and of some related interest rate instruments and in particular of the dates involved. We look at the details of a vanilla LIBOR coupon, a Forward Rate Agreement (FRA) and an Overnight Indexed Swap (OIS). We use those examples as typical representatives of interest rate derivatives; we could have selected other products and present similar arguments. More complex products, such as caps/floors, would potentially generate more complex issues, including the transformation of European options into Asian options; they are not the focus of this note. When examples are proposed, the USD-LIBOR-3M benchmark is used, but most of the material applies also to other tenors and similar benchmarks such as EUR-EURIBOR, GBP-LIBOR or CHF-LIBOR.

The terminology and notations of this note are the one used in Henrard (2014) where the standard pricing framework for derivatives under collateral is presented. A LIBOR fixing itself is characterised by three dates. The three dates are the fixing date θ, the effective date of the underlying deposit σ and the maturity date of the same deposit τ (we use Greek letters for the underlying deposit and later Latin letters for the derivatives). The fixing date is the one used to index the series of numbers in a time series and for LIBOR is also the figure's publication date. The effective date is typically two business days after the fixing and the maturity date is a given term after the effective date, typically a one-, three- or six-month term. The effective and maturity dates are adjusted to fall on good business dates in their respective financial centre. The effective and maturity dates are used by banks contributing data to the benchmark's administrator to estimate the contributed rate but are not used directly in the payoff's computation.

A vanilla LIBOR coupon referencing a LIBOR fixing is characterised by four dates: the fixing date θ, the coupon accrual start date u, the coupon accrual end date v and the payment date w. The LIBOR fixing date is the same for the fixing and the coupon and is the link between them. For vanilla coupons, the start accrual date is equal to the underlying deposit effective date, i.e., $\sigma = u$. Some swaps coupons, in particular with corporates, have an effective date delayed by a couple of days. For the deposit maturity date and the coupon end accrual date, one would like to say that they are also the same, but this is not always the case due to non-good business days adjustments. The coupons accrual dates are separated by a regular periods, e.g., three months, with each date in the list adjusted for non-good business days. When the start date of an accrual period is adjusted but the end date is adjusted by fewer days, the accrual period does not have a length equal to the theoretical period but a slightly shorter one. On the other side, the dates for the deposit underlying LIBOR are computed for each fixing separately, taking only into account the relevant start date and end date of the theoretical period, and not the adjustment done on the derivative. This can be described by "LIBOR means LIBOR" and LIBOR is not influenced by where it is used. In practice, the end accrual date and theoretical maturity dates coincide ($v = \tau$) except when a non-good business day intervenes. This non-coincidence appears roughly for two coupons out of seven (Saturdays and Sundays are non-good business days) where there is one day difference and $v = (\tau$ minus one business day). The payment is done at the end of the accrual period in $w = v$. The LIBOR fixing figure, which we denote $I^j(\theta)$, is known in θ, and the amount, which consists of the rate multiplied by the accrual factor, denoted as δ, is paid only in $w = v$. The different dates are represented in Figure 1.

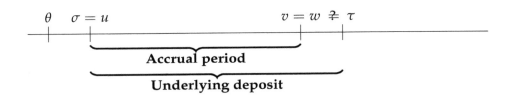

Figure 1. Representation of the dates associated to a LIBOR fixing and a LIBOR coupon in a vanilla IRS.

The option pricing in continuous time using the equivalent martingale measure approach provides a generic method to price contingent claims. The technical details of the approach can be found for example in (Hunt and Kennedy 2004, Corollary 7.34) for the underlying mathematics and in (Henrard 2014, Theorem 8.1) for the application in presence of collateral.

We apply the generic pricing approach to contingent claims referencing a LIBOR rate $I^j(\theta)$ fixed in θ and paid in w. Note that the fixing $I^j(\theta)$ is $\mathcal{F}_\theta$-measurable, even if paid only in $w \geq \theta$.

Theorem 1. *In a economy satisfying the standard conditions (see Hunt and Kennedy 2004), the present value of a contingent claim with payoff $f(I^j(\theta))$ in w is given in $s < \theta$ by*

$$N_s^c \, \mathrm{E}^{\mathbb{X}} \left[(N_w^c)^{-1} f(I^j(\theta)) \,\middle|\, \mathcal{F}_s \right] \tag{1}$$

where N_s^c is the collateral cash-account, $\mathbb{X}$ is the market-price-of-risk-adjusted (or risk-neutral) measure and $\mathcal{F}_s$ is the filtration representing the information available in s.

For a LIBOR coupon as described above, the valuation formula gives

$$N_s^c \, \mathrm{E}^{\mathbb{X}} \left[(N_w^c)^{-1} \delta I^j(\theta) \,\middle|\, \mathcal{F}_s \right]. \tag{2}$$

A FRA presents a picture similar to vanilla coupons in term of dates, except that the payment takes place in u (not in v) and the amount paid is adjusted by a discounting-like formula. For a fixed rate K, the amount paid in u is

$$\frac{\delta(I^j(\theta) - K)}{1 + \delta I^j(\theta)}.$$

Note that the formula above is not a valuation/modelling choice but part of the term sheet, the legal contract signed by the parties. The different dates associated with a FRA are represented in Figure 2.

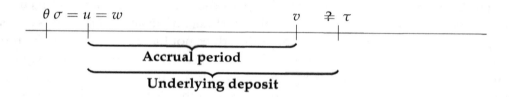

Figure 2. Representation of the dates associated to a LIBOR fixing and a FRA instrument.

The value of s is given in the standard option valuation framework by

$$N_s^c \, \mathrm{E}^{\mathbb{X}} \left[(N_u^c)^{-1} \frac{\delta(I^j(\theta) - K)}{1 + \delta I^j(\theta)} \,\middle|\, \mathcal{F}_s \right].$$

The FRAs are only one example of instruments with a similar date pattern where the payment takes place in σ, the deposit effective date, and not in τ, the maturity date. Other instruments include LIBOR-in-arrears and some exotics products such as range accruals. We emphasise that the payment date occurs in σ, which is several months before τ. As the fixing rate $I^j(\theta)$ is $\mathcal{F}_\theta$-measurable with $\theta \le \sigma$, the current FRA term sheets do not have a measurability problem. The $\mathcal{F}_\theta$-measurability of $I^j(\theta)$ allows instruments referencing them to use that information at any date on or after θ. Many instrument's term sheets use that flexibility and it seems natural that any replacement of I^j for exiting contracts should respect that feature.

The LIBOR-like benchmarks are currently the most important benchmarks in the interest rate derivative markets, but there exists another type of benchmarks that takes more and more importance and that is expected to replace the LIBOR benchmarks to some extent; they are the overnight benchmarks.

The overnight benchmarks are similar to LIBOR benchmarks in the sense that they measure some level of interest rate on a given deposit term. The main difference is that for overnight benchmarks the term is reduced to a single night; the rate is for a deposit from today to the next good business day.

Associated to those overnight benchmarks is a type of derivatives called Overnight Indexed Swaps (OIS). The floating coupons of those instruments are not paid on a daily basis, even if the underlying benchmark is for a single day. The rates are accumulated by composition and paid after a certain term. If we denote by $(t_i)_{i=0,\cdots,n}$ a set of $n+1$-consecutive business days, representing n one-day periods and $I^0(t_i)$ the overnight fixing for the period $[t_i, t_{i+1}]$ and δ_i^O the associated accrual factors, the amount paid on an OIS floating coupon (for a notional of 1) is the composition

$$\mathrm{Cmp}(I^O, (t_i)_{i=0,\cdots,n}) = \prod_{i=0}^{n-1} \left(1 + \delta_i^O I^O(t_i)\right) - 1. \tag{3}$$

The payment takes place in p which is usually one or two good-business days after the last day of the period t_n. This lag is required for a smooth settlement of the amount paid. The representation of the dates is proposed in Figure 3.

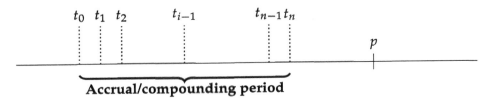

Figure 3. Representation of the dates associated to an OIS.

3. Fallback and Expected Value

The valuation formula (Equation (1)) is written as if the LIBOR benchmark $I^j(\theta)$ were always published in θ and thus available for payment in w. The current expectation, described in the Introduction, is that the benchmark may stop being published at some stage. We denote the announcement date of the discontinuation by a and the discontinuation date itself by d. Those dates are still unknown and can be modelled with stopping times. If a discontinuation were to take place, in today's legal wording of the contract, there is no guarantee that something meaningful would replace the LIBOR figure. The actual valuation formula should be

$$N_s^c \mathrm{E}^{\mathbb{X}} \left[(N_w^c)^{-1} f \left(\mathbb{1}\{d > \theta\} I^j(\theta) + \mathbb{1}\{d \le \theta\}? \right) \Big| \mathcal{F}_s \right]. \tag{4}$$

The question mark in the formula is not a typo, it is really an uncertainty related to the legal framework in the case of cessation of the LIBOR and the actual cash flow in that state of the universe would be highly uncertain.

Industry groups have gathered to find a practical way to replace that question mark by something manageable. Most of the derivative market is governed by ISDA master agreements or by CCP rule books inspired by it. ISDA (2018b) has launched a consultation on ways to amend the master agreements from July to October 2018 and the preliminary results of the consultation have been published on 27 November 2018 and later detailed in ISDA (2018a). This initial consultation was covering a limited number of currencies (AUD, CHF, GBP, and JPY). Another consultation ISDA (2019) took place from May to July 2019, mainly related to USD and its preliminary results have been published on 30 July 2019, while the full results have not been published yet at the time of writing. To some extent, what will be decided by the ISDA Benchmark Committee will become the de facto standard for the derivative market.

The general idea of the fallback would be to substitute the LIBOR fixing in the derivatives by a new quantity obtained as the sum of an *adjusted RFR* and an *adjustment spread*. The former would play the role of the floating rate; it would depend on an overnight benchmark and be known around the date θ where LIBOR should have been fixed (the precise rules are described below). The latter, the *adjustment spread*, would be decided when the discontinuation is announced and be seen as an adjustment to avoid value transfer between the original LIBOR fixing and the new fixing mechanism. The new pricing formula becomes

$$N_s^c \, \mathbb{E}^{\mathbb{X}} \left[(N_w^c)^{-1} f \left(\mathbb{1}\{d > \theta\} I^j(\theta) + \mathbb{1}\{d \leq \theta\} (\mathrm{FR}^j(\theta) + S(X, [a - l, a])) \right) \Big| \mathcal{F}_s \right]. \qquad (5)$$

The quantity $\mathrm{FR}^j(\theta)$ is the *adjusted RFR* that replaces $I^j(\theta)$; we use a notation with the date θ to indicate that the figure is associated to the original one fixed in θ but it should not be interpreted as being $\mathcal{F}_\theta$-measurable. We show below that, in the main ISDA proposal, it is actually not $\mathcal{F}_\theta$-measurable.

The spread S will be based on some historical mean or median. The notation for the spread $S(X, [a - l, a])$ contains two types of indications. The X and the length l represents a set of parameters that still have to be decided by the ISDA Benchmark Committee. Those parameters are not related to the derivatives themselves or the interest rate market; they are contractual descriptions such as the choice between mean and median, a potential trimming of the values and transitional period. To some extent, the contracts have been signed already by the market participants but some terms still have to be decided by the Committee. The spread will be fully known on the announcement date and will depend on historical data from a certain look back period l—which could be a 10-year period or another period to be decided—before the announcement. We have represented that period by the time interval $[a - l, a]$.

4. Adjusted RFR

The ISDA proposal for the adjusted RFR is to use a *compounding setting in arrears* approach. The composition is given by

$$\mathrm{FR}^j(\theta) = \mathrm{Cmp}(I^O, (t_i)_{i=0,\cdots,n}). \qquad (6)$$

The proposal sounds reasonable as it would replace a quantity that would no longer exist ($I^j(\theta)$) by an accumulation of elements that still exists ($I^O(t_i)$) using an accumulation mechanism (composition) familiar in the derivative market and natural for interest rates. Unfortunately, the proposal suffers major flaws that can be summarised as *lack of details* and *lack of measurability*[2]. The flaws described here are related only to the fallback procedure, not for new trades referencing directly the overnight benchmarks. For new trades, one can make sure that the term sheet has all the required details and that the dates are compatible.

In Equation (6), what would be the dates t_0 and t_n with respect to the dates θ, σ, τ, u, v and w described in Section 2? As the adjusted RFR is a replacement of LIBOR, it should be based only on LIBOR related dates and not on the derivative specific dates. The most natural ones would be that θ, the fixing date, is completely ignored and the overnight composition is done on the theoretical deposit period of the LIBOR, with $t_0 = \sigma$ and $t_n = \tau$. In this way, all the occurrences of LIBOR are replaced with the same figure. Even if this is natural, this precision is not given in the ISDA documents—neither in the consultation document, nor in the document describing the results. The reason of the absence of the precision can probably be seen in Figures 1 and 2. The payment date w is, in many cases, before the end of the theoretical deposit in τ. The minimal requirement is that the amount paid is known when paid, i.e., that $\mathrm{FR}^j(\theta)$ is $\mathcal{F}_w$-measurable. This requirement is not satisfied with the natural choice of dates described above. The measurability requirement may appear as a technical term of no practical importance, but it is not; it is only the precise description of a very practical requirement that before you are able to pay an amount, you need to know what amount should be paid.

A less natural approach to the date's choice would be to use $t_0 = u$ and $t_n = v$. This is less natural as such an approach would lack coherence. The same LIBOR figure would be replaced by different numbers, depending on where it is used. Moreover, even with the second approach, the issue of the upfront payment, as in the FRA case, could not be solved. In that case, the payment is done in u before

---

[2] Thanks to Andrea Macrina for pointing this way to describe the *measurability* problem.

any information about the composition figure is known. Without precise dates, the proposal cannot be implemented and when precise dates are used, it appears that the proposal is simply *not achievable*.

Several workarounds have been proposed unofficially to deal with this fundamental flaw. They include changing the term sheet of FRA to bring the payment to the end date v. It would solve the FRA problem in the most favourable case ($v = \tau$) but not the one of other products with a similar payment schedule like LIBOR in-arrears. Other proposed mechanisms include a "cut-off" period at the end of the composition, where a couple of days before the end date τ, the same rate would be used for a couple of days (k days) and the payment formula would become

$$\prod_{i=0}^{n-k} \left(1 + \delta_i^O I^0(t_i)\right) \prod_{i=n-k+1}^{n-1} \left(1 + \delta_i^O I^0(t_{n-k+1})\right) - 1 \tag{7}$$

with $t_0 = \sigma$ and $t_n = \tau$. This may solve the measurability question when there is only a couple of days discrepancy but would introduce significant valuation and risk management issues, e.g., curve intra-month seasonality and convexity adjustments. This does not appear to be a reasonable workaround.

Those issues have been publicly (e.g., Henrard 2019a) and privately mentioned and have been debated in industry magazine (e.g., Sherif 2019a, 2019b) and public podcast.[3] This is not simply an oversight of some trivial details, but a fundamental flaw in the proposal that has been exposed for a while and for which an answer is still missing. ISDA has indicated that the exact wording of the fallback will be published for consultation in 2019 and with a target implementation in 2020. Given the lack of attention to details in previous documents and the lack of answer to precise information requests, in the opinion of this author, it is doubtful that a satisfactory solution will be provided.

On the other side, a potential robust solution to the adjusted RFR rate in the fallback has been proposed by different working groups and this author. The solution is based on an *OIS benchmark*, also called *forward-looking rate* or *term RFR*. The solution has the favour of the majority of the market participants, when offered the possibility to chose it. On the EUR side, this was in particular the result of a recent consultation organised by the Working Group EUR Risk-free Rates (2019). On the GBP side, a recent statement of the Working Group on Sterling Risk-Free Reference Rates published on the Bank of England website indicated that *"the RFRWG also supports work currently underway to develop a term benchmark based on the sterling risk-free rate"*. This solution was surprisingly not included in the ISDA consultation. A recent letter by the same institution to the FSB[4] appears to warn participants with harsh (and possibly unwarranted) words against this solution. At this stage, this new benchmark does not exist and one has to be prudent not to recreate the issue we are trying to escape from. The inclusion of term rate could be done through a waterfall fallback as the one recommended by ARRC working groups for FRN[5], securitisation and business loans with the term rate the waterfall's first step. This single step is not a panacea, but to obtain a realistic solution, one has to accept to discuss the problem's full complexity, its constraints and review all the potential solutions.

The alternative solution is based on forward looking OIS rates. On the fixing date θ, the fair fixed rate for an OIS with effective date $t_0 = \sigma$ and maturity date $t_n = \tau$ is measured. The adjusted RFR would be that OIS rate, i.e.,

$$\mathrm{FR}^j(\theta) = \frac{N_\theta^c \, \mathrm{E}^{\mathbb{X}}\left[(N_p^c)^{-1} \left(\prod_{i=0}^{n-1} \left(1 + \delta_i^O I^O(t_i)\right) - 1\right) \Big| \mathcal{F}_\theta \right]}{\delta P^c(\theta, p)}. \tag{8}$$

---

3   See https://www.risk.net/derivatives/6495206/podcast-mercurio-and-henrard-on-libor-transition-and-the-need-to-involve-quants-early-in-discussions.

4   Letter available at https://www.isda.org/a/Y6SME/April-2019-Letter-to-FSB-OSSG.pdf.

5   Document available at https://www.newyorkfed.org/medialibrary/Microsites/arrc/files/2019/FRN_Fallback_Language.pdf.

This is a forward-looking or market expectation view of the same composition quantity used in the officially proposed method. If we ignore the difference between the maturity date τ and the payment date p, the value of the rate can be computed simply from (pseudo-)discount factors by

$$\mathrm{FR}^j(\theta) = \frac{1}{\delta}\left(\frac{P^c(\theta,\sigma)}{P^c(\theta,\tau)} - 1\right) \tag{9}$$

as proved in (Henrard 2014, Section 8.3.3). The impact of the payment in p instead of τ on the rate was proved to be negligible in practice in Henrard (2004).

Those instruments are fairly liquid in the market and the numbers above are quoted continuously on Swap Execution Facilities (SEF) and Multilateral Trading Facilities (MTF). To incorporate this approach in practice, one would need to discuss the difference between the end accrual date τ and the OIS payment date p (and adjust or not for it). However, in general, this approach is well-defined with the measurability of $\mathrm{FR}^j(\theta)$ the same as the one of $I^j(\theta)$—both are $\mathcal{F}_\theta$-measurable—and the mechanism from which the number is obtained is very familiar to the derivative market (OIS fair rate).

The solution has clear advantages and the support of a large part of market participants. Its main disadvantage is that such a benchmark does not exist yet. However, similar benchmarks, such as the ICE Swap rate [6], are widely used and there is a general consensus that such an OIS benchmark would be viable, including by A. Bailey as reported in Rega-Jones (2019).

Note that, when both approaches—the *compounded setting in arrears* and the *forward looking term rate*—are achievable in practice, the valuation and risk management of both approaches before the fixing date θ are the same. It is only after the fixing date that the approaches differ; the OIS benchmark is achievable, has the same measurability and has a similar risk profile to the one of the original LIBOR coupon while the compounded setting in-arrears may not be achievable and generate a significantly different risk profile.

We prove that the two approaches are equivalent in valuation terms before the fixing date θ.

Theorem 2. *The prices of a overnight linked coupon with compounding setting in-arrear or a standard coupon fixing on the OIS benchmark are equal before the fixing date θ of the OIS benchmark:*

$$\mathrm{E}^{\mathbb{X}}\left[(N_\tau^c)^{-1}\delta\mathrm{FR}^j(\theta)\right] = \mathrm{E}^{\mathbb{X}}\left[(N_\tau^c)^{-1}\left(\prod_{i=0}^{n-1}\left(1 + \delta_i I^O(t_i)\right) - 1\right)\right] \tag{10}$$

Proof. The present value of the OIS benchmark approach is, using the measure associated to the collateral account,

$$
\begin{aligned}
\mathrm{E}^{\mathbb{X}}\left[(N_\tau^c)^{-1}\delta\mathrm{FR}^j(\theta)\right] &= \mathrm{E}^{\mathbb{X}}\left[(N_\theta^c)^{-1}\delta N_\theta^c\,\mathrm{E}^{\mathbb{X}}\left[(N_\tau^c)^{-1}\delta\mathrm{FR}^j(\theta)\,\middle|\,\mathcal{F}_\theta\right]\right] \\
&= \mathrm{E}^{\mathbb{X}}\left[(N_\theta^c)^{-1}\left(\frac{P^c(\theta,\sigma)}{P^c(\theta,\tau)} - 1\right)P^c(\theta,\tau)\right] \\
&= \mathrm{E}^{\mathbb{X}}\left[(N_\theta^c)^{-1}\left(P^c(\theta,\sigma) - P^c(\theta,\tau)\right)\right] \\
&= P^c(0,\sigma) - P^c(0,\tau)
\end{aligned}
$$

The first equality uses the tower property of conditional expectation. The second equality uses the fact that $\mathrm{FR}^j(\theta)$ is $\mathcal{F}_\theta$-measurable (Equation (9)) for the adjusted RFR and the definition of $P^c(\theta,\tau)$. The last equality uses the martingale property of $P^c(.,x)$.

---

[6] See the administrator website at https://www.theice.com/iba/ice-swap-rate.

The cash flow in the backward-looking option is also paid in $v = \tau$ but based on the composition of the daily rates $I^O(t_i)$ compounded over the period. Today's value of the payment is given by

$$
\begin{aligned}
E^{\mathbb{X}}\left[(N_\tau^c)^{-1}\left(\prod_{i=0}^{n-1}\left(1 + \delta_i I^O(t_i)\right) - 1\right)\right] &= P^c(0,\tau)\left(\frac{P^c(0,\sigma)}{P^c(0,\tau)} - 1\right) \\
&= P^c(0,\sigma) - P^c(0,\tau)
\end{aligned}
$$

The first equality is obtained from (Henrard 2014, Theorem 2.4) and is the pricing of vanilla OIS. The reasoning leading to that result is a little bit long and involves multiple nested conditional expectations and for that reason is not reproduced here; we refer to the above reference for the details. □

5. Adjustment Spread

The adjustment spread is denoted by $S(X, [a - l, a])$. This is to indicate that it depends on methodology parameters X still to be decided and on some market data obtained in the period $[a - l, a]$ preceding the announcement date with l the look back period. In some sense, all the LIBOR derivatives are now path dependent up to the discontinuation's announcement date.

The expected methodology to compute the spread S is based on historical data, and in particular the daily spread (difference) between $I^j(\theta)$ and $\mathrm{Cmp}(I^O, (t_i)_{i=0,\cdots,n})$ with $t_0 = \sigma$ and $t_n = \tau$. Note the already mentioned difference in measurability between $I^j(\theta)$ which is $\mathcal{F}_\theta$-measurable and $\mathrm{Cmp}(I^O, (t_i)_{i=0,\cdots,n})$ which is $\mathcal{F}_{t_{n-1}}$-measurable. The computed spread is coming from a difference in credit riskiness between the two different types of benchmarks but also from a difference between forecasted and realised rates. The spread is more volatile than a simple credit analysis would suggest and embeds unexpected monetary policy actions, as seen recently in the US. Figure 4 displays historical data where this volatility can be observed.

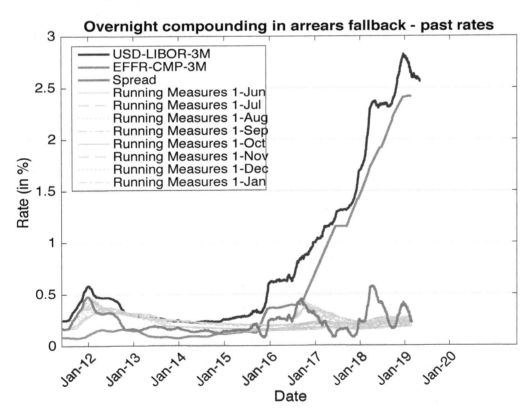

Figure 4. Historical time series for USD-LIBOR-3M and EFFR compounded on three-month periods. Running mean and median are for 5-, 7 -and 10-year look back periods and different announcement dates.

The fallback mechanism includes some market information—in Equation (5), we formally represent the information available by the filtration $\mathcal{F}_s$—but also some information about the methodology as discussed by the Committee members. That information about the discussion is generally not available to the public and is only available to the people privy to the methodology selection process. The existence of those different sets of information is not only a theoretical hypothesis but a fact recognised in practice by ISDA. In a recent letter [7], the association indicates the valuation sensitivity of those parameters and the requirement to hide it from market participants[8].

It means that there are in fact at least two filtrations, the pure financial market one, which we denote $\mathcal{F}_s$, and a second one, containing more information and that we denote from now on by $\mathcal{G}_s$: $\mathcal{F}_s \subset \mathcal{G}_s$. The second filtration contains the information related to the methodology choices. Some people have access to $\mathcal{G}$ and generic market participants only to $\mathcal{F}$. Applying the two filtrations in Equation (5) would generate different prices. It is not clear in general which value will be higher, as the hidden information can lead to lower or higher estimates of the spread. However, better information allows the market participant privy to that information to buy or sell at a better price. This situation can be compared, from an information point of view, to the situation of material non-public information in the securities market.

Note that the expected date for the LIBOR discontinuation is around the end of 2021 and the look back period could be ten years. This would means that from the period $[a - l, a]$, almost 80% of the relevant data—the period [2011, 2019]—is already known. It makes the value of the information in the hidden parameters X even higher.

Equation (5)—and similar formulas writing the present value as an expectation of future cash flows—emphasises one element which appears misunderstood. The changes on the amounts $\mathrm{FR}^j(\theta)$ or $S(X, [a - l, a])$, even if the exact quantities will be known only in a or in w, have already an impact on the present value of the instruments today. There is no need to wait the actual discontinuation in d to feel the changes of value. In the standard valuation framework used in this note, the present value of derivatives is the expectation of the discounted payoff; changing the payoff has an immediate impact on the present value and creates immediate *value transfer*. The value transfer started as soon as the discussions on the changes in the fallback wording started.

Each new information, in $\mathcal{G}_s$ or $\mathcal{F}_s$, has a direct impact on the present value. If one market participant has the information $\mathcal{G}_s$ and acts on it, he will change the market value immediately by his demand or offer. Even if the only information one other participant has is $\mathcal{F}_s$, he will be able to see a discrepancy of value between his estimation of value from $\mathrm{E}^X[\cdot \mid \mathcal{F}_s]$ and the market value partly based on $\mathrm{E}^X[\cdot \mid \mathcal{G}_s]$. It does not provide him the full information contained in $\mathcal{G}_s$ but at least an indication that such an information may exist and be known by other market participants. It is important that a strong governance procedure is in place to avoid the extra information contained in $\mathcal{G}$ to be abused.

This is a situation that some market participants may have felt last November. The market value of some instruments started to deviate significantly from their previous value without new economical information beside the small and natural incoming of incremental information from the passing of time. In a couple of days, we went from $\mathcal{F}_{26 \text{ November } 2018}$ to $\mathcal{F}_{3 \text{ December } 2018}$ with limited important economic news. On the other side, the price of some derivatives linked to LIBOR, in particular the basis spread between LIBOR and OIS, changed dramatically in that couple of days. This could be an indication that a particular discrepancy between $\mathcal{F}_{3 \text{ December } 2018}$ and $\mathcal{G}_{3 \text{ December } 2018}$ had appeared. This change of price is represented in Figure 5. The graph displays the spread of basis

---

[7] Text available at https://www.isda.org/a/Y6SME/April-2019-Letter-to-FSB-OSSG.pdf.
[8] The exact wording is: *ISDA to work with The Brattle Group and other external experts to analyse and perform sensitivity analysis on the "historical mean/median approach" to the spread adjustment (without input from ISDA working groups or market participants during this time period given the sensitivity of the parameters).*

swaps between USD-LIBOR-3M and average EFFR[9]. The spread moved significantly in the days after 26 November 2018 when the results of the consultation were known and the change of spread continued for the several months following that date, always in the same direction. It is only if a new set of information, not related to the economy in general but related to the information contained in the ISDA consultation results, is introduced that the market moves make sense. The graph depicts the market data of the spread—in dark blue thick line—and this author's best guess of what the spread would be based on past data and hints in the ISDA documents. The best guess is based on 48 scenarios (median/mean, eight potential announcement dates and three potential look back periods). For each scenario, a thin line represents the mean/median computed with past data on that date, i.e., it is the information about S available using public information about the methodology. The choice of the historical approach was public only on 26 November 2018, and we reproduce the running average only from that date onward. In some sense, the lines represent the part of $\mathcal{G}$ available to this author on any given date. As the methodology is further clarified in the future, the number of scenarios will decrease and the range of possibilities will narrow.

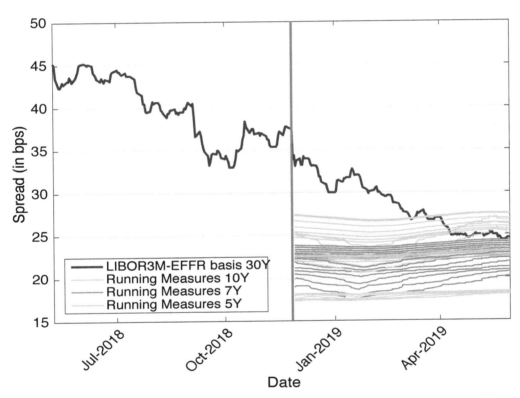

Figure 5. Historical time series for long tenor (30-year) basis swaps USD-LIBOR-3M/EFFR around the ISDA consultation period. The red vertical line is the consultation result date. The different thin lines are the author's estimates using scenarios with different methodologies.

The historical data related to the spread is depicted in Figure 4. A large part of the historical average/median for the 5, 7 or 10 years preceding the potential announcement is already known. The market that was pricing the spread at around 37 basis points for USD-LIBOR-3M/EFFR just before the consultation results—already down from around 45 basis points a couple of months before—has now moved to 25 basis points. It appears that it took roughly three months for the market participants to move their valuation paradigm from $\mathcal{F}$ to $\mathcal{G}$. It is likely that some market participants had access

---

9 The target replacement for USD-LIBOR is SOFR, but the liquidity of SOFR based swaps is currently very limited and it is proxied here with EFFR. The difference in the current market is a couple of basis points.

to the information but did not figure its impact on pricing immediately. Incorporating the extra information from the consultation explains the market move with surprisingly good precision[10]. A brief summary of figures for USD and GBP with three- and six-month tenors is provided in Table 1. All the spreads have move significantly over the last months. The GBP ten-year means are strongly impacted by the 2012 period. We can expect the mean to decrease slightly in the coming months.

Table 1. Spread between the different LIBOR indices and overnight composition. The spreads at the different dates are the market spreads for 30-year tenor basis swaps similar to those reported in Figure 5 for USD-LIBOR-3M. The ranges represent the author's estimates for the different scenarios.

Index	July 2018	November 2018	May 2019	Range
USD-LIBOR-3M	45	38	25	(18–28)
USD-LIBOR-6M	57	50	35	(30–40)
GBP-LIBOR-3M	27	22	17	(10–17)
GBP-LIBOR-6M	33	28	24	(18–32)

Spreads in basis points.

According to the author's data, the standard deviation of the USD-LIBOR-3M/EFFR spread has been divided by 2.5 between the period before November 2018 and the last three months. It is difficult to unentangle the macro-economic situation from instruments specific movements. One cannot prove the origin of those movements, but the joint movements in different currencies and the significant jump on a specific date are presumptions in favour of the explanation provided above. The coming months will show if the spreads stabilise at the expected fallback levels.

Note also that the historical spreads that will be used are between the forward-looking LIBOR and the backward-looking composition on overnight. It includes the past credit spread but also the past misestimations of future monetary policy decisions. If the *adjustment spread* is to obtain a neutral value transfer for the introduction of the fallback, it should be computed between the forward-looking LIBOR and a measure of forward-looking OIS when the fallback is introduced. Viewed from today or from the announcement date, both rates are forward looking and the adjustment spread should be based on forward-looking methodologies. Even if the past is a perfect estimator of the future, it is not clear that the spread methodology proposed is the correct one. The forward-looking OIS versus backward-looking composition can be hedged at zero cost with market swaps and should probably not be included in the spread computation.

6. Options and Hedging

The fallback introduces a new payoff for products currently linked to LIBOR. Some natural questions related to this new payoff type are: Which parts of it can be hedged? What is the dynamic of the different parts of the payoff (I^j, $S(X, [a - l, a])$, d, and $FR^j(\theta)$)? Can we obtain enough information about the implied dynamics from the market?

The easiest part to start with is $FR^j(\theta)$. In both approaches discussed in Section 4, the figure is based on compounding overnight rates. One is setting in arrears and one is forward-looking, but, as proved in Theorem 2, in term of valuation and risk management before the fixing, the two are equivalent. The OIS market exists and is liquid to some extent. Hedging this part is not an issue. The dynamic side is more involved. Currently, there is no liquidity in option-like products—cap/floor or swaptions—with overnight benchmarks as an underlying. It is impossible to obtain directly precise implied dynamic from the market.

---

[10] Similar results have been obtained for the CHF, GBP markets and and USD-LIBOR-6M. The CHF data are described in Pomberg and Willems (2019). The GBP and some USD data are not depicted in this note but can be found on the author's blog at http://multi-curve-framework.blogspot.com/.

The second observation is regarding the LIBOR with fallback inside Equation (5). If we take the full quantity, including the pure LIBOR and the overnight alternatives, the associated market is liquid. Swaps, cap/floor and swaptions on LIBOR with fallback are still the most liquid interest rate instruments. Even if the actual fallback wording has not been penciled explicitly yet and no contract includes this to-be-created wording yet, the general expectation is that, as soon as the wording is definitive and included in new contracts through updated master agreements, CCPs will change their rule books to include the fallback, for legacy trades as well as new contracts as described in LCH (2018). It is also expected that the large banks will sign protocols to apply the new wording/payoff to their legacy contracts. Even if the contracts have not been written yet and even less signed, from a valuation perspective, one can consider that the new payoff is already in place. If one believes that the discontinuation will actually take place by 2022, he has to consider that the long-term instruments are actually already overnight benchmarks-based and the dynamic of the LIBOR with fallback is actually the dynamic of the overnight-linked products. This provide a positive indirect answer to the question of the previous paragraph that had a negative direct answer: for post-2021 payoffs, the prices and implied dynamics of LIBOR linked products are actually prices and implied dynamics of OIS-like products.

We can try to go further into the details of those payoffs. For the announcement date a and the discontinuation date d themselves, there is a market expectation, at least for the ICE LIBOR in different currencies, that the discontinuation will take place around the beginning of 2022—1 January 2022 was used in the scenarios presented in the previous section—and the announcement date will be a couple of months before that. However, there is no instrument depending on that outcome on its own. There are no such things as binary swaps on those dates, e.g., an instrument paying a fixed amount if LIBOR exists and nothing otherwise. A similar reasoning can be done for the methodology parameters X and l; there is no market instrument where each component can be priced in isolation. The fact that most bilateral derivatives trade under similar master agreements and that CCPs will transfer the wording in their rule books means that there is uniformity of payoff among all liquid derivatives. If there were several fallback methodologies planned, for example with different spread approaches, one could try to extract from the differences in price the market implied values of some of those elements. However, from the uniformity, we can only price LIBOR and its fallback as a combined item and not each component separately.

Maybe going outside the derivative world, e.g., to Floating Rate Notes (FRN) or securitisation, could offer more information on the fallback elements as their fallback wording is different. However, for each individual FRN, there is an underlying credit and convenience yield impact. Even if the fallback is different, this difference, which is expected to be relatively small, will be lost in the idiosyncratic features of each note. It seems there is no practical possibility to extract information on the fallback from them.

Obviously, there will be no LIBOR after its discontinuation and asking what would be the value of $I^j(\theta)$ for $\theta > d$ does not make sense. However, we could try to use a proxy to estimate the credit risk impact that is removed by the fallback. Some benchmark providers have started to publish benchmarks that somehow represent bank credit and could be used as a proxy, e.g., US Dollar ICE Bank Yield Index[11] or Ameribor®[12], but there is no derivative trading currently on those indices and there is also no practical possibility to extract any information from them.

Consequently, there is no real hope to obtain the market implied information on the fallback details for the derivatives. There is no real hope to compute a precise amount for the value transfer resulting from the disappearance of LIBOR and its fallback choice and even less to hedge it. The valuation

---

[11] See description at https://www.theice.com/iba/Bank-Yield-Index-Test-Rates.

[12] https://ameribor.net/.

impact, positive or negative, from the fallback choice on end-users with a net exposure to LIBOR will probably remain unknown.

7. Conclusions

The LIBOR fallback is first and foremost a legal challenge. Nevertheless, writing it in the language of quantitative finance helps not only to estimate the potential impacts in term of value transfer, but also to understand what is possible and what is not. In the opinion of this author, this approach that helps clarify the issues has been neglected in the current discussions. The ensuing *lack of precision* has pushed the discussions to an impasse. The current proposals cannot be implemented in practice due to *lack of measurability*. A fundamental revision of the foundations of the fallback is required. Each workaround not taking into account the quantitative finance foundations of the problem leads to further issues that appear to be without simple and elegant solution. A simple and elegant solution to the fallback has been proposed, under the form of an OIS benchmark adjusted RFR, but appears to be resisted for derivatives.

On the other hand, the difference in access to information related to the fallback methodology by different market participants has created a non-level playing field that can be described technically by the existence of *two parallel filtrations* for the pricing of financial instruments. If some participants were allowed to act on the richer filtration, an uncontrolled value transfer between market participants may ensue.

The goal of this note is to describe requirements for a technically achievable fallback process. To reach the goal of implementing an achievable fallback, one has to accept to discuss the problem full complexity, its constraints and review all the potential solutions. If the note achieves that goal it will quickly become de facto obsolete; an achievable precise fallback mechanism will be implemented and its origin can be forgotten.

For quantitative analysts, a second phase, consisting in developing model specific estimation of value transfers and developing new payoffs and models compatible with the new market, will start.

Abbreviations

The following abbreviations are used in this manuscript:

ISDA   International Swaps and Derivatives Association
LIBOR   London InterBank Offered Rate
EFFR   Effective Federal Fund Rate
SOFR   Secured Overnight Financing Rate
FRA   Forward Rate Agreement
OIS   Overnight Indexed Swap

References

1. Bailey, Andrew. 2017. The Future of LIBOR. Speech at Bloomberg London. Available online: https://www.fca. org.uk/news/speeches/the-future-of-libor (accessed on 11 August 2019).
2. Duffie, Darrell. 2018. *Compression Auctions with an Application to LIBOR-SOFR Swap Conversion.* Technical Report. Stanford: Graduate School of Business, Stanford University.
3. Henrard, Marc. 2004. *Overnight Indexed Swaps and Floored Compounded Instrument in HJM One-Factor Model.* Ewp-fin 0402008, Economics Working Paper Archive. Munich: University Library of Munich.
4. Henrard, Marc. 2014. *Interest Rate Modelling in the Multi-Curve Framework: Foundations, Evolution and Implementation.* Applied Quantitative Finance. London: Palgrave Macmillan. ISBN 978-1-137-37465-3.
5. Henrard, Marc. 2019a. Fallback Compounding in Arrears Won'T Work! Multi-Curve Framework Blog Post. Available online: http://multi-curve-framework.blogspot.com/2019/03/fallback-compounding-in-arrears- wont.html (accessed on 11 August 2019).
6. Henrard, Marc. 2019b. A Quant Perspective on IBOR Fallback Consutation Results. Market Infrastructure Analysis. muRisQ Advisory. Available online: https://ssrn.com/abstract=3308766 (accessed on 11 August 2019).
7. Hunt, Philip J., and Joanne E. Kennedy. 2004. *Financial Derivatives in Theory and Practice,* 2nd ed. Wiley Series in Probability and Statistics. Wiley: Hoboken, NJ, USA.

8. ISDA. 2018a. *Anonymized Narrative Summary of Responses to the ISDA Consultation on Term Fixings and Spread Adjustment Methodologies.* Consultation Results. New York: The Brattle Group—ISDA.

9. ISDA. 2018b. Consultation on Certain Aspects of Fallbacks for Derivatives Referencing GBP LIBOR, CHF LIBOR, JPY LIBOR, TIBOR, Euroyen TIBOR and BBSW. Consultation, ISDA. Available online: https://www.isda.org/ 2018/07/12/interbank-offered-rate-ibor-fallbacks-for-2006-isda-definitions (accessed on 11 August 2019).

10. ISDA. 2019. Supplemental Consultation on Spread and Term Adjustments for Fallbacks in Derivatives Referencing USD LIBOR, CDOR and HIBOR and Certain Aspects of Fallbacks for Derivatives Referencing SOR. Consultation, ISDA. Available online: https://www.isda.org/a/n6tME/Supplemental-Consultation-on- USD-LIBOR-CDOR-HIBOR-and-SOR.pdf (accessed on 11 August 2019).

11. LCH. 2018. LCH's Position in Respect of ISDA's Recommended Benchmark Fallback Approaches. LCH Circular No. 3999. Available online: https://www.lch.com/membership/ltd-membership/ltd-member-updates/ lchs-position-respect-isdas-recommended-benchmark (accessed on 11 August 2019).

12. Lyashenko, Andrei, and Fabio Mercurio. 2019. *Looking Forward to Backward-Looking Rates: A Modeling Framework for Term Rates Replacing LIBOR.* Technical Report. Amsterdam: Elsevier.

13. Pomberg, Stefan, and Sander Willems. 2019. Back to a single curve? State of play of alternative risk-free rates. Paper presented at the QuantMinds International 2019, Hamburg, Germany, May 11–15.

14. Rega-Jones, Natasha. 2019. FCA: Sonia Derivatives Liquid Enough to Create Term Rates. Available online: https:// www.risk.net/ derivatives/6712261/fca-sonia-derivatives-liquid-enough-to-create-term-rates (accessed on 11 August 2019).

15. Schrimpf, Andreas, and Vladyslav Sushko. 2019. *Beyond LIBOR: A Primer on the New Reference Rates.* BIS Quarterly Review. Basel: Bank for International Settlements.

16. Sherif, Nazneen. 2019a. FRAs Won't Work with Standard Libor Fallback, Experts Say. Available online: https:// www.risk.net/ derivatives/6453341/fras-wont-work-with-standard-libor-fallback-experts-say(accessed on 11 August 2019).

17. Sherif, Nazneen. 2019b. LIBOR-In-Arrears Swaps Face Unwinds on Benchmark Death. Available online: https:// www.risk.net/ derivatives/6572906/libor-in-arrears-swaps-face-unwinds-on-benchmark-death (accessed on 11 August 2019).

18. Working Group EUR Risk-Free Rates. 2019. Second Public Consultation by the Working Group on Euro Risk-Free Rates: On Determining an ESTER-Based Term Structure Methodology as a Fallback in EURIBOR-Linked Contracts. Consultation, European Central Bank. Available online: https://www.ecb.europa.eu/paym/ cons/html/wg_ester_term_structure_methodology.en.html (accessed on 11 August 2019).

19. Zhu, Haoxiang. 2019. The Clock Is Ticking: A Multi-Maturity Clock Auction Design for LIBOR Transition. Presentation at Planning for the end of LIBOR, Cass Business School. Available online: https://www. cass.city.ac.uk/ data/assets/pdf_file/0004/471757/15h_ Haoxiang-Zhu_LIBORCass.pdf (accessed on 11 August 2019).

Machine Learning for Quantitative Finance Applications: A Survey

Francesco Rundo [1],*[ID], **Francesca Trenta** [2][ID], **Agatino Luigi di Stallo** [3] **and Sebastiano Battiato** [2][ID]

1   STMicroelectronics Srl-ADG Central R&D, 95121 Catania, Italy
2   IPLAB—Department of Mathematics and Computer Science, University of Catania, 95121 Catania, Italy;
     francesca.trenta@unict.it (F.T.); battiato@dmi.unict.it (S.B.)
3   GIURIMATICA Lab, Department of Applied Mathematics and LawTech, 97100 Ragusa, Italy;
     distallo@distallo.it
*   Correspondence: francesco.rundo@st.com

Featured Application: The described approaches can be used in various applications in the field of quantitative finance from HFT trading systems to financial portfolio allocation and optimization systems, etc.

Abstract: The analysis of financial data represents a challenge that researchers had to deal with. The rethinking of the basis of financial markets has led to an urgent demand for developing innovative models to understand financial assets. In the past few decades, researchers have proposed several systems based on traditional approaches, such as autoregressive integrated moving average (ARIMA) and the exponential smoothing model, in order to devise an accurate data representation. Despite their efficacy, the existing works face some drawbacks due to poor performance when managing a large amount of data with intrinsic complexity, high dimensionality and casual dynamicity. Furthermore, these approaches are not suitable for understanding hidden relationships (dependencies) between data. This paper proposes a review of some of the most significant works providing an exhaustive overview of recent machine learning (ML) techniques in the field of quantitative finance showing that these methods outperform traditional approaches. Finally, the paper also presents comparative studies about the effectiveness of several ML-based systems.

Keywords: machine learning; time-series; financial domain

1. Introduction

In recent years there has been increasing interest in predicting the future behavior of complex systems by involving a temporal component [1]. Researchers have investigated this problem modelling a convenient representation for financial data, the so-called time series (i.e., numerical data points observed sequentially through time). Previous studies have highlighted the difficulty studying financial time series accurately due to their non-linear and non-stationary patterns. In [2] the authors presented a comparative study in order to demonstrate the inadequacy of classical approaches in capturing the evolution of real-time time series. Furthermore, they discussed the advantages of applying machine learning (ML) techniques in the field of quantitative finance. Despite achieving effective outcomes, classical approaches have been widely employed in stationary systems, which represent an approximation of the complex real-world observations.

The progressive automatization of certain processes and rapid development in technology has led to the use of ML-based methods in several fields, including the financial one. Despite skepticism about the effectiveness of these approaches, researchers have proven that one of the main benefits of ML solutions is to analyze a large amount of data in a short period of time with greater accuracy and effectiveness. Due to unclear dependencies within data, identifying significant information from irrelevant information is a very difficult task that can be tackled properly by ML-based systems.

The remainder of this paper is organized as follows. Section 2 describes how the research investigation has been conducted. Section 3 introduces main differences between two principal approaches in which surveyed studies fall into. In Section 4, we discuss the performance of auto-regressive models developed for financial market applications. Section 5 provides a description of studies based on Machine Learning algorithm, selected for our review. In addition, we discuss a class of deep learning algorithm, which achieved impressive results in time series forecast. Section 6 provides an exhaustive comparison between ML-based approaches and traditional models (such as autoregressive integrated moving average (ARIMA), generalized autoregressive conditional heteroskedasticity (GARCH), etc.). Section 7 devises some of significant hybrid approaches to identify the effective combination for improving accuracy in time-series forecasting. Section 8 lists existing work in the area of sentiment analysis. Section 9 illustrates reinforcement learning and quantum finance approaches applied in financial domain. Section 10 illustrates comparison between traditional and ML-based approaches. In Section 11, we report the final considerations of this paper.

2. Research Methodology

In this survey, we selected studies and/or research works based on the ML-based approach or classical method in order to analyze time series problem in financial domain.

In this paper, we shed light on the promising results achieved by machine learning approaches for time-series forecasting in the financial sector. Unlike relevant existing review articles [3], this survey not only focuses on summarizing several approaches suitable for solving financial market problems, but also compares ML-based approaches and traditional ones in order to discuss which method could be more effective considering the current financial scenario.

Also, we provided results of selected studies in order to highlight the better overall performance of ML-based systems over traditional approaches.

3. Technical and Fundamental Analysis

In the financial field we can distinguish two different approaches: Technical and Fundamental Analysis. The goal is to identify patterns in order to predict time-series movements and improve accuracy. The technical approach is based on analyzing stock market considering previous observed patterns with the aim to determine future time series values. In fundamental analysis (FA), the basic idea focuses on evaluating intrinsic value (i.e., perceived or calculated value of a stock or a company). Technical analysis (TA) gained a considerable attention due to the efficient market hypothesis which claims that stock movements are not a stochastic process but reveal repeated patterns over time. In fact, this approach is based on studying prices movements through analyzing historical data. Despite being a basis for several financial applications, TA presents cons related to the fact that market is highly variable. Although the use of indicators parameters and tools to achieve a high accuracy, using real data could affect the overall performance in negative perspective. On the other hand, FA consists of studying factors which may affect the future trend. The main problem regards the fact that it incurs considerable computational cost due to the poor result in performing rapid decision.

The proposed work illustrated some of the main methods that fall into each category of analysis in order to define cons and pros of each methods and evaluate what algorithm is convenient to use according to the current scenario.

4. Autoregressive Models

A considerable amount of literature has examined the most promising techniques for time series forecasting. The outcomes have highlighted that these approaches could be subdivided into two separate macro-categories, which include statistical and machine-learning methods.

The ARIMA model represents a generalization of the auto-regressive moving average (ARMA) model, suitable to describe non-stationary time-series. More specifically, the main benefit in using the ARIMA model is to transform a non-stationary series into a series without seasonality or trend, by applying finite differencing of data points [4].

By definition, a time series is stationary if its statistical properties are all constant over time. If a stationary series has no trend, its variations around its mean have a constant amplitude. Furthermore, the time-series autocorrelations remain constant over time. Based on these assumptions, a time series of this form can be considered as a combination of signal and noise. An ARIMA model manages the signal by separating it from the noise. After removing noise from the signal, the output of ARIMA model is the signal step-ahead to obtain forecasts. In order to select an appropriate model to improve time-series forecasting, the Box–Jenkins model [4] has been developed to determine best ARIMA model to fit to a given time-series.

The Box–Jenkins model has gained momentum in forecasting time-series not only in financial sector but also to improve prediction of future values of a time-series considering electricity prices or traffic data observations [5,6].

In order to demonstrate the effectiveness of the ARIMA model, we surveyed a set of works where the ARIMA process was applied to perform stock price forecasting.

In [7] the authors investigated the problem to produce accurate prediction of stock market time series data by using ARIMA and the GARCH model. However, they indicate that a major class of works in literature used these classical approaches for solving a one-step ahead forecasting problems. In the case of a multi-step or N-step ahead prediction, the aforementioned model does not perform accurately. In particular, authors have been concerned about the decrease of accuracy and lack of maintenance of data trend or dynamics. In order to overcome these limitations, a linear hybrid model combining ARIMA and GARCH was proposed. First, they used a simple moving average filter in order to decompose the stock-market time series into two different series. One of these data streams is modeled by using ARIMA and GARCH model respectively. Finally, the outcomes from both models are then combined to perform the values predictions. Results have shown that the proposed hybrid model is suitable for multi-step ahead forecasting of high-volatile time-series.

In [8] the authors have applied a statistical model based on ARIMA to the New York Stock Exchange (NYSE) and Nigeria Stock Exchange (NSE) for predicting future daily stock prices. The experimental results showed that the model has reached satisfactory results for both stock indexes.

Despite preserving the data trend and obtaining good predictions in terms of accuracy, the ARIMA model has definite limitations when dealing with financial time series data which present asymmetries, irregular time intervals and high/low volatility. In fact, the main assumption of the ARIMA model regards constant variance. Considering this fact, an integrated model represents a suitable solution when dealing to data which reveal a non-complex structure.

Since we have shed light to the limitation of statistical models for the analyzed time series, the next step consists in reviewing models of the machine-learning family which achieve effective results for financial data prediction. Table 1 summarizes surveyed studies in this section.

Table 1. Summary of studies based on auto-regressive models. ARIMA: autoregressive integrated moving average. GARCH: generalized autoregressive conditional heteroskedasticity.

Article	Techniques	Main Goal	Dataset
Babu et al. (2014) [7]	Hybrid ARIMA-GARCH model	Multi-step ahead forecasting	NSE India data
Adebiyi et al. (2014) [8]	ARIMA model	Stock price prediction	Nokia stock index/Zenith bank stock index

5. Machine-Learning Approaches

5.1. *Support Vector Machine (SVM)*

Support vector machine (SVM) is a technique of Machine Learning for data classification. The objective of SVM is to find a separation hyperplane to correctly classify data with the maximum margin [9]. The SVM finds a decision function which maximizes the margin between classes. SVM is a supervised classification technique; this means that there are two main steps to be performed. First, a set of labelled data (training data) is provided to the SVM. During this step the algorithms performs a mathematical optimization based on the labelled data. The train examples that limit the maximum margin defined by the SVM during the training are called support vectors.

A significant work based on the SVM model is [10], in which the authors aimed to develop an efficient system to gain high profits by analyzing stock markets. Specifically, the authors employed the SVM model to select the stock that exceed the percentage return of the market only selecting stocks that outperform it. The results confirmed the effectiveness of the proposed SVM, in fact the selected range of stocks reported a total return of 208% over 5 years.

The work developed by Cao et al. [11] was motivated by the fact that SVM achieved consistent results for forecasting financial time series. This document provides a comparison between SVM, a retro-propagation multilayer neural network (BP) and a regularized radial base function (RBF) neural network. These models have been evaluated by taking as input five datasets listed in the Chicago Mercantile Market. Results showed that SVM excels and achieves effective results considering both adaptive and free parameters.

Nayak et al. [12] presented a framework which combines the SVM and K-approach (KNN) for predicting Indian stock indices. Specifically, the authors applied the proposed model by using different SVM kernel functions for estimating profits and losses. In order to improve the stock value prediction, the author used the output, computed by SVM, to calculate the best neighbor from a training set. Furthermore, they used two indices, the Bombay Stock Exchange (BSE Sensex) and CNX Nifty, to evaluate the proposed model, taking advantages of closing price forecast, volatility and stock market momentum related to data. To provide a complete study, the authors compared the hybrid model with Functional Link Interval Type 2 Fuzzy Neural System (FLIT2NS) and Computationally Efficient Functional Link Artificial Neural Networks (CEFLANN) by analyzing mean squared error (MSE) results. Despite significantly complex procedure to update weight, the developed SVM-KNN hybrid model is relatively suitable for solving financial prediction problems.

In [13], the authors explained a new approach called the state box method which consists of selecting a group of stock points and subdividing them into three different boxes. Each box refers to a category that indicates the stock status. In this approach, the authors implemented a new method incorporating the AdaBoost algorithm, the probabilistic vector support machine (PSVM) and the genetic algorithm (GA) with the aim to improve the classification of status boxes. Each box includes a limited number of points which indicates the share price trend over a specific time period. The authors investigated the effectiveness of the proposed model by selecting a group of shares listed in the Shenzhen Stock Exchange (SZSE) and the National Association of Securities Dealers Automated Quotations (NASDAQ) as inputs. By analyzing the results, the authors confirm that ensemble classifier achieves remarkable results and outperforms other approaches based on using only the PSVM or the back-propagation neural network (BPN).

One of the major issues related to financial field is the limitation in learning the pattern because of high complexity and strong non-linear trend of stock data. In order to avoid inconsistent and unpredictable performance on noisy data, Support Vector Machine has been proposed to overcome limitations of classical approaches. Recently, SVM was not only applied for pattern recognition problems but also to solve non-linear regression problems. SVM implements the so-called structural risk minimization principle (SRM) which is an inductive principle used for model selection based on balancing the model's complexity against its success at fitting the training data. In fact, the main benefit of SVM model is due to the fact it achieves higher generalization performance than traditional neural network models. From the results reported in this section, it can be observed that the performance of SVM exceeds the overall performance of classical neural networks approaches. In particular, the superior performance is guaranteed by the fact that SVM implements the SRM principle which is based on minimizing upper bound of the generalization error instead of minimizing the training error. This eventually leads to better generalization than other ML-approaches (such as the BP neural network). Also, advantages in applying SVM model not only includes a major improvement in terms of generalization of neural networks performance, but also successfully overcome the defeats of other models. Unlike existing ML models, SVM present a finite number of controlling parameters, prevents overfitting problem and reaches convergence faster.

In Table 2, we report surveyed studies based on applying SVM model.

Table 2. Summary of studies based on the support vector machine (SVM) model. KNN: K-nearest neighbors.

Article	Techniques	Main Goal	Dataset
Fan et al. (2001) [10]	Support Vector Machine	Stock selection	Australian Stock Exchange (1992–2000)
Cao et al. (2003) [11]	Support Vector Machine	Forecasting	Chicago Mercantile Market
Nayak et al. (2015) [12]	Hybrid SVM-KNN model	Stock market prediction	Indian stock market indices
Zhang et al. (2016) [13]	Status box method (Hybrid AdaBoost algorithm, genetic algorithm and probabilistic SVM)	Stock trend prediction	20 shares from SZSE/ 16 shares from NASDAQ

5.2. Deep Learning

Deep learning (DL) is a part of the machine-learning methods based on using data to train a model to make predictions from new data. In general, DL methods allow to perform difficult task without human involvement. In particular, DL methods represent an effective solution in solving financial market problems which are different from typical deep learning applications. For example, selecting a stock that is likely to perform well in future could represent a challenging task for a human. For this reason, the tools of deep learning may be useful in such selection problems, because deep learning techniques represent the best solution to compute any function mapping data (which include returns, economic data, accounting date, etc.) into the value of the return.

This document [14] deals with stock market index forecasting. The experiments were carried out by considering two indices, namely CNX Nifty and S&P Bombay Stock Exchange (BSE) Sensex of the Indian stock markets. The main contribution of this work is the development of a two-phase fusion approach which involves the use of support vector regression (SVR) in the first phase. The second stage defined three different combination of SVR with other models including an artificial neural network (ANN), random forest (RF) and SVR. Thus, the authors provide a comparison between the resulting prediction models and single models ANN, RF and SVR for estimating the accuracy in forecasting time series 1–10, 15 and 30 days in advance.

The authors of [15] presented a long short-term memory (LSTM) neural networks for modeling and predicting the return of Chinese shares. Furthermore, they compared their LSTM model with random forecasting method in order to verify the applicability and superiority of the proposed model. The input data of the model are data related to Chinese stock market. In order to evaluate the proposed model, the authors considered 30-day sequences of historical data with 10 learning features and labeling functions of the earnings rate in 3 days. Results confirmed the superior performance of LSTM over random forecasting method and its ability to improve the accuracy related to stock returns forecasting.

In this document [16], the authors provided an innovative model called the bat-neural network multi-agent system (BNNMAS) aimed to perform stock prices prediction. In particular, the goal of the proposed method is to predict eight years of Deutscher Aktienindex (DAX) stock indices. Furthermore, the results of BNNMAS have been compared with the results of the genetic algorithm-neural network (GANN) and teh general regression neural network (GRNN). Efforts have demonstrated the power of BNNMAS in predicting stock prices in the long term accurately.

In [17] the authors investigated the problem of applying LSTM for financial time series forecasting. They proposed a cutting-edge technique in order to distribute LSTM for predicting off-directional movements. Stocks of the S&P 500 from 1992 to 2015 have been used as input data to validate the proposed model. The results not only reveal that LSTM performs better without taking advantage of classification methods such as random forest or deep neural network (DNN) but also shedding light on the common pattern of securities presents high volatility and a short-term inversion return profile.

In Table 3, we summarize surveyed studies based on DL models.

5.3. Recurrent Neural Network (RNN) for Financial Forecasting

Recurrent Neural Networks (RNN) are a class of neural networks which uses internal memory to process arbitrary sequence of inputs. Recurrent networks differ from feedforward networks by taking as their input not just the current input example they analyze, but also what they have perceived previously in time. In fact, recurrent networks preserve sequential information through a hidden state which allows them to store information about the past efficiently. On the other hand, feedforward networks transform input examples into an output. For example, considering a supervised learning problem, the output would be a label, a name applied to the input.

A significant variant of RNN is LSTM which represents a well suitable solution in regression problem such as forecasting time series. Considering their ability to capture hidden nonlinear correlations between input data, the model was applied successfully to increase the accuracy forecast. In this section, we provide a list of works based on using the LSTM/RNN model to solve financial time-series forecasting.

LSTM architecture has proven to be stable and powerful for modeling long-range dependencies in various previous studies [18–20]. The major benefit of LSTM is the ability to store useful information by using its memory cell. In fact, LSTM represents a considerable improvement of the classic RNN model because not only is it able to evaluate the hidden non-linear correlations between input data but also it takes advantages of LSTM main unit and "gates" to prevent the so called vanishing gradient problem which represents a drawback in RNN model.

Table 3. Summary of studies based on machine-learning (ML)/deep-learning (DL) models. ANN: artificial neural network. SVR: support vector regression. RF: Random Forest.

Article	Techniques	Main Goal	Dataset
Patel et al. (2014) [14]	Fusion approach involving ANN, RF and SVR models	Stock prices prediction	Indian Stock market indices
Chen et al. (2015) [15]	LSTM model	Stock returns prediction	China Stock Market data
Hafezi et al. (2015) [16]	bat-neural network multi-agent system (BNNMAS)	Stock price prediction	DAX stock price
Fischer et al. (2017) [17]	LSTM model	Large-scale financial market prediction	S&P 500 (1992–2015)
Yümlü et al. (2005) [21]	Global, recurrent and smoothed-piecewise neural models	Financial time series prediction	Istanbul Stock Exchange (1990–2002)
Selvin et al. (2017) [22]	LSTM-RNN-CNN sliding window-ARIMA	Short term future prediction	NSE listed companies' data (2014–2015)
Samarawickrama et al. (2017) [23]	RNN model	Daily stock prices prediction	Sri Lankan Stock Exchange
Siami-Namini et al. (2018) [24]	LSTM vs. ARIMA	Comparison	N225, IXIC, HIS, GSPC, DJ
Rundo et al. (2019) [25]	LSTM model	Forecasting	ENEL.MI ISP.MI UCG.MI CVAL.MI MPS.MI
Rundo et al. (2019) [26]	Grid algorithmic trading system (Non-linear Regression Network)	Forecasting	FX market (EUR/USD)

A significant work that provides a comparative study on evaluating the performance of three different architectures is [21], in which the authors compare a global, feedback and smoothed-wise model in order to solve the financial forecast problem. The three models include a multilayer perceptron (MLP) feedback model by a RNN and smoothed-piecewise model by a "mixture of experts" (MoE) structure. The evaluation of the aforementioned models is performed considering 12 years (from 1990 to 2002) of the Istanbul Stock Exchange (ISE) index (XU100). Furthermore, the authors implemented an exponential generalized autoregressive conditional heteroscedastic (EGARCH) model aiming to provide an exhaustive comparison based on estimating index return series such as hit rate (HR), positive hit rate (HR+), negative hit rate (HR-), MSE, mean absolute error (MAE) and correlation. The analysis of experiment results has highlighted that smoothed-piecewise model outperforms the other ones, including EGARCH model.

Selvin et al. [22] investigated how a DL architecture could be applied to predict stock index movement. Contrary to existing methods which are based on linear autoregressive (AR), moving average (MA), ARIMA and non-linear algorithms, the proposed approach is based on three different neural networks (LSTM, RNN and convolutional neural network (CNN)) to predict National Stock Exchange of India (NSE)-listed companies. In order to evaluate the proposed methods, the authors defined a sliding window strategy which includes overlapped data referring to minute wise data. The results of error percentage value confirm that CNN is able to capture the dynamical change of the data compared to other models that present a lack of accuracy.

Samarawickrama et al. [23] proposed the use of RNN to improve the accuracy of financial time series prediction. Closing, High and Low prices of selected listed companies of Colombo Stock Exchange were analyzed in order to predict future prices considering the past two days values. In this approach, the comparison involved feedforward, simple recurrent neural network (SRNN), gated recurrent unit (GRU) and LSTM architecture and make comparison between them. The prediction results showed that structural recurrent neural network (SRNN) and LSTM neural networks performed high accuracy contrary to feedforward networks. Despite the effectiveness of the two proposed models, they present some drawbacks in different contexts whereas feedforward present a lower error. To conclude, it has been noted that GRU networks do not perform stock price forecasting accurately.

The work proposed by Siami-Namini et al. [24] conducted a comparative study with the aim of investigating if ML based approaches can be superior to traditional methods in terms of accuracy. In this work, the authors compared a LSTM, a deep-learning architecture, with the ARIMA model which falls into the class of statistical models. In this approach, historical monthly financial time series from Jan 1985 to Aug 2018 from the Yahoo finance Web have been considered as input of the proposed models in order to predict the trend of the stock exchanges. The experiment results reported that LSTM, compared to the ARIMA model, provided the best overall performance, confirmed by RMSE values.

Rundo et al. [25] proposed an innovative LSTM-based framework in order to perform careful stock price prediction. The proposed approach includes two pipelines: the first is defined to perform Trend prediction and the second is developed to predict stock price values. Regarding stock close price prediction, the proposed system is based on the usage of LSTM together with mathematical price correction approach performed by Markov statistical model. Results revealed that the proposed framework is able to perform stock price forecasting accurately. Furthermore, the proposed method outperforms statistical model such as SMA, in terms of accuracy.

In [26], the authors presented an innovative framework composed by a non-linear regression network which performs close price forecasting. The output, computed by Regression Network, is fed to a trend classifier block which estimates the most probable short-term financial trend. After organizing the trading grid by analyzing the current state of trading, the block called the basket equity system manager evaluates the financial exposure of the trading grid.

Despite demonstrating high accuracy in predicting the next lags of time series, Integrated model represents an inappropriate solution considering the newly developed deep learning-based algorithms for forecasting time series data.

In particular, the surveyed studies conducted and reported in this article show that deep learning-based algorithms such as LSTM outperform traditional-based algorithms such as the ARIMA model. More specifically, the average reduction in error rates obtained by LSTM present a higher percentage in term of accuracy when compared to auto-regressive models indicating the superiority of LSTM to statistical models.

6. Comparisons

In literature, there are a huge number of papers which provide comparison between the AR model with ARIMA methodology or BPANN aiming to define the suitable model for time-series forecasting. Other related works have also analyzed the performance of SVMs and the traditional back propagation (BP) model that seem to provide a better overall performance of these models compared to AR models. In [27], the authors investigated the stock market indices forecasting applying a GARCH model in order to compare it with standard BP. Defining a proper strategy should be provided to fit an adequate model for the time series prediction. In the past few decades, several works have applied ARMA approach for univariate time series forecasting. A time series represents a process where observations are sequences of equally spaced points in time. But in financial domain, time series present large volatility and non-linearity which are difficult to process by classical methods which their assumptions are based on linearity. Several ML techniques were proposed to overcome some drawbacks of classical methods by taking advantage of their ability to capture hidden patterns between input and output data. The authors analyzed the performance of ARMA, GARCH and BP models in predicting four stock market values. The results reported that GARCH and BP models offer a performance superior to the ARMA model by using deviation performance as a criterion. However, the ARMA model is extremely effective compared to other models in terms of direction and weighted direction performance criteria. Finally, the authors observed that GARCH fitting line is closer than BP one except for the Financial Times (FT) market.

A similar comparison was approached in [28] in which the authors demonstrate that ANN can be engaged to improve financial time-series forecasting. The authors focused on applying ANN and ARIMA models to predict PT Aneka Tambang Tbk (ANTM) by using historical daily values. The authors also referred to previous works in which ANN is employed to predict stock movement with a satisfactory result. In this paper, the most interesting observation that emerges from the comparison of the two models is that ANN outperformed the auto regressive method. These experimental results provide further justification to apply ANN model for solving a time-series forecasting problem considering its ability to detect non-linear data pattern. In this paper, the authors reported as benchmark the each sum square (ESS) result achieved by ARIMA and by ANN, confirming the effectiveness of ML-based methods.

In [29], the ISE Index has been considered to perform time-series forecasting. The authors provide a complete study for estimating the overall performance of an ANN and SVM model. To evaluate both models, ten technical indicators have been employed including SMA etc. After establishing the best combination of parameters for both models, the authors plugged the data into ANN and SVM model aiming to forecasting the future values of the stock market. The experiments revealed that ANN is more effective than the SVM model. However, the authors shed light that both models present lower accuracy in forecasting stock market related to year 2001 in which the economic and financial crises had an immense adverse impact on the Turkish financial market.

In [30], the authors examine the results of ARIMA and ANN models in forecasting the NYSE stock data. By comparing all empirical results, ANN are more efficient than the statistical model, ARIMA.

According to [31], a random forest model can be engaged to predict stock market trend achieving good results. In particular, the authors compared the performance of ANN, SVM, random forest and naive Bayes using Reliance Industries and Infosys Ltd., in addition to CNX Nifty and S&P Bombay Exchange (BSE) Sensex. The core idea is based on transforming data from continuous to discrete values of a fixed number (i.e., 10) of technical parameters. The authors have set up the conversion of the two first parameters, simple moving average (SMA) and weighted moving average (WMA), by comparing their value to current price. The trend is determined by setting the discrete value equal to −1 in case of the parameter value is lower than current price value which indicates a decreasing trend, +1 otherwise. The experimental results highlighted that ANN, random forest and SVM model present good performance by using discrete values as input. In general, the results illustrated that the model produces poor results for the trend prediction when considering continuous data. Technical indicators provide intrinsic information about the data trend, so they represent the adequate representation of data as input for each model. Thus, the model must find a relationship between the input trend and the output trend, which requires a lower level of complexity than that required when analyzing continuous data. By contrast, when continuous data are used, the model is not able to obtain information about the trend of the data which represents intrinsic information in these indicators.

Another example of work which focuses on applying artificial neural networks is [32]. A range of companies listed in the São Paulo Stock Exchange Brazilian Mercantile and Futures Exchange Bovespa (BM&FBovespa) were analyzed with the purpose to forecast the minimum and maximum daily prices of the shares. In particular, the proposed pipeline is based on extracting relevant attributes for improving the forecast prediction. The authors tested the developed algorithm by using MAE, mean absolute percentage error (MAPE) and root mean square error (RMSE) metrics. Results showed that the model is effective.

Li et al. [33] compared the use of LSTM and SVM in predicting the price movements of stocks. The authors focused on analyzing a range of stocks including Shanghai Stock Exchange 50 (SSE 50) Index and which are affected by different volatility. The overall performance reveal that SVM model achieves significant results for all stocks including the SSE 50 which presents values that does not fluctuate dramatically. Despite the effectiveness of SVM, it has been noted that the LSTM presents consistent results in forecasting SSE 50 Index affected by high volatility. Considering the low-volatility stock exchanges, LSTM reported an averaged accuracy of 51.78% which is higher than the SVM results (50.82%).

The surveyed studies of this section are reported in Table 4.

Table 4. Summary of comparative studies. GARCH: Generalized Autoregressive Conditional Heteroskedasticity.

Article	Method	Main Goal	Dataset
Hossain et al. (2008) [27]	GARCH vs. Neural Network	Comparison	Nikkei 225, Hang Seng, FTSE 100 and DAX
Wijaya et al. (2010) [28]	ARIMA vs. ANN	Comparison	Indonesia Stock data (ANTM)
Kara et al. (2011) [29]	ANN and SVM model	Stock price index movement prediction	Istanbul Stock Exchange (ISE)
Adebiyi et al. (2014) [30]	ARIMA vs. ANN	Comparison	New York Stock Exchange
Patel et al. (2015) [31]	ANN, SVM, RF, Naïve Bayes	Comparison (direction of movement for stock)	Indian Stock Exchange
Laboissiere et al. (2015) [32]	ANN	Forecasting	São Paulo Stock Exchange BM&FBovespa.
Li et al. (2017) [33]	RNN, SVM	Stock prediction	Shanghai Stock Exchange 50 (SSE 50)

7. Hybrid Systems

A new hybrid approach [34] have been devised in order to forecast trend by using Taiwan stock exchange weighted stock index (abbreviated TSEWSI). The hybrid system was developed by combining a RNN model which uses features extracted by ARIMA model as input data. To improve the overall performance, neural networks have been fed with the difference of predictions sequence in order to adjust the connection weights during backpropagation training. Experiments revealed that the prediction performed by the proposed model was significant and reliable. In fact, it has the capability to predict 6 weeks ahead the market trend.

Another work that takes advantages from both linear and non-linear models is [35]. In this work, the authors developed a hybrid method involving ARIMA and ANN models. The results confirmed that the proposed model is well suited to improve forecasting accuracy. The aim of the proposed models was to predict 35 and 67-period ahead. Results reported that neither the neural network nor the ARIMA model have the capability to understand the patterns within data. But it has been noted that the hybrid model combining two models is able to reduce the overall forecasting errors for 67-period forecasting. With regard to 35-period forecasting, the ANN achieved better results.

The authors of [36] presented a new hybrid asymmetric volatility approach based on artificial neural networks. In particular, they focused on improving the forecasting ability of derivative securities prices. The benefit of using the proposed method is due to not only its ability to capture asymmetric volatility but also the ability to reduce the stochastic and non-linearity of the error term sequence.

Lee et al. [37] provides a mixture of the SVM model and hybrid feature selection method aiming to predicting the trend of stock markets. To improve the trend prediction, a hybrid selection approach has been defined as a method to select the optimal features. The experiments were carried out by performing a comparison between SVM model with F-score and supported sequential forward search (F_SSFS) feature selection methods and BPNN along with information gain, symmetrical uncertainty, and correlation-based feature selection. The final results indicated not only that SVM achieved better results than BPN in terms of stock trend prediction but also the proposed SVM incorporating F_SSFS shows a reliable level of accuracy.

In [38], the authors present a hybrid system to forecast financial time-series. The proposed method combines an ARIMA model and fuzzy logic in order to demonstrate that proposed model could overcome data limitations of individual ARIMA model.

A reliable work based on applying hybrid method to solve stock index forecasting is [39]. Since ESM, ARIMA and BPNN models have been widely used with remarkable results to forecast time-series, this document proposed a hybrid approach involving the aforementioned models. In particular, the authors shed light on hybrid methods performs better than all three models in a single scenario in which they have been considered in the original form. Also, the proposed model achieves better results than the equal weight hybrid model (EWH), and the random walk model (RWM).

In [40] the authors have devised a hybrid system by using a genetic fuzzy system with an ANN model. The main contribution of this work is the stepwise regression analysis which has been developed to identify the factors that affect stock prices. To evaluate the overall performance of the proposed model, the experiments were carried out considering the data related to the stock of IBM and DELL corporations as well as Ryanair data, already used in previous studies. In general, it has been noted that the artificial neural networks as well as the fuzzy algorithms have been applied successfully to solve forecasting problems since they are able to obtain better results than using a single model.

In [41], the authors assembled a new hybrid approach combining the ARIMA with ANN model in order to predict financial time-series. Before applying the proposed hybrid model, the nature of financial time series has been explored in order to analyze its volatility. Numerical results showed that the hybrid model excels over the individual ARIMA and ANN models, and existing hybrid ARIMA-ANN models.

Panigrahi et al. [42] have elaborated a high-efficiency methodology combining ETS and ANN model. The proposed hybrid model takes advantages of linear as well as non-linear modeling capability. In this approach, the ETS model performs prediction of a given time series in order to capture data linear patterns. To evaluate the accuracy of predictions, the authors calculated the residual error by considering the difference between ETS predictions series and original time-series. The second stage used ETS-predictions and ANN-predictions in order to merge them. To verify the applicability and superiority of the proposed model, the authors compared this approach with some existing methods such as ARIMA, ETS, MLP and other ARIMA-ANN models. The experiments confirmed the promising results achieved by the ETS-ANN model.

In [43], the authors presented an innovative hybrid system which consists of a long short-term memory (LSTM) to forecast stock price volatility with GARCH-type models. In order to conduct the experiments, the authors used KOSPI 200 index data. The prediction performance confirmed that the proposed model yield to consistent results.

In Table 5, we reported the surveyed studies based on applying hybrid systems.

Table 5. Summary of studies based on hybrid models. IBM: International Business Machines NASDAQ: National Association of Securities Dealers Automated Quotation ESM: Exponential Smoothing Model.

Article	Techniques	Main Goal	Dataset
Wang et al. (1996) [34]	ARIMA-based Recurrent Neural Network	Market trend prediction	Taiwan stock exchange
Zhang et al. (2003) [35]	Hybrid ARIMA-ANN model	Forecasting	Wolf's sunspot data, Canadian lynx data/British Pound/USD exchange rate data
Wang et al. (2009) [36]	Hybrid asymmetric volatility approach (Grey-GJR–GARCH)	Forecasting	Taiwan stock index
Ming-Chi Lee (2009) [37]	SVM with Hybrid feature selection method (F_SSFS)	Stock trend prediction	NASDAQ Index
Khashei et al. (2009) [38]	Hybrid ARIMA-ANN-Fuzzy Logic model	Forecasting	Exchange rate (US dollars/Iran Rials), Gold price (Gram/US dollars), Exchange rate (Euro/Iran Rials)

Table 5. *Cont.*

Article	Techniques	Main Goal	Dataset
Wang et al. (2012) [39]	ESM, ARIMA, BPNN	Forecasting	Shenzhen Integrated Index (SZII), Dow Jones Industrial Average Index (DJIA)
Hadavandi et al. (2013) [40]	Hybrid Genetic Fuzzy Systems–ANN model	Stock price forecasting	IBM, British Airlines, RyanAir, DELL
Babu et al. (2014) [41]	Hybrid ARIMA–ANN model	Forecasting	Sunspot data, electricity data, L&T stock market
Panigrahi et al. (2017) [42]	Hybrid ETS–ANN model	Forecasting	IBM
Kim et al. (2018) [43]	Hybrid LSTM–multiple GARCH-type model	Volatility prediction	KOSPI 200 index

8. Sentiment Analysis

As already mentioned, social media usage has increased over the last 10 years, becoming the first place to obtain news. In particular, it has been noted that social media can affect not only public opinion but also political and economic events. Many researchers have investigated how social media could affect financial market in order to gain information for forecasting financial time-series.

Satisfactory results have been achieved by analyzing textual analysis of breaking financial news. The proposed method [44] collected more than 9000 financial news articles and 10,000,000 S&P 500 stock quotes for a period of 5 weeks. The core idea is to estimate a discrete share price by analyzing news 20 min after its release. Several textual representations have been used to analyze news accurately: bag of words, noun phrases and named entities. Furthermore, the authors developed a SVM-based system to perform discrete numerical prediction. The experiments demonstrated not only that Bag of Words is the representation that works better than others but also SVM is extremely accurate according to MSE values.

Another significant work in which a machine learning-based system is applied to analyze Twitter data in the financial domain is [45]. The authors suggest that the stock market trend is high correlated with public opinion. In particular, they focused on analyzing users' tweets using two different textual representations, called Word2vec [46] and N-gram [47]. The first representation was used to map each single word in a vector, the second one is used to match the corpus of a text. The experimental results confirmed the strong correlation existing between stock market trend and public opinion expressed in tweets. In Table 6, we provide a summary of surveyed studies focused on sentiment analysis.

Table 6. Summary of studies based on sentiment analysis.

Article	Techniques	Main Goal	Dataset
Schumaker et al. (2009) [44]	SVM	Discrete stock price estimation	S&P 500
Pagolu et al. (2016) [45]	Sentiment Analysis	Stock market movements prediction	Dow Jones Industrial Average Index (DJIA)

9. Reinforcement Learning (RL)

In this section, we surveyed some considerable approaches based on reinforcement learning. Reinforcement learning refers to a machine-learning paradigm which involves an "agent" in order to perform a task. The goal of agent is to maximize a numerical reward by interacting with an unknown environment. In financial field, this emerging paradigm has gained attention due to their ability to develop portfolio construction including prediction in one integrated step. Basically, the goal of the agent is to include some constraints such as liquidity and transactions cost when a decision-making process is performed.

In [48] the authors presented a time-driven feature-aware jointly deep reinforcement learning (RL) model (TFJ-DLR) in order to learn features representation considering noisy financial time series. Furthermore, the proposed method is developed to perform a decision-making system by taking advantage of environmental representation. Specifically, the authors selected various features of financial time series in order to summarize the useful values through analyzing historical data. Results demonstrated the robustness and effectiveness of the proposed TFJ-DLR system by using real-world financial data. In particular, the proposed method is able to increase investment returns.

A recent work is [49], in which the author implemented an algorithm based on supervised DL and reinforcement learning algorithm. The main goal is to forecast the short-term trend in the currency FOREX (FOReign EXchange) market with the aim to maximize the return of investment in a high-frequency trend (HFT) algorithm. Also, the author proposed a grid trading engine to perform high frequency operations. In order to validate the proposed model, the trading system has been validated over several financial years and on the EUR/USD cross. The value of return of investment (98.23%) and reduced drawdown (15.97%) confirmed the effectiveness of the proposed trading system. Table 7 reports surveyed articles based on RL approach.

In [50], the author proposed a model that combines dynamic programming (DP) and RL techniques. The proposed Q-Learner in the Black-Scholes (QLBS) model is developed to estimate future changes for stock market using Black–Scholes–Merton's model. After comparing fitted Q iteration to the DP model in order to evaluate the performance, the author formulated an inverse reinforcement learning (IRL) setting for the QLBS model aimed at analyzing prices and actions. Finally, the author discussed the usage of QLBS model for option portfolios.

Recently, the increasing request of developing intelligent financial systems has led to the development of trading systems which integrate quantum finance theory to solve financial problems [51,52]. The main benefit of applying quantum technology to financial problem is related to the ability of making calculations that reveal dynamic arbitrage possibilities that competitors are unable to see. Quantum computing not only could be applied to an asset management or trading problem, but it could perform trading optimization, risk profiling and prediction.

Table 7. Summary of studies based on reinforcement learning (RL) models. TFJ-DRL: Time-Driven Feature-aware Jointly Deep Reinforcement Learning.

Article	Techniques	Main Goal	Dataset
Lei et al. (2020) [48]	TFJ-DRL model	Financial signal representation	S&P 500
Rundo (2019) [49]	Deep Learning/ Reinforcement Learning	Forecasting	EUR/USD
Halperin (2019) [50]	Dynamic Programming/ Reinforcement Learning	Trading	Simulated stock price histories
Baaquie (2019) [53]	Quantum Finance	Range accrual swap	90-day Libor
Lee (2019) [54]	CT2TFDNN model	Financial prediction	Data provided by Quantum Finance Forecast Center (QFFC)
Lee (2019) [55]	COSMOS model	Forecasting	Data provided by Quantum Finance Forecast Center (QFFC)

In this context, the work of Baaquie [53] represents an innovative solution. The objective of this study [53] consists in taking advantage of quantum finance theory to price the rate range accrual swaps which refer to the exchange of one set of cash flows for another.

With the exponential growth of RL solutions, several hybrid systems based on fuzzy logic, genetic algorithms and chaotic theory have become a crucial topic in the fintech field. One of the most recent work is [54], in which the author presented a chaotic type-2 transient-fuzzy deep neuro-oscillatory network with retrograde signaling (CT2TFDNN) to perform financial prediction. The proposed model is intended as extension of the prior work of the same author in which a chaotic oscillatory multi-agent-based neuro-computing system (COSMOS) has been proposed [55].

In [54], the main contribution consists in providing an effective solution to preserve systems by dealing with deadlock problems which are very common in recurrent neural networks solution. Moreover, a chaotic deep neuro-oscillatory network with retrograde signaling (CDNONRS) is designed to improve time-series prediction.

10. Discussion

In this survey, we described some of the most promising directions adopted to solve financial problems. We started our investigation selecting the main approaches based on traditional methods, commonly used for time-series forecasting. In Table 1, we summarized studies based on ARIMA and GARCH models. First, linear models have been suggested to perform time-series forecasting taking advantage of their effectiveness and quite simple implementation. Then, non-linear models (such as ARIMA) have drawn attention due to their ability to transform non-linear data into stationary one. By comparing the results, it can be observed that surveyed methods based on traditional models, showed several weaknesses in processing a huge set of heterogenous data and identifying specific hidden patterns. This has led to an increasing demand to adopt more efficient algorithms which are able to capture hidden relationships between data, such as Machine Learning algorithms.

In recent years, several machine-learning methods have been developed for modeling financial time-series. The SVM model belongs to this category of algorithms. In SVM, the basic idea is to define an optimal hyperplane through mapping the data into higher-dimensional spaces, in which they are linearly separable.

Despite achieving remarkable results, SVM presents some problem concerning the definition of its hyper-parameters along the issue of selecting SVM training data from large datasets which could increase the time complexity and affect the overall performance of the SVM classifier in practice.

Considering these facts, other ML approaches (including ANN, LSTM and RNN) have gained a considerable uptake for time-series forecasting in last few years. One of the primary approaches was the ANN model. ANNs have been developed in order to mimic the intelligence of the human brain automatically. More specifically, ANNs try to recognize patterns in the input data attempting to provide generalized results based on their known previous knowledge. As confirmed by reported results, ANNs have largely applied in the financial domain. Their main advantage consists in not providing any a priori assumption about the data. In fact, the model is suitable to fit a given time-series by analyzing the features extracted from complex data, as opposed to traditional models, such as ARIMA.

Recently, a considerable amount of literature has investigated the use of RNN and its variants, such as LSTM, for time-series forecasting. Compared to the classical ANN model, these models achieved better results in forecasting problems due to their powerful ability to capture hidden relationships within data. More specifically, LSTM architecture has been designed to learn long-term dependencies. LSTM is able to manage the input/output data flow through its fundamental unit: the cell. A LSTM cell is composed by three different "gates", called input, forget and output gate, which establish to store or discard data by using sigmoid function, called "activation function". Also, the input and status of the cell is updated through applying the "tanh function".

Advances in natural language processing (NLP) and DL fields have brought the development of sentiment analysis approaches to transform upcoming web news, tweets and financial reports into relevant features. After extracting useful information from data in textual format, they are processed as input time series to perform forecasting.

The studies reported in this work confirmed further the effectiveness of sentiment analysis methods in predicting financial trend.

Finally, we investigated the problem to define a profitable trading system by applying RL approaches. Thus, recent development in this field combing both DL and RL approaches taking advantage of their powerful ability to elaborate complex data.

In particular, RL approaches have been applied to deal with the prediction of medium-short term trend which represents an issue of the HFT systems. In Figure 1, we reported a timeline of strategies adopted for financial time-series modelling.

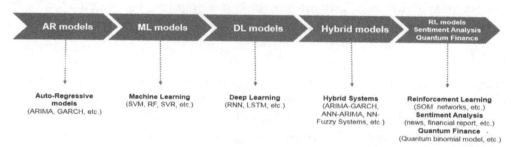

Figure 1. Timeline of adopted approaches for time-series analysis. AR: Auto-Regressive. ML: Machine Learning. DL: Deep Learning. RL: Reinforcement Learning. SVM: Support Vector Machine. RF: Random Forest. SVR: Support Vector Regression. ARIMA: Autoregressive Integrated Moving Average. GARCH: Generalized Autoregressive Conditional Heteroskedasticity. RNN: Recurrent Neural Network. LSTM: Long Short-Term Memory. SOM: Self-Organising Map.

The objective of this survey has been to discuss how machine-learning approaches outperform methods based on non-linear algorithm underlying their pros and cons. The main benefit on applying ML-based systems is to automatize trading operations and reduce computing time, ensuring to perform with high level in terms of accuracy. For this reason, we focused on ML algorithms such as SVM or random forest and DL models (LSTM or RNN). We compared some of these methods and evaluated the approaches, which obtained the best results related to time-series modeling.

Our investigation suggested that a quite considerable number of investigated studies provide an evaluation by using the following stock market data:

- **Bombay SE:** The Bombay Stock Exchange (BSE) is one of the largest exchanges in the world which includes around 6000 companies. A large part of these companies is also listed on the National Stock Exchange of India.

- **S&P 500:** Standard & Poor's 500 Index is a market-capitalization-weighted index of the 500 largest U.S. publicly traded companies.

- **DAX indices:** DAX is a stock index for German companies that trade on the Frankfurt Exchange. In order to calculate the DAX Index, an electronic trading system, called Xetra, is used. Unlike most indexes, the DAX is updated using futures prices for the next day.

- In a different twist from most indexes, the DAX is updated with futures prices for the next day, even after the main stock exchange has closed.

- **Shangai stock exchange:** The Shanghai Stock Exchange (SSE) represents the largest stock exchange in China. It is a non-profit organization run by the China Securities Regulatory Commission (CSRC). Stocks, funds, bonds, and derivatives are all traded on the exchange.

- **NASDAQ index:** The NASDAQ is the world's fast electronic stock exchange which operates through computer and telephones, as opposite to traditional method. NASDAQ lists only technology-based companies.

However, the proposed investigation highlighted the need to define a unique benchmark dataset. We observed that investigated methods conducted experiments by using different datasets. Benchmarks are important for researchers in order to measure the performance of an algorithm on a specific problem. Without the definition of a unique dataset and appropriate performance indicators, researchers cannot make a complete comparison between the proposed studies in order to select a suitable solution for a specific problem. Also, the majority of investigated primary studies provide different evaluation metrics for time-series forecasting.

In this work, we examined several proposed studies reporting the use of both traditional linear model and machine-learning approaches. Despite facing issues such as lack of a benchmark dataset and performance indicators, we attempted to provide a comparison between traditional and ML-based approaches, reported in this survey. Specifically, Table 8 summarizes experimental results regarding two of the investigated approaches [7,22]. The work of Babu et al. [7] proposed a hybrid system based on ARIMA and GARCH models. The authors collected data from January 2010 to January 2011 to define the first dataset (TD1) used for evaluating the performance of their model. As reported in [7], they compared results between the proposed approach and other autoregressive models such as ARIMA, GARCH etc. The corresponding errors measures (MAPE, MAE, MaxAPE and RMSE) show that the proposed approach outperforms other models. Furthermore, the authors considered SB1 shares from January 2010 to December 2010 to test the performance of proposed approach. The error performance measures (MAE, MaxAPE, etc.) confirmed that the proposed method obtains better results among others model (ARIMA and GARCH single scenario etc.). Also, the proposed hybrid system minimizes error performance. Despite achieving considerable results, autoregressive models present several limitations for stock price prediction compared to ML-based techniques.

Table 8. Summary of studies based on ML/DL models. MAPE: mean absolute percentage error. MAXAPE: maximum absolute percentage error MAE: mean absolute error. RMSE: root mean square error. NSE: Nigeria Stock Exchange.

	Techniques	MAPE	MAXAPE	MAE	RMSE	Dataset
Babu et al. (2014) [7]	Hybrid ARIMA-GARCH	0.1976 *	0.4285 *	0.5533	0.7514	NSE (TSD1)
		3.41	7.04	55.5303	66.1981	NSE (TSD2)
	ARIMA	2.4 *	5.3657 *	6.3765	6.7195	NSE (TSD1)
		9.8	15.73	160.9963	169.7036	NSE (TSD2)
Selvin al. (2017) [22]			Error Percentage			
	RNN		3.90			NSE (Infosys)
			7.65			NSE (TCS)
			3.83			NSE (Cipla)
	LSTM		4.18			NSE (Infosys)
			7.82			NSE (TCS)
			3.94			NSE (Cipla)
	CNN		2.36			NSE (Infosys)
			8.96			NSE (TCS)
			3.63			NSE (Cipla)
	ARIMA		31.91			NSE (Infosys)
			21.16			NSE (TCS)
			36.53			NSE (Cipla)

* The values shown in fractions instead of percentages.

In [22], the authors chose stock prices of National Stock Exchange (NSE) India data to evaluate the proposed pipeline. More specifically, they collected Infosys data for the period from July 2014 to October 2014 as training data and they used stock price for Infosys, Tata Consultancy Service (TCS) and Chemical Industrial and Pharmaceutical Laboratories (CIPLA) from October 2014 to November 2014. The reported results in Table 8 are related to Error Percentage. In particular, they compared results achieved by RNN, LSTM and CNN to ARIMA model. They observed that the ARIMA model present a higher error percentage value than other models, confirming that neural models are more suitable for the prediction of stock markets affected by high volatility.

In order to confirm the effectiveness of DL, we reported performance results of two surveyed works [17,48] based on applying a recurrent model (LSTM) and the RL approach, respectively. The work of Fischer et al., proposed a LSTM-based model. The authors reported performance results in terms of risk characteristics considering S&P 500 data before and after transaction costs. In Table 9, we summarized the performance results of the LSTM model. As reported in [17], LSTM shows the lowest maximum drawdown compared to other models.

In terms of annualized risk-return, LSTM achieves highest returns (0.8229) compared to random forest, DNN, etc. We reported results of [48] in which the authors applied a time-driven feature-aware jointly deep reinforcement-learning model (TFJ-DRL) to improve the financial signal representation learning. They considered stocks from S&P 500 to evaluate the proposed model which takes advantages of Reinforcement Learning paradigm. The evaluation metrics, total profits (TP), annualized rate of return (AR), annualized Sharpe ratio (SR) and transaction times (TT), highlighted that the proposed TFJ-DRL outperforms other competitors. Also, the reported results in [48] confirmed that the proposed framework could be applied on real data stock market to achieve reliable results.

Table 9. Summaries of results achieved by a ML-based approach and a reinforcement learning (RL)-based approach considering S&P 500.

	Techniques	MAX DrawDown (DD)	SR p.a	Return p.a		Dataset
Fischer et al. (2017) [17]	LSTM	0.4660	5.8261	2.0127		S&P 500 (before transaction costs)
		0.5233	2.336	0.8229		S&P 500 (after transaction costs)
		TP	**AR (%)**	**SR**	**TT**	
Lei et al. (2020) [48]	TFJ-DRL	3431.87	20.92	1.09	609	S&P 500 (rising)

Further interesting results in the field of HFT trading algorithms and time-series forecasts, have been recently obtained by applying some deep-learning approaches based on the morphological-temporal analysis of the data initially applied in the medical and industrial sector for the study of one-dimensional aperiodic physiological signals (very close to financial time-series) [56–58]. In this perspective, as already anticipated in the work proposed by the authors in [49], the aforementioned innovative approaches are able to significantly improve both the trend forecasting capability as well as the overall performance of the developed trading system.

11. Conclusions

In this survey, we have reviewed some of the most promising approaches applied in financial domain. Specifically, the contribution of our work reaches multiple goals. Firstly, we defined the problems related to analyzing time-series and how traditional approaches, such as AR methods, represented an effective solution to achieve satisfactory results in financial problems. However, we provided a comparison between traditional approaches and a ML-based system in order to highlight how ML-based algorithms outperform classical approaches in terms of accuracy. Also, we demonstrated the advantages related to DL models providing an exhaustive discussion on current approaches in the RL, sentiment analysis and quantum finance fields.

Author Contributions: Conceptualization & Investigation, F.R., F.T.; Validation, F.R., S.B.; Writing-Review and Editing, S.B. and A.L.d.S.

References

1. Hamilton, J.D. *Time Series Analysis*; Princeton University Press: Princeton, NJ, USA, 1994; Volume 2, pp. 690–696.
2. Cheng, C.; Sa-Ngasoongsong, A.; Beyca, O.; Le, T.; Yang, H.; Kong, Z.; Bukkapatnam, S.T. Time series forecasting for nonlinear and non-stationary processes: A review and comparative study. *IIE Trans.* **2015**, *47*, 1053–1071. [CrossRef]
3. Cavalcante, R.C.; Brasileiro, R.C.; Souza, V.L.; Nobrega, J.P.; Oliveira, A.L. Computational intelligence and financial markets: A survey and future directions. *Expert Syst. Appl.* **2016**, *55*, 194–211. [CrossRef]
4. Box, G.E.P.; Jenkins, G.M. *Time Series Analysis: Forecasting and Control*; Holden-Day: San Francisco, CA, USA, 1970.
5. Contreras, J.; Espinola, R.; Nogales, F.J.; Conejo, A.J. ARIMA models to predict next-day electricity prices. *IEEE Trans. Power Syst.* **2003**, *18*, 1014–1020. [CrossRef]
6. Williams, B.M.; Hoel, L.A. Modeling and forecasting vehicular traffic flow as a seasonal ARIMA process: Theoretical basis and empirical results. *J. Transp. Eng.* **2003**, *129*, 664–672. [CrossRef]
7. Babu, C.N.; Reddy, B.E. Selected Indian stock predictions using a hybrid ARIMA-GARCH model. In Proceedings of the 2014 International Conference on Advances in Electronics Computers and Communications, Bangalore, India, 10–11 October 2014; pp. 1–6.
8. Adebiyi, A.A.; Adewumi, A.O.; Ayo, C.K. Stock price prediction using the ARIMA model. In Proceedings of the 2014 UKSim-AMSS 16th International Conference on Computer Modelling and Simulation, Cambridge, UK, 26–28 March 2014; pp. 106–112.
9. Cortes, C.; Vapnik, V. Support vector machine. *Mach. Learn.* **1995**, *20*, 273–297. [CrossRef]
10. Fan, A.; Palaniswami, M. Stock selection using support vector machines. In Proceedings of the International Joint Conference on Neural Networks (IJCNN'01), Washington, DC, USA, 15–19 July 2001; Volume 3, pp. 1793–1798.
11. Cao, L.J.; Tay, F.E.H. Support vector machine with adaptive parameters in financial time series forecasting. *IEEE Trans. Neural Netw.* **2003**, *14*, 1506–1518. [CrossRef] [PubMed]
12. Nayak, R.K.; Mishra, D.; Rath, A.K. A Naïve SVM-KNN based stock market trend reversal analysis for Indian benchmark indices. *Appl. Soft Comput.* **2015**, *35*, 670–680. [CrossRef]
13. Zhang, X.D.; Li, A.; Pan, R. Stock trend prediction based on a new status box method and AdaBoost probabilistic support vector machine. *Appl. Soft Comput.* **2016**, *49*, 385–398. [CrossRef]
14. Patel, J.; Shah, S.; Thakkar, P.; Kotecha, K. Predicting stock market index using fusion of machine learning techniques. *Expert Syst. Appl.* **2015**, *42*, 2162–2172. [CrossRef]
15. Chen, K.; Zhou, Y.; Dai, F. A LSTM-based method for stock returns prediction: A case study of China stock market. In Proceedings of the 2015 IEEE International Conference on Big Data (Big Data), Santa Clara, CA, USA, 29 October–1 November 2015; pp. 2823–2824.
16. Hafezi, R.; Shahrabi, J.; Hadavandi, E. A bat-neural network multi-agent system (BNNMAS) for stock price prediction: Case study of DAX stock price. *Appl. Soft Comput.* **2015**, *29*, 196–210. [CrossRef]
17. Fischer, T.; Krauss, C. Deep learning with long short-term memory networks for financial market predictions. *Eur. J. Oper. Res.* **2018**, *270*, 654–669. [CrossRef]
18. Hochreiter, S.; Schmidhuber, J. Long short-term memory. *Neural Comput.* **1997**, *9*, 1735–1780. [CrossRef] [PubMed]
19. Sutskever, I.; Vinyals, O.; Le, Q.V. Sequence to sequence learning with neural networks. *arXiv* **2014**, arXiv:1409.3215v3.
20. Yue-Hei Ng, J.; Hausknecht, M.; Vijayanarasimhan, S.; Vinyals, O.; Monga, R.; Toderici, G. Beyond short snippets: Deep networks for video classification. In Proceedings of the IEEE Conference on Computer Vision and Pattern Recognition, Boston, MA, USA, 7–12 June 2015; pp. 4694–4702.
21. Yümlü, S.; Gürgen, F.S.; Okay, N. A comparison of global, recurrent and smoothed-piecewise neural models for Istanbul stock exchange (ISE) prediction. *Pattern Recognit. Lett.* **2005**, *26*, 2093–2103. [CrossRef]
22. Selvin, S.; Vinayakumar, R.; Gopalakrishnan, E.A.; Menon, V.K.; Soman, K.P. Stock price prediction using LSTM, RNN and CNN-sliding window model. In Proceedings of the 2017 International Conference on Advances in Computing, Communications and Informatics (ICACCI), Udupi, India, 13–16 September 2017; pp. 1643–1647.

23. Samarawickrama, A.J.P.; Fernando, T.G.I. A recurrent neural network approach in predicting daily stock prices an application to the Sri Lankan stock market. In Proceedings of the 2017 IEEE International Conference on Industrial and Information Systems (ICIIS), Peradeniya, Sri Lanka, 15–16 December 2017; pp. 1–6.

24. Siami-Namini, S.; Tavakoli, N.; Namin, A.S. A Comparison of ARIMA and LSTM in Forecasting Time Series. In Proceedings of the 2018 17th IEEE International Conference on Machine Learning and Applications (ICMLA), Orlando, FL, USA, 17–20 December 2018; pp. 1394–1401.

25. Rundo, F.; Trenta, F.; Di Stallo, A.; Battiato, S. Advanced Markov-Based Machine Learning Framework for Making Adaptive Trading System. *Computation* **2019**, *7*, 4. [CrossRef]

26. Rundo, F.; Trenta, F.; di Stallo, A.L.; Battiato, S. Grid Trading System Robot (GTSbot): A Novel Mathematical Algorithm for trading FX Market. *Appl. Sci.* **2019**, *9*, 1796. [CrossRef]

27. Hossain, A.; Nasser, M. Comparison of GARCH and neural network methods in financial time series prediction. In Proceedings of the 2008 11th International Conference on Computer and Information Technology, Khulna, Bangladesh, 24–27 December 2008; pp. 729–734.

28. Wijaya, Y.B.; Kom, S.; Napitupulu, T.A. Stock price prediction: Comparison of Arima and artificial neural network methods—An Indonesia Stock's Case. In Proceedings of the 2010 Second International Conference on Advances in Computing, Control, and Telecommunication Technologies, Jakarta, Indonesia, 2–3 December 2010; pp. 176–179.

29. Kara, Y.; Boyacioglu, M.A.; Baykan, Ö.K. Predicting direction of stock price index movement using artificial neural networks and support vector machines: The sample of the Istanbul Stock Exchange. *Expert Syst. Appl.* **2011**, *38*, 5311–5319. [CrossRef]

30. Adebiyi, A.A.; Adewumi, A.O.; Ayo, C.K. Comparison of ARIMA and artificial neural networks models for stock price prediction. *J. Appl. Math.* **2014**, *2014*, 614342. [CrossRef]

31. Patel, J.; Shah, S.; Thakkar, P.; Kotecha, K. Predicting stock and stock price index movement using trend deterministic data preparation and machine learning techniques. *Expert Syst. Appl.* **2015**, *42*, 259–268. [CrossRef]

32. Laboissiere, L.A.; Fernandes, R.A.; Lage, G.G. Maximum and minimum stock price forecasting of Brazilian power distribution companies based on artificial neural networks. *Appl. Soft Comput.* **2015**, *35*, 66–74. [CrossRef]

33. Li, Z.; Tam, V. A comparative study of a recurrent neural network and support vector machine for predicting price movements of stocks of different volatilites. In Proceedings of the 2017 IEEE Symposium Series on Computational Intelligence (SSCI), Honolulu, HI, USA, 27 November–1 December 2017; pp. 1–8.

34. Wang, J.H.; Leu, J.Y. Stock market trend prediction using ARIMA-based neural networks. In Proceedings of the International Conference on Neural Networks (ICNN'96), Washington, DC, USA, 3–6 June 1996; Volume 4, pp. 2160–2165.

35. Zhang, G.P. Time series forecasting using a hybrid ARIMA and neural network model. *Neurocomputing* **2003**, *50*, 159–175. [CrossRef]

36. Wang, Y.H. Nonlinear neural network forecasting model for stock index option price: Hybrid GJR–GARCH approach. *Expert Syst. Appl.* **2009**, *36*, 564–570. [CrossRef]

37. Lee, M.C. Using support vector machine with a hybrid feature selection method to the stock trend prediction. *Expert Syst. Appl.* **2009**, *36*, 10896–10904. [CrossRef]

38. Khashei, M.; Bijari, M.; Ardali, G.A.R. Improvement of auto-regressive integrated moving average models using fuzzy logic and artificial neural networks (ANNs). *Neurocomputing* **2009**, *72*, 956–967. [CrossRef]

39. Wang, J.J.; Wang, J.Z.; Zhang, Z.G.; Guo, S.P. Stock index forecasting based on a hybrid model. *Omega* **2012**, *40*, 758–766. [CrossRef]

40. Hadavandi, E.; Shavandi, H.; Ghanbari, A. Integration of genetic fuzzy systems and artificial neural networks for stock price forecasting. *Knowl. Based Syst.* **2010**, *23*, 800–808. [CrossRef]

41. Babu, C.N.; Reddy, B.E. A moving-average filter based hybrid ARIMA–ANN model for forecasting time series data. *Appl. Soft Comput.* **2014**, *23*, 27–38. [CrossRef]

42. Panigrahi, S.; Behera, H.S. A hybrid ETS–ANN model for time series forecasting. *Eng. Appl. Artif. Intell.* **2017**, *66*, 49–59. [CrossRef]

43. Kim, H.Y.; Won, C.H. Forecasting the volatility of stock price index: A hybrid model integrating LSTM with multiple GARCH-type models. *Expert Syst. Appl.* **2018**, *103*, 25–37. [CrossRef]

44. Schumaker, R.P.; Chen, H. Textual analysis of stock market prediction using breaking financial news: The AZFin text system. In Proceedings of the ACM Transactions on Information Systems (TOIS), Honolulu, HI, USA, 8–12 March 2009; Volume 27, p. 12.

45. Pagolu, V.S.; Reddy, K.N.; Panda, G.; Majhi, B. Sentiment analysis of Twitter data for predicting stock market movements. In Proceedings of the 2016 International Conference on Signal Processing, Communication, Power and Embedded System (SCOPES), Paralakhemundi, India, 3–5 October 2016; pp. 1345–1350.

46. Mikolov, T.; Sutskever, I.; Chen, K.; Corrado, G.S.; Dean, J. Distributed representations of words and phrases and their compositionality. In Proceedings of the Advances in Neural Information Processing Systems, Lake Tahoe, NV, USA, 5–10 December 2013; pp. 3111–3119.

47. Daniel, J.; Martin, J.H. *Speech and Language Processing. Computational Linguistics, and Speech Recognition*; Prentice-Hall Inc.: Edinburgh, UK, 2000; pp. 22–105.

48. Lei, K.; Zhang, B.; Li, Y.; Yang, M.; Shen, Y. Time-driven feature-aware jointly deep reinforcement learning for financial signal representation and algorithmic trading. *Expert Syst. Appl.* **2020**, *140*, 112872. [CrossRef]

49. Rundo, F. Deep LSTM with Reinforcement Learning Layer for Financial Trend Prediction in FX High Frequency Trading Systems. *Appl. Sci.* **2019**, *9*, 4460. [CrossRef]

50. Halperin, I. The QLBS Q-Learner goes NuQLear: Fitted Q iteration, inverse RL, and option portfolios. *Quant. Finance* **2019**, *19*, 1543–1553. [CrossRef]

51. Baaquie, B.E. *Quantum Finance*; Cambridge University Press: Cambridge, UK, 2004.

52. Lee, R.S. *Quantum Finance-Intelligent Financial Forecast and Program Trading Systems*; Springer NATURE: Singapore, 2019.

53. Baaquie, B.E.; Du, X.; Tang, P.; Cao, Y. Pricing of range accrual swap in the quantum finance Libor Market Model. *Phys. A Stat. Mech. Its Appl.* **2014**, *401*, 182–200. [CrossRef]

54. Lee, R.S. Chaotic Type-2 Transient-Fuzzy Deep Neuro-Oscillatory Network (CT2TFDNN) for Worldwide Financial Prediction. *IEEE Trans. Fuzzy Syst.* **2019**. [CrossRef]

55. Lee, R.S. COSMOS trader–Chaotic Neuro-oscillatory multiagent financial prediction and trading system. *J. Finance Data Sci.* **2019**, *5*, 61–82. [CrossRef]

56. Banna, G.L.; Camerini, A.; Bronte, G.; Anile, G.; Addeo, A.; Rundo, F.; Zanghi, G.; Lal, R.; Libra, M. Oral metronomic vinorelbine in advanced non-small cell lung cancer patients unfit for chemotherapy. *Anticancer Res.* **2018**, *38*, 3689–3697. [CrossRef]

57. Rundo, F.; Petralia, S.; Fallica, G.; Conoci, S. A nonlinear pattern recognition pipeline for PPG/ECG medical assessments. In *CNS Sensors, Lecture Notes in Electrical Engineering*; Springer: Cham, Switzerland, 2018; Volume 539, pp. 473–480.

58. Vinciguerra, V.; Ambra, E.; Maddiona, L.; Romeo, M.; Mazzillo, M.; Rundo, F.; Fallica, G.; di Pompeo, F.; Chiarelli, A.M.; Zappasodi, F.; et al. PPG/ECG Multisite Combo System Based on SiPM Technology. In *CNS Sensors, Lecture Notes in Electrical Engineering*; Springer: Cham, Switzerland, 2018; Volume 539, pp. 353–360.

On the Relationship of Cryptocurrency Price with US Stock and Gold Price using Copula Models

Jong-Min Kim [1], Seong-Tae Kim [2] and Sangjin Kim [3,*

[1] Statistics Discipline, University of Minnesota at Morris, Morris, MN 56267, USA; jongmink@morris.umn.edu
[2] Department of Mathematics, North Carolina A&T State University, Greensboro, NC 27411, USA; skim@ncat.edu
[3] Department of Management and Information Systems, Dong-A University, Busan 49236, Korea
* Correspondence: skim10@dau.ac.kr

Abstract: This paper examines the relationship of the leading financial assets, Bitcoin, Gold, and S&P 500 with GARCH-Dynamic Conditional Correlation (DCC), Nonlinear Asymmetric GARCH DCC (NA-DCC), Gaussian copula-based GARCH-DCC (GC-DCC), and Gaussian copula-based Nonlinear Asymmetric-DCC (GCNA-DCC). Under the high volatility financial situation such as the COVID-19 pandemic occurrence, there exist a computation difficulty to use the traditional DCC method to the selected cryptocurrencies. To solve this limitation, GC-DCC and GCNA-DCC are applied to investigate the time-varying relationship among Bitcoin, Gold, and S&P 500. In terms of log-likelihood, we show that GC-DCC and GCNA-DCC are better models than DCC and NA-DCC to show relationship of Bitcoin with Gold and S&P 500. We also consider the relationships among time-varying conditional correlation with Bitcoin volatility, and S&P 500 volatility by a Gaussian Copula Marginal Regression (GCMR) model. The empirical findings show that S&P 500 and Gold price are statistically significant to Bitcoin in terms of log-return and volatility.

Keywords: cryptocurrency; gold; S&P 500; GARCH; DCC; copula

1. Introduction

Knowing the relationships of the cryptocurrency market with either the US stock market or commodity market will be very useful to manage investors' portfolios and how many portions of their investment money will be allocated to cryptocurrency for their secure and profitable investment plan. Cryptocurrency is a digital or virtual currency that is exchanged between peers without the need for a third party [1]. The key features of the cryptocurrency include that there is no central system to manage the transactions of cryptocurrencies, and they are classified as a commodity by the U.S. Commodity Futures Trading Commission (CFTC). The first cryptocurrency, Bitcoin, operates with block-chain technology, in which a secure system of accounting is used that transfers ownership. The cryptocurrency market is an attractive emerging market for investment, but this market revealed downfalls such as cryptocurrency hacking news. For example, in May 2019, hackers stole $40 million worth of Bitcoin from Binance, one of the largest cryptocurrency exchanges in the world. Therefore, investors themselves have to take a high risk from cryptocurrency investment. However, the recent cryptocurrency market is a bull market where the Bitcoin price is equal to the USD 10,806.90 as of 30 September 2020, but the Bitcoin price has severely fluctuated since the maximum Bitcoin price at the USD 19,783.06 on 17 December 2017. Despite a series of negative events in this market, investing cryptocurrency is gaining popularity among investors to make their own money. Consequently, economic entities are interested in the dynamic relationships among the cryptocurrency market, commodity market, and stock market.

There have been many studies on the analysis of the exchange rates of cryptocurrency [2]. Recently, Hyun et al. [3] examined dependence relationships among the five well-known cryptocurrencies (Bitcoin, Ethereum, Litecoin, Ripple, and Stella) using a copula directional dependence. Kim et al. [4] studied the volatility of nine well-known cryptocurrencies—Bitcoin, XRP, Ethereum, Bitcoin Cash, Stella, Litecoin, TRON, Cardano, and IOTA using several GARCH models and Bayesian Stochastic Volatility (SV) models. Klein et al. [5] employed the BEKK [6] GARCH model to estimate time-varying conditional correlations between gold and Bitcoin. In terms of portfolio management, Aslanidisa, Barivierab and Martínez-Ibañeza [7] considered Dynamic Conditional Correlation (DCC) with daily price data (21 May 2014, to 27 September 2018), pairs of four cryptocurrencies (Bitcoin, Dash, Monero, and Ripple), and three traditional financial assets (Standard & Poors 500 Composite (SP500), S&P US Treasury bond 7-10Y index (BOND), and Gold Bullion LBM) [8–11]. Guesmi et al. [12] examined the dynamics of Bitcoin and other financial assets using the VARMA (1, 1)-DCC-GJR-GARCH model and found that Bitcoin provides diversification and hedging opportunities for investment. Hyun et al. [3] already applied the copula approach to cryptocurrency because no assumption is needed such as normality, linearity, and independence of the errors from the proposed model.

In this study, we aim to apply the copula-based GARCH-DCC models [3,13,14] to see the recent time varying correlations between the cryptocurrency market and US stock price or between the cryptocurrency market and commodity market price after the slump of the cryptocurrency market price since 2018. The copula-based GARCH-DCC models are compared to the GARCH-DCC models in the empirical data analysis [8,15–17] which shows that copula-based GARCH-DCC models has better model than GARCH-DCC models. A copula is a multivariate distribution function described on the unit $[0, 1]^n$ with uniformly distributed marginal [18]. Our result also leaded to the same conclusion as the previous researches. Furthermore, because of the failure of the ordinary least regression to capture the heteroscedasticity with high volatility financial data, we use the Gaussian Copula Marginal Regression (GCMR) models [19] which can consider the heteroscedasticity and non-normality of the financial data to test our alternative hypothesis that Bitcoin is statistically significant by log-returns of S&P 500 and Gold price in terms of log-return. We also test the current volatility of log-returns of Bitcoin can be statistically significant with the current and lagged volatilities of the other assets (S&P 500 and Gold price). We also test that the time varying correlations of log-returns of Bitcoin and S&P 500 can be statistically significant with the current volatilities of the Bitcoin and S&P 500.

The paper is organized as follows. Section 2 reviews econometric methodologies that will be used in this paper. Section 3 describes data and discusses empirical data analysis. Section 4 provides the conclusion and our related future study.

2. Econometrical Methods

This section introduces the volatility model, dynamic correlation coefficient, copula, and their combinations. The description of econometric models is not comprehensive but selective to understand the dynamic relationships among the three markets.

2.1. GARCH Models

Let S_t be a price time series at time t. For a log return series $r_t = log\left(\frac{S_t}{S_{t-1}}\right)$, we let $a_t = r_t - E_{t-1}[r_t]$ be the innovation at time t. Then a_t follows a GARCH (p, q) model if $a_t = h_t \epsilon_t$

$$h_t^2 = \alpha_0 + \sum_{i=1}^{q} \alpha_i a_{t-i}^2 + \sum_{j=1}^{p} \beta_j h_{t-j}^2 \qquad (1)$$

where $\{\epsilon_t\}$ is a sequence of independent and identically distributed random variables with mean 0 and variance 1, $\alpha_0 > 0$, $\alpha_i \geq 0$, $\beta_j \geq 0$, and $\sum_{i=1}^{\max(p,q)}(\alpha_i + \beta_j) \leq 1$. All members of the family of GARCH models can be obtained from a transformation of the conditional standard deviation, h_t, determined by the transformation of the innovations, a_t, and lagged transformed conditional standard deviations. An extensive discussion on the nested GARCH models is given in Hentschel [20]. Since the conditional variance in the GARCH model did not properly respond to positive and negative shocks, Engel and Ng [21] also proposed one of the popular nonlinear asymmetric GARCH (NAGARCH) models as follows:

$$h_t^2 = \alpha_0 + \sum_{i=1}^{q} \alpha_i(a_{t-i} - \gamma_i h_{t-i})^2 + \sum_{j=1}^{q} \beta_j h_{t-j}^2,$$ (2)

where $\alpha_0 > 0$, $\alpha_i \geq 0$, $\beta_j \geq 0$ for $i = 1, 2, \ldots, p$ and $j = 1, 2, \ldots, q$. In the model, the distance $\gamma_i h_{t-i}$ moves the news impact curve to the right, and the parameter γ_i of stock returns is estimated to be positive. It indicates that negative returns increase future volatility with larger amounts than positive returns of the same magnitude.

The T-GARCH model, which can capture the asymmetric effect in the volatility is given by

$$h_t^2 = \alpha_0 + \sum_{i=1}^{q} \alpha_i(|a_{t-i}| - \eta_i a_{t-i})^2 + \sum_{j=1}^{p} \beta_j h_{t-j}^2,$$ (3)

where the asymmetric parameter η satisfies the condition $-1 < \eta < 1$. For the model selection of the GARCH (1, 1) models considered, we use the Akaike Information Criterion (AIC). Besides, this study also considers the Student-t errors to take into account the possible fatness of the distribution tails of a_t.

2.2. DCC and Copula DCC Models

To investigate the time-varying correlations among multivariate returns, we adopt the DCC model, which incorporates the flexibility of univariate GARCH models and the harmonicity of correlation estimation functions. In the DCC model in [6,22], the correlation matrix is time-varying, and the covariance matrix can be decomposed into:

$$H_t = D_t R D_t = \rho_{ij}\sqrt{h_{ij,t}h_{ij,t}}, \quad \text{where } D_t = diag\left(\sqrt{h_{11,t}},\ldots,\sqrt{h_{nn,t}}\right)$$ (4)

containing the time-varying standard deviations is obtained from GARCH models, and R is the constant conditional correlation (CCC) proposed by Bollerslev [23], which is defined as $R = T^{-1}\sum_{i=t}^{T}v_t v_t'$, where $v_t = \frac{r_t - \mu}{\sigma_t}$, and μ is a vector of expected returns. The DDC in [24] is a time-varying extension of the CCC, which has the following structure:

$$R_t = diag(Q_t)^{-\frac{1}{2}}Q_t diag(Q_t)^{-\frac{1}{2}},$$ (5)

where $Q_t = R + \alpha\left(v_{t-1}v_{t-1}' - R\right) + \beta(Q_{t-1} - R)$.

Note that to ensure stationarity, nonnegative α and β satisfy the constraint $\alpha+\beta < 1$, and Q_t is positive definite which makes R_t positive definite. Off-diagonal elements in the covariance matrix Q_t are the correlation coefficients between pairwise indexes among Bitcoin, Gold, and S&P 500 at time t. In this paper, we use the "dcc.estimation" function in the "ccgarch" on R package [24,25] to estimate each conditional correlation.

We consider another statistical approach to address the correlation among multivariate time series. Sklar [26] suggested copular functions to build joint multivariate distributions. The copula models we consider here are Gaussian copulas which are used to estimate the time-varying correlation matrix of the DCC model. A copula is an efficient way to characterize and model correlated multivariate random variables. Therefore, we consider the time-varying conditional correlation in the copula framework. Let a random vector $(X_1, \ldots, X_p)$ have marginal distribution functions $F_i(x_i) = P(X_i \leq x_i)$ for $i = 1, \ldots, p$. The dependence function, C, for all $u_1, \ldots, u_n \in [0,1]^n$ can be defined as:

$$C(u_1, \ldots, u_n) = P(F_1(X_1) \leq u_1, \ldots, F_n(X_n) \leq u_n)$$
$$C(u_1, \ldots, u_n) = F\left(F_1^{-1}(u_1), \ldots, F_1^{-1}(u_n)\right). \tag{6}$$

In this study, we estimate $\mathrm{DCC}(\hat{\rho}_t)$ by a Gaussian copula function whose conditional density is defined as:

$$c_t(u_{1t}, \ldots, u_{nt}|R_t) = \frac{f_t(F_1^{-1}(u_{1t}), \ldots, F_1^{-1}(u_{nt})|R_t)}{\prod_{i=1}^n f_i(F_1^{-1}(u_{it}))}, \tag{7}$$

where R_t is the correlation matrix implied by the covariance matrix, $u_{it} = F_{it}(r_{it}|\mu_{it}, h_{it}, v_t, \tau_i)$ is the probability integral transformed values estimated by the GARCH process, and $F_1^{-1}(u_{it}|\tau)$ represents the quantile transformation. We estimate each conditional correlation via the "cgarchspec" function in the R package "rmgarch" implementing the Gaussian copula [27,28]. In particular, our model applies the Gaussian copula to estimate the conditional covariance matrix. We propose four different DCC-related models: the GARCH-DCC (DCC) model, Nonlinear Asymmetric-GARCH-DCC (NA-DCC) model, Gaussian copula-based GARCH-DCC (GC-DCC) model, and Gaussian copula-based nonlinear asymmetric GARCH-DCC (GCNA-DCC) model to see the dynamic conditional correlations between Bitcoin and S&P 500 and between Bitcoin and Gold.

2.3. Gaussian Copula Marginal Regression (GCMR) Model

Gaussian Copula Marginal Regression (GCMR) is another methodology used in this study to capture the relationship, where dependence is expressed in the correlation matrix of a multivariate Gaussian distribution [19,29]. Let $F(\cdot|x_i)$ be a marginal cumulative distribution depending on a vector of covariates x_i. If a set of n dependent variables in Y_i is considered, then the joint cumulative distribution function is in the Gaussian copula regression defined by

$$\Pr(Y_1 \leq y_1, \ldots, Y_1 \leq y_1) = \Phi_n\{\varepsilon_1, \ldots, \varepsilon_n; P\}, \tag{8}$$

where $\varepsilon_i = \Phi^{-1}\{F(y_i|x_i)\}$. $\Phi(\cdot)$ and $\Phi_n(\cdot; P)$ indicate the univariate and multivariate standard normal cumulative distribution functions, respectively. P denotes the correlation matrix of the Gaussian copula. Masarotto and Varin [19] propose an equivalent formulation of the Gaussian copula model linking each variable Y_i to a vector of covariates x_i as follows:

$$Y_i = h(x_i, \varepsilon_i), \tag{9}$$

where ε_i indicates a stochastic error. In particular, the Gaussian copula regression model assumes that $h(x_i, \varepsilon_i) = F^{-1}\{\Phi(\varepsilon_i)|x_i\}$ and ε has a multivariate standard normal distribution with correlation matrix P. The advantages of using GCMR are to keep the marginal univariate distributions for each variable and to have multivariate normal errors for the joint distribution.

3. Empirical Analysis and Results

In this section, we apply the proposed methods to the three selected price time series. Given the sensitivity of the periods in predicting the volatility of financial time-series return data such as cryptocurrencies, we examine two different periods, more recent and short- and long-term periods. The sample consists of the daily log-returns of the nine cryptocurrencies over the period from 2 January 2018 to 21 September 2020. The log-returns of Bitcoin (BTC) and S&P 500 are denoted by LBTC and LSP, respectively. We obtained our Bitcoin data from a financial website [30], Gold data from Prof. Werner Antweiler's website [31] at the University of British Columbia Sauder School of Business, and S&P 500 data from the Yahoo finance website [32].

Figure 1 compares the pattern of prices of Bitcoin, Gold, and S&P 500 at the original scale since January 2018. The graphs appear to have a significant pairwise positive relationship after the COVID-19 pandemic occurrence. Therefore, with the log-returns of prices of Bitcoin, Gold, and S&P 500 (LBTC, LGD, LSP), we test if there is the significant pairwise correlation among LBTC, LGD, and LSP in this period using three correlations measures, the Pearson correlation method with the linear relationship assumption and Spearman and Kendall rank correlations as non-parametric methods. The data provided no statistically significant pairwise relationships among the three variables of prices as seen in Table 1. We also summarized descriptive statistics of the log return data of the cryptocurrencies such as mean, skewness, and kurtosis as well as the five-number summary statistics in Table 2. In Table 2, it is recognized that the standard deviation of LBTC is larger than those of LGD and LSP, which means that LBTC has a higher risk than LGD and LSP in terms of investment. Besides, the value of kurtosis in LBTC is greater than 3, meaning heavy tails while LGD and LSP have values less than 3, meaning light tails compared to a normal distribution. The LBTC and LSP are left-skewed while LGD is right-skewed. It means that the prices of Bitcoin and the S&P 500 will more likely be decreased soon, but the price of Gold will more likely be increased shortly.

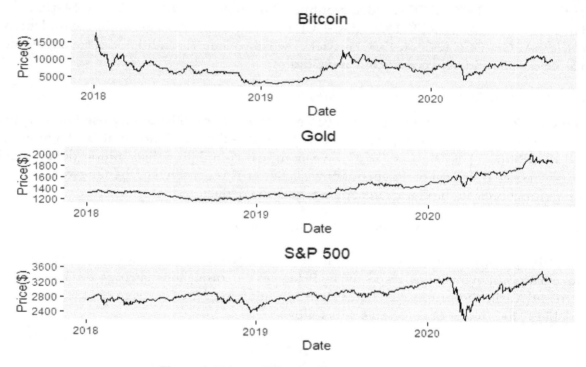

Figure 1. Prices of Bitcoin, Gold, and S&P 500.

Table 1. Correlation coefficients of log-return of Bitcoin (LBTC), log-return of Gold (LGD), and log-returns of S&P 500 (LSP) with Pearson, Spearman, and Kendall.

		LBTC	LGD	LSP
Pearson	LBTC	1	0.202	0.240
	LGD	0.202	1	0.255
	LSP	0.240	0.255	1
Spearman	LBTC	1	0.134	0.095
	LGD	0.134	1	0.084
	LSP	0.095	0.084	1
Kendall	LBTC	1	0.090	0.064
	LGD	0.090	1	0.060
	LSP	0.064	0.063	1

Table 2. Summary statistics of the log-return of Bitcoin (LBTC), log-return of Gold (LGD), and log-returns of S&P 500 (LSP).

	LBTC	LGD	LSP
Min	−0.465	−0.053	−0.128
Q1	−0.016	−0.004	−0.004
Q2	0.001	0.0004	0.001
Mean	−0.0005	0.0006	0.0003
Q3	0.019	0.005	0.007
Max	0.203	0.051	0.090
SD	0.049	0.009	0.015
Skewness	−1.579	−0.268	−1.067
Kurtosis	17.662	9.311	18.960

Since a causality between two variables may exist although there is no correlation as in Table 1, we tested if there is linear Granger causality with each lag of 1, 2, and 3 using the *"grangertest"* function in the *"lmtest"* R package [33]. That is, we consider the causality from LBTC to LSP and vice versa and from LBTC to LGD and vice versa. Table 3 shows the results of linear Granger causality tests at lag 1, 2, and 3, respectively. As seen in Table 3, there is no statistically significant causality among LBTC, LSP and LGD at the lag 1 but there is statistically significant causality among (LBTC, LSP) and (LBTC, LGD) at the lag 2 and the lag 3.

Table 3. The result of linear Granger causality with lag of 1, 2, and 3. There is no Granger causality between the log-returns of Bitcoin (LBTC) and S&P 500 (LSP) and Bitcoin (LBTC) and Gold (LGD), respectively.

	Lag 1		Lag 2		Lag 3	
Causality	F-stat	p-val	F-stat	p-val	F-stat	p-val
Bitcoin → S&P 500	2.656	0.104	8.153	0.000	5.520	0.001
S&P 500 → Bitcoin	0.530	0.467	0.120	0.887	0.257	0.857
Bitcoin → Gold	0.034	0.854	4.217	0.015	3.788	0.010
Gold → Bitcoin	0.868	0.352	1.882	0.153	2.413	0.066

Figure 2 shows the volatilities of log-returns of Bitcoin, Gold, and S&P 500 with the models of GARCH and NAGARCH. The GARCH volatilities are larger than those of the NAGARCH, while the pattern of volatility is similar between the two models. In each of the two plots, the level of volatilities (or risk) among the log-returns of Bitcoin, Gold, and S&P 500 is in the order of Bitcoin, S&P 500, and Gold.

To investigate the volatilities of the LBTC, LGD, LSP, we consider three different GARCH models which include two asymmetric GARCH models, T-GARCH (1, 1), and Nonlinear Asymmetric-GARCH (1, 1), and one standard-GARCH (1, 1). Table 4 reports the result of log-likelihood to choose an optimal model among the three models. The standard-GARCH (1, 1) model achieved the minimum AIC scores meaning a better fit across LBTC, LSP, and LGD.

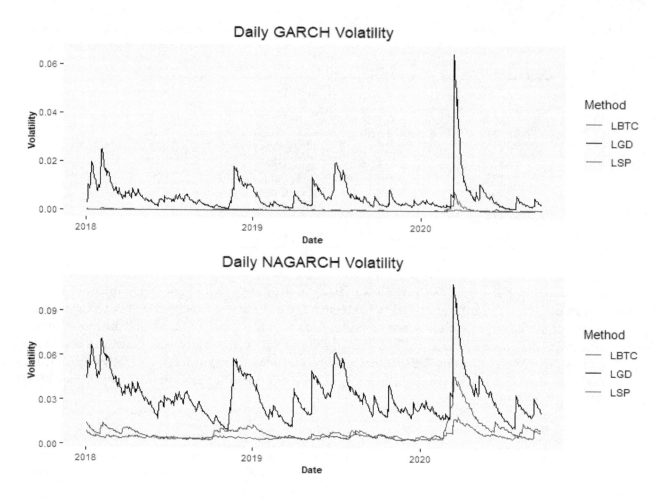

Figure 2. Daily volatility plots for LBTC, LSP, LGD with GARCH (1, 1), and Nonlinear Asymmetric-GARCH (1, 1).

Table 4. The result of Akaike Information Criterion (AIC) scores to select the best model among three different GARCH models. The Standard-GARCH (1, 1) model has maximum values of log-likelihood (LH) from the log-return of Bitcoin (LBTC), log-return of Gold (LGD), and log-returns of S&P 500 (LSP). A higher LH indicates a better fit.

	LBTC	LSP	LGD
T-GARCH (1, 1)	1568.405	1702.325	797.6006
NA-GARCH (1, 1)	2014.815	2139.722	1163.852
Standard-GARCH (1, 1)	2106.239	2246.397	1206.569

We apply a standard-GARCH (1, 1) model to LBTC, LSP, and LGD to check if there exists volatility clustering. Table 5 shows the results of the model fits based on the standard-GARCH (1, 1) model. The coefficient β_1 is the effect of the conditional variance at time t-1 on the conditional variance at time t, so a high value close to one indicates a longer persistency of the volatility shock. Hence, the estimates of $\beta_1's$ in the table explain the amount of volatility clustering. Likewise, there exist consistent volatility clusterings throughout all models since all p values of β_1s are closed to 0 at $\alpha = 0.05$.

Table 5. The results of the standard-GARCH (1, 1) model with the log-return of Bitcoin (LBTC), log-return of Gold (LGD), and log-returns of S&P 500 (LSP) where α_0, α_1, and β_1 are from Equation (1).

	Estimate	S.E	t-Value	p-Value
Standard-GARCH Model Fit with LBTC				
α_0	0.000	0.000	2.700	0.007
α_1	0.244	0.051	4.794	0.000
β_1	0.755	0.040	18.707	0.000
t-distribution parameter	5.547	1.167	4.752	0.000
Standard-GARCH Model Fit with LSP				
α_0	0.000	0.000	2.026	**0.043**
α_1	0.097	0.029	3.319	**0.000**
β_1	0.867	0.039	22.494	**0.000**
t-distribution parameter	6.260	1.522	4.111	**0.000**
Standard-GARCH Model Fit with LGD				
α_0	0.000	0.000	0.964	0.335
α_1	0.277	0.148	1.560	0.084
β_1	0.878	0.033	32.097	0.000
t-distribution parameter	2.315	0.337	10.516	0.000

Note: β_1 is statistically significant in the table. It means there exists consistent volatility clustering.

Furthermore, we checked the normality of the data and determined if a good fit had been achieved based on the Ljung-Box test which is a classical hypothesis test whose null hypothesis is that the autocorrelations between the population series values are zero. Table 6 shows the results of the Jarque–Bera and Sapiro–Wilk tests for normality and the Ljung–Box and LM-ARCH conditional heteroscedasticity tests for residuals. According to the statistical tests in the table, the residuals appear to be non-normal since the p-values of the two normality tests are less than $\alpha = 0.05$, and they show no serial correlations in the series since the p-values of the Ljung–Box tests are greater than $\alpha = 0.05$.

Table 6. The residual test results of the standard-GARCH (1, 1) model. It shows that the residuals are not normal and there is volatility clustering.

Standardized Residuals (R) Tests	Statistic	p-Value
Jarque-Bera Test on R	6760.294	0.000
Shapiro-Wilk Test on R	0.824	0.000
Ljung-Box Test on R Q(10)	10.668	0.384
Ljung-Box Test on R Q(15)	12.946	0.606
Ljung-Box Test on R Q(20)	16.334	0.696
Ljung-Box Test on R Squared Q(10)	10.223	0.421
Ljung-Box Test on R Squared Q(15)	11.416	0.723
Ljung-Box Test on R Squared Q(20)	12.765	0.887
LM-ARCH Test on R	10.217	0.597

We also consider nonlinear asymmetric GARCH to model LBTC, LSP, and LGD. Table 7 reports that there exists consistent volatility clustering since the p values of β_1s are all significant at $\alpha = 0.05$, which is consistent with the results in Table 5, and there is no volatility asymmetry in leverage effect in this period because all p values of γ_1s are not significant over each of the LBTC, LGD, LSP.

We built four different dynamic conditional correlation (DCC) models for LBTC and LSP and three different DCC models for LBTC and LGD. Figure 3 represents the DCC of four different models with DCC, NA-DCC, GC-DCC, and GCNA-DCC for log-returns of Bitcoin and S&P 500. The patterns of the four models are almost similar to each other. However, the top two graphs for DCCs without Gaussian copulas are slightly different from the bottom two graphs for DCCs with Gaussian copulas for which NA-DCC using Gaussian copulas has relatively smaller values than those of using NA-DCC alone. In

Figure 3, the highest positive DCC between LBTC and LSP was observed during the cryptocurrency crash in early 2018. In particular, we need to pay attention to that there exists a postive time-varying correlation between LBTC and LSP from March 2020 to September 2020 which is the COVID-19 pandemic period.

Table 7. Model fit of NA-GARCH (1, 1) where α_0, α_1, and β_1 are from Equation (2). Each of all β_1s has significance indicating there exists consistent volatility clustering and all γ_1s have no significance meaning there is no leverage effect (not asymmetric).

	Estimate	S.E	t-Value	p-Value
NA-GARCH Model Fit with LBTC				
α_0	0.000	0.000	0.298	0.765
α_1	0.050	0.006	8.385	0.000
β_1	0.900	0.010	89.068	0.000
γ_1	0.050	0.068	0.737	0.461
t-distribution parameter	4.000	0.215	18.605	**0.000**
NA-GARCH Model Fit with LSP				
α_0	0.000	0.000	0.073	0.942
α_1	0.050	0.006	8.266	0.000
β_1	0.900	0.012	73.973	0.000
γ_1	0.051	0.059	0.861	0.389
t-distribution parameter	4.000	0.208	19.215	0.000
NA-GARCH Model Fit with LGD				
α_0	0.000	0.000	0.923	0.356
α_1	0.050	0.009	5.753	0.000
β_1	0.900	0.019	48.154	0.000
γ_1	−0.003	0.089	−0.037	0.971
t-distribution parameter	4.000	0.268	14.921	0.000

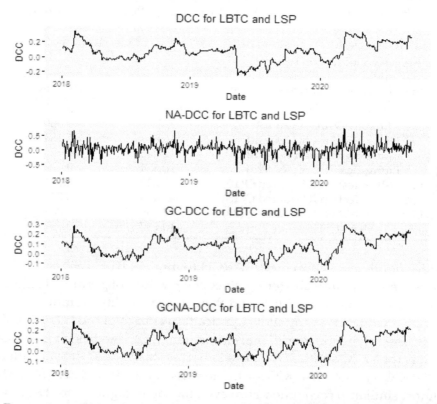

Figure 3. Dynamic conditional correlation between LBTC and LSP with GARCH-DCC (DCC),

Nonlinear Asymmetric GARCH-DCC (NA-DCC), Gaussian copula-based GARCH-DCC (GC-DCC), and Gaussian copula-based Nonlinear Asymmetric GARCH-DCC (GCNA-DCC).

Figure 4 shows the plots describing the three models of DCC, GC-DCC, and GCNA-DCC for log-returns of Bitcoin and Gold. From the patterns of GC-DCC and GCNA-DCC in Figure 4, we also found that there exists a postive time-varying correlation between LBTC and LGD from March 2020 to September 2020 which is the COVID-19 pandemic period.

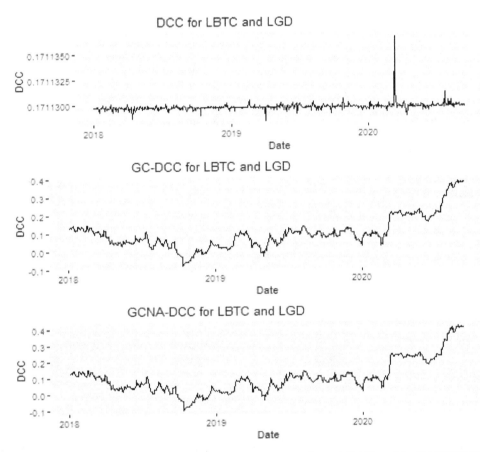

Figure 4. Dynamic conditional correlation between LBTC and LGD with GARCH-DCC (DCC), Gaussian copula-based GARCH-DCC (GC-DCC), and Gaussian copula-based Nonlinear Asymmetric GARCH-DCC (GCNA-DCC).

Log-likelihood is a measure of model fit. The higher the value, the better the fit. This is usually obtained from statistical output. For the pair of LBTC and LSP, the log-likelihood values of the DCC and NA-DCC models are smaller than the values of GC-DCC and GCNA-DCC in Table 8. Therefore, we can say that GC-DCC and GCNA-DCC are better models than DCC and NA-DCC to show relationship of Bitcoin with Gold and S&P 500 in terms of log-likelihood. In addition, there is a computation difficulty to compute NA-DCC with LBTC and LGD. Therefore, we can conclude that our proposed method is a better statistical method to look at the relationship among financial assets compared with DCC and NA-DCC. In addition, the estimates of alpha and beta for GC-DCC and GCNA-DCC are statistically significant at the 5% significance level but the estimates of alpha and beta for DCC and NA-DCC are not statistically significant at the 5% significance level. We can see that there is a computation difficulty to apply DCC and NA-DCC to high volatility financial data. The standard errors of the estimates from the DCC and NA-DCC models are much smaller than the standard errors from GC-DCC and GCNA-DCC. Especially, NA-DCC for Bitcoin and Gold cannot be computed from the *"fGarch"* R package [34] even though the log-likelihood value of DCC is larger than GC-DCC and GCNA-DCC. Based on these results, GC-DCC and GCNA-DCC are better models than DCC and NA-DCC. It is a strong motivation to apply the Gaussian copula DCC models for cryptocurrency to US stock and Gold market prices. We also investigate the relationship of the volatilities of cryptocurrency and US stock market with the GC-DCC or GCNA-DCC.

Table 8. The results of DCC with LBTC and LSP and with LBTC and LGD. Alpha and beta are the parameters for DCC, NA-DCC, GC-DCC and GCNA-DCC.

DCC		**DCC Alpha**	**DCC Beta**
	Estimate	0.025	0.953
Bitcoin and S&P 500	S.E	0.038	0.067
	Log-likelihood	3179.215	
	Estimate	0.000	0.227
Bitcoin and Gold	S.E	0.009	59,386
	Log-likelihood	3326.434	
NA-DCC		**NA-DCC Alpha**	**NA-DCC Beta**
	Estimate	0.334	0.188
Bitcoin and S&P 500	S.E	0.109	0.591
	Log-likelihood	2754.319	
	Estimate	NA	NA
Bitcoin and Gold	S.E	NA	NA
	Log-likelihood	NA	
GC-DCC		**GC-DCC Alpha**	**GC-DCC Beta**
	Estimate	0.069	0.910
Bitcoin and S&P 500	S.E	0.013	0.019
	Log-likelihood/AIC	3286.216/−10.0129	
	Estimate	0.069	0.910
Bitcoin and Gold	S.E	0.013	0.019
	Log-likelihood/AIC	3437.459/−10.475	
GCNA-DCC		**GCNA-DCC Alpha**	**GCNA-DCC Beta**
	Estimate	0.068	0.899
Bitcoin and S&P 500	S.E	0.015	0.063
	Log-likelihood/AIC	3293.257/−10.028	
	Estimate	0.068	0.899
Bitcoin and Gold	S.E	0.015	0.063
	Log-likelihood/AIC	2143.902/−10.028	

NA means no computational result because of an optimization error from the "*fGarch*" R package.

We have two hypotheses from this research. The first hypothesis is that we want to test the alternative hypothesis that Bitcoin is statistically significant by log-returns of S&P 500 and Gold price in terms of log-return. The second hypothesis is that we also test another alternative hypothesis that the current volatility of log-returns of Bitcoin can be statistically significant with the current and lagged volatilities of the other assets (S&P 500 and Gold price).

To perform the first alternative hypothesis that Bitcoin is statistically significant by log-returns of S&P 500 and Gold price in terms of log-return, we consider building an optimal Autoregressive Moving Average (ARMA) model based on AIC criteria among four different combinations of p and q: (0, 0), (0, 1), (1, 0), and (1, 1). Table 9 shows the result of the selection of p and q for the ARMA model. The ARMA (0, 0) turned out to be the best model with a minimum AIC value and Table 9 shows the result of the GCMR model fit of LBTC with LSP and LGD with error dependence structure of ARMA (0, 0). The reason we employ GCMR for the modeling is that GCMR has a Sigma dispersion parameter which accounts for heteroscedasticity of error. The GCMR model is more flexible to model the data which do not follow normality or heteroscedasticity of errors. Table 9 shows that there exists a statistical significance between LSP and LGD to LBTC in terms of price. And the Sigma dispersion parameter is statistically significant at the 5% significance level.

Table 9. Selection of p and q for ARMA based on AIC of 4 cases of (0, 0), (0, 1), (1, 0), and (1, 1). ARMA (0, 0) is selected based on AIC criteria. CMR model fit of LBTC with LSP and LGD with error dependence structure ARMA (0, 0).

Model	$LBTC = Intercept + \alpha_1 \times LSP + \beta_1 \times LGD$			
ARMA (p,q)	ARMA (0,0)	ARMA (0,1)	ARMA (1,0)	ARMA (1, 1)
AIC	−2140.6	−2139.7	−2139.8	−2138.5
ARMA (0,0)	$LBTC = Intercept + \alpha_1 \times LSP + \beta_1 \times LGD$			
	Estimate	S.E	Z-value	p-value
Intercept	−0.001	0.002	−0.653	0.514
LSP	0.645	0.124	5.182	0.000
LGD	0.803	0.208	3.860	0.000
Sigma	0.047	0.001	36.163	0.000

With volatilities by both standard-GARCH (1, 1) and nonlinear asymmetric GARCH (1, 1), we compare the values of both AIC and Log Likelihood for LBTC Volatility(t) = Intercept + $\alpha_1 \times$ LSP Volatility(t) + $\alpha_2 \times$ LGD Volatility(t)+ $\alpha_3 \times$ LSP Volatility(t-1) + $\alpha_4 \times$ LGD Volatility(t-1) where t-1 is one day before and t = 2, . . . , 401 in Tables 10 and 11.

Table 10. With standard-GARCH (1, 1) volatilities, GCMR model fit of LBTC volatility with LSP volatility(t), LGD volatility (t), volatility (t-1) and LGD volatility (t-1) with error dependence structure ARMA (0, 0).

Model	LBTC Volatility (t) = Intercept + $\alpha_1 \times$ LSP Volatility (t) + $\alpha_2 \times$ LGD Volatility (t) + $\alpha_3 \times$ LSP Volatility (t-1) + $\alpha_4 \times$ LGD Volatility (t-1)			
	Estimate	S.E.	Z-value	p-value
Intercept	−6.698	0.262	−25.570	0.000
LSP Volatility (t)	1341.294	0.015	90993.019	0.000
LGD Volatility (t)	17.942	3.303	5.431	0.000
LSP Volatility (t-1)	6350.534	0.008	771671.098	0.013
LGD Volatility (t-1)	−11.556	3.662	−3.156	0.001
Shape	0.800	0.209	3.818	0.000
Log Likelihood			−5799.7	
AIC			−11583	

Table 11. With nonlinear asymmetric GARCH (1, 1) volatilities, GCMR model fit of LBTC volatility with LSP volatility(t), LGD volatility (t), volatility (t-1) and LGD volatility (t-1) with error dependence structure ARMA (0, 0).

Model	LBTC Volatility (t) = Intercept+$\alpha_1 \times$ LSP Volatility (t) + $\alpha_2 \times$ LGD Volatility (t) + $\alpha_1 \times$ LSP Volatility (t-1) + $\alpha_2 \times$ LGD Volatility (t-1)			
	Estimate	S.E.	Z-value	p-value
Intercept	−6.085	0.109	−55.757	0.000
LSP Volatility (t)	24.313	0.032	760.170	0.000
LGD Volatility (t)	5.092	0.583	8.739	0.000
LSP Volatility (t-1)	89.167	0.021	4291.506	0.000
LGD Volatility (t-1)	−2.085	0.636	−3.279	0.001
Sigma	1.388	0.091	15.295	0.000
Log Likelihood			−3837.7	
AIC			−7661.5	

The GCMR model fit of LBTC volatility (t) with LSP volatility (t), LGD volatility (t), volatility (t-1), and LGD volatility (t-1) with standard-GARCH (1, 1) volatilities and error dependence structure ARMA (0, 0) is better than the GCMR model fit of LBTC volatility (t) with LSP volatility (t), LGD volatility (t), volatility (t-1), and LGD volatility (t-1) with nonlinear asymmetric GARCH (1, 1) volatilities and error dependence structure ARMA (0, 0).

We chose the statistical output from Table 10 so that LSP volatility (t), LGD volatility (t) and LSP volatility (t-1) are statistically significant, and they have a positive statistical effect to LBTC volatility (t), but LGD volatility (t-1), one day before volatilities, has a statistically significant negative effect to LBTC volatility (t) at the 5% significance level. The Sigma dispersion parameter is also statistically significant at the 5% significance level in both Tables 10 and 11.

The following statistical output is another interesting result in our paper. We want to see the relationship of the Gaussian copula time-varying correlation (GC-DCC or GCNA-DCC) with the volatilities of LBTC and LSP. With volatilities by both standard-GARCH (1, 1) and nonlinear asymmetric GARCH (1, 1) with an error dependence structure of ARMA (1, 0), we also compared the log-likelihood of GC-DCC = Intercept + $\alpha_1 \times$ LBTC Volatility + $\beta_1 \times$ LSP Volatility with GCNA-DCC = Intercept + $\alpha_1 \times$ LBTC Volatility + $\beta_1 \times$ LSP Volatility in Tables 12 and 13.

Table 12. Gaussian Copula Marginal Regression (GCMR) with standard-GARCH (1, 1) volatilities. Selection of p and q for ARMA based on AIC of 4 cases of (0, 0), (0, 1), (1, 0), and (1, 1). ARMA (0, 0) is selected based on AIC criteria. GCMR Model fit of GC-DCC with LBTC Volatility, and LSP Volatility of Error dependence structure ARMA (1, 1).

Model	GC-DCC = Intercept + $\alpha_1 \times$ LBTC Volatility + $\beta_1 \times$ LSP Volatility			
ARMA(p,q)	ARMA(0, 0)	ARMA(0, 1)	ARMA(1, 0)	ARMA(1, 1)
AIC	−1312.2	−1960.7	NA	−3014.6
ARMA (1, 1)	GC-DCC = Intercept + $\alpha_1 \times$ LBTC Volatility + $\beta_1 \times$ LSP Volatility			
	Estimate	S.E	z-value	P-value
Intercept	0.068	0.026	2.580	0.010
LBTC Volatility	1.912	4.698	0.407	0.684
LSP Volatility	371.367	0.269	1379.714	0.000
Sigma	0.089	0.013	6.625	0.000
Log-likelihood		−1513.3		

Table 13. Gaussian Copula Marginal Regression with nonlinear asymmetric GARCH (1, 1) volatilities. Selection of p and q for ARMA based on AIC of 4 cases of (0, 0), (0, 1), (1, 0), and (1, 1). ARMA (1, 0) is selected based on AIC criteria. GCMR Model fit of GCNA-DCC with LBTC Volatility, and LSP Volatility of Error dependence structure ARMA (1, 1).

Model	GCNA-DCC = Intercept + $\alpha_1 \times$ LBTC Volatility + $\beta_1 \times$ LSP Volatility			
ARMA(p,q)	ARMA(0, 0)	ARMA(0, 1)	ARMA(1, 0)	ARMA(1, 1)
AIC	−678.24	−1994.3	NA	−3070.4
ARMA(1, 1)	GCNA-DCC = Intercept + $\alpha_1 \times$ LBTC Volatility + $\beta_1 \times$ LSP Volatility			
	Estimate	S.E	z-value	P-value
Intercept	0.087	0.027	3.223	0.001
LBTC Volatility	16.698	4.572	3.652	0.000
LSP Volatility	131.869	0.264	499.807	0.000
Sigma	0.088	0.014	6.377	0.000
Log-likelihood		−1541.2		

From the relationship among time-varying conditional correlation with LBTC volatility, and LSP volatility by the Gaussian Copula Marginal Regression (GCMR) Model in Tables 12 and 13, we find that there exists a statistically significant and positive effect to time-varying conditional correlation by the volatility of LBTC and the volatility of LSP.

4. Conclusions

We applied the copula-based GARCH-DCC models to the financial assets, Bitcoin, Gold, and S&P 500. We showed that the proposed method for the relationships among time-varying conditional correlation with Bitcoin volatility, and S&P 500 can overcome the difficulty which cannot be computed by the GARCH-DCC models. Our empirical study showed the time-varying relationship between the cryptocurrency market and the US stock market or the gold market price. Recent data showed that there was a positive time-varying relationship between these two markets since the COVID-19 occurrence. Our Gaussian copula marginal regression modeling the volatility of the most popular cryptocurrency, Bitcoin, with Gold price and US stock market price has more performance compared to competitors such as DCC and NA-DCC to show that a volatility relationship exists among the three market prices with the current day and one-day lagged prices. Our findings provide important implications for both investors and policymakers. In our future study, we will apply state-space modeling for the most popular cryptocurrency with the Gold price and US stock market to see a time-varying relationship in terms of a time-varying intercept and slope. The limitation of this research is that our proposed copula DCC methodology to the high volatility finance assets is not multivariate data analysis but pairwise data analysis. In order to overcome this limitation, our future study will be based on multivariable time series data by using vine copula based multivariate time varying correlation analysis so that we will be able to look at the multivariate time varying correlation behavior among several financial assets simultaneously.

Author Contributions: Formal analysis and investigation, J.-M.K. and S.K.; writing—original draft preparation, S.K., J.-M.K. and S.-T.K.; supervision and reviewing, S.K. All authors have read and agreed to the published version of the manuscript.

Acknowledgments: We would like to thank the editor and reviewers for their insightful comments and helpful suggestions.

References

1. Nakamoto, S. Bitcoin: A Peer-to-Peer Electronic Cash System. Available online: https://bitcoin.org/bitcoin.pdf (accessed on 3 May 2018).
2. Katsiampa, P. An empirical investigation of volatility dynamics in the cryptocurrency market. *Res. Int. Bus. Finance* **2019**, *50*, 322–335. [CrossRef]
3. Hyun, S.; Lee, J.M.; Kim, J.; Jun, C. What coins lead in the cryptocurrency market? Using Copula and Neural Network Models. *J. Risk Financ. Manag.* **2019**, *12*, 132. [CrossRef]
4. Kim, J.-M.; Jun, C.; Lee, J. Forecasting the volatility of the cryptocurrency market using GARCH and Stochastic Volatility. *Econ. Model.* **2019**. under review.
5. Klein, T.; Thu, H.P.; Walther, T. Bitcoin is not the New Gold—A comparison of volatility, correlation, and portfolio performance. *Int. Rev. Financ. Anal.* **2018**, *59*, 105–116. [CrossRef]
6. Baba, Y.; Engle, R.F.; Kraft, D.F.; Kroner, K.F. Multivariate simultaneous generalized ARCH. *Econ. Theory* **1995**, *11*, 122–150.
7. Aslanidisa, N.; Barivierab, A.F.; Martínez-Ibañeza, O. An analysis of cryptocurrencies conditional cross correlations. *Financ. Res. Lett.* **2019**, *31*, 130–137. [CrossRef]
8. Ghosh, I.; Sanyal, M.K.; Jana, R.K. Co-movement and Dynamic Correlation of Financial and Energy Markets: An Integrated Framework of Nonlinear Dynamics, Wavelet Analysis and DCC-GARCH. *Comput. Econ.* **2020**. [CrossRef]
9. Maraqa, B.; Bein, M. Dynamic Interrelationship and Volatility Spillover among Sustainability Stock Markets, Major European Conventional Indices, and International Crude Oil. *Sustainability* **2020**, *12*, 3908. [CrossRef]
10. Chen, Y.; Qu, F. Leverage effect and dynamics correlation between international crude oil and China's precious metals. *Phys. A Stat. Mech. Appl.* **2019**, *534*. [CrossRef]
11. Lee, N.; Kim, J.-M. Dynamic functional connectivity analysis of functional MRI based on copula time-varying correlation. *J. Neurosci. Methods* **2019**, *323*, 32–47. [CrossRef]
12. Guesmi, K.; Saadi, S.; Abid, I.; Ftiti, Z. Portfolio diversification with virtual currency: Evidence from bitcoin. *Int. Rev. Financ. Anal.* **2019**, *63*, 431–437. [CrossRef]
13. Denkowska, A.; Wanat, S. A Tail Dependence-Based MST and Their Topological Indicators in Modeling Systemic Risk in the European Insurance Sector. *Risks* **2020**, *8*, 39. [CrossRef]
14. Chen, H.; Liu, Z.; Zhang, Y.; Wu, Y. The Linkages of Carbon Spot-Futures: Evidence from EU-ETS in the Third Phase. *Sustainability* **2020**, *12*, 2517. [CrossRef]

15. Lee, N.; Kim, J.-M. Dynamic functional connectivity analysis based on time-varying partial correlation with a copula-DCC-GARCH model. *Neurosci. Res.* **2020**. [CrossRef]

16. John, M.; Wu, Y.; Narayan, M.; John, A.; Ikuta, T.; Ferbinteanu, J. Estimation of Dynamic Bivariate Correlation Using a Weighted Graph Algorithm. *Entropy* **2020**, *22*, 617. [CrossRef]

17. Amrouk, E.M.; Grosche, S.C.; Heckelei, T. Interdependence between cash crop and staple food international prices across periods of varying financial market stress. *Appl. Econ.* **2020**, *52*. [CrossRef]

18. Kim, J.M.; Jun, S. Graphical causal inference and copula regression model for apple keywords by text mining. *Adv. Eng. Inform.* **2015**, *29*, 918–929. [CrossRef]

19. Masarotto, G.; Varin, C. Gaussian Copula Marginal Regression. *Electron. J. Stat.* **2012**, *6*, 1517–1549. [CrossRef]

20. Hentschel, L. All in the Family Nesting Symmetric and Asymmetric GARCH Models. *J. Financ. Econ.* **1995**, *39*, 71–104. [CrossRef]

21. Engle, R.F.; Ng, V.K. Measuring and Testing the Impact of News on Volatility. *J. Financ.* **1993**, *48*, 1749–1778. [CrossRef]

22. Tse, Y.K.; Tsui, A.K.C. A multivariate generalized autoregressive conditional heteroscedasticity model with time-varying correlations. *J. Bus. Econ. Stat.* **2002**, *20*, 351–362. [CrossRef]

23. Bollerslev, T. Modeling the coherence in short-run nominal exchange rates: A multivariate generalized ARCH model. *Rev. Econ. Stat.* **1990**, *72*, 498–505. [CrossRef]

24. Engle, R. Dynamic conditional correlation: A simple class of multivariate generalized autoregressive conditional heteroskedasticity models. *J. Bus. Econ. Stat.* **2002**, *20*, 339–350. [CrossRef]

25. Engle, R.F.; Sheppard, K. *Theoretical and Empirical Properties of Dynamic Conditional Correlation Multivariate GARCH*; Working Paper 8554; National Bureau of Economic Research: Cambridge, MA, USA, 2011. [CrossRef]

26. Sklar, M. *Fonctions de Répartition À N Dimensions et Leurs Marges*; Université Paris: Paris, France, 1959.

27. Joe, H. *Multivariate Models and Dependence Concepts*; Chapman & Hall: London, UK, 1997.

28. Genest, C.; Ghoudi, K.; Rivest, L. A semiparametric estimation procedure of dependence parameters in multivariate families of distributions. *Biometrica* **1995**, *82*, 543–552. [CrossRef]

29. Song, P. Multivariate Dispersion Models Generated from Gaussian Copula. *Scand. J. Stat.* **2000**, *27*, 305–320. [CrossRef]

30. Crypto—Defi Wallet—CoinMarketCap. Available online: https://coinmarketcap.com/coins/ (accessed on 2 April 2018).

31. University of British Columbia, Sauder School of Business. Pacific Exchange Rate Service. Available online: http://fx.sauder.ubc.ca/data.html (accessed on 5 January 2020).

32. Yahoo Finance. Available online: https://finance.yahoo.com/ (accessed on 5 January 2020).

33. Dumitrescu, E.I.; Hurlin, C. Testing for Granger non-causality in heterogeneous panels. *Econ. Model.* **2012**, *29*, 1450–1460. [CrossRef]

34. Bollerslev, T. Generalized Autoregressive Conditional Heteroscedasticity. *J. Econ.* **1986**, *31*, 307–327. [CrossRef]

4

The Net Worth Trap: Investment and Output Dynamics in the Presence of Financing Constraints

Jukka Isohätälä [1], Alistair Milne [2,*] and Donald Robertson [3]

[1]   Institute of Operations Research and Analytics, National University of Singapore, 3 Research Link, Innovation 4.0 04-01, Singapore 117602, Singapore; jukka.isohatala@gmail.com

[2]   School of Business and Economics, Loughborough University, Epinal Way, Loughborough LE11 3TU, UK

[3]   Faculty of Economics, University of Cambridge, Cambridge CB3 9DD, UK; dr10011@cam.ac.uk

*   Correspondence: a.k.l.milne@lboro.ac.uk

Abstract: This paper investigates investment and output dynamics in a simple continuous time setting, showing that financing constraints substantially alter the relationship between net worth and the decisions of an optimizing firm. In the absence of financing constraints, net worth is irrelevant (the 1958 Modigliani–Miller irrelevance proposition applies). When incorporating financing constraints, a decline in net worth leads to the firm reducing investment and also output (when this reduces risk exposure). This negative relationship between net worth and investment has already been examined in the literature. The contribution here is providing new intuitive insights: (i) showing how large and long lasting the resulting non-linearity of firm behaviour can be, even with linear production and preferences; and (ii) highlighting the economic mechanisms involved—the emergence of shadow prices creating both corporate prudential saving and induced risk aversion. The emergence of such pronounced non-linearity, even with linear production and preference functions, suggests that financing constraints can have a major impact on investment and output; and this should be allowed for in empirical modelling of economic and financial crises (for example, the great depression of the 1930s, the global financial crisis of 2007–2008 and the crash following the Covid-19 pandemic of 2020).

Keywords: cash flow management; corporate prudential risk; the financial accelerator; financial distress; induced risk aversion; liquidity constraints; liquidity risk; macroeconomic propagation; multiperiod financial management; non-linear macroeconomic modelling; Tobin's q; precautionary savings

1. Introduction

This paper examines the impacts of financing constraints on firm operations and finances using the tools of continuous time dynamic stochastic optimisation. The introduction of a threshold whereat the firm faces costly refinancing or liquidation, changes the behaviour of a firm, even when the firm's shareholders are risk neutral. As the threshold is approached, there emerges an increasing premium on the value of cash held inside the firm (relative to the outside cost of capital) and an increasing aversion to risk.

This modelling builds on the dynamic analyses of [1,2]. Following [2] firms have constant returns to scale, i.e., linear production technology, and seek to maximise the value of cash dividends paid to share- holders whilst facing convex costs of adjusting their capital stock. With these assumptions the solution to the firm's optimisation problem can be expressed in terms of a single state variable, the ratio of balance sheet net worth to productive capital. Cash held internally reduces shareholder returns but also lowers the expected future costs of refinancing or liquidation. It is the interplay between these two forces that drives behaviour.

The financing constraint is assumed to be an exogenous (to the firm) lower boundary for this state variable at which the firm must undertake costly refinancing or bankruptcy occurs and the firm is liquidated. An upper bound appears as part of the optimal solution and marks the threshold where the firm pays out cash flow dividends to its impatient shareholders. As shocks drive the firm closer to the liquidation threshold, its presence increasingly affects the optimal decisions of the firm.

An analogy for this mechanism is provided by Whittle [3] pages 287–288:

> This might be termed the "fly-paper" effect... A deterministic fly, whose path is fully under its own control, can approach arbitrarily closely to the fly-paper with impunity, knowing he can avoid entrapment ... A stochastic fly cannot guarantee his escape; the nearer he is to the paper, the more certain it is that he will be carried onto it. This also explains why the fly tries so much harder in the stochastic case than in the deterministic case to escape the neighbourhood of the fly-paper... One may say that the penalty of ending on the fly-paper "propagates" into the free-flight region in the stochastic case, causing the fly to take avoiding action while still at a distance from the paper.

Whittle is pointing out that in dynamic settings with (i) uncertainty in the equations of motion for state variables (the position of the fly); and (ii) constraints on state (the fly paper), then (in the language of economic theory) non-zero shadow prices appear even for values of the state where the constraints are not currently binding.

In the setting of this paper there are two routes by which this mechanism affects firm decisions:

(1)   A shadow price of internal funds creates a wedge between the internal and external cost of capital. This reduces the marginal valuation of investment in terms of internal funds (Tobin's marginal-q). A firm invests less and less as its net worth declines. The consequence is corporate prudential saving, analogous to the household prudential saving extensively discussed in the literature on the consumption function (surveyed in [4]).

(2)   A shadow price of risk creates an "induced risk aversion" leading to firms reducing their risk exposure. A variation of the model allows firms to respond by renting out more and more of their capital as net worth declines below a threshold level. It is this mechanism which, if sufficiently powerful, creates the "net worth trap."

Since the firm cannot raise new equity capital, declines in net worth are financed by increases in firm borrowing. When this state variable is comparatively high, near the upper boundary where dividends are paid, then these shadow prices are close to those that would apply for a financially unconstrained firm that can raise new equity. As the state variable falls closer to its minimum level at which no further borrowing is possible, these shadow prices rise. Even with the assumed linear production technology and the risk-neutrality of firm shareholders, the resulting dynamics of corporate output and investment are highly non-linear, depending on both the direction and size of shocks: negative shocks to productivity or net worth have a larger impact than positive shocks; small negative shocks self-correct relatively quickly; larger negative shocks (or a succession of smaller negative shocks) can result in extended periods of high shadow prices and contractions of output and investment.

The remainder of the paper is set out as follows. Section 2 locates the paper in the economics, finance and mathematical insurance literature. Section 3 presents a simplified version of the model in which capital cannot be rented out. For high values of the fixed cost of recapitalisation, firms do not recapitalise instead liquidating on the lower net worth boundary; but for lower values firms choose to exercise their option to recapitalise on the lower boundary and so avoid liquidation. In either case, investment is reduced below unconstrained levels by the state dependent shadow price of internal funds.

Section 4 then introduces the possibility that firms, by mothballing or renting capital to outsiders, are able to reduce their risk exposure, but at the expense of a decline in their expected output.

The extent to which this is done depends on the magnitude of a shadow price of risk capturing an effective induced risk aversion for other wise risk-neutral shareholders. This is where the possibility of a net worth trap emerges. Section 5 provides a concluding discussion considering the macroeconomic implications of these findings. While the model solution is numerical, not closed form, we have developed convenient and rapid solution routines in Mathematica. (We have created a standalone module which can be used by any interested reader to explore the impact of parameter choice on model outcomes. This, together with the Mathematica notebook used for creating the Figures reported in the paper, can be downloaded via http://leveragecycles.lboro.ac.uk/networthtrap.html and run using the free Mathematica Player software https://www.wolfram.com/player/). Four appendices contain supporting technical details. (Appendix A solves the situation in which there is no non-negativity constraint on dividend payments; or equivalently when uncertainty vanishes. Appendix B provides proofs of the propositions in the main text. Appendix D derives the asymptotic approximations used to incorporate the singularities that arise in the model with rent. Appendix C details the numerical solution, noting how this must be handled differently in the two possible cases, wherein a "no Ponzi" condition applies to the unconstrained model of Appendix A; and when this condition does not).

2. Related Literature

There is a substantial body of literature examining firm operations, financing and risk management over multiple periods. Central to this work is the inventory theoretic modelling (initiated by [5,6]) of both financial (cash, liquidity and capitalisation) and operational (inventory, employment, fixed capital investment) decisions subject to fixed (and sometimes also proportional or convex) costs of replenishment or investment.

Most dynamic models of corporate behaviour focus either on financial or operational decisions without considering their interaction. Well known contributions include work on the dynamics of fixed capital investment in the presence of adjustment costs (including [7,8]); and on applying standard tools of inventory modelling to study corporate cash holdings and money demand [9–11]. Dynamic modelling methods are also employed in the contingent claims literature, to examine both the pricing of corporate liabilities [12] and the possibility of strategic debt repudiation [13,14] and the interaction of the choice of asset risk and capital structure, taking account of the implications for the cost of debt [15]. However, this line of research does not address the dynamic interaction of financing and investment.

The interaction of financial and operational decisions is often considered in a static framework. This allows an explicit statement of the informational asymmetries and strategic interactions that lead to departures from the [16] irrelevance proposition (for a unified presentation of much of this literature, see [17]). This is widely used in the corporate finance literature. Take, for example, the pecking order theory of capital structure in which costs of equity issuance result in discrepancies between the costs of inside funds (retained earnings), debt and outside equity [18,19]. In [20] such a static framework was applied to develop a joint framework of the determination of investment and risk management decisions.

There is a smaller body of literature on the dynamic interactions of financial and operational decisions. The negative relationship between net worth and the shadow price of internal funds that appears in the present paper is not a new finding; it appears in a number of other contributions to the literature. In [21] the costly state verification problem of [22] is extended into a recursive model of dynamic stochastic control wherein one period debt contract can be refinanced through a new debt contract. His analysis does not establish an explicit solution for the optimal contract, but it does show how if debt contracts are used to dynamically finance a productive investment opportunity, then the value function has a "characteristic" convex shape, with a negative second derivative with respect to net worth, reflecting a departure from [16] capital structure irrelevance and a resulting shadow price of internal funds. In consequence, as net worth declines so does investment and output.

Progress has been made more recently on analysing optimal financial contracts in a dynamic principal agent context (see [23,24] and references therein), yielding similar divergence between the cost of funds. In [24] it is shown that it can be optimal for a firm to use, simultaneously, both long term debt and short term lines of credit, in order to create incentives for managerial effort, but this work has not been extended to modelling the interactions of financial and operational decisions.

Most other work on the dynamic interactions of financial and operational decisions has proceeded, as in this paper, by imposing costly financial frictions (rather than establishing an optimal contract). Many of these papers employ continuous time modelling techniques. An early example is [25] exploring the bond financing of a project subject to fixed costs both of opening and shutting the project (hence creating real option values) and of altering capital structure through bond issuing. Four papers written independently [1,26–28] explore cash flow management and dividend policy in a context where cash holdings evolve stochastically (as a continuous time diffusion) resulting in a need for liquidity management. This leads to the simple boundary control for dividends that is inherited by the model of the present paper: paying no dividends when net cash holdings are below a target level and making unlimited dividend payments on this boundary.

This cash flow management framework was subsequently employed in a variety of different contexts. These include the risk exposure decisions of both insurance companies and non-financial corporates (see [29–31]). In a sequence of papers [32–35] bank capital regulation and bank behaviour are analysed. Other related work examined how intervention rules affect market pricing in exchange rates and in money markets; for example, [36–38] provides a survey article linking this work to portfolio allocation and cash management problems faced by companies and insurance firms.

Other recent and closely related studies exploring the interactions of financing, risk management and operational decisions include [39–44]. While employing differing assumptions, these papers have a great deal in common. The resulting dynamic optimisation again yielded a value function with the "characteristic" convex shape reported by [21] and appearing also in this paper, and hence resulted in internal "shadow prices" which reduce risk exposure, output and investment as net worth or cash holdings decline.

Similar findings emerged in discrete time models, such as those of [45,46], who considered risk management and firm decision making in the presence of taxation and imposed costs of financial transactions. They incorporated a wide range of determining factors and firm decision variables, again finding that a reduction in net worth leads to reduced of risk exposure and increased incentives to hedge risks.

While the literature offers a consistent account of the dynamic interactions of corporate financing and operational decisions, the macroeconomic implications are less fully explored. Capital market frictions, in particular the high costs of external equity finance and the role of collateral values have been proposed as an explanation of macroeconomic dynamics (see, e.g., [47,48]). The most widely used implementation of these ideas is the "financial accelerator" introduced into macroeconomics by [49,50]. This is based on a static model of underlying capital market frictions, in which the macroeconomic impact of financing constraints comes through assuming a costly state verification (as in [22]) and modelling the resulting difficulties entrepreneurs face in obtaining external finance for new investment projects. The resulting propagation mechanism operates through an "external financing premium", i.e., a additional cost that must be paid by investors in fixed capital projects in order to overcome the frictional costs of external monitoring whenever they raise external funds, rather than internal shadow prices such as appear in this paper.

An alternative perspective on the propagation of macroeconomic shocks is found in the literature on endogenous risk in traded asset markets (see [51–53] in which asset price volatility limits access to external finance. In their overview of the impacts of financing constraints on macrofinancial dynamics using continuous-time modelling [54] highlighted some further recent analysis of this kind [2,55,56] that focused on the impacts of financial constraints on asset prices.

In [55,56] "specialists" were able to better manage financial assets but their ability to invest in these assets was constrained by their net worth. The outcome was two regimes: one of higher net worth wherein the constraint does not bind and the pricing and volatility of assets are determined by fundamental future cash flows; the other of lower net worth wherein asset prices fall and asset price volatility rises relative to fundamental levels. This approach is developed further in [2], treating physical capital as a tradable financial asset and showing how endogenous volatility can then limit investment and create the possibility of a "net worth" trap with extended declines in output and investment following a major negative shock.

The analysis of this paper shows that such a net worth trap can also emerges through the operation of internal shadow prices, rather than, as in [2], through external market pricing. Thus there is a potential net worth trap for all firms, large and small and regardless of the extent to which they participate in external financial and asset markets. This paper also extends [2] by allowing not just for shocks to capital productivity (these can be interpreted as supply shocks such as those that have resulted from the Covid-19 pandemic) but also for shocks to net worth (these can be interpreted as demand and financial market shocks, such as those that occurred during the global financial crisis). As in [2], in order to limit the number of state variables and obtain tractable results, this paper considers only serially uncorrelated shocks represented in continuous time by a Wiener process.

This paper contributes to this literature in two further ways. First, building on [1] it distinguishes the impact on firm decisions of the shadow price of internal funds (the first derivative of the value function in net worth) from the shadow price of risk (the scaled second derivative of the value function). Second, it develops efficient numerical solution methods which support convenient exploration of the effect of changing parameters on firm decisions.

3. A Basic Model

This section solves a basic model in which firms decide only on investment and dividend payments. We delay to Section 4 consideration of a broader model in which firms can reduce their risk exposure by selling or renting capital to outsiders, and the circumstances in which a net worth trap might then appear.

Section 3.1 sets out the model assumptions. Section 3.2 discusses its numerical solution. Section 3.3 presents some illustrative simulations of the numerical solution.

3.1. Model Assumptions

Firms produce output sold at price unity through a constant returns to scale production function ($y = ak$) and seek to maximise a flow of cash dividends ($\lambda \geq 0$) to risk neutral owners/shareholders. There are two state variables, capital k, which is augmented by investment at rate i and reduced by depreciation at rate δ, and cash, which increases with sale of output and is reduced by capital investment (subject to quadratic adjustment costs) and dividend payouts. Cash c held internally (which can be negative if borrowing) attracts an interest rate r. Additionally, the firm can recapitalise (increase its cash) at any time τ by an amount $\epsilon(\tau)$ where τ can be chosen by the firm. Cash holdings are disturbed by an amount $\sigma k dz$ with dz a Wiener process.

The state variables evolve according to:

$$dc = \left[-\lambda + ak + rc - ik - \frac{1}{2}\theta(i-\delta)^2 k \right] dt + \epsilon(\tau) + \sigma k dz \tag{1a}$$

$$dk = (i-\delta)k dt \tag{1b}$$

where the coefficient θ captures costs of adjustment of the capital stock (increasing with the net rate of investment $i - \delta$).

The firm seeks to maximise the objective:

$$\Omega = \max_{\{i_t\},\{\lambda_t\},\{\epsilon_\tau\}} E \int_{t=0}^{\infty} e^{-\rho t} \lambda dt - \sum_{\tau=\tau_1}^{\tau_\infty} e^{-\rho\tau} (\epsilon_\tau + \chi k) \qquad (2)$$

where $\chi > 0$ represents the cost to shareholders of recapitalisation, arising from any associated due-diligence or dilution of interests. These are assumed proportional to k.

The only other agents are outside investors ("households" in the terminology of [2] who lend to firms, but do not take credit risks; instead, they require that lending is secured against the firm's assets, limiting the amount of credit available to the firm, and they become the residual owner of the firm's assets if and when the debt is not serviced. Like firm owners, these investors are risk-neutral and seek to maximise the present discounted value of current and future consumption. Unlike firms, there is no non-negativity constraint on their cash flow. Since they are the marginal suppliers of finance, and there is no risk of credit losses, they lend to or borrow from firms at a rate of interest r reflecting their rate of time discount. Investors are more patient than firms, i.e., $r < \rho$ (without this assumption firms will build up unlimited cash holdings instead of paying dividends). Fixed capital held directly by outside investors generates an output of $\bar{a}k$.

Further assumptions are required in order to obtain a meaningful solution: (i) capital is less productive in the hands of outside investors than when held by firms (otherwise, firms will avoid using capital for production), $\bar{a} < a$; (ii) upper bounds on both a and $\bar{a}$ to ensure that the technology does not generate sufficient output to allow self-sustaining growth faster than the rates of shareholder or household discount; (iii) a further technical condition (a tighter upper bound on a) ensuring that there is a solution in which dividends are paid to firm shareholders.

3.2. Solution

3.2.1. Characterisation of the Solution

The form of the solution is summarised in the following propositions:

Proposition 1. *The firm can borrow (hold $c < 0$) up to a maximum amount determined by the valuation of the firm by outside investors:*

$$c > \bar{\eta}k = -\left[1 + \theta\left(r - \sqrt{r^2 - 2\theta^{-1}[\bar{a} - \delta - r]}\right)\right]k \qquad (3)$$

Proof. Appendix A. □

This maximum amount of borrowing $(-\bar{\eta}k)$ is exogenous to the the firm but endogenous to the model. It increases with the net productivity of firms' assets in the hands of outside investors $(\bar{a} - \delta)$ and decreases with the costs of investing in new capital (θ) and with the discount rate of outside investors (r) which is also the available rate of interest on cash holding/cash borrowing by the firm. It would be possible to generalise the model by enforcing either a lower exogenous limit on borrowing or a higher exogenous limit on borrowing with an interest rate on borrowing of $\bar{r}(c) > r$ for $c < 0$ that compensates lenders for the liquidated value of the firm—that being less than the amount borrowed at liquidation. We do not explore these extensions.

If c reaches this bound then the firm has a choice: either liquidate (in which case its assets are acquired by the lenders and there is no further payment to shareholders); or recapitalise (at a cost to shareholders of χk).

Proposition 2. *Sufficient conditions for an optimal policy for choice of $\{i_t\}$, $\{\lambda_t\}$, $\{\epsilon_\tau\}$ as functions of the single state variable $\eta = ck^{-1}$ to exist and satisfy $i_t - \delta < \rho$, $\forall t$ are*

$$a - \delta < \rho + \frac{1}{2}\theta\rho^2 - (\rho - r)\left[1 + \theta\left(r - \sqrt{r^2 - 2\theta^{-1}[\bar{a} - \delta - r]}\right)\right], \qquad (4a)$$

$$\bar{a} - \delta < r + \frac{1}{2}\theta r^2. \qquad (4b)$$

Further, if Equation (4a) is satisfied, the growth rate of the capital stock $g(\eta)$ and the optimal investment rate $i(\eta)$ always satisfies the constraints

$$\bar{g} = \left(r - \sqrt{r^2 - 2\theta^{-1}[\bar{a} - \delta - r]}\right) \leq g(\eta) = i(\eta) - \delta < \rho.$$

Proof. Appendix B. □

If a solution exists then it is characterised by the following further proposition:

Proposition 3. *An optimal policy choice for $\{i_t\}$, $\{\lambda_t\}$, $\{\epsilon_\tau\}$ as functions of the single state variable $\eta = ck^{-1}$, if it exists and takes the following form: (i) making no dividend payments a long as $\bar{\eta} < \eta < \eta^*$ for some value η^* of η, while making dividend payments at an unlimited rate if $\eta > \eta^*$; (ii) investing at a rate*

$$i = \delta + \theta^{-1}(q - 1)$$

where $W(\eta)k$ is the value of Ω under optimal policy; and $q(\eta)$ representing the valuation of fixed assets by the firm (the cash price it would be willing to pay for a small increase in k) is given by:

$$q = \frac{W}{W'} - \eta, \qquad q' = -\frac{WW''}{W'W'}, \qquad (5)$$

with $q' > 0$ whenever $\eta < \eta^*$; and $W(\eta)$ is the unique solution to the second-order differential equation over $\eta \in [\bar{\eta}, \eta^*]$:

$$\rho\frac{W}{W'} = a - \delta + r\eta - \frac{1}{2}\sigma^2\left(-\frac{W''}{W'}\right) + \frac{1}{2}\theta^{-1}\left(\frac{W}{W'} - \eta - 1\right)^2 \qquad (6)$$

obtained subject to three boundary conditions: (i) an optimality condition for payment of dividends at η^* $W''(\eta^*) = 0$ (ii) a scaling condition $W'(\eta^*) = 1$; and (iii) the matching condition:

$$W(\bar{\eta}) = \max\left[W(\eta^*) - (\eta^* - \bar{\eta} + \chi), 0\right]. \qquad (7)$$

Finally, the firm recapitalises only on the lower boundary and only if $W(\bar{\eta}) > 0$ in which case it recapitalises by increasing η immediately to η^*.

Proof. Appendix B. □

This solution combines barrier control at an upper level of the state variable with either impulse control or absorption at a lower level.

- Barrier control is applied at an upper level of cash holding/borrowing $\eta^* k$, retaining all earnings when below this level and paying out all earnings that would take it beyond this level (a form of barrier control). It never holds more cash (or conducts less borrowing) than this targeted amount, and below this level no dividends are paid (as discussed in Section 2, similar barrier control appears in a number of earlier papers studying corporate decision making subject to external financing constraints).
- Impulse control through recapitalisation at a lower boundary $\bar{\eta}k$, but only if the cost to shareholders of recapitalisation is less than their valuation of the recapitalised firm. Net worth is then restored to the upper impulse control level $\eta^* k$. The value of the firm at the lower boundary $W(\bar{\eta})$ is the value at the upper boundary $W(\eta^*)$ less the total costs of recapitalisation $(\eta^* - \bar{\eta} + \chi)$.
- Absorption if instead the cost of recapitalisation at the lower boundary representing the maximum level of borrowing exceeds the valuation of the recapitalised firm. It then liquidates and the value obtained by shareholders is zero.

In the absence of financing constraints (as discussed in Appendix A), impulse control is exerted for all values of $\eta \neq 0$ to immediately enforce $\eta = 0$, leverage is no longer relevant to the decisions of the firm (the Modigliani–Miller [16] proposition applies) and the value function is linear in η and given by $\Omega = k(W_0 + \eta)$, $W' = 1$ and $q = W/W' - \eta = W_0$.

The outcome is very different in the presence of financing constraints. The value function is then distorted downward. As η declines towards the maximum level of borrowing, an increasing marginal valuation of cash results (the slope of W) because $W'' < 0$. This increasing marginal valuation of cash as the firm comes closer to liquidation is reflected in a curvature of the value function $\Omega = kW(\eta)$ characteristic of dynamic models of financing constraints (see the upper panel of Figure 1 and discussion in Section 2). See [1] for further discussion).

This higher marginal valuation of cash results in a reduction of q, the marginal or the internal cost of cash (Ω_c) relative to the marginal benefits of capital (Ω_k). The further η falls below the target η^*, the more investment is reduced in order to realise cash and stave off costly liquidation or recapitalisation.

The implications of the model for dynamic behaviour can be analysed using the steady state "ergodic distribution." The ergodic distribution, if it exists, represents both the cross-sectional distribution of many firms subject to independent shocks to cash flow and the unconditional time distribution of a single firm across states. It indicates the relative amount of time in which a firm stays in any particular state. When this is high, it visits this state often; when it is low then it visits this state rarely.

If a firm is liquidated at the lower boundary, i.e., if there is no recapitalisation, and it is not replaced by new firms, then no ergodic density exists. In order to compute an ergodic distribution and for comparability with the case of recapitalisation, an additional assumption is required: that liquidated firms are replaced at the upper dividend paying boundary. The following proposition then applies:

Proposition 4. *The pdf of the ergodic distribution is described the following first-order ODE:*

$$\frac{1}{2}\sigma^2 f' - \left[a + r\eta - \delta - \theta^{-1}(1+\eta)(q-1) - \frac{1}{2}\theta^{-1}(q-1)^2 \right] f = -d. \tag{8}$$

and can be computed subject to the boundary conditions

$$f(\bar{\eta}) = 0 \tag{9}$$

and $F(\eta^*) = 1$ where $F(\eta) = \int_{u=\bar{\eta}}^{\eta} f(u)\, du$.

Proof. Appendix B.   □

Here d is a constant representing the net flow of companies through the non-dividend paying region, until they exit at the lower boundary $\bar{\eta}$ through liquidation or recapitalisation and are replaced at the upper boundary η^*.

The interpretation of this ergodic distribution is slightly different in the two cases of recapitalisation and of liquidation. In the case of recapitalisation this represents the steady state cross-sectional distribution of firm net worth for firms hit by independent shocks *and* the proportion of time spent by a firm at each level of net worth. In the case of liquidation, it represents only the cross-sectional distribution of firm net worth and only when liquidated firms are indeed replaced at the upper boundary. (Other replacement assumptions are possible, for example, replacement at different levels of net worth in proportion to the steady state distribution of firms in which case the right-hand side of Equation (8) is replaced by $-df$. The ergodic density still represents only a cross-sectioaln distribution).

3.2.2. Numerical Solution

Appendix C presents the methods of numerical solution. The outline of these is as follows, utilising the function $q(\eta)$. Equation (6) can be written as:

$$q' = \frac{2}{\sigma^2}\left[a - \delta - (\rho - r)\eta - \rho q + \frac{1}{2}\theta^{-1}(q-1)^2\right](q + \eta). \tag{10}$$

requiring only two boundary conditions for solution: the optimality condition locating the upper boundary $q'(\eta^*) = 0$ together with the condition on the lower boundary Equation (7).

In the case of liquidation no iteration is necessary. This is because $W(\bar{\eta}) = 0$ implying from Equation (5) that $q(\bar{\eta}) = -\bar{\eta}$, i.e., the maximum amount of lending is the valuation of capital by outsiders and this determines the value of q on the lower boundary. Equation (10) is simply computed directly beginning from the lower boundary with $q = -\eta$ and continuing for higher values of η until $q' = 0$ and the upper boundary, if it exists, is located.

Iteration is required when there is recapitalisation rather than liquidation. This is because in this case $q(\bar{\eta})$ is not known, but must be determined from the matching condition $W(\bar{\eta}) = W(\eta^*) - (\eta^* - \bar{\eta} + \chi)$. Given any initial starting value for $q(\bar{\eta})$ it is possible to jointly compute both $q(\eta)$ and the accompanying value function $W(\eta)$. Iteration on the starting value $q(\bar{\eta})$ then yields the solution with recapitalisation (if one exists) with $W(\bar{\eta}) > 0$. While numerical solution is straightforward, it may fail to locate an upper boundary η^* for some combinations of parameters. This happens, for example, when the productivity of capital a is so high, and the adjustment costs of capital increase θ are so low, that output can be reinvested to increase the stock of capital faster than the discount rate of firms. (See Appendix A) for a discussion of the parameter restrictions required to prevent this in the deterministic case $\sigma = 0$). In this case the value function is unbounded and there is no meaningful solution. Extreme parameter values, for example, very low values of σ, can also result in numerical instability and failure to find a solution.

3.3. Simulation Results

Numerical solution is rapid, allowing extensive simulations of the model equations. Focusing on the shape of the ergodic distribution $f(\eta)$, one question is whether it has two peaks and can therefore help explain a transition from a high output boom to a low output slump, or instead has a single peak. In this first version of the model in this section there is always a single peak located at the maximum value η^*, i.e., the model without rental or sale of capital does not create long lasting periods with output and investment below normal levels.

Typical value functions W together with the corresponding ergodic densities f are presented in Figure 1. For that, the chosen parameters were:

$$\rho = 0.06, \quad r = 0.05, \quad \sigma = 0.2,$$
$$\theta = 15.0, \quad \chi = 0.75,$$
$$a = 0.1, \quad \bar{a} = 0.04, \quad \delta = 0.02. \tag{11}$$

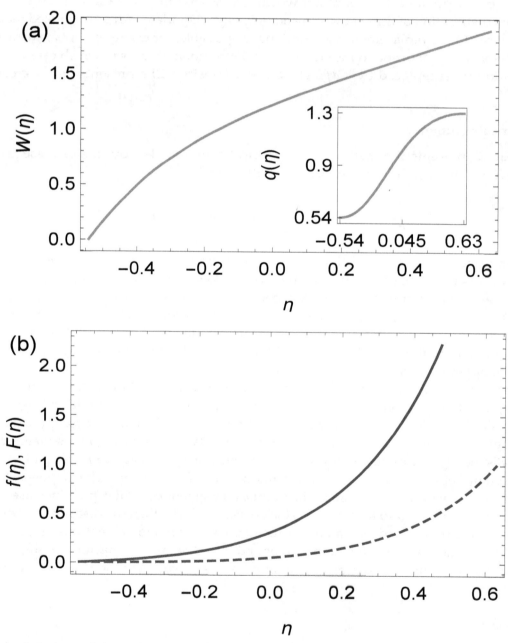

Figure 1. Solutions of the model equations of Section 3 for baseline parameters $\rho = 0.06$, $r = 0.05$, $\sigma = 0.2$, $a = 0.1$, $\bar{a} = 0.04$, $\delta = 0.02$, $\theta = 15$ and $\chi = 0.75$. Subfigure (**a**): value function W, inset shows the function q over the same η range; (**b**) the ergodic density f (solid curve) and the cumulative density function F (dashed).

Note the shape of these plots, with a monotonically increasing value function W, and a single-peaked ergodic density with a maximum at η^*. Across a wide range of parameter space search, only single-peaked distributions of this kind emerge. Although double peaks were not found, in some simulations the main peak normally at η^* can migrate into the central part of the η range. This occurs when choosing parameters for which cash-flows are non-positive ($d\eta \leq 0$). We do not report these simulations here.

4. An Extended Model

This section extends the model of Section 4 by assuming that capital can be rented by firms to outside investors. The structure of this section parallels that of Section 3, with subsections on assumptions (Section 4.1), the solution (Section 4.2) and simulation results (Section 4.3).

4.1. Additional Assumptions

In this extended setting, firms continue to manage the same two "state" variables, net cash c and capital k, but these now evolve according to:

$$dc = \left\{ -\lambda + [\psi a + (1 - \psi)\bar{a}]k + rc - ik - \frac{1}{2}\theta(i - \delta)^2 k \right\} dt \tag{12a}$$

$$+ \epsilon\left(\tau\right) + \psi\sigma_1 k\, dz_1,$$

$$dk = (i - \delta)k\, dt + \psi\sigma_2 k\, dz_2. \tag{12b}$$

There are now two independent diffusion terms ($\psi\sigma_1 k\, dz_1$ and $\sigma_2\psi k\, dz_2$) and an additional third control variable, the proportion of capital ψ firms themselves manage (with remaining capital $1 - \psi$ rented to households). All the other assumptions of Section 3 continue to apply.

Due to competition amongst households to acquire this capital, the amount households are willing to pay and hence the income from renting out a unit of capital is $\bar{a}$ the productivity of capital when managed by households. A special case is when $\bar{a} = 0$. In this case the renting of capital can be understood as "mothballing," taking a proportion $1 - \psi$ capital out of production. In either case, whether renting or mothballing, the firm benefits from a reduction in the diffusion terms from σk to $\psi\sigma k$, protecting it from the risk of fluctuations in net worth.

The introduction of a second diffusion term is a modest extension of the model. This introduces a dependency of diffusion on the level of net worth with $\sigma^2(\eta) = \sigma_1^2 + \sigma_2^2\eta^2$ instead of a constant σ^2. The introduction of renting is a more fundamental change, leading to the possibility of a double-peaked ergodic density and the possibility of persistence of a sequence of negative shocks that push net worth down to very low levels (the "net worth trap").

4.2. Solution

4.2.1. Characterisation of Solution

Propositions 1 and 2 apply to the generalised model with renting. Proposition 3 applies in the following amended form:

Proposition 5. *An optimal policy choice for* $\{i_t\}$, $\{\psi_t\}$, $\{\lambda_t\}$, $\{\epsilon_\tau\}$ *as functions of the single state variable* $\eta = ck^{-1}$, *if it exists, takes the following form. The rules for* $i(\eta), \lambda(\eta)$ *are exactly as stated in Proposition 3;*

optimal policy for $\psi(\eta)$ renting of fixed capital is that for lower values of η, in the range $\bar{\eta} \le \eta < \tilde{\eta}$ where $\bar{\eta} \le \tilde{\eta} < \eta^*$, firms retain a proportion $\psi < 1$ of fixed capital given by:

$$\psi = \frac{a - \bar{a}}{\sigma^2(\eta)} \left[-\frac{W''}{W'} \right]^{-1} \tag{13}$$

and rent the remaining proportion $1 - \psi > 0$ to firms; and for $\eta \ge c$, firms retain all fixed capital, i.e., $\psi = 1$ and none is rented out. Here $\sigma^2(\eta) = \sigma_1^2 + \sigma_2^2 \eta^2 \, W(\eta)$; the unique solution to the second-order differential equation over $\eta \in [\tilde{\eta}, \eta^*]$, now obeys:

$$\rho \frac{W}{W'} = \bar{a} + (a - \bar{a})\psi - \delta + r\eta - \frac{\sigma^2(\eta)}{2} \psi^2 \left[-\frac{W''}{W'} \right]$$

$$+ \frac{1}{2\theta} \left[\frac{W}{W'} - 1 - \eta \right]^2 \tag{14}$$

Solution for W is found subject to same boundary conditions as in Proposition 3

Proof. Appendix B. □

Here $-W''/W'$ expresses the induced risk aversion created by the presence of financing constraints (Section 4 of [1] has further discussion of this induced risk aversion and a comparison with the risk loving behaviour that emerges in many standard discrete time models as a result of moral hazard). $-W''/W'$ appears also in Proposition 3, the solution for the model with no option to rent out capital. There though, while it appears in Equation (6) the second-order differential equation for the value function, it has no direct impact on firm decisions. Now in Proposition 5, induced risk aversion $-W''/W'$ has a direct impact on firm decisions once net worth η falls below $\tilde{\eta}$. Renting out productive capital to households then reduces both the drift and the diffusion of η.

The introduction of the option to rent out capital introduces a second component to the behaviour of the firm. Now, and with the reduction of investment in the basic model because of a higher internal cost of capital, they can also reduce their employment of capital as a response to higher induced risk aversion. As a consequence of reduction in the employment of capital, in effect a "shrinking" of the size of operations, the firm can get "stuck" near the bankruptcy threshold, leading to a second peak in the ergodic distribution.

The resulting ergodic density can be computed using this Proposition (an indirect statement is used because of the dependency of ψ and σ on η. While ϕ can be substituted out from Equation (15) the resulting ODE for f is rather cumbersome):

Proposition 6. *The pdf of the ergodic distribution is described by the following first-order ode:*

$$\phi' - \left[\frac{1}{2}\psi^2\sigma^2(\eta) \right]^{-1} \left[a + (a - \bar{a})\psi + r\eta - \delta - \theta^{-1}(1 + \eta)(q - 1) - \frac{1}{2}\theta^{-1}(q - 1)^2 \right] \phi = -d \tag{15}$$

where $\phi = \psi^2\sigma^2 f/2$ and satisfies the boundary conditions

$$\begin{cases} f(\bar{\eta}) = 0, & \text{if } W(\bar{\eta}) > 0 \\ d = 0 & \text{if } W(\bar{\eta}) = 0 \end{cases} \tag{16}$$

and $F(\eta^*) = 1$ where $F(\eta) = \int_{u=\bar{\eta}}^{\eta} f(u)\, du$.

Proof. Appendix B. □

4.2.2. Numerical Calculation

Numerical solution methods are again detailed in Appendix C. This proceeds in the same way as for the first model without renting of Section 3, by re-expressing Equation (14) as a differential equation in q. Over the lower region $\eta < \bar{\eta}$ (Equation (14)) becomes:

$$q' = -\frac{1}{2}\frac{(a-\bar{a})^2}{\sigma_1^2 + \eta^2\sigma_2^2}\frac{q+\eta}{\bar{a} - \delta + r\eta - \rho(q+\eta) + \frac{1}{2}\theta^{-1}(q-1)^2} \qquad (17)$$

while in the upper region Equation (10) continues to apply (except that now $\sigma^2 = \sigma_1^2 + \sigma_2^2\eta^2$ is a function of η).

If there is no recapitalisation then the model can again be solved without iteration, commencing the calculation at $\eta = \bar{\eta}$ and continuing until the intermediate values $\eta = \tilde{\eta}$ and $\eta = \eta^*$ are located. However, in this case $q(\bar{\eta}) = -\bar{\eta}$ and hence $\psi(\bar{\eta}) = 0$, with the consequence that there are singularities in f, q and W at $\bar{\eta}$. We incorporate these singularities using asymptotic approximations summarised in the following further proposition.

Proposition 7. W, q and ϕ close to $\bar{\eta}$ are described by:

$$W = C_W(\eta - \bar{\eta})^\beta(1 + \mathcal{O}(\eta - \bar{\eta})), \qquad (18)$$

where C_W is a constant and $\beta = 1/(1 + q'(\bar{\eta})) \in (0, 1]$;

$$q = \bar{q} + q'(\bar{\eta})(\eta - \bar{\eta}). \qquad (19)$$

and;

$$\phi = C_\phi(\eta - \bar{\eta})^\alpha, \qquad (20)$$

where α is given by Equation (A34) of Appendix D and C_ϕ is another constant.

This further implies that $-W''/W'$ (our measure of induced risk aversion) is divergent at $\bar{\eta} = -\bar{q}$,

$$-\frac{W''}{W'} \simeq \frac{1-\beta}{\eta - \bar{\eta}}.$$

(consistent with $\psi(\bar{\eta}) = 0$), and the ergodic density is approximated by

$$f \propto (\eta - \bar{\eta})^{\alpha-2} \qquad (21)$$

and thus diverges if $\alpha < 2$ and becomes degenerate, with the entire probability mass at $\bar{\eta}$ if $\alpha \leq 1$.

Proof. Appendix D. □

In the case of recapitalisation $q(\bar{\eta}) > -\bar{\eta}$ and there is are no singularities in the solution; so, while iteration ia again required to determine $q(\bar{\eta})$, this can be conducted in exactly the same way as described in Section 3.2.2 for the model without renting.

4.3. Simulation Results

As expected from the power-law shape of f, Equation (21), the option to rent can have a strong impact on the shape of the ergodic density. As an example of this, in Figure 2 plots the value function W together with q, and the probability and cumulative densities, now using baseline parameters $\rho = 0.06$, $r = 0.05$, $\sigma_1 = 0.2$, $\sigma_2 = 0.0$, $a = 0.1$, $\bar{a} = 0.04$, $\delta = 0.02$, $\theta = 15$ and $\chi = 0.75$ (identical parameters to those used in Figure 1). Whereas the value function W and q show little change when renting is introduced, the density function f changes dramatically. This time a second peak is clearly present near the left-hand side range of η values. Note that with these particular parameter values the firm chooses not to recapitalise, with χ being slightly above the critical value of around 0.74 at which recapitalisation is not worthwhile, and $W(\bar{\eta}) \approx 0.05$. The interested reader can observe, using our standalone application, how increasing χ to above this critical level results in the emergence of singularities and the divergence of $f(\eta)$ to $+\infty$ at $\eta = \bar{\eta}$.

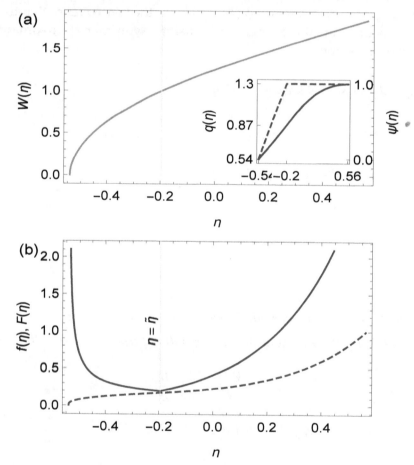

Figure 2. Solutions of the model of Section 4 with option to rent, using baseline parameters $\rho = 0.06$, $r = 0.05$, $\sigma_1 = \sigma = 0.2$, $\sigma_2 = 0.0$, $a = 0.1$, $\bar{a} = 0.04$, $\delta = 0.02$, $\theta = 15$ and $\chi = 0.75$. Contrast this to Figure 1 where identical parameters were used, but without renting. Subfigure (**a**): value function W, inset shows the functions q and ψ over the same η range; (**b**) the ergodic density f (solid curve) and the cumulative density function F (dashed). Notice the prominent peak in f towards the left-hand side boundary.

This ergodic instability (a second peak towards in the ergodic density associated with low values of the state variable η representing the ratio of cash-to-capital) is parameter dependent. This parameter dependence emerges in two different ways: (i) through the power-law exponent α, and (ii) dependence on the cost of recapitalisation χ. The ability to recapitalise or not has a major impact on the ergodic distribution. For any given parameters, there is a threshold χ, $\bar{\chi}$, above which recapitalisation is no longer worthwhile. If χ is equal to or greater than this value, then $\psi(\bar{\eta}) = 0$, and the density diverges and the ergodic density follows the power-law $f \propto (\eta - \bar{\eta})^{\alpha-2}$ near $\bar{\eta}$, which in turn can lead to infinite densities. Hence, the strength of the instability (*i.e.* the amount of probability mass near $\bar{\eta}$) is strongly controlled by the parameter χ.

This is illustrated in Figure 3 showing how the ergodic density changes as χ is varied. For low values of χ, there is no left-hand side peak in the model with rent (Figure 3a) and f largely resembles that of the model without the option to rent (Figure 3b). As χ approaches $\bar{\chi}$ (indicated by the dotted lines on the floor of the two panels of this figure, where $\bar{\chi} \simeq 0.74$ with rent, $\bar{\chi} \simeq 0.73$ without), in the model with renting a probability mass starts to appear near $\bar{\eta}$. Crossing $\bar{\chi}$, recapitalisation becomes no longer an option, and the density at $\bar{\eta}$ diverges. Above $\bar{\chi}$ there is no longer χ dependence. Note that the distribution f changes quite sharply; when approaching $\bar{\chi}$ is crossed, with a second peak of the distribution emerging close to $\eta = \bar{\eta}$, a robust result across a variety of simulations.

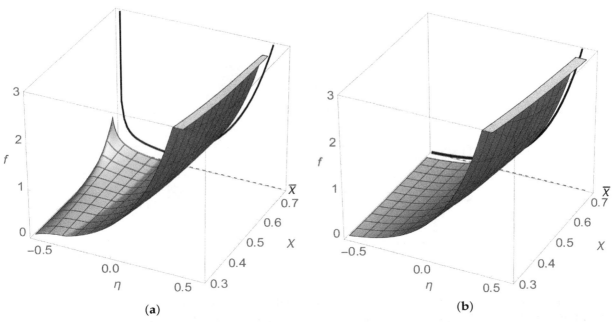

(a)   (b)

Figure 3. Comparison of ergodic densities f given the option to rent (**a**) and no option to rent (**b**) as the financing constraint χ is varied. Other parameters were set to baseline values. The lower boundary is recapitalising unto $\chi = \bar{\chi}$ ($\bar{\chi} \simeq 0.74$ in (**a**) and 0.73 in (**b**)), indicated by the thick solid line on the graph and dashed line on the axis. In (**a**) a left-boundary peak emerges for χ just less than $\bar{\chi}$. Density is infinite at $\bar{\eta}$ for $\chi > \bar{\chi}$. Note the complete absence of the left-hand side peak in (**b**).

To further explore this parameter dependence consider how the median of f depends on various parameters. Since the values of $\bar{\eta}$ and η^*, the range on which the distribution is defined, also vary with the parameters, it is convenient to scale the median on to the interval $[0, 1]$: Let m be the median; then the scaled median is defined as

$$\tilde{m} = \frac{m - \bar{\eta}}{\eta^* - \bar{\eta}}, \qquad F(m) = \frac{1}{2}. \tag{22}$$

A value of $\tilde{m} \sim 0$ implies that most of the probability mass is concentrated near $\bar{\eta}$, while $\tilde{m} \sim 1$ suggests that firms are more probably found near η^*. While this is a somewhat crude measure (e.g., the median cannot distinguish between distributions that are $\cup$ or $\cap$-shaped), nonetheless, $\tilde{m} \lesssim 1/2$ is a strong indicator of large mass of probability near the lower boundary, hence the long lasting response to a large initial shock found by [2].

In Figure 4 presents a contour plot $\tilde{m}$ as a function of the financing constraint χ and the volatility σ (note that Figure 3 represents a small slice of data presented in this figure). Three roughly distinct regimes can be seen:

(i) The low volatility range $\sigma \lesssim 0.2$, in which the firm always prefers to recapitalise and where $\tilde{m} \gtrsim 0.8$ and so most of the probability is found near the dividend paying boundary.

(ii) A region where $\sigma \gtrsim 0.3$ and at the same time $\chi \gtrsim 0.5$, i.e., red region to the top right, where $\tilde{m} \sim 0$, and much of the probability mass is located near the left-hand boundary.

(iii) An intermediate transition range wherein small changes in either σ or χ result in a very substantial change in $\tilde{m}$. This transition is especially abrupt for high values of σ.

Exploring the behaviour of $\tilde{m}$ as a function of other model parameters yields remarkably similar contour plots. For example, as the relative impatience of shareholders $\rho - r$ is increased from relatively low to high values, there are also two distinct regions similar to those of Figure 4, with a relatively sharp transition in the balance of the probability distribution from near the upper boundary η^* to the lower boundary $\bar{\eta}$.

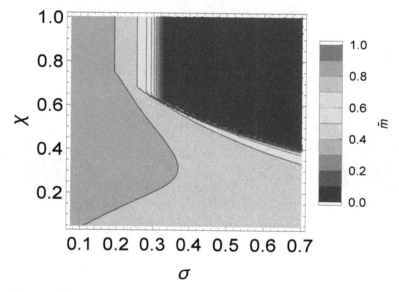

Figure 4. The scaled median $\tilde{m}$ as a function of χ and σ. $\tilde{m}$ is the median of the distribution of η relative to its range. $\tilde{m}$ close to one indicates that the mass of the distribution is located near the upper dividend paying boundary. $\tilde{m}$ close to zero indicates that the mass is located near the lower liquidation or recapitalisation boundary. $\sigma_2 = 0.0$ (the baseline value from earlier figures) so $\sigma_1 = \sigma$. Other parameters were set to baseline values; $\rho = 0.06$, $r = 0.05$, $a = 0.1$, $\bar{a} = 0.04$, $\delta = 0.02$ and $\theta = 15$. Contours are plotted at level values of $\tilde{m}$ and are spaced at intervals of 0.1.

One further finding concerns induced aversion to cash flow risk $-\frac{W''}{W'}$. This induced risk aversion is, like ergodic instability, strongly parameter and model structure dependent. In the model with renting, when firms do not recapitalise they become extremely risk-averse close to the lower boundary $\bar{\eta}$. This is revealed by an analysis of power-law behaviour of W at the lower boundary $\bar{\eta}$ (see Proposition 7). This extreme risk aversion does not arise in the model with renting or if recapitalisation is not costly.

This finding is illustrated in Figure 5 which compares induced risk-aversion for the two versions of the model, with and without the option to rent. The parameters here are the same as in Figures 1 and 2. For relatively large values of η close to η^* the option to rent provides protection against cash flow risk and induced risk aversion $-\frac{W''}{W'}$ is lower for the model with renting; but as η falls down towards $\bar{\eta}$, the model with renting induced risk aversion $-\frac{W''}{W'}$ diverges upwards—rising increasingly rapidly as η approaches $\bar{\eta}$, whereas it rises only slightly in the model without renting.

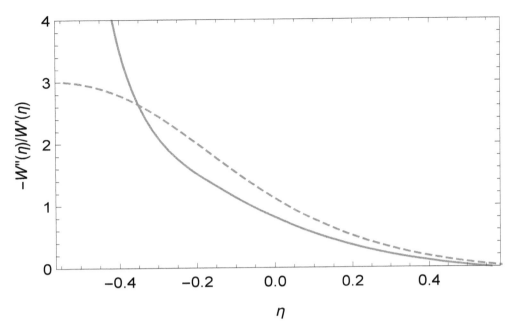

Figure 5. Induced risk aversion $-W''/W'$ as a function of η. Parameters were set to baseline. Solid curve: model with option to rent; dashed curve: model without option to rent. Significantly, the risk aversion diverges strongly near $\bar{\eta}$ in the model without renting, in contrast to the model with renting.

5. Conclusions

This paper investigated the impact of financing constraints on corporate output and investment in a simple continuous time setting with linear production and preferences. Firms face liquidation or costly recapitalisation, if their net worth (relative to capital) falls to a minimum level following a shock to cash flows or productivity. The boundary conditions resulting from these financing constraints generate potentially large and long-lasting non-linearities in the response of firm output and investment to external shocks, even in this otherwise linear setting. A fall of net worth leads to a decline of investment below normal levels. Moreover, if firms can rent out or mothball their capital stock, output also declines along with investment, and this may continue for an extended period of time: the "net worth trap".

Several further insights emerged. One is the importance of "corporate prudential saving", analogous to the household prudential saving extensively discussed in the literature on the consumption function. As their net worth declines, firms invest less and less (a fall in marginal q). The second is "induced risk aversion": firms with sufficiently high net worth have the same attitude to risk as their share holders (assumed for simplicity to be risk-neutral); but as net worth declines then firms behave increasingly as if they were averse to risk in order to reduce the probability of future liquidation or costly recapitalisation, here by mothballing or renting out more and more of their capital. Figures 4 and 5 show how resulting behaviour can vary markedly (both qualitatively and quantitatively) with parametrisation and model specification.

The finding that financing constraints mean that firm decisions can be highly non-linear functions of their indebtedness means that both the size and direction of shocks matter. This in turn helps to clarify when a linearisation—of the kind routinely employed in new Keynesian DSGE macroeconomic models—provides a reasonable approximation to the fully dynamic optimal behaviour

In normal times when shocks are comparatively small, aggregate behaviour can be sufficiently well captured in standard linearised specifications. This is illustrated by Figures 1a and 2a. In normal times most firms are located near the right-hand sides of these figures, close to the upper dividend payment boundary η^* where the value function $W(\eta)$ is approximately linear. The reserve of net worth provides and adequate hedge against both aggregate and idiosyncratic risk. Moreover, in normal times, external equity capital can, if necessary, be raised at relatively low cost; i.e., the cost of recapitalisation parameter χ is low. As a result, impulse responses, expressed as a percentage of initial shock are then approximately the same regardless of the size or direction of the initial disturbance; linearisation of impulse responses based on past data provides a convenient and reliable summary of macroeconomic behaviour.

In times of extreme financial and economic stress, such as the Great Depression of the 1930s or the Global Financial Crisis of 2007–2008, the situation can be quite different. Uncertainty σ and the cost of recapitalisation χ rises. Large shocks push many firms towards the lower minimum level of net worth $\bar{\eta}$, where as illustrated in Figures 1a and 2a, the value function $W(\eta)$ is concave not linear and both corporate prudential saving and induced risk aversion emerge. Impulse responses based on past data are no longer a reliable guide to the response to shocks. As our Figure 4 illustrates, such an adverse change in the economic environment can lead to a "phase change," with a shift to a regime where the net worth trap emerges. The response to the Covid-19 pandemic may provide another such episode.

Most striking here, as illustrated in our Figure 4, is that relatively small parameter changes can lead to this phase change. A small increase in perceived uncertainty (our parameter σ) leads to a large change in behaviour, from relatively rapid rebuilding of physical and financial capacity following the emergence of financial distress to a slow rebuilding with a long lasting period of reduced output and investment. Small changes in the external environment faced by firms can lead to the emergence of the persistent "net worth trap." Policy makers and regulators need to be aware that whilst linear approximations may provide a good description of usual events, they can give misleading insights in more turbulent times.

Author Contributions: The mathematical modelling, proofs and the selection of illustrative figures reported in the paper are the joint work of all the authors. J.I. conducted the numerical solution and wrote most of the supporting Mathematica code, including the free standing numerical solver. A.M. and D.R. wrote the review of the literature and the economic interpretation of the model's results. All authors have read and agreed to the published version of the manuscript.

Acknowledgments: The authors are grateful for comments from Jussi Keppo, Feo Kusmartsev, Tassos Malliaris, Jean-Charles Rochet and Javier Suarez; and for feedback from audiences at the Bank of England, the Bank of Finland, the IBEFA January 2013 meetings, IFABS 2014 meeting, the University of Durham, Bristol University, the London School of Economics, the Bank of Japan, the National University Singapore, the University of Tasmania and internal seminar and conference presentations at Loughborough University. Remaining shortcomings are our responsibility alone.

Appendix A. Solution in the Absence of the Non-Negativity Constraint on Dividends

This appendix considers the solution to the model of this paper in the baseline case wherein dividend payments can be negative, or equivalently, there is no uncertainty. This provides a benchmark for studying and solving the case of the constrained firm for which there is uncertainty and dividends are required to be non-negative. It also yields a convenient formula for the maximum amount of borrowing provided by households to firms.

A crucial intuition emerges from this benchmark model, relevant to the model with a non-negativity constraint on dividend payments. The rate of growth preferred by firms is an increasing function of the ratio of debt to capital (this is because debt increases at the same rate of growth of capital, creating an additional cash flow that can be used for investment, and the higher the ratio of debt to capital, the greater this cash flow). If the financing constraint is sufficiently lax then it is possible for firms to achieve a growth rate equal to their own rate of discount while still being able to pay dividends. In this case the objective of this firm (expected discounted dividend payments) is unbounded and the solution is no longer meaningful. Therefore, some financing constraint is required in order for the model to have a meaningful solution.

To solve this benchmark, note that since firm owners can freely transfer funds into or out of the firm, optimal policy is to maintain the ratio of cash balances $\eta = c/k$ at whatever rate is preferred by borrowers, subject to the highest level of indebtedness allowed by lenders $\eta \geq \bar{\eta}$. If the initial time $t = 0$ ratio η_0 differs from the desired ratio η then an instantaneous dividend payment of $(\eta_0 - \eta)\, k$ is immediately made to bring the cash to capital ratio to the desired value of η.

There is therefore now only a single state variable k. The value function (the value of the objective function under optimal policy) is linearly homogeneous in k and so can be written as $V = kW$, where W is a constant that depends on the parameters representing preferences and the evolution of the state variable k. This in turn implies that $V_k = W$ and $V_{kk} = 0$. Expected dividend payments will be determined by the expected net cash flow of the firm plus any additional borrowing possible because k and hence c are growing. The remaining policy decision is to choose a rate of investment i and hence expected growth of the capital stock $g = i - \delta$ to maximise Ω, Equation (2)

The solution can be summarised in the following proposition.

Proposition A1. *Assuming $\rho > r$, then an optimal policy yielding positive pay-offs for the owners of the firm can be found provided that:*

$$-2\frac{\rho - (a - \delta) + (\rho - r)\bar{\eta}}{\rho^2} < \theta < \begin{cases} \infty & \text{if } a + r\bar{\eta} \geq \delta \\ \dfrac{1}{2}\dfrac{(1 + \bar{\eta})^2}{\delta - r\bar{\eta} - a} & \text{if } a + r\bar{\eta} < \delta \end{cases} \tag{A1}$$

in which case an instantaneous dividend payment of $\eta_0 - \bar{\eta}$ is made so that $\eta = \bar{\eta}$, the growth rate of the capital stock is constant (state independent) and is given by:

$$g = \rho - \sqrt{\rho^2 - 2\theta^{-1}[a - \delta - \rho + (r - \rho)\bar{\eta}]} < \rho, \tag{A2}$$

while the value of the maximised objective is given by:

$$V(\eta_0, k) = (\eta_0 - \bar{\eta})\, k + \frac{(a - \delta) + (r - g)\bar{\eta} - g - \frac{1}{2}\theta g^2}{\rho - g} k = (1 + \eta_0 + g\theta)\, k \tag{A3}$$

where $\left[(a - \delta) + (r - g)\bar{\eta} - g - \frac{1}{2}\theta g^2\right] k$ is the expected flow of dividends per period of time paid to shareholders.

Proof. The firm has two choice variables, η and g (with investment expenditure given by $ik = (g + \delta)\, k$ and associated quadratic adjustment costs of $\frac{1}{2}\theta (i - \delta)^2 = \frac{1}{2}\theta g^2$). The equations of motion (1) still apply and dividends are paid according to:

$$\lambda\, dt = \left[(a - \delta) + (r - g)\,\eta - g - \frac{1}{2}\theta g^2\right] k\, dt + \sigma k\, dz$$

Substituting for λ the discounted objective can be written as:

$$\Omega = \max_{\eta, g}\left\{\mathbb{E}\int_0^\infty e^{-\rho t}\left[(a - \delta) + (r - g)\,\eta - g - \frac{1}{2}\theta g^2\right] k\ dt + (\eta_0 - \eta)\, k_0 + \int e^{-\rho t}\sigma k\ dz\right\} \tag{A4}$$

yielding, since $\mathbb{E}[k] = k(0)\exp(gt)$ and $e^{-\rho t}\sigma k = 0$:

$$\Omega = k(0)\max_{\eta, g}\left[\eta_0 - \eta + \frac{(a - \delta) + (r - g)\,\eta - g - \frac{1}{2}\theta g^2}{\rho - g}\right]. \tag{A5}$$

The growth rate g that maximises the right-hand side of this expression is determined by the first-order condition with respect to g:

$$\frac{1}{2}g^2 - \rho g - \theta^{-1}\left[\rho - (a - \delta) + (\rho - r)\eta\right] = 0 \tag{A6}$$

yielding the solution (the positive root of the quadratic can be ruled out because $g < \rho$ to ensure that the value function is finite and that the second-order condition for maximisation is satisfied):

$$g = \rho - \sqrt{\rho^2 + 2\theta^{-1}[\rho - (a - \delta) + (\rho - r)\eta]}. \tag{A7}$$

Writing $\rho - g = \sqrt{\rho^2 + 2\theta^{-1}[\rho - (a - \delta) + (\rho - r)\eta]} = R$, implying $g^2 = \rho^2 - 2\rho R + R^2$, and substitution into Equation (A5) then yields: (A3).

The indebtedness is determined by the first-order condition in (A5) with respect to η:

$$\frac{r - g}{\rho - g} - 1 = \frac{r - \rho}{\rho - g} < 0$$

establishing that the firm will seek to borrow as much as it possibly can. Hence, the firm will make an instantaneous dividend at time $t = 0$ to reduce η as far as possible, until the borrowing constraint binds so $\eta = \bar{\eta}$. The first inequality on θ in the proposition ensures that the borrowing constraint does indeed bind at a level of borrowing at which Equation (A6) has real roots.

The remaining inequality conditions on θ ensure that it is possible to achieve positive dividends per unit of capital (these are relatively weak conditions since normally $a > \delta$ in which case a policy of zero growth $g = 0$ and no indebtedness will always yield positive dividends; but if depreciation is larger than the productivity of capital then a further restriction on θ is required). To establish these further conditions note that expected dividends per unit of capital $a - \delta + r\bar{\eta} - (1 + \bar{\eta})g - \frac{1}{2}\theta g^2$ are maximised by choosing $g = -(1 + \bar{\eta})\theta^{-1}$ resulting in expected dividend payments of $\lambda = a - \delta + r\bar{\eta} + \frac{1}{2}\theta^{-1}(1 + \bar{\eta})^2$. This is always greater than zero if $a > \delta$; otherwise this requires that $\theta < (1 + \bar{\eta})^2/2(\delta - a - r\bar{\eta})$. $\square$

This proof also shows that the Modigliani–Miller [16] proposition on the irrelevance of capital structure to the value of the firm applies, in this case when negative dividends are allowed. It does so in the sense that any net worth in excess of the minimum level $\bar{\eta}k$ is immediately paid out to shareholders and the firm always operates with maximum leverage. The value function is additive in $\bar{\eta}k$.

Finally, note that the fundamental valuation of a firm's capital by outside investors can be obtained by substituting $\rho = r$, $a = \bar{a}$ and $\bar{\eta} = 0$ into this solution. A finite positive valuation is obtained provided the parameters satisfy:

$$2\frac{\bar{a} - \delta - r}{r^2} < \theta < \begin{cases} \infty & \text{if } \bar{a} \geq \delta \\ \dfrac{1}{2}\dfrac{1}{\delta - \bar{a}} & \text{if } \bar{a} < \delta \end{cases}$$

in which case the growth rate (when held by outside investors) is given by

$$\bar{g} = r - \sqrt{r^2 - 2\theta^{-1}[\bar{a} - \delta - r]},$$

and the value of the maximised objective by

$$V = \frac{\bar{a} - \bar{g} - \delta - \frac{1}{2}\theta\bar{g}^2}{r - \bar{g}}k = (1 + \theta\bar{g})k.$$

This provides an immediate proof of Proposition 1 in Section 3.

Proof of Proposition 1. This valuation of the firm's assets by outside investors is also the maximum amount of debt that it can borrow from these investors, implying that the lower boundary for η is given by Equation (3). □

Appendix B. Proofs of Propositions in Sections 3 and 4

Proof of Proposition 5. (Proposition 3 requires no separate proof, since it is the special case when $\sigma_2 = 0$ and $\psi = 1$). While uniqueness of solution can be established using standard arguments based on the non-convexity of the optimisation program, the proof provided here is geometric proof, offering some additional insights into both the existence of solution and its numerical calculation.

Applying standard methods of stochastic dynamic programming, with two state variables k and c, the optimal policy by firms, at times when there is no recapitalisation ($\epsilon_t = 0$), satisfies the Hamilton–Jacobi–Bellman equation:

$$\rho V = \max_{i,\lambda,\psi} \left\{ \lambda + \left[-\lambda + (\bar{a} + (a - \bar{a})\psi) k + rc - ik - \frac{1}{2}\theta(i - \delta)^2 k \right] V_c \right. \tag{A8}$$

$$\left. + (i - \delta)kV_k + \frac{1}{2}\sigma_1^2\psi^2k^2V_{cc} + \frac{1}{2}\sigma_2^2\psi^2k^2V_{kk} \right\}, \tag{A9}$$

with three first-order conditions for maximisation. The first is:

$$\left\{ \begin{array}{ll} \lambda \geq 0 \text{ of unbounded magnitude,} & V_c = 1 \\ \lambda = 0, & V_c > 1 \end{array} \right.,$$

there is "bang-bang" control with two distinct regions of dividend behaviour: one when $c \geq c^*(k)$ with $V_c = 1$ in which case the policy is to payout a discrete dividend to reduce cash holdings immediately to the dividend paying boundary c^*; the other when $c < c^*(k)$ wherein there is no payment of dividends and $V_c > 1$. The second first-order condition is:

$$(1 + \theta(i - \delta)) V_c = V_k$$

yielding the investment rule:

$$i = \delta + \theta^{-1}\left(\frac{V_k}{V_c} - 1\right). \tag{A10}$$

The third first-order condition for maximisation (subject to the constraint $0 \leq \psi \leq 1$) is:

$$(a - \bar{a})kV_c + \psi k^2 \left(\sigma_1^2 V_{cc} + \sigma_2^2 V_{kk}\right) = 0$$

yielding the final control rule:

$$\psi = \max\left\{ \min\left\{ (a - \bar{a})\left[-k\frac{\sigma_1^2 V_{cc} + \sigma_2^2 V_{kk}}{V_c} \right]^{-1}, 1 \right\}, 0 \right\}. \tag{A11}$$

Due to the linearity of production the value function is linearly homogeneous in k and so value can be expressed as a function W of a single state variable $\eta = c/k$:

$$W(\eta) = k^{-1}V(c,k) = V(\eta,1) \tag{A12}$$

implying the substitutions $V = kW$, $V_c = W'$, $V_k = W - \eta W'$, $q = V_k/V_c = W/W' - \eta$, $V_{cc} = k^{-1}W''$, $V_{ck} = -k^{-1}\eta W''$ and $V_{kk} = k^{-1}\eta^2 W''$ Substituting for both optimal policy and for V and its derivatives yields Equation (14). The maximisation in this second boundary condition reflects the choice available to the firm when η falls to $\bar{\eta}$; it may choose either to liquidate, in which case $W(\bar{\eta}) = 0$, or to recapitalise, which is worth doing if it can achieve a higher valuation by paying the fixed cost of recapitalisation χk and increasing η to η^*. The firm will never choose to recapitalise to a value of $\eta < \eta^*$. This is because when $\eta < \eta^*$, $V_c = W' > 1$, so the maximum possible value of $W(\bar{\eta})$ in Equation (7) is achieved by a full recapitalisation up to η^*. Turning to the uniqueness of this solution, note that as discussed in Appendix C solution of the upper boundary η^* is characterised by Equation (10) (itself obtained from

Equation (6) using $q = W/W' - \eta$ which yields $q' = -WW''/(W')^2$). Equation (10) can be written (allowing for dependencies of σ on η) as:

$$q' = \frac{2}{\sigma_1^2 + \eta^2 \sigma_2^2} Q(q, \eta)(q + \eta)$$

from which, since $\sigma_1^2 + \eta^2 \sigma_2^2 > 0$ and $q^* + \eta^* > \bar{q} + \bar{\eta} \geq 0$ and $Q(q, \eta) = a - \delta - (\rho - r)\eta - \rho q + \frac{1}{2}\theta^{-1}(q - 1)^2$ is a quadratic function of q and linear function of η. This in turn implies that the possible locations of q^* are given by $Q(q, \eta) = 0$, i.e., a parabola in (q, η) space, which when solved yields the location of η on the dividend paying boundaries as a function of q^*:

$$\eta^* = \frac{a - \delta - \rho q^* + \frac{1}{2}\theta^{-1}(q^* - 1)^2}{\rho - r} \tag{A13}$$

Inverting this equation to solve for $q = q^*$ on the dividend paying boundary yields:

$$q^* = 1 + \theta\left(\rho \pm \sqrt{\rho^2 - 2\theta^{-1}\{a - \delta - \rho - \eta^*(\rho - r)\}}\right) \tag{A14}$$

The uniqueness of the solution then follows (assuming continuity of $q(\eta)$) from noting that the value of $q = q^*$ is a function of the value of $q(\bar{\eta}) = \bar{q}$ on the lower boundary. Given any starting value $\bar{q}$ the ODE characterising the solution can be computed (with $q' > 0$) until it meets $Q(q, \eta) = 0$. There can only be one such intersection. Having crossed $Q(q, \eta) = 0$, $q' < 0$ until there is another intersection, and this means any potential second intersection can only take place on the lower branch of $Q(q, \eta) = 0$. However, in order for there to be an intersection on this lower branch it is necessary that the q-curve falls faster than the lower branch, i.e., that on the point of intersection:

$$q' < \left.\frac{\partial q}{\partial \eta}\right|_{Q(q,\eta)=0} < 0$$

which contradicts the requirement that $q' = 0$ on $Q(q, \eta) = 0$. This contradiction shows that any solution of the ODE has at most one unique intersection with $Q(q, \eta) = 0$. $\square$

This proof does not establish existence. While there can only be one solution to the ODE for W satisfying the boundary conditions of Proposition 5, the existence of this solution is dependent on parameter values. Proposition 2 gave sufficient conditions for a solution to exist.

Proof of Proposition 2. First note that Equation (4a) is equivalent to

$$\bar{\eta} > \eta^*_{\min} = -\frac{\rho - (a - \delta) + \frac{1}{2}\theta\rho^2}{\rho - r}, \tag{A15}$$

where $\eta^*_{\min}$ is the minimum value of η on the dividend paying boundary. This condition can be described as the "no-Ponzi" condition because, as stated in Proposition A1 in Appendix A when $\bar{\eta} > \eta^*_{\min}$ is satisfied, then the solution to the problem in the deterministic limit $\lim_{\sigma \downarrow 0}$ exists, in which the growth of the fixed capital stock is less than the discount rate of firm shareholders $g < \rho$, and the value to shareholders comes from both growth of the capital stock and dividend payments.

The idea of proof is illustrated in Figure A1. Consider possible solutions of the ODE for $q(\eta)$. In the case of no recapitalisation, $\bar{q} = -\bar{\eta}$ and the lower intersection of $Q(q, \eta) = 0$ with $\eta = \bar{\eta}$ is at $q = q^*_- = 1 + \theta(\rho - \sqrt{\rho^2 - 2\theta^{-1}\{a - \delta - \rho - \bar{\eta}(\rho - r)\}})$. This implies (using Equation (3)) that:

$$q^*_- - \bar{q} = 1 + \theta\left(\rho - \sqrt{\rho^2 - 2\theta^{-1}\{a - \delta - \rho - \bar{\eta}(\rho - r)\}}\right) + \bar{\eta} > 0$$

This shows that a solution with no recapitalisation exists, because the ODE begins at a point strictly below q^*_-, and since $q' > 0$ must eventually intersect with $Q(q, \eta) = 0$. This in turn implies the existence of solutions with recapitalisation, since these are associated with higher values of $\bar{q}$ satisfying

$-\bar{\eta} < \bar{q} < q_-^*$, in all cases with the ODE eventually intersecting with the lower branch of $Q(q, \eta) = 0$; and with values of $\chi > 0$. Eventually in the limit $\lim_{\chi \downarrow 0} \bar{q} = q_-^*$. $\square$

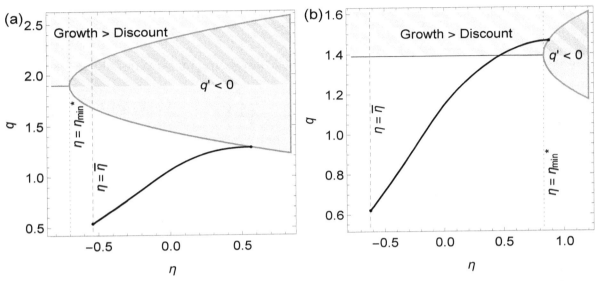

Figure A1. Illustration of Proof of Proposition 2. In subfigure (a), the "no-Ponzi" condition, Equation (A15), holds: the initial η is below the dividend paying boundary, and so the solution is guaranteed to hit it. Subfigure (b) shows a scenario wherein the condition does not hold: The solution starts from a point to the left of η_{min}^*, and grows fast enough to miss the lower branch of $q' = 0$ curve, entering a region where growth exceeds the discount rate. In (a), parameters are set to baseline, $\rho = 0.06$, $r = 0.05$, $\sigma_1 = 0.2$, $\sigma_2 = 0.0$, $a = 0.1$, $\bar{a} = 0.04$, $\delta = 0.02$, $\theta = 15$ and $\chi = 0.75$; in (b), parameters are the same, except that $\theta = 6.5$.

Some additional intuition into the factors that determine whether the "no-Ponzi" condition is satisfied or not can be obtained by re-expressing Equation (A15) as

$$\bar{g}^* < \left[\frac{1}{2} (\rho - g^*)^2 / (\rho - r) - \theta^{-1} \right]$$

where

$$\bar{g}^* = \left(r - \sqrt{r^2 - 2\theta^{-1}[\bar{a} - \delta - r]} \right) < r$$

is the rate of growth when capital stock is owned by external investors and

$$g^* = \left(\rho - \sqrt{\rho^2 - 2\theta^{-1}[\bar{a} - \delta - \rho]} \right) < \rho$$

the rate of growth of the capital stock in the situation where firms can costlessly issued equity ($\chi = 0$) but are unable to borrow (see Appendix A). This expression indicates that in order for the "no-Ponzi" to be satisfied requires that the difference between the discount rates of firms and outside investors $\rho - r$ is comparatively small, or the net productivity of capital either in the hands of firms or investors ($a - \delta$, $\bar{a} - \delta$) relative to the maximum values given by the constraints of Equations (4a) and (4b) is comparatively small, or the costs of adjustment of capital θ are comparatively high.

What about solution in the stochastic case if the "no-Ponzi" condition is not satisfied? A numerical solution can still be obtained and indicate that an optimal policy for choice of $\{i_t\}$, $\{\lambda_t\}$, $\{\epsilon_\tau\}$ satisfying the conditions of Proposition 3, i.e., with future dividend payments after any initial dividend payment to reduce η to the desired target level η^*, may still exist, provided that g^* is not too close to ρ.

Finally there are the propositions about the ergodic density.

Proof of Proposition 4. (Proposition of Section 3 can again be obtained by imposing appropriate parameter restrictions.) Denote the density function for the location of firms across the possible values of η at the moment t by $f(t, \eta)$, with the corresponding cumulative density:

$$F(t, \eta) = \int_{\bar\eta}^{\eta} f(t, \eta')\, d\eta', \quad F(t, \eta^*) = 1$$

The evolution of $f(t, \eta)$ is then determined by the Kolmogorov forward or Fokker-Planck equation:

$$\frac{\partial f}{\partial t}(t, \eta) = -\frac{\partial}{\partial \eta}\left[\mu^\eta(\eta) f(t, \eta)\right] + \frac{1}{2}\frac{\partial^2}{\partial \eta^2}\left[\sigma^\eta(\eta)^2 f(t, \eta)\right], \tag{A16}$$

where η follows the equation of motion

$$d\eta = \mu^\eta\, dt + \sigma^\eta\, dz.$$

with coefficients obtained simply by Itô differentiating $\eta = c/k$:

$$d\eta = \frac{1}{k}\left[\mu^c - \eta\mu^k + \frac{\eta}{k}(\sigma^k)^2\right] dt + \frac{\sigma^c}{k}\, dz_1 - \eta\frac{\sigma^k}{k}\, dz_2, \tag{A17}$$

where $\mu^{c,k}$ and $\sigma^{c,k}$ are respectively the drift and diffusion terms for c and k: $dc = \mu^c dt + \sigma^c dz_1$, $dk = \mu^k dt + \sigma^k dz_2$; i.e.,

$$\mu^c = [\psi a + (1-\psi)\bar a - \delta + r\eta - \theta^{-1}(q-1) - \frac{1}{2}\theta^{-1}(q-1)^2]k,$$
$$\mu^k = \theta^{-1}(q-1)k,$$
$$\sigma^c = \sigma_1\psi k, \quad \sigma^k = \sigma_2\psi k.$$

The increments dz_1, dz_2 are independent and normally distributed, and so the noise sources in $d\eta$ can be combined into a single term,

$$k^{-1}\sigma^c dz_1 - k^{-1}\eta\sigma^k dz_2 = k^{-1}\sqrt{(\sigma^c)^2 + \eta^2(\sigma^k)^2}\, dz.$$

Substituting in the expressions for $\mu^{c,k}$ and $\sigma^{c,k}$ yields

$$d\eta = \left[\bar a + (a - \bar a)\psi - \delta + r\eta - (1+\eta)\theta^{-1}(q-1)\right.$$
$$\left. -\frac{1}{2}\theta^{-1}(q-1)^2 + \eta\sigma_2^2\psi^2\right] dt + \sqrt{\sigma_1^2 + \eta^2\sigma_2^2}\,\psi\, dz. \tag{A18}$$

The ergodic probability density is then the stationary, $\partial f/\partial t = 0$, solution of Equation (A16), also denoted by $f(\eta)$. Integration of the Kolmogorov forward equation in η yields

$$d = \mu^\eta(\eta)f(\eta) - \frac{1}{2}\frac{\partial}{\partial\eta}\left[\sigma^\eta(\eta)^2 f(\eta)\right]. \tag{A19}$$

It is convenient to write this in terms of ϕ,

$$\phi = \frac{(\sigma^\eta)^2}{2}f,$$

so this becomes:

$$d = \left[\frac{(\sigma^\eta)^2}{2}\right]^{-1}\mu^\eta(\eta)\phi(\eta) - \frac{1}{2}\frac{\partial}{\partial\eta}\phi(\eta). \tag{A20}$$

and this yields Equation (15). $\square$

Appendix C. Numerical Solution

Appendix C.1. Preliminary Considerations and Some Economic Intuition

The ordinary differential equation governing q (Equation (17) for $\eta \leq \bar{\eta}$ and Equation (10) for $\eta \geq \bar{\eta}$) can be solved by forward integration using standard methods starting from any given initial condition $q(\bar{\eta}) = \bar{q}$. The solution is completed by finding an intersection with $Q(q, \eta) = 0$ on which $q' = 0$, if one exists, or establishing that there is no such intersection (moreover, any solution with an intersection with $Q(q, \eta) = 0$). Any initial value $\bar{q} \geq 1 + \theta\rho$ can be ruled out, since it implies that $g > \rho$ for all η.

The inequality in Equation (A15), which is required if the special case of the model with no uncertainty ($\sigma = 0$) is to a be one with no "Ponzi-borrowing" and also ensures the existence of solution, leads to extremely straightforward numerical solution, since intersection with the lower branch of $Q(q, \eta) = 0$ is guaranteed.

If however this inequality is not satisfied then for some values of $\bar{q}$, a value of q^* whereat the ODE interacts with $Q(q, \eta) = 0$ may be located on the upper boundary (if the ODE "misses" the lower branch, in which case it may or may not hit the upper branch). This considerably complicates the search for numerical solution because it is no longer possible to restrict the initial values $\bar{q}$ to a range of values for which intersection with $Q(q, \eta) = 0$ is guaranteed.

Such solutions with upper branch intersections are of less economic interest than those where intersection is on the lower branch. It is possible that investment close to η^* is so high that the firm has negative cash flow. This can be seen by substituting Equation (A13), $\psi = 1, q = q^*$ and $\eta = \eta^*$ into Equation (A18), yielding the following expression for cash flow on the dividend paying boundary:

$$\mu^\eta = \frac{(a - \delta)\rho - \rho r + \left[(r - (a - \delta))\theta^{-1} - \rho r\right](q^* - 1)}{\rho - r}$$
$$+ \frac{\frac{1}{2}(2r + \rho)\theta^{-1} - \frac{1}{2}\theta^{-2}(q^* - 1)}{\rho - r}(q^* - 1)^2 + \eta^*\sigma_2^2 \quad \text{(A21)}$$

which, for sufficiently high q^*, is negative. The economic intuition in this case is similar to that applicable to the "Ponzi" solution of the model with no non-negativity constraint on dividends in Appendix A. The firm creates the most value not by dividend payments but from growing the capital stock at a rate close to and often above the shareholder's rate of discount, and this very high rate of investment can generate the negative expected cash flows.

The function $W(\eta^*)$ is obtained by substitution into Equation (A14) on the boundary η^*, using the boundary conditions $W' = 1$, to yield:

$$W^* = (q^* + \eta^*)W' = 1 + \eta^* + \rho\theta \pm \sqrt{2\theta\left\{(\eta^* - \eta_{\min}^*)(\rho - r)\right\}} \quad \text{(A22)}$$

with the positive root applying on the upper branch of q^* and the negative root on the lower branch.

This in turn results in some useful insights into the solution. In the case of recapitalisation, Equation (7) can be written:

$$0 < W^* - (\eta^* - \bar{\eta} + \chi) = 1 + \rho\theta + \bar{\eta} - \chi \pm \sqrt{2\theta\left\{(\eta^* - \eta_{\min}^*)(\rho - r)\right\}} < 1 + \rho\theta + \bar{\eta} \quad \text{(A23)}$$

where the first inequality is required by the maximisation in Equation (7) and the second because the presence of financing constraints must lower value $W(\bar{\eta})$ relative to the valuation for the case of no non-negativity constraint on dividend payments given by Equation (A3)). This establishes the following further proposition:

Proposition A2. *A solution with recapitalisation (for some sufficiently low value of χ) exists. Let $\chi = \chi_0$ be the critical value of χ at which the firm is indifferent between recapitalisation and liquidation. Then: (i) If $\eta^*_{min} \leq \bar{\eta}$ a solution exists with η^* on the lower branch of $Q(q, \eta) = 0$, $\bar{q}$ satisfies:*

$$-\bar{\eta} \leq \bar{q} < \bar{q}_{max} = 1 + \theta \left(\rho - \sqrt{\rho^2 - 2\theta^{-1} \left\{ a - \delta - \rho - \bar{\eta}\,(\rho - r) \right\}} \right) > \bar{q} \qquad (A24)$$

and the maximum possible value of η^* satisfies:

$$\eta^*_{min} \leq \eta^* < \eta^*_{min} + \frac{\left((\rho - r) + \sqrt{r^2 - 2\theta^{-1}[\bar{a} - \delta - r]} - \theta^{-1}\chi_0 \right)^2}{2\,(\rho - r)} \qquad (A25)$$

(ii) If instead $\eta^*_{min} > \bar{\eta}$ then $-\bar{\eta} \leq \bar{q} < 1 + \rho\theta$; a solution may or may not exist solution may be on the upper branch of $Q(q, \eta) = 0$, in which case η^* satisfies:

$$\eta^*_{min} < \eta^* \leq \eta^*_{min} + \frac{\chi^2}{2\theta\,(\rho - r)} \qquad (A26)$$

Proof. The existence of a solution with recapitalisation is guaranteed because $1 + \rho\theta + \bar{\eta} = (\rho - r)\theta + \theta\sqrt{r^2 - 2\theta^{-1}[\bar{a} - \delta - r]} > 0$. As noted above, solutions for which $\bar{q} > 1 + \theta\rho$ can be ruled out, and hence all possible solutions, with recapitalisation or without, are with an intersection of the ODE for q on the lower branch of $Q(q, \eta) = 0$; and (the value that applies when cost of recapitalisation $\chi = 0$ and hence the maximum possible value of $\bar{q}$) is given by the intersection of this lower branch of Equation (A14) with $\eta = \bar{\eta}$. If solution is on the lower branch then the largest possible value of η^* and the smallest value of $\bar{q}$ ($\bar{q} = -\bar{\eta}$) arise when $\chi = \chi_0$ (the same solution also applies if χ is higher than this critical value and no-recapitalisation takes place). If $\chi = \chi_0$ then the first inequality in Equation (A23) binds and this implies the second inequality in Equation (A25). If instead solution is on the upper branch, then the largest possible value is when $\chi < \chi_0$, so that Equation (A23) binds and this implies the second inequality in Equation (A26). □

Proposition A2 helps guide the numerical solution. If $\eta^*_{min} \leq \bar{\eta}$ then a solution with a bounded value function exists and an intersection is guaranteed on the lower branch of $Q(q, \eta) = 0$. A first calculation of the case with no recapitalisation determines χ_0 and this can then be used to limit the scope of iteration on $\bar{q}$ (using Equation (A24)) in the search for solution in the case of recapitalisation. If instead $\eta^*_{min} > \bar{\eta}$ then a solution with a bounded value function and finite η^* may not exist. The existence of a solution for the case of no-recapitalisation can be established by computing the ODE Equation (10) upwards. If η exceeds the upper bound given by Equation (A26) then there is no intersection and no solution) is not satisfied, then while there is an intersection there is no finite solution to the value function. A solution with recapitalisation will exist for at least some values of χ if there is a solution for no-recapitalisation. The proposition then provides a slightly different limits on the scope of iteration on $\bar{q}$ and the same criteria can be applied to establish if there is an intersection with $Q(q, \eta) = 0$, and if so whether this represents a finite value for the value function.

Appendix C.2. Model without Option to Rent

For any given $\bar{q}$, the right-hand side boundary at $\eta = \eta^*$ wherein $q'(\eta^*) = 0$ is found by evaluating the function $q'(\eta)$ during the integration. After a single integration step is found to bracket a root of $q'(\eta)$, the critical value of η is pin-pointed using standard root finding methods, here the Brent's method.

The value function W can be solved from $W' = W/(\eta + q)$ parallel to integrating the equation for q. The boundary condition $W''(\eta^*) = 0$ will be satisfied since the q variable integration is stopped at $q' = 0$. In order to also satisfy the boundary condition $W'(\eta^*) = 1$, solve W for an arbitrary initial value at $\bar{\eta}$. Let the resulting solution be $\tilde{W}$. Since the ODE for W is linear and homogeneous, simply multiply $\tilde{W}$ ex post by $[\tilde{W}'(\eta^*)]^{-1}$ to get a solution for which $W'(\eta^*) = 1$.

In the case of liquidation, the lower boundary is $\bar{\eta} = -\bar{q}$, and consequently, the derivative of W, $W' = W/(\eta + q)$ cannot be evaluated. Appendix D shows that $W \propto \eta - \bar{\eta}$, and so $W'(\bar{\eta})$ is finite. Thus, if $\bar{\eta}$ is indeed liquidating, we simply set $\tilde{W}'(\bar{\eta}) = 1$ and $W(\bar{\eta}) = 0$.

Solving for the ergodic density with an absorbing boundary requires determining the constant of integration (the rate of flow across the boundary) d and this requires two boundary conditions. These conditions are that the absorbing boundary must have a zero density, i.e., $f(\bar{\eta}) = 0$, and the cumulative density must satisfy $F(\eta^*) = 1$.

The following method enforces these conditions. Solve two independent differential equations for two densities f_0 and f_1 satisfying:

$$f_0'(\eta) = \frac{2\mu(\eta)}{\sigma^2} f_0(\eta), \quad f_1'(\eta) = \frac{2\mu(\eta)}{\sigma^2} f_1(\eta) + 1. \tag{A27}$$

These are obtained by integration starting from arbitrary non-zero initial conditions. Let F_0 and F_1 be the resulting corresponding cumulative functions, with $F_0' = f_0$, $F_1' = f_1$ and $F_0(\bar{\eta}) = F_1(\bar{\eta}) = 0$. This determines values for $F(\eta^*)$ and $F_1(\eta^*)$.

Then find the ergodic density by choosing appropriate constants a_0 and a_1 in the following function f:

$$f(\eta) = a_0 f_0(\eta) + a_1 f_1(\eta), \tag{A28}$$

These coefficients a_0, a_1 are determined by the conditions $f(\bar{\eta}) = 0$ and $F(\eta^*) = 1$ as follows. Upon substituting the trial solution (A28), one obtains

$$a_0 f_0(\bar{\eta}) + a_1 f_1(\bar{\eta}) = 0, \quad a_0 F_0(\eta^*) + a_1 F_1(\eta^*) = 1.$$

yielding a pair of linear equations that can be solved for a_0 and a_1. To obtain d differentiate (A28) and use Equation (A27), to get:

$$f'(\eta) = \frac{2\mu}{\sigma^2} f(\eta) + a_1,$$

so $a_1 = -2d/\sigma^2$ (cf. Equation (A19)).

The possibility for recapitalisation is tested by finding roots of

$$G(\bar{q}) = W[\bar{q}, \eta^*(\bar{q})] - W(\bar{q}, \bar{\eta}) - [\eta^*(\bar{q}) - \bar{\eta}] - \chi,$$

making explicit the dependence of the location of the upper dividend paying boundary $\eta = \eta^*$ and the function $W(\eta)$ on the value of q on the lower boundary $q(\bar{\eta}) = \bar{q}$. Clearly $G = 0$ is equivalent to achieving Equation (7). Functions η^*, q and W are all obtained using the same method outlined above (i.e., jointly computing the two odes for q and W using $\bar{q}$ and an arbitrary value of W on $\bar{\eta}$, locating η^* from $q' = 0$, and rescaling W to enforce $W' = 1$).

The task then is to iterate on the starting value $\bar{q}$ to find the root of $G(\bar{q})$. First a coarse root bracketing is attempted by evaluating G at $\bar{q}_i = -\bar{\eta} + (q_1 + \bar{\eta})i/n_q$, where $i = 0 \ldots n_q$ and n_q an integer (using $n_q = 10$), and q_1 is q as given by Equation (A14) if that value is real, or $1 + \theta\rho$ if it is not. If sign of G changes across a bracketing interval $(\bar{q}_i, \bar{q}_{i+1})$, the root is pin-pointed using standard root finding algorithms. This locates a recapitalisation solution. If no roots are found, or a root is found with $\bar{q} < -\bar{\eta}$ or $q^* > 1 + \theta\rho$ then the solution is identified as liquidation with $\bar{q} = -\bar{\eta}$.

Appendix C.3. Model with Option to Rent

The algorithm outline is same as in the model without the rental option. However, the solution near the lower boundary is more involved when recapitalisation is not undertaken, and so $\psi(\bar{\eta}) = 0$.

The differential equations for q can again be solved by simple forward integration starting from $q(\bar{\eta}) = \bar{q}$. If recapitalisation is available ($\bar{q} > -\bar{\eta}$), no singularities are present, and the equation for q, Equation (17), can be integrated directly to obtain $q(\eta)$, η^* and now also $\tilde{\eta}$. The point $\tilde{\eta}$ is found in the same way as η^*, i.e., by monitoring the function $\psi - 1$ as integration advances and polishing the root after a coarse approximation is found. Initial $\bar{q}$ is found the same way as for the model without renting (but with q, W computed slightly differently as described below).

If $\bar{q} = -\bar{\eta}$, then $\psi = 0$ and singularities appear. As is shown in Appendix D, the derivative $q'(\bar{\eta})$ is finite. In order to evaluate it numerically, use Equation (A32) since Equation (17) is indeterminate at $\bar{\eta}$ (in practice, numerical round-off would cause significant error in $\bar{q}$). Otherwise the solution of q proceeds the same way as with a recapitalising lower boundary.

Using ϕ, and expanding the resulting equation in the renting ($0 < \psi < 1$) and not renting regimes ($\psi = 1$), yields

$$\phi' = \begin{cases} \dfrac{\bar{a} + (a - \bar{a})\psi - \delta + r\eta + \sigma_2^2\psi^2\eta - \theta^{-1}(q-1)[\eta + \frac{1}{2}(q+1)]}{\frac{1}{2}(\sigma_1^2 + \eta^2\sigma_2^2)\psi^2}\phi - d, \\ \qquad \text{when } \psi \in (0,1), \\ \dfrac{a - \delta + r\eta + \sigma_2^2\eta - \theta^{-1}(q-1)[\eta + \frac{1}{2}(q+1)]}{\frac{1}{2}(\sigma_1^2 + \eta^2\sigma_2^2)}\phi - d, \\ \qquad \text{when } \psi = 1. \end{cases} \qquad (A29)$$

When there are no recapitalisation, equations for f' and W', unlike that for q', do not tend to finite values at $\bar{\eta}$, since $\psi(\bar{\eta}) = 0$ if $q(\bar{\eta}) = -\bar{\eta}$, $q'(\bar{\eta}) > 0$. Due to this divergence, the point $\bar{\eta}$ cannot be reached by directly integrating the model equations, which in principle could be done backwards from, say, $\tilde{\eta}$ down to $\bar{\eta} + \epsilon$, $0 < \epsilon \ll 1$. Cutting the integration short in this way would lead to severe underestimation of the probability mass near $\bar{\eta}$ if f diverges fast enough at this edge.

This issue is resolved using the analytically obtained power-law solutions, $f_a \propto (\eta - \bar{\eta})^{\alpha-2}$ (Equation (21)) and $W_a \propto (\eta - \bar{\eta})^\beta$ (Equation (18)), from $\bar{\eta}$ up to a cross-over value $\eta_\times$. Numerical solutions are matched to the analytic ones so that the resulting functions are continuous. The cross-over point can determined by requiring that

$$\left| \frac{f_a'(\eta_\times)}{f_a(\eta_\times)} \right| = \epsilon^{-1}, \qquad (A30)$$

where $0 < \epsilon \ll 1$, implying that the divergent terms dominate the expression for the derivative of f. However, since W' also tends to infinity, the same condition applies to W_a as well. This gives two different cross-over values; the smallest is chosen:

$$\eta_\times = \epsilon \min(|\alpha|, \beta) + \bar{\eta}, \qquad (A31)$$

where α is given by Equation (A34) and $\beta = 1/(1 + q'(\bar{\eta}))$, with $q'(\bar{\eta})$ from Equation (A32). The results reported here use the value $\epsilon = 1.0 \times 10^{-3}$ and the analytic solution for f to obtain the cumulative density F below $\eta_\times$.

If the lower boundary is at $\bar{q} = -\bar{\eta}$, then directly integrate Equation (A29) with $d = 0$ from $\eta_\times$ to η^*. The obtained solution can then be multiplied by a constant to make the cumulative distribution satisfy $F(\eta^*) = 1$. If $\bar{\eta}$ is absorbing (recapitalisation), use the same trick as in the model without rent: solve for ϕ_0 and ϕ_1 satisfy Equation (A29) with $d = 0$ and $d = 1$, respectively. The final ϕ is then constructed as a superposition of these two, $\phi = a_0\phi_0 + a_1\phi_1$. Coefficients a_0 and a_1 are determined from

$$\phi(\bar{\eta}) = 0, \qquad \int_{\bar{\eta}}^{\eta^*} \frac{2}{(\sigma^\eta(\eta))^2}\phi(\eta)\,\mathrm{d}\eta = 1.$$

When needed, the same analytic solution, Equation (21), can be used for both ϕ_0 and ϕ_1 ($\phi_{0,1} \propto (\eta - \bar{\eta})^\alpha / (\sigma^\eta)^2$), since d term is negligible near $\bar{\eta}$.

Note that reverting to the analytic solution for f is equivalent to using a truncated integration range with an additional correction term coming from the analytical solution near $\bar{\eta}$. Numerical simulations confirm that this approach is sound: (i) the analytical and numerical solutions are in very good agreement across a wide range of η, (ii) the obtained solutions are independent of ϵ, provided it is small enough while keeping the numerical solution from reaching the singularity, and (iii) qualitative features of the solution do not change if the analytical correction is omitted.

Appendix D. Behaviour of Solutions Near Boundaries

This Appendix provides the derivation of the asymptotic approximations summarised in Proposition 7.

Appendix D.1. Model without Option to Rent

While no singularities emerge in the model with no option to rent, it is still useful to begin with this simple case. The evolution of the value function W is given by $W'/W = 1/(q + \eta)$, which in the case of liquidation tends to infinity as the point of maximum borrowing where $q(\bar{\eta}) = -\bar{\eta}$ is approached. This means there is a potential singularity in W at $\bar{\eta}$. It can be shows that in the model without the option to rent this does not occur and W is linear close to $\eta = \bar{\eta}$.

Suppose now that q is of the form $q(\eta) = -\bar{\eta} + q'(\bar{\eta})(\eta - \bar{\eta}) + \mathcal{O}((\eta - \bar{\eta})^2)$. Near the boundary, W follows

$$W' = \frac{1}{1 + q'(\bar{\eta})} \frac{W}{\eta - \bar{\eta}} + \mathcal{O}(\eta - \bar{\eta}).$$

The solution is then given by Equation (18) in the main text. In the case of the model without renting, it is clear from Equation (10) that $q'(\bar{\eta}) = 0$ and so W is linear near $\bar{\eta}$.

Appendix D.2. Model with Option to Rent

Turning to the model with option to rent, again a singularity can occur only on the lower boundary and only when there is no recapitalisation, i.e., when $q(\bar{\eta}) = -\bar{\eta}$ and $\psi(\bar{\eta}) = 0$.

Note now that in the equation for q', Equation (17), both the numerator and the denominator vanish. Applying the l'Hopital's rule, the derivative can be solved as:

$$q'(\bar{\eta}) = \frac{-(\rho - r - \gamma) \pm \sqrt{(\rho - r - \gamma)^2 + 4\gamma\theta^{-1}[1 + \theta\rho - \bar{q}]}}{2\theta^{-1}[1 + \theta\rho - \bar{q}]}, \tag{A32}$$

where $\gamma = (a - \bar{a})^2/2(\sigma_1^2 + \bar{\eta}^2\sigma_2^2)$. Above, only the plus sign applies. This can be seen by recalling that $\bar{q} < q_{max} = 1 + \rho\theta$ must apply (see above for the reasoning), in which case only the plus sign gives a positive q'. Thus, the solution near $\bar{\eta}$ is given by Equation (19) in the main text.

The power-law form of W given in Equation (18) holds here as well. Since now $q'(\bar{\eta}) > 0$, the exponent $\beta = 1/(1 + q'(\bar{\eta}))$ is always less than one, in contrast to the model without option to rent, implying that $\lim_{\eta\downarrow\bar{\eta}} W' = \lim_{\eta\downarrow\bar{\eta}} (-W''/W') = +\infty$.

To find the behaviour of the ergodic density near $\bar{\eta}, \bar{q}$, requires ψ. This time $\eta - \bar{\eta}$ is not negligible compared to $q - \bar{q}$. A straight-forward calculation gives:

$$\psi = \psi'(\bar{\eta})(\eta - \bar{\eta}) \tag{A33}$$

where

$$\psi'(\bar{\eta}) = \frac{2}{a - \bar{a}} \left\{ \rho - r + \theta^{-1} [1 + \theta\rho - \bar{q}] q'(\bar{\eta}) \right\}.$$

Next, the $\eta \to \bar{\eta}$ limiting forms of q and ψ are substituted into Equation (A20), and only terms up to $\mathcal{O}(\eta - \bar{\eta})$ are kept. Notice that the numerator vanishes in the leading order, and hence $\phi' \propto (\eta - \bar{\eta})^{-1}$ and not $\propto (\eta - \bar{\eta})^{-2}$:

$$\phi' = \alpha \frac{\phi}{\eta - \bar{\eta}},$$

where

$$\alpha = \frac{(a - \bar{a})\psi'(\bar{\eta}) + r - \frac{1}{2}\theta^{-1}q'(\bar{\eta})(\bar{\eta} + 1) + \theta^{-1}(\bar{\eta} + 1)(1 + q'(\bar{\eta})/2)}{\frac{1}{2}(\sigma_1^2 + \bar{\eta}^2\sigma_2^2)\psi'(\bar{\eta})^2}. \tag{A34}$$

This gives the power-law solution Equation (20) in the main text. Finally using Equation (A33) yields Equation (21) of the main text.

References

1.   Milne, A.; Robertson, D. Firm Behaviour Under the Threat of Liquidation. *J. Econ. Dyn. Control* **1996**, *20*, 1427–1449. [CrossRef]

2.   Brunnermeier, M.K.; Sannikov, Y. A Macroeconomic Model with a Financial Sector. *Am. Econ. Rev.* **2014**, *104*, 379–421. [CrossRef]

3.   Whittle, P. *Optimization over Time: Dynamic Programming and Stochastic Control*; Wiley-Blackwell: New York, NY, USA, 1982; Volume 1.

4.   Carroll, C.D. A theory of the consumption function, with and without liquidity constraints. *J. Econ. Perspect.* **2001**, *15*, 23–45. [CrossRef]

5.   Arrow, K.J.; Harris, T.; Marschak, J. Optimal inventory policy. *Econometrica* **1951**, *19*, 250–272. [CrossRef]

6.   Scarf, H. *The Optimality of (sS) Policies in the Dynamic Inventory Problem. Mathematical Methods in the Social Science*; Arrow, K.J., Karlin, S., Suppes, P., Eds.; Stanford University Press: Stanford, CA, USA, 1960; Chapter 22.

7.   Jorgenson, D.W. Capital Theory and Investment Behavior. *Am. Econ. Rev.* **1963**, *53*, 247–259. [CrossRef]

8.   Lucas, R.E., Jr.; Prescott, E.C. Investment under Uncertainty; Princeton University Press: Princeton, NJ, USA, 1971; Volume 39, pp. 659–681.

9.   Miller, M.H.; Orr, D. A Model of the Demand for Money by Firms. *Q. J. Econ.* **1966**, *80*, 413–435. [CrossRef]

10. Constantinides, G.M. Stochastic Cash Management with Fixed and Proportional Transaction Costs. *Manag. Sci.* **1976**, *22*, 1320–1331. [CrossRef]

11. Frenkel, J.A.; Jovanovic, B. On Transactions and Precautionary Demand for Money. *Q. J. Econ.* **1980**, *95*, 25–43. [CrossRef]

12. Merton, R.C. On the Pricing of Corporate Debt: The Risk Structure of Interest Rates. *J. Financ.* **1974**, *29*, 449–470.

13. Anderson, R.W.; Sundaresan, S. Design and valuation of debt contracts. *Rev. Financ. Stud.* **1996**, *9*, 37–68. [CrossRef]

14. Mella-Barral, P.; Perraudin, W. Strategic debt service. *J. Financ.* **1997**, *52*, 531–556. [CrossRef]

15. Leland, H.E. Agency Costs, Risk Management, and Capital Structure. *J. Financ.* **1998**, *53*, 1213–1243. [CrossRef]

16. Modigliani, F.; Miller, M.H. The Cost of Capital, Corporation Finance and the Theory of Investment. *Am. Econ. Rev.* **1958**, *48*, 261–297. [CrossRef]

17. Tirole, J. *The Theory of Corporate Finance*; Princeton University Press: Princeton, NJ, USA, 2006.

18. Myers, S.C. The Capital Structure Puzzle. *J. Financ.* **1984**, *39*, 574–592. [CrossRef]

19. Myers, S.C.; Majluf, N.S. Corporate financing and investment decisions when firms have information that investors do not have. *J. Financ. Econ.* **1984**, *13*, 187–221. [CrossRef]

20. Froot, K.; Scharfstein, D.; Stein, J.C. Risk Management: Coordinating Corporate Investment and Financing Policies. *J. Financ.* **1993**, *48*, 1629–1658. [CrossRef]

21. Gertler, M. Financial Capacity and Output Fluctuations in an Economy with Multi-Period Financial Relationships. *Rev. Econ. Stud.* **1992**, *59*, 455. [CrossRef]

22. Townsend, R.M. Optimal contracts and competitive markets with costly state verification. *J. Econ. Theory* **1979**, *21*, 265 – 293. [CrossRef]

23. Sannikov, Y. A Continuous-Time Version of the Principal—Agent Problem. *Rev. Econ. Stud.* **2008**, *75*, 957–984. [CrossRef]

24. De Marzo, P.M.; Sannikov, Y. Optimal Security Design and Dynamic Capital Structure in a Continuous-Time Agency Model. *J. Financ.* **2006**, *61*, 2681–2724. [CrossRef]

25. Mauer, D.C.; Triantis, A.J. Interactions of corporate financing and investment decisions: A dynamic framework. *J. Financ.* **1994**, *49*, 1253–1277. [CrossRef]

26. Radner, R.; Shepp, L. Risk vs. profit potential: A model for corporate strategy. *J. Econ. Dyn. Control* **1996**, *20*, 1373–1393. [CrossRef]

27. Jeanblanc-Picqué, M.; Shiryaev, A.N. Optimization of the flow of dividends. *Russ. Math. Surv.* **1995**, *50*, 257–277. [CrossRef]

28. Asmussen, S.; Taksar, M. Controlled diffusion models for optimal dividend pay-out. *Insur. Math. Econ.* **1997**, *20*, 1–15. [CrossRef]

29. Taksar, M.I.; Zhou, X.Y. Optimal risk and dividend control for a company with a debt liability. *Insur. Math. Econ.* **1998**, *22*, 105–122. [CrossRef]

30. Jgaard, B.H.; Taksar, M. Controlling risk exposure and dividends payout schemes: Insurance company example. *Math. Financ.* **1999**, *9*, 153–182. [CrossRef]

31. Asmussen, S.; Højgaard, B.; Taksar, M. Optimal risk control and dividend distribution policies. Example of excess-of loss reinsurance for an insurance corporation. *Financ. Stochastics* **2000**, *4*, 299–324. [CrossRef]

32. Milne, A.; Whalley, A.E. Bank Capital and Risk Taking; Bank of England Working Paper: London, UK, 1999.

33. Milne, A.; Whalley, A.E. Bank Capital Regulation and Incentives for Risk Taking; Cass Business School Research Paper: London, UK, 2002.

34. Milne, A. The Inventory Perspective on Bank Capital; Cass Business School Research Paper: London, UK, 2004.

35. Peura, S.; Keppo, J. Optimal Bank Capital With Costly Recapitalization. *J. Bus.* **2006**, *79*, 2163–2201. [CrossRef]

36. Krugman, P.R. Target Zones and Exchange Rate Dynamics. *Q. J. Econ.* **1991**, *106*, 669–682. [CrossRef]

37. Mundaca, G.; Øksendal, B. Optimal stochastic intervention control with application to the exchange rate. *J. Math. Econ.* **1998**, *29*, 225–243. [CrossRef]

38. Korn, R. Some applications of impulse control in mathematical finance. *Math. Methods Oper. Res. (ZOR)* **1999**, *50*, 493–518. [CrossRef]

39. Rochet, J.C.; Villeneuve, S. Liquidity management and corporate demand for hedging and insurance. *J. Financ. Intermediation* **2011**, *20*, 303–323. [CrossRef]

40. Bolton, P.; Chen, H.; Wang, N. A Unified Theory of Tobin's q, Corporate Investment, Financing, and Risk Management. *J. Financ.* **2011**, *66*, 1545–1578. [CrossRef]

41. Bolton, P.; Chen, H.; Wang, N. Market timing, investment, and risk management. *J. Financ. Econ.* **2013**, *109*, 40–62. [CrossRef]

42. Rampini, A.A.; Viswanathan, S. Collateral and capital structure. *J. Financ. Econ.* **2013**, *109*, 466–492. [CrossRef]

43. Palazzo, B. Cash holdings, risk, and expected returns. *J. Financ. Econ.* **2012**, *104*, 162–185. [CrossRef]

44. Anderson, R.W.; Carverhill, A. Corporate Liquidity and Capital Structure. *Rev. Financ. Stud.* **2011**, *25*, 797–837. [CrossRef]

45. Gamba, A.; Triantis, A. The Value of Financial Flexibility. *J. Financ.* **2008**, *63*, 2263–2296. [CrossRef]

46. Gamba, A.; Triantis, A.J. Corporate Risk Management: Integrating Liquidity, Hedging, and Operating Policies. *Manag. Sci.* **2014**, *60*, 246–264. [CrossRef]

47. Greenwald, B.; Stiglitz, J.E.; Weiss, A. Informational imperfections in the capital market and macroeconomic fluctuations. *Am. Econ. Rev.* **1984**, pp. 194–199.

48. Kiyotaki, N.; Moore, J. Credit Cycles. *J. Political Econ.* **1997**, *105*, 211–248. [CrossRef]

49. Bernanke, B.S.; Gertler, M. Agency Costs, Net Worth, and Business Fluctuations. *Am. Econ. Rev.* **1989**, *79*, 14–31.

50. Bernanke, B.; Gertler, M.; Gilchrist, S. The Financial Accelerator in a Quantitative Business Cycle Framework. In *Handbook of Macroeconomics, Volume 1C*; Taylor, J.B.; Woodford, M., Eds.; Elsevier Science: North-Holland, The Netherlands, 1999; pp. 1341–1393.

51. Danielsson, J.; Shin, H.S.; Zigrand, J.P. The impact of risk regulation on price dynamics. *J. Bank. Financ.* **2004**, *28*, 1069–1087. [CrossRef]

52. Brunnermeier, M.K.; Pedersen, L.H. Market Liquidity and Funding Liquidity. *Rev. Financ. Stud.* **2008**, *22*, 2201–2238. [CrossRef]

53. Adrian, T.; Boyarchenko, N. Intermediary Leverage Cycles and Financial Stability; Federal Reserve Bank of New York Staff Reports No 567; Federal Reserve Bank of New York: New York, NY, USA, 2013.

54. Isohätälä, J.; Klimenko, N.; Milne, A. *Post-Crisis Macrofinancial Modeling: Continuous Time Approaches*; Palgrave Macmillan UK: London, UK, 2016. [CrossRef]

55. He, Z.; Krishnamurthy, A. A Model of Capital and Crises. *Rev. Econ. Stud.* **2012**, *79*, 735–777. [CrossRef]

56. He, Z.; Krishnamurthy, A. Intermediary Asset Pricing. *Am. Econ. Rev.* **2013**, *103*, 732–770. [CrossRef]

5

Some Notes on the Formation of a Pair in Pairs Trading

José Pedro Ramos-Requena [1], Juan Evangelista Trinidad-Segovia [1,*] and Miguel Ángel Sánchez-Granero [2]

[1] Department of Economics and Business, University of Almería, Ctra. Sacramento s/n, La Cañada de San Urbano, 04120 Almería, Spain; jpramosre@ual.es

[2] Department of Matematics, University of Almería, Ctra. Sacramento s/n, La Cañada de San Urbano, 04120 Almería, Spain; misanche@ual.es

* Correspondence: jetrini@ual.es

Abstract: The main goal of the paper is to introduce different models to calculate the amount of money that must be allocated to each stock in a statistical arbitrage technique known as pairs trading. The traditional allocation strategy is based on an equal weight methodology. However, we will show how, with an optimal allocation, the performance of pairs trading increases significantly. Four methodologies are proposed to set up the optimal allocation. These methodologies are based on distance, correlation, cointegration and Hurst exponent (mean reversion). It is showed that the new methodologies provide an improvement in the obtained results with respect to an equal weighted strategy.

Keywords: pairs trading; hurst exponent; financial markets; long memory; co-movement; cointegration

1. Introduction

Efficient Market Hypothesis (EMH) is a well-known topic in finance. Implications of the weak form of efficiency is that information about the past is reflected in the market price of a stock and therefore, historical market data is not helpful for predicting the future. An investor in an efficient market will not be able to obtain a significant advantage over a benchmark portfolio or a market index trading based on historical data (for a review see Reference [1,2]).

On the opposite way, some researchers have shown that the use of historical data as well as trading techniques is sometimes possible due to temporal markets anomalies. Despite that most of economists consider that these anomalies are not compatible with an efficient market, recent papers have shown new perspectives called Fractal Market Hypothesis (FMH) and Adaptive Market Hypothesis (AMH), that tries to integrate market anomalies into the efficient market hypothesis.

The EMH was questioned by the mathematician Mandelbrot in 1963 and after the economist Fama showed his doubts about the Normal distribution of stock returns, essential point of the efficient hypothesis. Mandelbrot concluded that stock prices exhibit long-memory, and proposed a Fractional Brownian motion to model the market. Di Matteo [3,4] considered that investors can be distinguished by the investment horizons in which they operate. This consideration allows us to connect the idea of long memory and the efficiency hypothesis. In the context of an efficient market, the information is considered as a generic item. This means that the impact that public information has over each investor is similar. However, the FMH assumes that information and expectations affect in a different way to traders, which are only focused on short terms and long term investors [5,6].

The idea of a AMH has been recently introduced by Lo [7] to reflect an evolutionary perspective of the market. Under this new idea, markets show complex dynamics at different times which make that some arbitrage techniques perform properly in some periods and poorly in others.

In an effort of conciliation, Sanchez et al. [8] remarks that the market dynamic is the results of different investors interactions. In this way, scaling behavior patterns of a specific market can characterize it. Developed market price series usually show only short memory or no memory whereas emerging markets do exhibit long-memory properties. Following this line, in a recent contribution, Sanchez et al. [9] proved that pairs trading strategies are quite profitable in Latin American Stock Markets whereas in Nasdaq 100 stocks, it is only in high volatility periods. These results are in accordance with both markets hyphotesis. A similar result is obtained by Zhang and Urquhart [10] where authors are able to obtain a significant exceed return with a trading strategy across Mainland China and Hong kong but not when the trading is limited to one of the markets. The authors argue that this is because of the increasing in the efficiency of Mainland China stock market and the decreasing of the Hong Kong one because of the integration of Chinese stock markets and permission of short selling.

These new perspectives of market rules explain why statistical arbitrage techniques, such as pairs trading, can outperform market indexes if they are able to take advantage of market anomalies. In a previous paper, Ramos et al. [11] introduced a new pairs trading technique based on Hurst exponent which is the classic and well known indicator of market memory (for more details, References [8,12] contain an interesting review). For our purpose, the selection of the pair policy is to choose those pairs with the lowest Hurst exponent, that is, the more anti-persistent pairs. Then we use a reversion to the mean trading strategy with the more anti-persistent pairs according with the previously mentioned idea that developed market prices show short memory [3,13–15].

Pairs trading literature is extensive and mainly focused on the pair selection during the trading period as well as the developing of a trading strategy. The pioneer paper was Gatev et al. [16] where authors introduced the distance method with an application to the US market. In 2004, Vidyamurthy [17] presented the theoretical framework for pair selection using the cointegration method. Since then, different analysis have been carried out using this methodology in different markets, such us the European market [18,19], the DJIA stocks [20], the Brazilian market [21,22] or the STOXX 50 index [23]. Galenko et al. [24] made an application of the cointegration method to arbitrage in fund traded on different markets. Lin et al. [25] introduced the minimum profit condition into the trading strategy and Nath [26] used the cointegration method in intraday data. Elliott et al. [27] used Markov chains to study a mean reversion strategy based on differential predictions and calibration from market observations. The mean reversion approach has been tested in markets not considered efficient such us Asian markets [28] or Latin American stock markets [9]. A recent contribution of Ramos et al. [29] introduced a new methodology for testing the co-movement between assets and they tested it in statistical arbitrage. However, researchers did not pay attention to the amount of money invested in every asset, considering always a null dollar market exposition. This means that when one stock is sold, the same amount of the other stock is purchased. In this paper we propose a new methodology to improve pairs trading performance by developing new methods to improve the efficiency in calculating the ratio to invest in each stock that makes up the pair.

2. Pair Selection

One of the topics in pairs trading is how to find a suitable pair for pairs trading. Several methodologies have been proposed in the literature, but the more common ones are co-movement and the distance method.

2.1. Co-Movement

Baur [30] defines co-movement as the shared movement of all assets at a given time and it can be measured using *correlation* or *cointegration* techniques.

Correlation technique is quite simple, and the higher the correlation coefficient is, the greatest they move in sync. An important issue to be considered is that correlation is intrinsically a short-run measure, which implies that a correlation strategy will work better with a lower frequency trading strategy.

In this work, we will use the Spearman correlation coefficient, which is a nonparametric range statistic which measure the relationship between two variables. This coefficient is particularly useful when the relationship between the two variables is described by a monotonous function, and does not assume any particular distribution of the variables [31].

The Spearman correlation coefficient for a sample A_i, B_i of size n can be described as follows: first, consider the ranks of the samples rgA_i, rgB_i, then the Spearman correlation coefficient r_s is calculated as:

$$r_s = \rho_{rg_A, rg_B} = \frac{cov(rg_A, rg_B)}{\sigma_{rg_A} * \sigma_{rg_B}},$$

(1)

where

- ρ denotes the Pearson correlation coefficient, applied to the rank variables
- $cov(rg_A, rg_B)$, is the covariance of the rank variables.
- σ_{rg_A} and σ_{rg_B}, are the standard deviations of the rank variables.

Cointegration approach was introduced by Engle and Granger [32] and it considers a different type of co-movement. In this case, cointegration refers to movements in prices, not in returns, so cointegration and correlation are related, but different concepts. In fact, cointegrated series can perfectly be low correlated.

Two stocks A and B are said to be cointegrated if there exists γ such that $P_t^A - \gamma P_B^t$ is a stationary process, where P_t^A and P_B^t are the log-prices A and B, respectively. In this case, the following model is considered:

$$P_t^A - \gamma P_B^t = \mu + \epsilon_t,$$

(2)

where

- μ is the mean of the cointegration model
- ϵ_t is the cointegration residual, which is a stationary, mean-reverting process
- γ is the cointegration coefficient.

We will use the ordinary least squares (OLS) method to estimate the regression parameters. Through the Augmented Dickey Fuller test, we will verify if the residual ϵ_t is stationary or not, and with it we will check if the stocks are co-integrated.

2.2. The Distance Method

This methodology was introduced by Gatev et al. [16]. It is based on minimizing the sum of squared differences between somehow normalized price series:

$$ESD = \sum_t (S_A(t) - S_B(t))^2,$$

(3)

where $S_A(t)$ is the cumulative return of stock A at time t and $S_B(t)$ is the cumulative return of stock B at time t.

The best pair will be the pair whose distance between its stocks is the lowest possible, since this means that the stocks moves in sync and there is a high degree of co-movement between them.

An interesting contribution to this trading system was introduced by Do and Faff [33,34]. The authors replicated this methodology for the U.S. CRSP stock universe and an extended period. The authors confirmed a declining profitability in pairs trading as well as the unprofitability of the trading strategy due to the inclusion of trading costs. Do and Faff then refined the selection method to improve the pair selection. The authors restricted the possible combinations only within the 48 Fama-French industries and they looked for pairs with a high number of zero-crossings to favor the pairs with greatest mean-reversion behavior.

2.3. Pairs Trading Strategy Based on Hurst Exponent

Hurst exponent (H from now on) was introduced by Hurst in 1951 [35] to deal with the problem of reservoir control for the Nile River Dam. Until the beginning of the 21st century, the most common methodology to estimate H was the R/S analysis [36] and the DFA [37], but due to accuracy problems remarked by several studies (see for example References [38–41]), new algorithms were developed for a more efficient estimation of the Hurst exponent, some of them with its focus on financial time series. One of the most important methodologies is the GHE algorithm, introduced in Reference [42], which is a general algorithm with good properties.

The GHE is based on the scaling behavior of the statistic

$$K_q(\tau) = \frac{<|X(t+\tau) - X(t)|^q>}{<|X(t)|^q>}$$

which is given by

$$K_q(\tau) \propto \tau^{qH}\cdot, \tag{4}$$

where τ is the scale (usually chosen between 1 and a quarter of the length of the series), H is the Hurst exponent, $< \cdot >$ denotes the sample average on time t and q is the order of the moment considered. In this paper we will always use $q = 1$.

The GHE is calculated by linear regression, taking logarithms in the expression contained in (4) for different values of τ [3,43].

The interpretation of H is as follow: when H is greater than 0.5, the process is persistent, when H is less than 0.5, it is anti persistent, while Brownian motion has a value of H equal to 0.5.

With this technique, pairs with the lowest Hurst exponent has to be chosen in order to apply reversion to the mean strategies which is also the base of correlation and cointegration strategies.

2.4. Pairs Trading Strategy

Next, we describe the pairs trading strategy, which is taken from Reference [11]. As usual, we consider two periods. The first one is the formation period (one year), which is used for the pair selection. This is done using the four methods defined in this section (distance, correlation, cointegration and Hurst exponent). The second period is the execution period (six months), in which all selected pairs are traded as follows:

- In case $s > m + \sigma$ the pair will be sold. The position will be closed if $s < m$ or $s > m + 2\sigma$.
- In case $s < m - \sigma$ the pair will be bought. The position will be closed if $s > m$ or $s < m - 2\sigma$.

where m is a moving average of the series of the pair and s is a moving standard deviation of m.

3. Forming the Pair: Some New Proposals

As we remarked previously, all works assume that the amount purchased in a stock is equal to the amount sold in the other pair component. The main contribution of this paper is to analyse if not assuming an equal weight ratio in the formation of the pair improves the performance of the different pair trading strategies. In this section different methods are proposed.

When a pair is formed, we use two stocks A and B. This two stocks have to be normalized somehow, so we introduce a constant b such that stock A is comparable to stock bB. Then, to buy an amount T of the pair AB means that we buy $\frac{1}{b+1}T$ of stock A and sell $\frac{b}{b+1}T$ of stock B, while to sell an amount T of the pair AB means that we sell $\frac{1}{b+1}T$ of stock A and buy $\frac{b}{b+1}T$ of stock B.

We will denote by $p_X(t)$ the logarithm of the price of stock X in time t minus the logarithm of the price of stock X at time $t = 0$, that is $p_X(t) = \log(price_X(t)) - \log(price_X(0))$, and by $r_X(t)$ the log-return of stock X between times $t - 1$ and t, $r_X(t) = p_X(t) - p_X(t - 1)$.

In this paper we discuss the following ways to calculate the weight factor b:

1. Equal weight (EW).

    In this case $b = 1$. This is the way used in most of the literature. In this case, the position in the pair is dollar neutral. This method was used in Reference [16], and since then, it has become the more popular procedure to fix b.

2. Based on volatility.

    Volatility of stock A is $std(r_A)$ and volatility of stock B is $std(r_B)$. If we want that A and bB have the same volatility then $b = std(r_A)/std(r_B)$. This approach was used in Reference [11] and it is based on the idea that both stocks are normalized if they have the same volatility.

3. Based on minimal distance of the log-prices.

    In this case we minimize the function $f(b) = \sum_t |p_A(t) - bp_B(t)|$, so we look for the weight factor b such that p_A and bp_B has the minimum distance. This approach is based on the same idea that the distance as a selection method. The closer is the evolution of the log-price of stocks A and bB, the more reverting to the mean properties the pair will have.

4. Based on correlation of returns.

    If returns are correlated then r_A is approximately equal to br_B, where b is obtained by linear regression $r_A = br_B$. In this case, if returns of stocks A and B are correlated, then the distribution of r_A and br_B will be the same, so we can use this b to normalize both stocks.

5. Based on cointegration of the prices.

    If the prices (in fact, the log-prices) of both stocks A and B are cointegrated then $p_A - bp_B$ is stationary, whence b is obtained by linear regression $p_A = bp_B$. In this case, this value of b makes the pair series stationary so we can expect reversion to the mean properties of the pair series. Even if the stocks A and B are not perfectly cointegrated, this method for the calculation of b may be still valid, since, thought $p_A - bp_B$ may be not stationary, it can be somehow close to it or still have mean-reversion properties.

6. Based on lowest Hurst exponent of the pair.

    The series of the pair is defined as $s(b)(t) = p_A(t) - bp_B(t)$. In this case, we look for the weight factor b such that the series of the pair $s(b)$ has the lowest Hurst exponent, what implies that the series is as anti-persistent as possible. So we look for b which minimizes the function $f(b) = H(s(b))$, where $H(s(b))$ is the Hurst exponent of the pair series $s(b)$. The idea here is similar to the cointegration method, but from a theoretical point of view, we do not expect $p_A - bp_B$ to be stationary (which is quite difficult with real stocks), but to be anti-persistent, which is enough for our trading strategy.

4. Experimental Results

For testing the results through the different models introduced in this paper, we will use the components of the Nasdaq 100 index technological sector (see Table A1 in Appendix A),for the period between January 1999 and December 2003, coinciding with the "dot.com" bubble crash and the period between January 2007 and December 2012, this period coincides with the financial instability caused by the "subprime" crisis. These periods are choosen based on the results showed by Sánchez et al. [9].

We use Pairs Trading traditional methods (Distance Method, Correlation and Cointegration) in addition to the method developed by Ramos et al. [11] based on the Hurst exponent.

In Appendix B, it is shown the results obtained for different selection methods and different ways to calculate b, for the two selected periods. In addition to the returns obtained for each portfolio of pairs, we include two indicators of portfolio performance and risk, the Sharpe Ratio and the maximum Drawdown.

In the first period analyzed, the EW method to calculate b is never the best one. The best methods to calculate b seems to be the cointegration method and the minimization of the Hurst exponent. Also note that the Spearman correlation, the cointegration and the Hurst exponent selection methods provide strategies with high Sharpe ratios for several methods to calculate b.

In the second period analyzed, the EW method to calculate b works fine with the cointegration selection method, but it is not so good with the other ones, while the correlation method to calculate b is often one of the best ones.

Note that, in both periods, the Sharpe ratio when we use EW to calculate b are usually quite low with respect to the other methods.

Figures 1–4 show the cumulative log-return of the strategy for different selection methods and different ways to calculate b.

Figure 1 shows the returns obtained for the period 1999–2003 using the co-integration approach as a selection method. We can observe that during the whole period, the best option is to choose to calculate the b factor by means of the lowest value of the Hurst exponent, while the EW method is the worst.

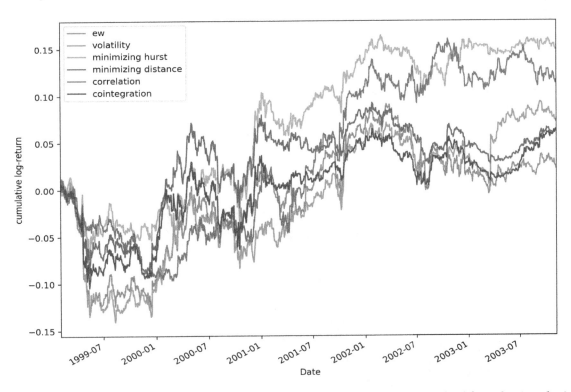

Figure 1. Comparative portfolio composed of 30 pairs using cointegration method for selection during the period 1999–2003.

Figure 2 represents the returns obtained for each of the b calculation methods for the 1999–2003 period, using the Hurst exponent method for the selection of pairs and a portfolio composed of 20 pairs. It can be observed that during the period studied, the results obtained using the EW method are also negative, while the Hurst exponent method is again the best option.

For the period 2007–2012, for a portfolio composed of 20 pairs selected using the distance method, Figure 3 shows the cumulative returns for the different methods proposed. In this case we can highlight the methods of correlation, minimizing distance and cointegration, as the methods to calculate b that provide the highest returns. Again, we can observe that the worst options would be the EW method together with the volatility one.

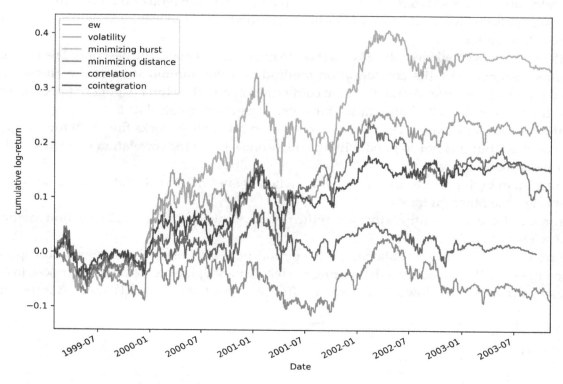

Figure 2. Comparative portfolio composed of 20 pairs using the Hurst exponent method for selection during the period 1999–2003.

Figure 3. Comparative portfolio composed of 20 pairs using distance method for selection during the period 2007–2012.

Figure 4 shows the results obtained using the different models to calculate the b factor for a portfolio of 10 pairs by selecting them using the Spearman model. We can observe that all returns are positive throughout the period studied (2007–2012). The most outstanding are the methods of correlation, minimum distance and volatility, which move in a very similar way during this period. On the contrary, the method of the lowest value of the Hurst exponent and the EW one are the worst options during the whole period.

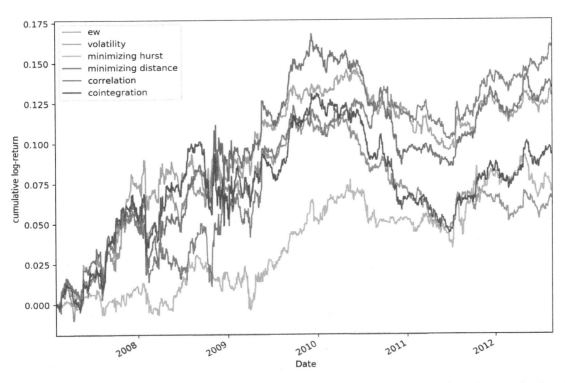

Figure 4. Comparative portfolio composed of 10 pairs using Spearman method for selection during the period 2007–2012.

Finally, we complete our sensitivity analysis by analyzing the influence of the strategy considered in Section 2.4. We consider the Hurst exponent as the selection method, 20 pairs in the portfolio and the period 1999–2003. We change the strategy by using 1 (as before), 1.5 and 2 standard deviations. That is, we modify the strategy as follows:

- In case $s > m + k\sigma$ the pair will be sold. The position will be closed if $s < m$ or $s > m + 2k\sigma$.
- In case $s < m - k\sigma$ the pair will be bought. The position will be closed if $s > m$ or $s < m - 2k\sigma$.

where $k = 1, 1.5, 2$. Table A2 shows that the EW, correlation and minimal distance obtain the worst results, while cointegration and the Hurst exponent obtain robust and better results for the different values of k.

Discussion of the Results

In Tables A3–A10, the results obtained with a pair trading strategy are shown. In those tables, we have consider four different methods for the pair selection (distance, correlation, cointegration and Hurst exponent), three different number of pairs (10, 20 and 30 pairs) and two periods (1999–2003 and 2007–2012). Overall, if we focus on the Sharpe ratio of the results, in 58% of the cases (14 out of 24) the EW method for calculating b obtains one of the three (out of seven) worst results. If we compare the EW method with the other methods proposed we obtain the following: minimal Hurst exponent is better than EW in 58% of the cases, minimal distance is better than EW in 58% of the cases, correlation is better than EW in 67% of the cases, cointegration is better than EW in 58% of the cases and volatility is better than *EW* in 50% of the cases. So, in general, the proposed methods (except the volatility one) tend to be better than the *EW* one.

However, since we are considering stocks in the technology sector, if we focus in the dot.com bubble (that is, the period 1999–2003) which affected more drastically to the stocks in the portfolio, we have, considering the Sharpe ratio of the results, that in 83% of the cases (10 out of 12) the *EW* method for calculating *b* obtains one of the three (out of seven) worst results. In this period, if we compare the *EW* method with the other methods proposed we obtain the following: minimal Hurst exponent is better than *EW* in 75% of the cases, minimal distance is better than *EW* in 83% of the cases, correlation is better than *EW* in 83% of the cases, cointegration is better than *EW* in 83% of the cases and volatility is better than *EW* in 58% of the cases. So, in general, the proposed methods (except the volatility one) tend to be much better than the *EW* one in this period.

On the other hand, in the second period (2007–2012), the *EW* performs much better than in the first period (1999–2003) and it does similarly or slightly better than the other methods.

Results show that these novel approaches used to calculate the factor *b* improve the results obtained compared with the classic *EW* method for the different strategies and mainly in the first period considered (1999–2003). Therefore, it seems that the performance of pairs trading can be improved not only acting on the strategy, but also on the method for the allocation in each stock.

In this section we have tested different methods for the allocation in each stock of the pair. Though we have used the different allocation methods with all the selection methods analyzed, it is clear that some combinations make more sense than others. For example, if the selection of the pair is done by selecting the pair with a lower Hurst exponent, the allocation method based on the minimization of the Hurst exponent of the pair should work better than other allocation methods.

One of the main goal of this paper is to point out that the allocation in each stock of the pair can be improved in the pairs trading strategy and we have given some ways to make this allocation. However, further research is needed to asses which of the methods is the best for this purpose. Even better, which of the combinations of selection and allocation method is the best. Though this problem depends on many factors, and some of them changes, depending on investor preferences, a multi-criteria decision analysis (see, for example References [44–46]) seems to be a good approach to deal with it.

In fact, in future research it can be tested if the selection method can be improved if we take into account the allocation method. For example, for the distance selection method, we can use the allocation method based on the minimization of the distance to normalize the price of the stocks in a different way than in the classical distance selection method, taking into account the allocation in each stock. Not all selection methods can be improved in this way (for example, the correlation selection method will not improve), but some of them, including some methods which we have not analyzed in this paper or future selection methods, could be improved.

5. Conclusions

In pairs trading literature, researchers have focused their attention in increasing pairs trading performance proposing different methodologies for pair selection. However, in all cases it is assumed that the amount invested in each stock of a pair (*b*) must be equal. This technique is called *Equally Weighted* (*EW*).

This paper presents a novel approach to try to improve the performance of this statistical arbitrage technique through novel methodologies in the calculation of *b*. Any selection method can benefit from these new allocation methods. Depending on the selection method used, we prove that the new methodologies for calculating the factor *b* obtain a greater return than those used up to the present time.

Results show that the classic EW method does not performance as well as the others. Cointegration, correlation and Hurst exponent give excellent results when are used to calculate factor *b*.

Author Contributions: Conceptualization, J.P.R.-R., J.E.T.-S. and M.Á.S.-G.; Methodology, J.P.R.-R., J.E.T.-S. and M.Á.S.-G.; Software, J.P.R.-R., J.E.T.-S. and M.Á.S.-G.; Validation, J.P.R.-R., J.E.T.-S. and M.Á.S.-G.; Formal Analysis, J.P.R.-R., J.E.T.-S. and M.Á.S.-G.; Investigation, J.P.R.-R., J.E.T.-S. and M.Á.S.-G.; Resources, J.P.R.-R., J.E.T.-S. and M.Á.S.-G.; Data Curation, J.P.R.-R., J.E.T.-S. and M.Á.S.-G.; Writing–Original Draft Preparation, J.P.R.-R., J.E.T.-S. and M.Á.S.-G.; Writing–Review & Editing, J.P.R.-R., J.E.T.-S. and M.Á.S.-G.; Visualization, J.P.R.-R., J.E.T.-S. and M.Á.S.-G.; Supervision, J.P.R.-R., J.E.T.-S. and M.Á.S.-G.; Project Administration, J.P.R.-R., J.E.T.-S. and M.Á.S.-G.; Funding Acquisition, J.P.R.-R., J.E.T.-S. and M.Á.S.-G. All authors have read and agreed to the published version of the manuscript.

Appendix A. Stocks Portfolio Technology Sector Nasdaq 100

Table A1. The Technology Sector Nasdaq 100.

Ticker	Company
AAPL	Apple Inc.
ADBE	Adobe Systems Incorporated
ADI	Analog Devices, Inc.
ADP	Automatic Data Processing, Inc.
ADSK	Autodesk, Inc.
AMAT	Applied Materials, Inc.
ATVI	Activision Blizzard, Inc.
AVGO	Broadcom Limited
BIDU	Baidu, Inc.
CA	CA, Inc.
CERN	Cerner Corporation
CHKP	Check Point Software Technologies Ltd.
CSCO	Cisco Systems, Inc.
CTSH	Cognizant Technology Solutions Corporation
CTXS	Citrix Systems, Inc.
EA	Electronic Arts Inc.
FB	Facebook, Inc.
FISV	Fiserv, Inc.
GOOG	Alphabet Inc.
GOOGL	Alphabet Inc.
INTC	Intel Corporation
INTU	Intuit Inc.
LRCX	Lam Research Corporation
MCHP	Microchip Technology Incorporated
MSFT	Microsoft Corporation
MU	Micron Technology, Inc.
MXIM	Maxim Integrated Products, Inc.
NVDA	NVIDIA Corporation
QCOM	QUALCOMM Incorporated
STX	Seagate Technology plc
SWKS	Skyworks Solutions, Inc.
SYMC	Symantec Corporation
TXN	Texas Instruments Incorporated
VRSK	Verisk Analytics, Inc.
WDC	Western Digital Corporation
XLNX	Xilinx, Inc.

Appendix B. Empirical Results

For each model (*Equal Weight, Volatility*, Minimal *Distance* of the log-prices, *Correlation* of returns, *Cointegration* of the prices, lowest *Hurst* exponent of the pair), we have considered 3 scenarios, depending on the amount of pairs included in the portfolio.

1.   Number of standard deviations.

Table A2. Comparison of results using the Hurst exponent selection method for the period 1999–2003 with 20 pairs and different numbers of standard deviations.

b Calculation Method	k [1]	Sharpe [2]	Profit TC [3]
Cointegration	1.0	0.39	14.55%
Cointegration	1.5	0.60	26.00%
Cointegration	2.0	0.59	24.08%
Correlation	1.0	0.15	6.10%
Correlation	1.5	0.17	8.21%
Correlation	2.0	0.31	13.82%
EW	1.0	−0.28	−11.25%
EW	1.5	0.38	15.49%
EW	2.0	0.21	7.74%
Lowest Hurst Exponent	1.0	0.70	40.51%
Lowest Hurst Exponent	1.5	0.51	28.00%
Lowest Hurst Exponent	2.0	0.57	28.51%
Minimal Distance	1.0	0.03	0.05%
Minimal Distance	1.5	0.39	15.70%
Minimal Distance	2.0	0.31	11.48%
Volatility	1.0	0.49	18.22%
Volatility	1.5	0.41	16.37%
Volatility	2.0	0.25	9.12%

[1] number of standard deviations; [2] Sharpe Ratio; [3] Profitability with transaction costs.

2.   Distance (1999–2003).

Table A3. Comparison of results using the distance selection method for the period 1999–2003.

b Calculation Method	N [1]	Oper [2]	AR [3]	%Profit TC [4]	Sharpe [5]	Max Drawdown
Cointegration	10	1375	0.40%	0.72%	0.05	13.70%
Correlation	10	1357	−0.60%	−4.36%	−0.07	18.60%
EW	10	1403	−1.30%	−7.30%	−0.15	19.60%
Minimal distancie	10	1389	−0.90%	−5.49%	−0.10	16.30%
Lowest Hurst Exponent	10	1352	−1.50%	−8.55%	−0.16	19.20%
Volatility	10	1370	−1.30%	−7.57%	−0.16	13.90%
Cointegration	20	2786	3.50%	16.31%	0.47	7.40%
Correlation	20	2630	2.80%	12.68%	0.36	9.20%
EW	20	2884	1.00%	3.36%	0.14	12.30%
Minimal distancie	20	2794	2.50%	11.00%	0.34	8.30%
Lowest Hurst Exponent	20	2685	0.60%	1.66%	0.08	12.00%
Volatility	20	2812	0.40%	0.39%	0.06	8.70%
Cointegration	30	4116	2.80%	12.83%	0.42	8.00%
Correlation	30	3830	2.00%	8.62%	0.27	12.60%
EW	30	4247	1.10%	4.18%	0.18	14.80%
Minimal distancie	30	4105	1.90%	7.93%	0.28	8.40%
Lowest Hurst Exponent	30	3861	0.30%	0.01%	0.04	11.80%
Volatility	30	4160	0,10%	-0,99%	0.01	9,20%

[1] Number of pairs; [2] Number of operations; [3] Annualised return; [4] Profitability with transaction costs; [5] Sharpe Ratio.

3. Distance (2007–2012).

Table A4. Comparison of results using the distance selection method for the period 2007–2012.

b Calculation Method	N [1]	Oper [2]	AR [3]	%Profit TC [4]	Sharpe [5]	Max Drawdown
Cointegration	10	1666	1.80%	8.73%	0.35	10.20%
Correlation	10	1594	3.50%	19.51%	0.55	12.10%
EW	10	1677	1.20%	5.42%	0.22	9.40%
Minimal distance	10	1649	2.80%	15.15%	0.56	8.80%
Lowest Hurst Exponent	10	1677	2.60%	13.42%	0.51	8.00%
Volatility	10	1684	1.20%	5.22%	0.24	11.90%
Cointegration	20	3168	2.60%	13.82%	0.60	6.50%
Correlation	20	2985	3.10%	16.91%	0.58	9.30%
EW	20	3219	1.70%	8.19%	0.36	4.20%
Minimal distance	20	3172	3.10%	17.01%	0.72	6.20%
Lowest Hurst Exponent	20	3116	2.20%	11.54%	0.51	7.20%
Volatility	20	3221	2.00%	9.89%	0.48	10.00%
Cointegration	30	4714	1.50%	7.33%	0.38	6.70%
Correlation	30	4453	1.40%	6.42%	0.29	10.90%
EW	30	4791	1.40%	6.50%	0.34	5.30%
Minimal distance	30	4709	1.70%	8.43%	0.44	5.90%
Lowest Hurst Exponent	30	4545	1.40%	6.48%	0.35	6.80%
Volatility	30	4785	1.60%	7.60%	0.43	9.00%

[1] Number of pairs; [2] Number of operations; [3] Annualised return; [4] Profitability with transaction costs; [5] Sharpe Ratio.

4. Spearman Correlation (1999–2003).

Table A5. Comparison of results using the Spearman correlation selection method for the period 1999–2003.

b Calculation Method	N [1]	Oper [2]	AR [3]	%Profit TC [4]	Sharpe [5]	Max Drawdown
Cointegration	10	1274	4.10%	19.93%	0.50	14.30%
Correlation	10	1432	3.00%	13.67%	0.36	11.20%
EW	10	1400	4.30%	20.80%	0.56	9.30%
Minimal distance	10	1219	4.00%	19.68%	0.51	12.50%
Lowest Hurst Exponent	10	1103	5.70%	29.20%	0.64	10.70%
Volatility	10	1405	3.30%	15.39%	0.45	8.40%
Cointegration	20	2583	4.70%	23.41%	0.69	12.30%
Correlation	20	2833	3.90%	18.78%	0.55	10.90%
EW	20	2814	2.80%	12.69%	0.45	8.30%
Minimal distance	20	2538	4.40%	21.63%	0.65	12.50%
Lowest Hurst Exponent	20	2176	3.50%	16.71%	0.48	10.40%
Volatility	20	2781	2.50%	11.01%	0.41	9.30%
Cointegration	30	3776	4.90%	24.54%	0.79	8.10%
Correlation	30	4196	2.80%	12.90%	0.41	8.60%
EW	30	4168	0.40%	0.71%	0.08	9.90%
Minimal distance	30	3717	4.20%	20.76%	0.69	8.30%
Lowest Hurst Exponent	30	3236	4.20%	20.72%	0.56	8.20%
Volatility	30	4125	1.20%	4.52%	0.22	9.50%

[1] Number of pairs; [2] Number of operations; [3] Annualised return; [4] Profitability with transaction costs; [5] Sharpe Ratio.

5.   Spearman Correlation (2007–2012).

Table A6. Comparison of results using the Spearman correlation selection method for the period 2007–2012.

b Calculation Method	N [1]	Oper [2]	AR [3]	%Profit TC [4]	Sharpe [5]	Max Drawdown
Cointegration	10	1614	1.70%	8.09%	0.38	8.30%
Correlation	10	1653	2.90%	15.75%	0.75	4.60%
EW	10	1620	1.20%	5.28%	0.37	7.00%
Minimal distancie	10	1551	2.50%	13.05%	0.58	7.80%
Lowest Hurst Exponent	10	1117	1.30%	6.18%	0.42	4.20%
Volatility	10	1668	2.30%	12.13%	0.72	5.00%
Cointegration	20	3022	1.00%	4.09%	0.29	6.80%
Correlation	20	3268	2.60%	13.77%	0.75	4.00%
EW	20	3236	1.40%	6.78%	0.46	5.70%
Minimal distance	20	2944	1.10%	4.93%	0.34	7.80%
Lowest Hurst Exponent	20	1966	0.40%	1.12%	0.14	3.90%
Volatility	20	3282	1.30%	5.76%	0.42	4.70%
Cointegration	30	4342	0.80%	3.15%	0.27	5.80%
Correlation	30	4872	2.60%	13.58%	0.74	4.30%
EW	30	4814	1.60%	7.80%	0.57	4.90%
Minimal distance	30	4222	0.90%	3.69%	0.30	7.00%
Lowest Hurst Exponent	30	2718	0.60%	2.49%	0.26	2.80%
Volatility	30	4864	1.90%	9.28%	0.67	3.60%

[1] Number of pairs; [2] Number of operations; [3] Annualised return; [4] Profitability with transaction costs; [5] Sharpe Ratio.

6.   Cointegration (1999–2003).

Table A7. Comparison of results using the cointegration selection method for the period 1999–2003.

b Calculation Method	N [1]	Oper [2]	AR [3]	%Profit TC [4]	Sharpe [5]	Max Drawdown
Cointegration	10	998	5.30%	26.80%	0.58	12.40%
Correlation	10	1015	7.30%	39.38%	0.78	9.30%
EW	10	1369	4.30%	20.83%	0.41	10.30%
Minimal distance	10	945	4.00%	19.45%	0.47	9.40%
Lowest Hurst Exponent	10	1123	7.70%	41.68%	0.79	11.90%
Volatility	10	1376	6.90%	36.62%	0.68	11.00%
Cointegration	20	1984	5.50%	28.41%	0.78	9.00%
Correlation	20	1985	5.50%	28.31%	0.76	6.40%
EW	20	2718	2.90%	13.24%	0.36	9.90%
Minimal distance	20	1876	4.50%	22.36%	0.67	8.10%
Lowest Hurst Exponent	20	2031	6.90%	36.88%	0.90	7.70%
Volatility	20	2688	4.10%	19.76%	0.50	11.50%
Cointegration	30	2957	0.90%	3.51%	0.14	11.00%
Correlation	30	3132	2.40%	11.06%	0.36	10.30%
EW	30	4064	−0.10%	−1.85%	−0.01	12.20%
Minimal distance	30	2783	0.70%	2.67%	0.12	9.40%
Lowest Hurst Exponent	30	2924	3.60%	17.23%	0.50	7.50%
Volatility	30	4040	0.90%	3.25%	0.12	13.00%

[1] Number of pairs; [2] Number of operations; [3] Annualised return; [4] Profitability with transaction costs; [5] Sharpe Ratio.

7.   Cointegration (2007–2012).

Table A8. Comparison of results using the cointegration selection method for the period 2007–2012.

b Calculation Method	N [1]	Oper [2]	AR [3]	%Profit TC [4]	Sharpe [5]	Max Drawdown
Cointegration	10	1516	−1.00%	−6.82%	−0.19	15.50%
Correlation	10	1512	−0.10%	−2.11%	−0.02	14.70%
EW	10	1604	1.40%	6.80%	0.30	9.60%
Minimal distance	10	1478	0.70%	2.32%	0.12	12.50%
Lowest Hurst Exponent	10	1502	−1.60%	−9.90%	−0.32	10.90%
Volatility	10	1635	−0.10%	−2.14%	−0.02	12.90%
Cointegration	20	2884	−0.70%	−5.44%	−0.19	9.90%
Correlation	20	2955	−0.70%	−5.28%	−0.16	11.70%
EW	20	3195	1.80%	8.90%	0.48	4.40%
Minimal distance	20	2709	0.20%	−0.15%	0.06	9.50%
Lowest Hurst Exponent	20	2666	−0.90%	−6.53%	−0.26	9.00%
Volatility	20	3189	0.50%	1.31%	0.14	8.90%
Cointegration	30	4142	0.00%	−1.38%	0.00	8.80%
Correlation	30	4373	0.20%	−0.56%	0.04	9.50%
EW	30	4720	2.70%	14.63%	0.75	4.90%
Minimal distance	30	3923	1.10%	4.69%	0.28	7.90%
Lowest Hurst Exponent	30	3694	−0.30%	−2.93%	−0.09	7.60%
Volatility	30	4742	1.30%	5.82%	0.36	7.00%

[1] Number of pairs; [2] Number of operations; [3] Annualised return; [4] Profitability with transaction costs; [5] Sharpe Ratio.

8.   Hurst exponent (1999–2003).

Table A9. Comparison of results using the Hurst exponent selection method for the period 1999–2003.

b Calculation Method	N [1]	Oper [2]	AR [3]	%Profit TC [4]	Sharpe [5]	Max Drawdown
Cointegration	10	1136	−0.60%	−3.94%	−0.06	15.60%
Correlation	10	1176	0.50%	1.32%	0.04	24.40%
EW	10	1334	2.80%	12.87%	0.29	12.20%
Minimal distance	10	1166	−1.20%	−6.87%	−0.12	13.50%
Lowest Hurst Exponent	10	1234	4.60%	22.77%	0.37	21.40%
Volatility	10	1401	7.40%	39.60%	0.72	14.40%
Cointegration	20	2104	3.10%	14.55%	0.39	11.10%
Correlation	20	2400	1.50%	6.10%	0.15	15.70%
EW	20	2695	-2.10%	−11.25%	−0.28	12.30%
Minimal distance	20	2093	0.20%	0.05%	0.03	10.60%
Lowest Hurst Exponent	20	2375	7.50%	40.51%	0.70	17.10%
Volatility	20	2755	3.80%	18.22%	0.49	8.90%
Cointegration	30	2984	3.10%	14.91%	0.48	7.80%
Correlation	30	3516	2.00%	8.83%	0.22	16.50%
EW	30	4066	−1.30%	−7.56%	−0.19	11.80%
Minimal distance	30	2915	2.70%	12.63%	0.41	6.50%
Lowest Hurst Exponent	30	3411	7.10%	37.86%	0.78	13.40%
Volatility	30	3994	4.40%	21.57%	0.63	6.50%

[1] Number of pairs; [2] Number of operations; [3] Annualised return; [4] Profitability with transaction costs; [5] Sharpe Ratio.

9.   Hurst exponent (2007–2012).

Table A10. Comparison of results using the Hurst exponent selection method for the period 2007–2012.

b Calculation Method	N [1]	Oper [2]	AR [3]	%Profit TC [4]	Sharpe [5]	Max Drawdown
Cointegration	10	1596	3.00%	16.40%	0.55	8.00%
Correlation	10	1587	3.70%	21.51%	0.57	9.80%
EW	10	1643	3.00%	16.26%	0.59	9.10%
Minimal distancie	10	1581	2.10%	11.02%	0.41	8.70%
Lowest Hurst Exponent	10	1649	4.80%	28.15%	0.83	8.30%
Volatility	10	1724	1.30%	5.98%	0.27	8.40%
Cointegration	20	2795	0.80%	3.40%	0.21	7.10%
Correlation	20	3001	2.60%	14.10%	0.50	7.50%
EW	20	3258	1.70%	8.27%	0.40	9.10%
Minimal distancie	20	2758	−0.40%	−3.48%	−0.10	10.60%
Lowest Hurst Exponent	20	3129	1.90%	9.84%	0.39	8.30%
Volatility	20	3204	0.40%	0.90%	0.11	6.40%
Cointegration	30	4100	−0.20%	−2.27%	−0.05	9.30%
Correlation	30	4418	2.00%	10.23%	0.43	8.10%
EW	30	4666	1.90%	9.34%	0.46	7.60%
Minimal distancie	30	4049	0.00%	−1.55%	−0.01	10.50%
Lowest Hurst Exponent	30	4248	0.40%	0.78%	0.09	9.20%
Volatility	30	4790	0.60%	1.50%	0.15	8.40%

[1] Number of pairs; [2] Number of operations; [3] Annualised return; [4] Profitability with transaction costs; [5] Sharpe Ratio.

References

1. Fama, E. Efficient capital markets: II. *J. Financ.* **1991**, *46*, 1575–1617. [CrossRef]
2. Dimson, E.; Mussavian, M. A brief history of market efficiency. *Eur. Financ. Manag.* **1998**, *4*, 91–193. [CrossRef]
3. Di Matteo, T.; Aste, T.; Dacorogna, M.M. Using the scaling analysis to characterize their stage of development. *J. Bank. Financ.* **2005**, *29*, 827–851. [CrossRef]
4. Di Matteo, T. Multi-scaling in finance. *Quant. Financ.* **2007**, *7*, 21–36. [CrossRef]
5. Peters, E.E. *Chaos and Order in the Capital Markets. A New View of Cycle, Prices, and Market Volatility*; Wiley: New York, NY, USA, 1991.
6. Peters, E.E. *Fractal Market Analysis: Applying Chaos Theory to Investment and Economics*; Wiley: New York, NY, USA, 1994.
7. Lo, A.W. The adaptive markets hypothesis: Market efficiency from an evolutionary perspective. *J. Portf. Manag.* **2004**, *30*, 15–29. [CrossRef]
8. Sanchez-Granero, M.A.; Trinidad Segovia, J.E.; García, J.; Fernández-Martínez, M. The effect of the underlying distribution in Hurst exponent estimation. *PLoS ONE* **2015**, *28*, e0127824.
9. Sánchez-Granero, M.A.; Balladares, K.A.; Ramos-Requena, J.P.; Trinidad-Segovia, J.E. Testing the efficient market hypothesis in Latin American stock markets. *Phys. A Stat. Mech. Its Appl.* **2020**, *540*, 123082. [CrossRef]
10. Zhang, H.; Urquhart, A. Pairs trading across Mainland China and Hong Kong stock Markets. *Int. J. Financ. Econ.* **2019**, *24*, 698–726. [CrossRef]
11. Ramos-Requena, J.P.; Trinidad-Segovia, J.E.; Sanchez-Granero, M.A. Introducing Hurst exponent in pairs trading. *Phys. A Stat. Mech. Its Appl.* **2017**, *488*, 39–45. [CrossRef]
12. Taqqu, M.S.; Teverovsky, V. Estimators for long range dependence: An empirical study. *Fractals* **1995**, *3*, 785–798. [CrossRef]
13. Kristoufek, L.; Vosvrda, M. Measuring capital market efficiency: Global and local correlations structure. *Phys. A Stat. Mech. Its Appl.* **2013**, *392*, 184–193. [CrossRef]
14. Kristoufek, L.; Vosvrda, M. Measuring capital market efficiency: Long-term memory, fractal dimension and approximate entropy. *Eur. Phys. J. B* **2014**, *87*, 162. [CrossRef]

15. Zunino, L.; Zanin, M.; Tabak, B.M.; Pérez, D.G.; Rosso, O.A. Complexity-entropy causality plane: A useful approach to quantify the stock market inefficiency. *Phys. A Stat. Mech. Its Appl.* **2010**, *389*, 1891–1901. [CrossRef]

16. Gatev, E.; Goetzmann, W.; Rouwenhorst, K. Pairs Trading: Performance of a relative value arbitrage rule. *Rev. Financ. Stud.* **2006**, *19*, 797–827. [CrossRef]

17. Vidyamurthy, G. *Pairs Trading, Quantitative Methods and Analysis*; John Wiley and Sons: Toronto, ON, Canada, 2004.

18. Dunis, L.; Ho, R. Cointegration portfolios of European equities for index tracking and market neutral strategies. *J. Asset Manag.* **2005**, *6*, 33–52. [CrossRef]

19. Figuerola Ferretti, I.; Paraskevopoulos, I.; Tang, T. Pairs trading and spread persistence in the European stock market. *J. Futur. Mark.* **2018**, *38*, 998–1023 [CrossRef]

20. Alexander, C.; Dimitriu, A. *The Cointegration Alpha: Enhanced Index Tracking and Long-Short Equity Market Neutral Strategies*; SSRN eLibrary: Rochester, NY, USA, 2002.

21. Perlin, M.S. Evaluation of Pairs Trading strategy at the Brazilian financial market. *J. Deriv. Hedge Funds* **2009**, *15*, 122–136. [CrossRef]

22. Caldeira, J.F.; Moura, G.V. *Selection of a Portfolio of Pairs Based on Cointegration: A Statistical Arbitrage Strategy*; Revista Brasileira de Financas (Online): Rio de Janeiro, Brazil, 2013; Volume 11, pp. 49–80.

23. Burgess, A.N. Using cointegration to hedge and trade international equities. In *Applied Quantitative Methods for Trading and Investment*; John Wiley and Sons: Chichester, UK, 2003; pp. 41–69.

24. Galenko, A.; Popova, E.; Popova, I. Trading in the presence of cointegration. *J. Altern. Investments* **2012**, *15*, 85–97. [CrossRef]

25. Lin, Y.X.; Mccrae, M.; Gulati, C. Loss protection in Pairs Trading through minimum profit bounds: A cointegration approach. *J. Appl. Math. Decis. Sci.* **2006**. [CrossRef]

26. Nath, P. *High frequency Pairs Trading with U.S Treasury Securities: Risks and Rewards for Hedge Funds*; SSRN eLibrary: Rochester, NY, USA, 2003.

27. Elliott, R.; van der Hoek, J.; Malcolm, W. Pairs Trading. *Quant. Financ.* **2005**, *5*, 271–276. [CrossRef]

28. Dunis, C.L.; Shannon, G. Emerging markets of South-East and Central Asia: Do they still offer a diversification benefit? *J. Asset Manag.* **2005**, *6*, 168–190. [CrossRef]

29. Ramos-Requena, J.P.; Trinidad-Segovia, J.E.; Sánchez-Granero, M.A. An Alternative Approach to Measure Co-Movement between Two Time Series. *Mathematics* **2020**, *8*, 261. [CrossRef]

30. Baur, D. What Is Co-movement? In *IPSC-Technological and Economic Risk Management*; Technical Report; European Commission, Joint Research Center: Ispra, VA, Italy, 2003.

31. Hauke, J.; Kossowski, T. Comparison of values of Pearson's and Spearman's correlation coefficients on the same sets of data. *Quaest. Geogr.* **2011**, *30*, 87–93. [CrossRef]

32. Engle, R.F.; Granger, C.W.J. Co-integration and error correction: Representation, estimation, and testing. *Econometrica* **1987**, *5*, 251–276. [CrossRef]

33. Do, B.; Faff, R. Does simple pairs trading still work? *Financ. Anal. J.* **2010**, *66*, 83–95. [CrossRef]

34. Do, B.; Faff, R. Are pairs trading profits robust to trading costs? *J. Financ. Res.* **2012**, *35*, 261–287. [CrossRef]

35. Hurst, H. Long term storage capacity of reservoirs. *Trans. Am. Soc. Civ. Eng.* **1951**, *6*, 770–799.

36. Mandelbrot, B.; Wallis, J.R. Robustness of the rescaled range R/S in the measurement of noncyclic long-run statistical dependence. *Water Resour. Res.* **1969**, *5*, 967–988. [CrossRef]

37. Peng, C.K.; Buldyrev, S.V.; Havlin, S.; Simons, M.; Stanley, H.E.; Goldberger, A.L. Mosaic organization of DNA nucleotides. *Phys. Rev. E* **1994**, *49*, 1685–1689. [CrossRef]

38. Lo, A.W. Long-term memory in stock market prices. *Econometrica* **1991**, *59*, 1279–1313. [CrossRef]

39. Sanchez-Granero, M.A.; Trinidad-Segovia, J.E.; Garcia-Perez, J. Some comments on Hurst exponent and the long memory processes on capital markets. *Phys. A Stat. Mech. Its Appl.* **2008**, *387*, 5543–5551. [CrossRef]

40. Weron, R. Estimating long-range dependence: Finite sample properties and confidence intervals. *Phys. A Stat. Mech. Its Appl.* **2002**, *312*, 285–299. [CrossRef]

41. Willinger, W.; Taqqu, M.S.; Teverovsky, V. Stock market prices and long-range dependence. *Financ. Stochastics* **1999**, *3*, 1–13. [CrossRef]

42. Barabasi, A.L.; Vicsek, T. Multifractality of self affine fractals. *Phys. Rev. A* **1991**, *44*, 2730–2733. [CrossRef]

43. Barunik, J.; Kristoufek, L. On Hurst exponent estimation under heavy-tailed distributions. *Phys. A Stat. Mech. Its Appl.* **2010**, *389*, 3844–3855. [CrossRef]

44. Goulart Coelho, L.M.; Lange, L.C.; Coelho, H.M. Multi-criteria decision making to support waste management: A critical review of current practices and methods. *Waste Manag. Res.* **2017**, *35*, 3–28. [CrossRef]

45. Meng, K.; Cao, Y.; Peng, X.; Prybutok, V.; Gupta, V. Demand-dependent recovery decision-making of a batch of products for sustainability. *Int. J. Prod. Econ.* **2019**, 107552. [CrossRef]

46. Roth, S.; Hirschberg, S.; Bauer, C.; Burgherr, P.; Dones, R.; Heck, T.; Schenler, W. Sustainability of electricity supply technology portfolio. *Ann. Nucl. Energy* **2009**, *36*, 409–416. [CrossRef]

6

Detection of Near-Multicollinearity through Centered and Noncentered Regression

Román Salmerón Gómez [1], Catalina García García [1,*] and José García Pérez [2]

[1]   Department of Quantitative Methods for Economics and Business, University of Granada,
     18010 Granada, Spain; romansg@ugr.es

[2]   Department of Economy and Company, University of Almería, 04120 Almería, Spain; jgarcia@ual.es

*   Correspondence: cbgarcia@ugr.es

Abstract: This paper analyzes the diagnostic of near-multicollinearity in a multiple linear regression from auxiliary centered (with intercept) and noncentered (without intercept) regressions. From these auxiliary regressions, the centered and noncentered variance inflation factors (VIFs) are calculated. An expression is also presented that relates both of them. In addition, this paper analyzes why the VIF is not able to detect the relation between the intercept and the rest of the independent variables of an econometric model. At the same time, an analysis is also provided to determine how the auxiliary regression applied to calculate the VIF can be useful to detect this kind of multicollinearity.

Keywords: centered model; noncentered model; intercept; essential multicollinearity; nonessential multicollinearity

1. Introduction

Consider the following multiple linear model with n observations and k regressors:

$$\mathbf{y}_{n \times 1} = \mathbf{X}_{n \times k} \cdot \boldsymbol{\beta}_{k \times 1} + \mathbf{u}_{n \times 1}, \tag{1}$$

where $\mathbf{y}$ is a vector with the observations of the dependent variable, $\mathbf{X}$ is a matrix containing the observations of regressors and $\mathbf{u}$ is a vector representing a random disturbance (that is assumed to be spherical). Generally, the first column of matrix $\mathbf{X}$ is composed of ones to denote that the model contains an intercept. Thus, $\mathbf{X} = [\mathbf{1} \, \mathbf{X}_2 \ldots \mathbf{X}_k]$ where $\mathbf{1}_{n \times 1} = (1\,1\ldots1)^t$. This model is considered to be centered.

When this model presents worrying near-multicollinearity (hereinafter, multicollinearity), that is, when the linear relation between the regressors affects the numerical and/or statistical analysis of the model, the usual approach is to transform the regressors (see, for example, Belsley [1], Marquardt [2] or, more recently, Velilla [3]). Due to the transformations (centering, typification or standardization) implying the elimination of the intercept in the model, the transformed models are considered to be noncentered. Note that even after transforming the data, it is possible to recover the original model (centered) from the estimations of the transformed model (noncentered model). However, in this paper, we refer to the centered and noncentered model depending on whether the intercept is initially included or not. Thus, it is considered that the model is centered if $\mathbf{X} = [\mathbf{1} \, \mathbf{X}_2 \ldots \mathbf{X}_k]$ and noncentered if $\mathbf{X} = [\mathbf{X}_1 \, \mathbf{X}_2 \ldots \mathbf{X}_k]$, given that $\mathbf{X}_j \neq \mathbf{1}$ with $j = 1, \ldots, k$.

From the intercept is also possible to distinguish between essential and nonessential multicollinearity:

Nonessential: A near-linear relation between the intercept and at least one of the rest independent variables.

Essential: A near-linear relation between at least two of the independent variables (excluding the intercept).

A first idea of these definitions was provided by Cohen et al. [4]: Nonessential ill-conditioning results simply from the scaling of the variables, whereas essential ill-conditioning results from substantive relationships among the variables. While in some papers the idea of distinguishing between essential and nonessential collinearity is attributed to Marquardt [5], it is possible to find this concept in Marquardt and Snee [6]. These terms have been widely used not only for linear models but also, for example, for moderated models with interactions and/or with a quadratic term. However, these concepts have been analyzed fundamentally from the point of view of the solution of collinearity. Thus, as Marquardt and Snee [6] stated: In a linear model, centering removes the correlation between the constant term and all linear terms.

The variance inflation factor is one of the most applied measures to detect multicollinearity. Following O'Brien [7], commonly a VIF of 10 or even one as low as 4 have been used as rules of thumbs to indicate excessive or serious collinearity. Salmerón et al. [8] show that the VIF does not detect the nonessential multicollinearity, while this kind of multicollinearity is detected by the index of Stewart [9] (see Salmerón Gómez et al. [10]). This index has been misunderstood in the literature since its presentation by Stewart, who wrongly identified it with the VIF. Even Marquardt [11] when published a comment of the paper of Stewart [9] stated: Stewart collinearity indices are simply the square roots of the corresponding variance inflation factor. It is not clear to me whether giving a new name to the square of a VIF is a help or a hindrance to understanding. There is a long and precisely analogous history of using the term "standard error" for the square root of the corresponding "variances". Given the continuing necessity for dealing with statistical quantities on both the scale of the observable and the scale of the observable squared, there may be a place for a new term. Clearly, the essential intellectual content is identical for both terms.

However, in Salmerón Gómez et al. [12] it is shown that the VIF and the index of Stewart are not the same measure. This paper analyzes in what cases use one measure or another, focusing on the initial distinction between centered and noncentered models. Thus, the algebraic contextualization provided by Salmerón Gómez et al. [12] will be complemented from an econometric point of view. This question was also presented by Jensen and Ramirez [13], striving to commit to a clarification of the misuse given to the VIF over decades since its first use, who insinuated: To choose a model, with or without intercept, is substantive, is specific to each experimental paradigm and is beyond the scope of the present study. It was also stated that: This differs between centered and uncentered diagnostics.

This paper, focused on the differences between essential and nonessential multicollinearity in relation to its diagnostic, analyzes the behaviour of the VIF depending on whether model (1) initially includes the intercept or not. For this analysis, it will be considered that the auxiliary regression used for its calculation is centered or not since as stated by Grob [14] (p. 304): Instead of using the classical coefficient of determination in the definition of VIF, one may also apply the centered coefficient of determination. As a matter of fact, the latter definition is more common. We may call VIF uncentered or centered, depending on whether the classical or centered coefficient of determination is used. From the above considerations, a centered VIF only makes sense when the matrix **X** contains ones as a column. Additionally, although initially in the centered version of model (1) it is possible to find these two kinds of multicollinearity, and in the noncentered version, it is only possible to find essential multicollinearity, this paper shows that this statement is subject to some nuances.

On the other hand, throughout the paper the following statement of Cook [15] will be illustrated: As a matter of fact, the centered VIF requires an intercept in the model but at the same time denies the status of the intercept as an independent "variable" being possibly related to collinearity effects. Furthermore, another statement was provided by Belsley [16] (p. 29): The centered VIF has no ability to discover collinearity involving the intercept. Thus, the second part of the paper analyzes why the centered VIF is unable to detect the nonessential multicollinearity and, for this, the centered coefficient of determination of the centered auxiliary regression to calculate the centered VIF is analyzed.

This analysis will be applied to propose a methodology to detect the nonessential multicollinearity from the centered auxiliary regression.

The structure of the paper is as follows: Section 2 presents the detection of multicollinearity in noncentered models from the noncentered auxiliary regressions, Section 3 analyzes the effects of high values of the noncentered VIF on the statistical analysis of the model and Section 4 presents the detection of multicollinearity in centered models from the centered auxiliary regressions. Section 5 illustrates the contribution of the paper with two empirical applications. Finally, Section 6 summarizes the main conclusions.

2. Auxiliary Noncentered Regressions

This section presents the calculation of the VIF uncentered, VIFnc, considering that the auxiliary regression is noncentered, that is, it has no intercept. First, the method regarding how to calculate the coefficient of determination for noncentered models is presented.

2.1. Noncentered Coefficient of Determination

Given the linear regression of Equation (1) with or without the intercept, the following decomposition for the sum of squares is verified:

$$\sum_{i=1}^{n} y_i^2 = \sum_{i=1}^{n} \widehat{y}_i^2 + \sum_{i=1}^{n} e_i^2, \tag{2}$$

where $\widehat{y}$ represents the estimation of the dependent variable of the model that is fit by employing ordinary least squares (OLS) and $\mathbf{e} = \mathbf{y} - \widehat{\mathbf{y}}$ are the residuals obtained from that fit. In this case, the coefficient of determination is obtained by the following expression:

$$R_{nc}^2 = \frac{\sum\limits_{i=1}^{n} \widehat{y}_i^2}{\sum\limits_{i=1}^{n} y_i^2} = 1 - \frac{\sum\limits_{i=1}^{n} e_i^2}{\sum\limits_{i=1}^{n} y_i^2}. \tag{3}$$

Comparing the decomposition of the sums of squares given by (2) with the traditionally applied method to calculate the coefficient of determination in models with the intercept, as in model (1):

$$\sum_{i=1}^{n} (y_i - \overline{y})^2 = \sum_{i=1}^{n} (\widehat{y}_i - \overline{y})^2 + \sum_{i=1}^{n} e_i^2, \tag{4}$$

it is noted that both coincide if the dependent variable has zero mean. If the mean is different from zero, both models present the same residual sum of squares but different explained and total sum of squares.

Thus, these models lead to the same value for the coefficient of determination (and, as a consequence, for the VIF) only if the dependent variable presents a mean equal to zero.

2.2. Noncentered Variance Inflation Factor

The VIFnc is obtained from the expression:

$$VIFnc(j) = \frac{1}{1 - R_{nc}^2(j)}, \quad j = 1, \ldots, k, \tag{5}$$

where $R_{nc}^2(j)$ is the coefficient of determination, calculated by following (3), of the noncentered auxiliary regression:

$$\mathbf{X}_j = \mathbf{X}_{-j}\delta + \mathbf{w}, \tag{6}$$

where $\mathbf{X}_{-j}$ is equal to the matrix $\mathbf{X}$ after eliminating the variable $\mathbf{X}_j$, for $j = 1, \ldots, k$, and it does not have a vector of ones representing the intercept.

In this case:

- $\sum_{i=1}^{n} X_{ij}^2 = \mathbf{X}_j^t \mathbf{X}_j$, and

- $\sum_{i=1}^{n} \widehat{X}_{ij}^2 = \widehat{\mathbf{X}}_j^t \widehat{\mathbf{X}}_j = \mathbf{X}_j^t \mathbf{X}_{-j} \cdot \left(\mathbf{X}_{-j}^t \mathbf{X}_{-j} \right)^{-1} \cdot \mathbf{X}_{-j}^t \mathbf{X}_j$ due to $\widehat{\mathbf{X}}_j = \mathbf{X}_{-j} \cdot \left(\mathbf{X}_{-j}^t \mathbf{X}_{-j} \right)^{-1} \cdot \mathbf{X}_{-j}^t \mathbf{X}_j$.

Then:

$$R_{nc}^2(j) = \frac{\mathbf{X}_j^t \mathbf{X}_{-j} \cdot \left(\mathbf{X}_{-j}^t \mathbf{X}_{-j} \right)^{-1} \cdot \mathbf{X}_{-j}^t \mathbf{X}_j}{\mathbf{X}_j^t \mathbf{X}_j},$$

$$1 - R_{nc}^2(j) = \frac{\mathbf{X}_j^t \mathbf{X}_j - \mathbf{X}_j^t \mathbf{X}_{-j} \cdot \left(\mathbf{X}_{-j}^t \mathbf{X}_{-j} \right)^{-1} \cdot \mathbf{X}_{-j}^t \mathbf{X}_j}{\mathbf{X}_j^t \mathbf{X}_j},$$

$$VIFnc(j) = \frac{\mathbf{X}_j^t \mathbf{X}_j}{\mathbf{X}_j^t \mathbf{X}_j - \mathbf{X}_j^t \mathbf{X}_{-j} \cdot \left(\mathbf{X}_{-j}^t \mathbf{X}_{-j} \right)^{-1} \cdot \mathbf{X}_{-j}^t \mathbf{X}_j}. \tag{7}$$

Thus, the VIFnc coincides with the expression given by Stewart [9] for the VIF and is denoted as k_j^2, that is, $VIFnc(j) = k_j^2$.

However, recently, Salmerón Gómez et al. [12] showed that the index presented by Stewart has been misleadingly identified as the VIF, verifying the following relation between both measures:

$$k_j^2 = VIF(j) + n \cdot \frac{\overline{\mathbf{X}}_j^2}{RSS_j}, \quad j = 2, \ldots, k, \tag{8}$$

where $\overline{\mathbf{X}}_j$ is the mean of the $j-$variable of $\mathbf{X}$. This expression is also shown by Salmerón Gómez et al. [10], where it is used to quantify the proportion of essential and nonessential multicollinearity existing in a concrete independent variable.

Note that the expression:

$$VIFnc(j) = VIF(j) + n \cdot \frac{\overline{\mathbf{X}}_j^2}{RSS_j}, \tag{9}$$

is obtained by Chennamaneni et al. [17] (expression (6) page 174), although it is also limited to the particular case of the moderated regression $\mathbf{Y} = \alpha_0 \cdot \mathbf{1} + \alpha_1 \cdot \mathbf{U} + \alpha_2 \cdot \mathbf{V} + \alpha_3 \cdot \mathbf{U} \times \mathbf{V} + \nu$ where $\mathbf{U}$ and $\mathbf{V}$ are ratio-scaled explanatory variables in n-dimensional data vectors. Indeed, these authors proposed a new measure to detect multicollinearity in moderated regression models that is derived from the noncentered coefficient of determination. However, this use of the noncentered coefficient of determination lacks of the statistical contextualization provided by this paper

Finally, from expression (9), it is shown that the VIFnc and the VIF only coincide if the associated variable has zero mean, analogously to what happens in the decomposition of the sum of squares. Note that this expression also clarifies why Stewart's collinearity indices diminish when the variables are centered, which the author attributed to errors in regression variables: This phenomenon is a consequence of the fact that our definition of collinearity index compels us to work with relative errors.

Example 1. *Considering $k = 4$ in model (1), we use the noncentered coefficient of determination, R_{nc}^2, to calculate the noncentered variance inflation factor, $VIFnc$. For it, we consider the values displayed in Table 1. Note that variables $\mathbf{y}$, $\mathbf{X}_2$ and $\mathbf{X}_3$ were originally used by Belsley [1] and we have added a new variable, $\mathbf{X}_4$, that has been randomly generated (from a normal distribution with a mean equal to 4 and a variance equal to 16) to obtain a variable that is linearly independent with respect to the rest.*

Table 1. Data set applied by Belsley [1].

y	1	X_2	X_3	X_4
2.69385	1	0.996926	1.00006	8.883976
2.69402	1	0.997091	0.998779	6.432483
2.70052	1	0.9973	1.00068	−1.612356
2.68559	1	0.997813	1.00242	1.781762
2.7072	1	0.997898	1.00065	2.16682
2.6955	1	0.99814	1.0005	4.045509
2.70417	1	0.998556	0.999596	4.858077
2.69699	1	0.998737	1.00262	4.9045
2.69327	1	0.999414	1.00321	8.631162
2.68999	1	0.999678	1.0013	−0.4976853
2.70003	1	0.999926	0.997579	6.828907
2.702	1	0.999995	0.998597	8.999921
2.70938	1	1.00063	0.995316	7.080689
2.70094	1	1.00095	0.995966	1.193665
2.70536	1	1.00118	0.997125	1.483312
2.70754	1	1.00177	0.998951	−1.053813
2.69519	1	1.00231	1.00102	−0.5860236
2.7017	1	1.00306	1.00186	−1.371546
2.70451	1	1.00394	1.00353	−2.445995
2.69532	1	1.00469	1.00021	5.731981

In these data, the existence of nonessential multicollinearity is intuited. This fact is confirmed by the small values of the coefficient of variation (CV) in two of the independent variables and the following conclusions obtained from the value of the condition indices and the proportions of the variance (see, for example, Belsley et al. [18] and Belsley [16] for more details) shown in Table 2:

- *Variables X_2 and X_3 present a CV lower than 0.06674082 and than 0.1002506 that were presented by Salmerón Gómez et al. [10] as thresholds to indicate that a variable may be related to the constant and the model will present strong and moderate nonessential multicollinearity, respectively.*
- *The second index is associated with a high proportion of the variance with the variable X_4, although it is not worrisome since it does not present a high value.*
- *The third index presents a value higher than the established thresholds (20 for moderate multicollinearity and 30 for strong multicollinearity), and it is also associated with high proportions in the variables X_2 and X_3.*
- *The last index identified as the condition number is clearly related to the intercept, and at the same time, it includes the relation between X_2 and X_3 as previously commented.*
- *Finally, the condition number, 1614.829, is higher than the threshold traditionally established as indicative of worrisome multicollinearity.*

Table 2. Diagnostic of collinearity of Belsley–Kuh–Welsch and coefficient of variation of the considered variables.

		Proportion of the Variance			
Eigenvalue	Index of Condition	1	X_2	X_3	X_4
3.517205	1.000	0	0	0	0.022
0.4827886	2.699	0	0	0	0.784
4.978345×10^{-6}	840.536	0	0.423	0.475	0.003
1.348791×10^{-6}	1614.829	1	0.577	0.525	0.191
Coefficients of variation			0.002	0.002	1.141

Now, other models are proposed apart from the initial model for $k = 4$:

- *Model 0 (**Mod0**): $y = \beta_1 \cdot 1 + \beta_2 \cdot X_2 + \beta_3 \cdot X_3 + \beta_4 \cdot X_4 + u$.*
- *Model 1 (**Mod1**): $y = \beta_1 \cdot 1 + \beta_2 \cdot X_2 + \beta_3 \cdot X_3 + u$.*
- *Model 2 (**Mod2**): $y = \beta_1 \cdot 1 + \beta_2 \cdot X_2 + \beta_4 \cdot X_4 + u$.*

- Model 3 (**Mod3**): $\mathbf{y} = \beta_1 \cdot \mathbf{1} + \beta_3 \cdot \mathbf{X}_3 + \beta_4 \cdot \mathbf{X}_4 + \mathbf{u}$.

*Table 3 presents the VIF and the VIFnc of these models. Note that by using the original variables applied by Belsley (**Mod1**), the traditional VIF (from the centered model, see Theil [19]) provides a value equal to 1 (its minimum possible value), while the VIFnc is equal to 100,032.1. If the additional variable $\mathbf{X}_4$ is included (**Mod0**), the traditional VIFs are also close to one while the noncentered VIFs present values higher than 100,000. The conclusion is that the VIF is not detecting the existence of nonessential multicollinearity (see Salmerón et al. [8]) while the VIFnc "does detect it". However, since the calculation of VIFnc excludes the constant term, the detected relation refers to the one between $\mathbf{X}_2$ and $\mathbf{X}_3$, and not to the relation between $\mathbf{X}_2$ and/or $\mathbf{X}_3$ with the intercept.*

*This fact is supported by the values obtained for the VIF and VIFnc of the second and fourth variables (**Mod2**) and for the third and fourth variables (**Mod3**).*

Table 3. Variance inflation factor (VIF) and VIF uncentered (VIFnc) of models proposed from Belsley [1] dataset.

		$\mathbf{X}_2$	$\mathbf{X}_3$	$\mathbf{X}_4$
Mod0	VIF	1.155	1.084	1.239
	VIFnc	100,453.8	100,490.6	1.737
Mod1	VIF	1	1	
	VIFnc	100,032.1	100,032.1	
Mod2	VIF	1.143		1.143
	VIFnc	1.765		1.765
Mod3	VIF		1.072	1.072
	VIFnc		1.766	1.766

2.3. What Kind of Multicollinearity Detects the VIFnc?

The results of Example 1 for **Mod0** suggest a new definition of nonessential multicollinearity as the relation between at least two variables with little variability. Thus, the particular case when one of these variables is the intercept leads to the definition initially given by Marquardt and Snee [6]. Then, the initial idea that in a noncentered model, is not possible to find nonessential collinearity is of a nuanced nature.

By following Salmerón et al. [8] and Salmerón Gómez et al. [10], it can be concluded that the VIF only detects the essential multicollinearity and, with these results, the VIFnc detects the nonessential multicollinearity but in its generalized definition since the intercept is eliminated in the corresponding auxiliary regression.

This fact is contradictory to the fact that the VIFnc coincides with the index of Stewart, see expression (7), since this measure is able to detect the nonessential multicollinearity (see Salmerón Gómez et al. [10]). This is because the VIFnc could be fooled, including the constant as an independent variable in a model without the intercept, that is:

$$\mathbf{y} = \beta_1 \cdot \mathbf{X}_1 + \beta_2 \cdot \mathbf{X}_2 + \cdots + \beta_k \cdot \mathbf{X}_k + \mathbf{u},$$

where $\mathbf{X}_1$ is a column of ones but is not considered as the intercept.

Example 2. *Now, we part from model 1 in the Belsley example but include the constant as an independent variable in a model without the intercept (**Mod4**) and two additional models (**Mod5** and **Mod6**):*

- Model 4 (**Mod4**): $\mathbf{y} = \beta_1 \cdot \mathbf{X}_1 + \beta_2 \cdot \mathbf{X}_2 + \beta_3 \cdot \mathbf{X}_3 + \mathbf{u}$.
- Model 5 (**Mod5**): $\mathbf{y} = \beta_1 \cdot \mathbf{X}_1 + \beta_2 \cdot \mathbf{X}_2 + \mathbf{u}$.
- Model 6 (**Mod6**): $\mathbf{y} = \beta_1 \cdot \mathbf{X}_1 + \beta_3 \cdot \mathbf{X}_3 + \mathbf{u}$.

Table 4 presents the VIFnc obtained from expression (5) in Models 4–6. Results indicate that, considering the centered model and calculating the coefficient of determination of the auxiliary regressions as if the model were noncentered, it is possible to detect the nonessential multicollinearity. Thus, the contradiction indicated at the beginning of this subsection is saved.

Table 4. VIFnc of Models 4–6 including the constant as an independent variable in a model without the intercept.

	X_1	X_2	X_3
Mod4	400,031.4	199,921.7	200,158.3
Mod5	199,921.7	199,921.7	
Mod6		200,158.3	200,158.3

3. Effects of the Vifnc on the Statistical Analysis of the Model

Given the model (1), the expression obtained for the variance of the estimator is given by:

$$var(\widehat{\beta}_j) = \frac{\sigma^2}{RSS_j}, \quad j = 1, \ldots, k, \tag{10}$$

where RSS_j is the residual sum of squares of the auxiliary regression of the $j-$independent variable as a function of the rest of the independent variables (see expression (6)).

From expression (10), and considering that expression (7) can be rewritten as:

$$VIFnc(j) = \frac{\mathbf{X}_j^t\mathbf{X}_j}{RSS_j},$$

it is possible to obtain:

$$var(\widehat{\beta}_j) = \frac{\sigma^2}{RSS_j} = \frac{\sigma^2}{\mathbf{X}_j^t\mathbf{X}_j} \cdot VIFnc(j), \quad j = 1, \ldots, k. \tag{11}$$

Establishing a model as a reference is required to conclude whether the variance has been inflated (see, for example, Cook [20]). Thus, if the variables in $\mathbf{X}$ are orthogonal, it is verified that $\mathbf{X}^t\mathbf{X} = diag(d_1, \ldots, d_k)$ where $d_j = \mathbf{X}_j^t\mathbf{X}_j$. In this case, $(\mathbf{X}^t\mathbf{X})^{-1} = diag(1/d_1, \ldots, 1/d_k)$, and consequently, the variance of the estimated coefficients in the hypothetical orthogonal case is given by the following expression:

$$var(\widehat{\beta}_{j,o}) = \frac{\sigma^2}{\mathbf{X}_j^t\mathbf{X}_j}, \quad j = 1, \ldots, k. \tag{12}$$

In this case:

$$\frac{var(\widehat{\beta}_j)}{var(\widehat{\beta}_{j,o})} = VIFnc(j), \quad j = 1, \ldots, k,$$

and it is then possible to state that the VIFnc is a factor that inflates the variance.

As consequence, high values of $VIFnc(j)$ imply high values of $var(\widehat{\beta}_j)$ and a tendency not to reject the null hypothesis in the individual significance test of model (1). Thus, the statistical analysis of the model will be affected.

Note from expression (11) that this negative effect can be offset by low values of the estimation of σ^2, that is, low values of the residual sum of squares of model (1) or high values of the number of observations, n. This is similar to what happen to the VIF (see O'Brien [7] for more details).

4. Auxiliary Centered Regressions

The use of the coefficient of determination of the auxiliary regression (6) where matrix $\mathbf{X}_{-j}$ contains a column of ones that represents the intercept is a very common approach to detect the linear relations between the independent variables of the model (1). This is motivated due to the higher relation between

X_j and the rest of the independent variables, that is, the higher the multicollinearity is, the higher the value of that coefficient of determination.

However, since the coefficient of determination ignores the role of the intercept, this measure is unable to detect the nonessential linear relations. The question is evident: Does another measure exist related to the auxiliary regression that allows detection of the nonessential multicollinearity?

4.1. Case When There Is Only Nonessential Multicollinearity

Example 3. *Suppose that 100 observations are simulated for variables* **X**, **Z** *and* **W** *from normal distributions with a mean of 5, 4 and -4 and a standard deviation of 0.01, 4 and 0.01, respectively. Note that* **X** *and* **W** *present light variability and, for this reason, it is expected that the model presents nonessential multicollinearity.*

Then, **y** $= 1 + $ **X** $+$ **Z** $-$ **W** $+$ **v** *is generated by simulating* **v** *as a normal distribution with a mean equal to 0 and a standard deviation equal to 2.*

The second column of Table 5 presents the results obtained after the estimation by ordinary least squares (OLS) of model **y** $= \beta_1 \cdot 1 + \beta_2 \cdot$ **X** $+ \beta_3 \cdot$ **Z** $+ \beta_4 \cdot$ **W** $+$ **u***. Note that the estimations of the coefficients of the model differ substantially from the real values used to generate* **y***, except for the coefficient of the variable* **Z** *(this situation illustrates the fact that if the interest is to estimate the effect of variable* **Z** *on* **y***, the analysis will not be influenced by the linear relations between the rest of the independent variables), which is the variable free of multicollinearity (indeed, it is the unique coefficient significantly different from zero, with a 5% significance—the value used by default in this paper).*

Table 5. Estimation by ordinary least squares (OLS) of the first simulated model and its corresponding auxiliary regressions (estimated standard deviation in parenthesis and coefficients significantly different from zero in bold).

Dependent Variable	$\widehat{y}$	$\widehat{X}$	$\widehat{Z}$	$\widehat{W}$
Intercept	173.135 (123.419)	**4.969** (0.369)	−27.63 (240.08)	**−3.953** (0.557)
X	−38.308 (20.035)		−17.05 (38.94)	−0.009 (0.111)
Z	0.939 (0.052)	−0.0001 (0.0002)		−0.0002 (0.0002)
W	−7.173 (18.2309)	−0.007 (0.092)	−29.34 (35.34)	
R^2	0.7773	0.001	0.008	0.007
VIF		1.001	1.008	1.007

This table also shows the results obtained from the estimations of the centered auxiliary regressions. Note that the coefficients of determination are very small, and consequently, the associated VIFs do not detect the degree of multicollinearity. However, note that in the auxiliary regressions corresponding to variables **X** *and* **W***:*

- *The estimation of the coefficient of the intercept almost coincides with the mean from which each variable was generated, 5 and −4, and, at the same time, the coefficients of the rest of the independent variables are almost zero.*
- *The estimations of the coefficients of the intercept are the unique ones that are significantly different from zero.*

Thus, note that the auxiliary regressions are capturing the existence of nonessential multicollinearity. The problem is that it is not transferred to its coefficient of determination but to another characteristic.

From this finding, it is possible to propose a way to detect the nonessential multicollinearity from the centered auxiliary regression traditionally applied to calculate the VIF:

Condition 1 (C1): Quantify the contribution of the estimation of the intercept to the total sum of the estimations of the coefficients of model (6), that is, calculate:

$$\frac{|\delta_1|}{\sum_{j=1}^{k-1} |\delta_j|} \cdot 100\%.$$

Condition 2 (C2): Calculate the number of independent variables with coefficients significantly different from zero and quantify the contribution of the intercept.

A Montecarlo simulation is presented considering the model (1) where $k = 3$ and the variable X_2 has been generated as a normal distribution with mean $\mu_2 \in \mathbf{A}$ and variance $\sigma_2^2 \in \mathbf{B}$, the variable X_3 has been generated as normal distribution with mean $\mu_3 \in \mathbf{A}$ and variance $\sigma_3^2 \in \mathbf{C}$ being $\mathbf{A} = \{0, 1, 2, 3, 4, 5, 10, 15, 20\}$, $\mathbf{B} = \{0.00001, 0.0001, 0.001, 0.1, \mathbf{C}\}$ and $\mathbf{C} = \{1, 2, 3, 4, 5, 10, 15, 20\}$. The results are presented in Table 6. Taking into account that the sample size has varied within the set $\{15, 20, 25, \ldots, 140, 145, 150\}$, 235872 iterations have been performed.

Table 6. Values of condition **C1** depending on the coefficient of variation (CV).

	P_5	P_{95}	Mean	Typical Deviation
$CV < 0.06674082$	99.402%	99.999%	99.512%	3.786%
$CV > 0.06674082$	52.678%	99.876%	89.941%	16.837%
$CV < 0.1002506$	95.485%	99.999%	98.741%	6.352%
$CV > 0.1002506$	51.434%	99.842%	89.462%	17.114%

Considering the thresholds established by Salmerón Gómez et al. [10], 90% of the simulations present values for condition **C1** between 99.402% and 99.999% if $CV < 0.06674082$ and between 95.485% and 99.999% if $CV < 0.1002506$. Thus, we can consider that values of condition **C1** higher than 95.485% will indicate that the auxiliary centered regressions are detecting the presence of nonessential multicollinearity.

Table 7 shows that a high value is obtained for the condition **C1**, even if any estimated coefficient is significantly different from zero (**C2** = NA).

Thus, the previous threshold, 95.485%, will be considered as valid if it is accompanied by a high value in the second condition.

Table 7. Values of condition **C1** depending on condition **C2**.

	C2	NA	50%	100%
	P_5	39.251%	67.861%	89.514%
C1	P_{95}	98.751%	99.984%	99.997%
	Mean	81.378%	91.524%	96.965%
	Typical Deviation	19.622%	13.598%	9.972%

Example 4. *Applying these criteria to the data of the Example 1 for **Mod1**, it is obtained that:*

- *In the auxiliary regression $X_2 = \delta_1 \cdot \mathbf{1} + \delta_3 \cdot X_3 + \mathbf{w}$, the estimation of the intercept is equal to 99.988% of the total, and the individual significance of the intercept corresponds to 100% of the significant estimated coefficients.*
- *In the auxiliary regression $X_3 = \delta_1 \cdot \mathbf{1} + \delta_2 \cdot X_2 + \mathbf{w}$, the estimation of the intercept is equal to 99.988% of the total, and the individual significance of the intercept corresponds to 100% of the significant estimated coefficients.*

Thus, the symptoms shown in the previous simulation also appear, and consequently, in both situations, the nonessential multicollinearity will be detected.

Replicating both situations where the VIFnc was not able to detect the nonessential multicollinearity, it is obtained that:

- For **Mod2** it is obtained that:

  - In the auxiliary regression $X_2 = \delta_1 \cdot 1 + \delta_4 \cdot X_4 + w$, the estimation of the intercept is equal to the 99.978% of the total, and the individual significance of the intercept corresponds to 100% of the significant estimated coefficients.
  - In the auxiliary regression $X_4 = \delta_1 \cdot 1 + \delta_2 \cdot X_2 + w$, the estimation of the intercept is equal to 50.138% of the total, and none of the estimated coefficients are significantly different from zero.

- For **Mod3** it is obtained that:

  - In the auxiliary regression $X_3 = \delta_1 \cdot 1 + \delta_4 \cdot X_4 + w$, the estimation of the intercept is equal to the 99.984% of the total, and the individual significance of the intercept corresponds to 100% of the significant estimated coefficients.
  - In the auxiliary regression $X_4 = \delta_1 \cdot 1 + \delta_3 \cdot X_3 + w$, the estimation of the intercept is equal to 50.187% of the total, and none of the estimated coefficients are significantly different from zero.

Once again, it was shown that with this procedure, it is possible to detect the nonessential multicollinearity and the variables that are causing it.

4.2. Relevance of a Variable in a Regression Model

Note that the conditions **C1** and **C2** are focused on measuring the relevance of one of the variables, in this case, the intercept, within the multiple linear regression model. It is interesting to analyze the behavior of other measures with this same goal as, for example, the index ι_j of Stewart [9]. Given model (1), Stewart defined the relevance of the j−variable as the number:

$$\iota_j = \frac{|\beta_j| \cdot ||X_j||}{||y||}, \quad j = 1, \ldots, p,$$

where $|| \cdot ||$ is the usual Euclidean norm. Stewart considered that a variable with a relevance higher than 0.5 should not be ignored.

Example 5. *Table 8 presents the calculation of ι_j for situations shown in Example 1. Note that in all cases, the intercept will be considered relevant, even when the variable X_4 is analyzed as a function of X_2 or X_3, despite that it was previously shown that the intercept was not relevant in these situations (at least in relation to nonessential multicollinearity).*

Table 8. Calculation of ι_j for situations **Mod1**, **Mod2** and **Mod3** shown in Example 1.

	Auxiliary Regression	ι_1	ι_2
Mod1	$X_2 = \delta_1 \cdot 1 + \delta_3 \cdot X_3 + w$	0.999	0.0001
	$X_3 = \delta_1 \cdot 1 + \delta_2 \cdot X_2 + w$	0.999	0.0001
Mod2	$X_2 = \delta_1 \cdot 1 + \delta_4 \cdot X_4 + w$	1.0006	0.001
	$X_4 = \delta_1 \cdot 1 + \delta_2 \cdot X_2 + w$	119.715	119.056
Mod3	$X_3 = \delta_1 \cdot 1 + \delta_4 \cdot X_4 + w$	1.0005	0.0007
	$X_4 = \delta_1 \cdot 1 + \delta_3 \cdot X_3 + w$	88.346	87.687

Thus, the application of ι_j seems not to be appropriate contrarily to what happens with conditions **C1** and **C2**.

4.3. Case When There Is Generalized Nonessential Multicollinearity

Example 6. *Suppose that the previous simulation is repeated, except for the generation of the variable Z, which, in this case, is considered to be given by $Z_i = 2 \cdot X_i - a_i$, for $i = 1, \ldots, 100$, where a_i is generated from a normal distribution with a mean equal to 2 and a standard deviation equal to 0.01.*

Table 9 presents the results of the estimation by OLS of the model $y = \beta_1 \cdot 1 + \beta_2 \cdot X + \beta_3 \cdot Z + \beta_4 \cdot W + u$ and its possible auxiliary regressions.

In this case, none of the coefficients are significantly different from zero and the coefficients are very far from the real values used in the simulation.

Table 9. Estimation by OLS of the second simulated model and its corresponding auxiliary regressions (estimated standard deviation in parenthesis and coefficients significantly different from zero in bold).

Dependent Variable	$\widehat{y}$	$\widehat{X}$	$\widehat{Z}$	$\widehat{W}$
Constant	−233.37 (167.33)	**1.977** (0.2203)	**−2.638** (0.673)	**−4.959** (0.715)
X	12.02 (56.98)		**2.213** (0.102)	−0.059 (0.298)
Z	8.89 (23.44)	**0.374** (0.017)		0.156 (0.121)
W	−29.96 (19.41)	−0.006 (0.034)	0.107 (0.107)	
R^2	0.034	0.838	0.841	0.073
VIF		6.172	6.289	1.078

In relation to the auxiliary regression, it is possible to conclude that:

- *When the dependent variable is **X**, the coefficients that are significantly different from zero are the ones of the intercept and the variable **Z**. At the same time, the estimation of the coefficient of the intercept differs from the mean from which the variable **X** was generated. In this case, the contribution of the estimation of the intercept is equal to 83.837% of the total and represents 50% of the coefficients significantly different from zero.*

- *When the dependent variable is **Z**, the coefficients significantly different from zero are the ones of the intercept and the variable **X**. In this case, the contribution of the estimation of the intercept is equal to 53.196% of the total and represents 50% of the coefficients significantly different from zero.*

- *When the dependent variable is **W**, the signs shown in the previous section are maintained. In this case, the contribution of the intercept is equal to 95.829% of the total and represents 100% of the coefficients significantly different from zero.*

- *Finally, although it will require a deeper analysis, the last results indicate that the estimated coefficient that is significantly different from zero in the auxiliary regression represents the variables responsible for the existing linear relation (intercept included).*

Note that the existence of generalized nonessential multicollinearity distorts the symptoms previously detected. Thus, the fact that in a centered auxiliary regression, the contribution (in absolute terms) of the estimation of the intercept to the total sum (in absolute value) of all estimations will be close to 100%, and the estimation of the intercept will be uniquely significantly different from zero, are indications of nonessential multicollinearity. However, it is possible that these symptoms are not manifested but there exists worrisome nonessential multicollinearity. Thus, these conditions are sufficient but not required.

However, in situations shown in Example 6 where conditions **C1** and **C2** are not verified, the VIFnc will be equal to 1109,259.3, 758,927.7 and 100,912.7. Thus, note that these results complement the results presented in the previous section in relation to the VIFnc. Thus, VIFnc detects generalized nonessential multicollinearity while conditions **C1** and **C2** detect the traditional nonessential multicollinearity given by Marquardt and Snee [6].

5. Empirical Applications

In order to illustrate the contribution of this study, this section presents two empirical applications with financial and economic real data. Note that in a financial prediction model, a financial variable with low variance means low risk and a better prediction, because the standard deviation and volatility are lower. However, as discussed above, a lower variance of the independent variable may mean greater nonessential multicollinearity in a GLR model. Thus, the existence of worrisome nonessential collinearity may be relatively common in financial econometric models and this idea can be extended in general to economic applications. Note that the objective is to diagnose the type of multicollinearity existing in the model and indicate the most appropriate treatment (without applying it).

5.1. Financial Empirical Application

The following model of Euribor (**100%**) is specified from the data set composed by 47 Eurozone observations for the period January 2002 to July 2013 (quarterly and seasonally adjusted data) and previously applied by Salmerón Gómez et al. [10]:

$$\textbf{Euribor} = \beta_1 + \beta_2 \cdot \textbf{HICP} + \beta_3 \cdot \textbf{BC} + \textbf{u}, \tag{13}$$

where **HICP** is the Harmonized Index of Consumer Prices (**100%**), **BC** is the Balance of Payments to net current account (millions of euros) and **u** is a random disturbance (centered, homoscedastic, and uncorrelated).

Table 10 presents the analysis of model (13) and its corresponding auxiliary regressions. The values of the VIFs which are very close to one will indicate that there is not essential multicollinearity. The correlation coefficient between **HICP** and **BC** is 0.231 and the determinant of the correlation matrix is 0.946. Both values indicate that there is no essential multicollinearity, see García García et al. [21] and Salmerón Gómez et al. [22].

However, the condition number is higher than 30 indicating a strong multicollinearity associated, see conditions **C1** and **C2**, with variable **HICP**. The values of conditions **C1** and **C2** are conclusive in the case of variable **HICP**. In the case of variable **BC**, although condition **C1** presents a high value, none of the coefficients of the auxiliary regression is significatively different from zero (condition **C2**). By following the simulation presented in subsection, this indicate that the variable **BC** is not related to the intercept. This conclusion is in line with the value of the coefficient of variation of variable **HICP** that is lower than 0.1002506, the threshold established by Salmerón Gómez et al. [10] for moderate nonessential multicollinearity.

Table 11 presents the calculation of the VIFnc. Note that it is not detecting the non-essential multicollinearity. As previously commented, the VIFnc only detects the essential and the generalized nonessential multicollinearity. This table also presents the VIFnc calculated in a model without intercept but including the constant as an independent variable (see Section 2.3). In this case, the VIFnc is able to detect the nonessential multicollinearity between the intercept and the variable **HIPC**.

In conclusion, this model will present nonessential multicollinearity caused by the variable **HICP**. This problem can be mitigated by centering that variable (see, for example, Marquardt and Snee [6] and Salmerón Gómez et al. [10]).

Table 10. Estimations by OLS of model (13) and its corresponding auxiliary regressions (estimated standard deviation in parenthesis and coefficients significantly different from zero in bold).

	Euribor	HICP	BC
Intercept	**8.442**	**104.8**	−64,955
	(1.963)	(1.09)	(43,868)
HICP	**−0.054**		663.3
	(0.018)		(415.9)
BC	**−3.493 × 10^{-5}**	8.065 × 10^{-5}	
	(6.513 × 10^{-6})	(5.057 × 10^{-5})	
R^2	0.517	0.053	0.053
VIF		1.055	1.055
CN	30.246		
Condition 1 (**C1**)		99.999%	98.98%
Condition 2 (**C2**)		100%	NA
Coefficients of variation		0.069	4.3403

Table 11. VIFnc of auxiliary regressions associated to model (13).

	X_1	HICP	BC
VIFnc		1.0609	1.0609
VIFnc	217.672	219.291	1.112

5.2. Economic Empirical Application

From French economy data from Chatterjee and Hadi [23], also analyzed by Malinvaud [24], Zhang and Liu [25] and Kibria and Lukman [26], among others, the following model is analyzed:

$$\mathbf{I} = \beta_1 + \beta_2 \cdot \mathbf{DP} + \beta_3 \cdot \mathbf{SF} + \beta_4 \cdot \mathbf{DC} + \mathbf{u}, \tag{14}$$

for years 1949 through 1966 where imports (**I**), domestic production (**DP**), stock formation (**SF**) and domestic consumption (**DC**), all are measured in billions of French francs and **u** is a random disturbance (centered, homoscedastic, and uncorrelated).

Table 12 presents the analysis of model (14) and its corresponding auxiliary regressions. The values of the VIFs of variables **DP** and **DC** indicate strong essential multicollinearity. The condition number is higher than 30 also indicating a strong multicollinearity.

Note that the values of condition **C1** for variables **DP** and **DC** are lower than threshold shown in the simulation. Only the variable **SF** presents a higher value but, in this case, condition **C2** indicates that none of the estimated coefficients of the auxiliary regression are significatively different from zero. This conclusion is in line with the coefficients of variation that are higher than the threshold established by Salmerón Gómez et al. [10] indicating that there is no nonessential multicollinearity.

Table 13 presents the calculation of the VIFnc. Note that it is detecting the essential multicollinearity. This table also presents the VIFnc calculated in a model without intercept but including the constant as an independent variable. In this case, the VIFnc is also detecting the essential multicollinearity between the variables **DP** and **DC**. From thresholds established by Salmerón Gómez et al. [10] for simple linear regression ($k = 2$), the value 60.0706 will not be worrisome and, consequently, the nonessential multicollinearity will not be worrisome.

Table 12. Estimations by OLS of Model (14) and its corresponding auxiliary regressions (estimated standard deviation in parenthesis and coefficients significantly different from zero in bold).

	I	DP	SF	DC
Intercept	**−19.725**	−18.052	2.635	**12.141**
	(4.125)	(3.28)	(3.234)	(2.026)
DP	0.032		0.025	**0.654**
	(0.186)		(0.149)	(0.007)
SF	0.414	0.075		−0.038
	(0.322)	(0.444)		(0.291)
DC	0.242	**1.525**	−0.029	
	(0.285)	(0.018)	(0.228)	
R^2	0.973	0.997	0.047	0.997
VIF		333.333	1.049	333.333
CN	247.331			
Condition 1 (**C1**)		91.85%	97.94%	94.6%
Condition 2 (**C2**)		50%	NA	50%
Coefficients of variation		0.267	0.473	0.248

Table 13. VIFnc of auxiliary regressions associated to Model (14).

	X_1	DP	SF	DC
VIFnc		2457.002	5.753	2512.562
VIFnc	60.0706	7424.705	6.008	8522.1308

To conclude, this model presents essential multicollinearity caused by the variables **DP** and **DC**. In this case, the problem will be mitigated by applying estimation methods other than OLS such as ridge regression (see, for example, Hoerl and Kennard [27], Hoerl et al. [28], Marquardt [29]), LASSO regression (see Tibshirani [30]), raise regression (see, for example, García et al. [31], Salmerón et al. [32], García and Ramírez [33], Salmerón et al. [34]), residualization (see, for example, York [35], García et al. [36]) or the elastic net regularization (see Zou and Hastie [37]).

6. Conclusions

The distinction between essential and nonessential multicollinearity and its diagnosis has not been not been adequately treated in either the scientific literature or in statistical software and this lack of information has led to mistakes in some relevant papers, for example Velilla [3] or Jensen and Ramirez [13]. This paper analyzes the detection of essential and nonessential multicollinearity from auxiliary centered and noncentered regressions, obtaining two complementary measures between them that are able to detect both kinds of multicollinearity. The relevance of the results is that they are obtained within an econometric context, encompassing the distinction between centered and noncentered models that is not only accomplished from a numerical perspective, as was the case presented, for example, in Salmerón Gómez et al. [12] or Salmerón Gómez et al. [10]. An undoubtedly interesting point of view of this situation is the one presented by Spanos [38] that stated: It is argued that many confusions in the collinearity literature arise from erroneously attributing symptoms of statistical misspecification to the presence of collinearity when the latter is misdiagnosed using unreliable statistical measures. That is, the distinction related to the econometric model provides confidence to the measures of detection and avoids the problems commented by Spanos.

From a computational point of view, this debate clarifies what is calculated when the VIF is obtained for centered and noncentered models. It also clarifies, see Section 2.3, what type of multicollinearity is detected (and why) when the uncentered VIF is calculated in a centered model. At the same time, a definition of nonessential multicollinearity is presented that generalizes the definition given by Marquardt and Snee [6]. Note that this generalization can be understood as a particular kind of essential multicollinearity:

A near-linear relation between two independent variables with light variability. However, it is shown that this kind of multicollinearity is not detected by the VIF, and for this reason, we consider it more appropriate to include it within the nonessential multicollinearity.

In relation to the application of the VIFnc, this paper shows that the VIFnc detects the essential and the generalized nonessential multicollinearity and even the traditional nonessential multicollinearity if it is calculated in a regression without the intercept but including the constant as an independent variable. Note that the VIF, although widely applied in many different fields, only detects the essential multicollinearity. This paper has also analyzed why the VIF is unable to detect the nonessential multicollinearity, and two conditions are presented as sufficient (but not required) to establish the existence of nonessential multicollinearity. Since these conditions, **C1** and **C2**, are based on the relevance of the intercept within the centered auxiliary regression to calculate the VIF, this scenario was compared to the measure proposed by Stewart [9], ι_j, to measure the relative importance of a variable within a multiple linear regression. It is shown that conditions **C1** and **C2** are preferable to the calculation of ι_j.

To summarize:

- A centered model can present essential, generalized nonessential and traditional nonessential collinearity (given by Marquardt and Snee [6]) while in a noncentered model only it is only possible to find the essential and the generalized nonessential collinearity.

- The VIF only detects the essential collinearity, the VIFnc detects the generalized nonessential and essential collinearity and the conditions **C1** and **C2** the traditional nonessential collinearity.

- When there is generalized nonessential collinearity it is understood that there is also traditional nonessential collinearity, but this is not detected by the conditions **C1** and **C2**. Thus, in this case it is necessary to use other alternative measures as the coefficient of variation of the condition number.

To conclude, in order to detect the kind of multicollinearity and its degree, the greatest number of measures must be used (variance inflation factors, condition number, correlation matrix and its determinant, coefficient of variation, conditions **C1** and **C2**, etc.) as in Section 5, and it is inefficient to limit oneself to the management of only a few. Similarly, it is necessary to know what kind of multicollinearity is capable of detecting each one of them.

Finally, the following will be interesting as future lines of inquiry:

- to establish the threshold for the VIFnc,
- to extend the Montecarlo simulation of Section 4.1 for models with $k > 3$ regressors,
- a deeper analysis to conclude if the variable responsible for the existing linear relation can be identified as the one whose estimated coefficient is significantly different from zero in the auxiliary regression (see Example 6) and
- the development of a specific package in R Core Team [39] to perform the calculation of VIFnc and conditions **C1** and **C2**.

Author Contributions: Conceptualization, R.S.G. and C.G.G.; methodology, R.S.G.; software, R.S.G.; validation, R.S.G., C.G.G. and J.G.P.; formal analysis, R.S.G. and C.G.G.; investigation, R.S.G., C.G.G. and J.G.P.; resources, R.S.G., C.G.G. and J.G.P.; writing—original draft preparation, R.S.G. and C.G.G. ; writing—review and editing, R.S.G. and C.G.G.; supervision, J.G.P.; project administration, R.S.G.; funding acquisition, J.G.P. All authors have read and agreed to the published version of the manuscript.

References

1. Belsley, D.A. Demeaning conditioning diagnostics through centering. *Am. Stat.* **1984**, *38*, 73–77.
2. Marquardt, D.W. A critique of some ridge regression methods: Comment. *J. Am. Stat. Assoc.* **1980**, *75*, 87–91. [CrossRef]
3. Velilla, S. A note on collinearity diagnostics and centering. *Am. Stat.* **2018**, *72*, 140–146. [CrossRef]

4.   Cohen, P.; West, S.G.; Aiken, L.S. *Applied Multiple Regression/Correlation Analysis for the Behavioral Sciences*; Psychology Press: London, UK, 2014.

5.   Marquardt, D. You should standardize the predictor variables in your regression models. Discussion of: A critique of some ridge regression methods. *J. Am. Stat. Assoc.* **1980**, *75*, 87–91.

6.   Marquardt, D.W.; Snee, R.D. Ridge regression in practice. *Am. Stat.* **1975**, *29*, 3–20.

7.   O'Brien, R. A caution regarding rules of thumb for variance inflation factors. *Qual. Quant.* **2007**, *41*, 673–690. [CrossRef]

8.   Salmerón, R.; García, C.; García, J. Variance Inflation Factor and Condition Number in multiple linear regression. *J. Stat. Comput. Simul.* **2018**, *88*, 2365–2384. [CrossRef]

9.   Stewart, G. Collinearity and least squares regression. *Stat. Sci.* **1987**, *2*, 68–84. [CrossRef]

10. Salmerón Gómez, R.; Rodríguez, A.; García García, C. Diagnosis and quantification of the non-essential collinearity. *Comput. Stat.* **2020**, *35*, 647–666. [CrossRef]

11. Marquardt, D.W. [Collinearity and Least Squares Regression]: Comment. *Stat. Sci.* **1987**, *2*, 84–85. [CrossRef]

12. Salmerón Gómez, R.; García García, C.; García Pérez, J. Comment on A Note on Collinearity Diagnostics and Centering by Velilla (2018). *Am. Stat.* **2019**, 114–117. [CrossRef]

13. Jensen, D.R.; Ramirez, D.E. Revision: Variance inflation in regression. *Adv. Decis. Sci.* **2013**, *2013*, 671204. [CrossRef]

14. Grob, J. *Linear Regression*; Springer: Berlin, Germany, 2003.

15. Cook, R. Variance Inflations Factors. *R News Newsl. R Proj.* **2003**, *3*, 13–15.

16. Belsley, D.A. A guide to using the collinearity diagnostics. *Comput. Sci. Econ. Manag.* **1991**, *4*, 33–50.

17. Chennamaneni, P.R.; Echambadi, R.; Hess, J.D.; Syam, N. Diagnosing harmful collinearity in moderated regressions: A roadmap. *Int. J. Res. Mark.* **2016**, *33*, 172–182. [CrossRef]

18. Belsley, D.A.; Kuh, E.; Welsch, R.E. *Regression Diagnostics: Identifying Influential Data and Sources of Collinearity*; Wiley: New York, NY, USA, 1980.

19. Theil, H. *Principles of Econometrics*; Wiley: New York, NY, USA, 1971; Volume 4.

20. Cook, R. [Demeaning Conditioning Diagnostics through Centering]: Comment. *Am. Stat.* **1984**, *38*, 78–79. [CrossRef]

21. García García, C.; Salmerón Gómez, R.; García García, C. Choice of the ridge factor from the correlation matrix determinant. *J. Stat. Comput. Simul.* **2019**, *89*, 211–231. [CrossRef]

22. Salmerón Gómez, R.; García García, C.; García García, J. A Guide to Using the R Package "multiColl" for Detecting Multicollinearity. *Comput. Econ.* **2020**. [CrossRef]

23. Chatterjee, S.; Hadi, A.S. *Regression Analysis by Example*; John Wiley & Sons: Hoboken, NY, USA, 2015.

24. Malinvaud, E. *Statistical Methods of Econometrics*; North Holland: New York, NY, USA, 1980.

25. Zhang, W.; Liu, L. A New Class of Biased Estimate in the Linear Regression Model. *J. Wuhan Univ. Nat. Sci. Ed.* **2006**, *52*, 281.

26. Kibria, B.; Lukman, A.F. A New Ridge-Type Estimator for the Linear Regression Model: Simulations and Applications. *Scientifica* **2020**, *2020*, 9758378 . [CrossRef]

27. Hoerl, A.E.; Kennard, R.W. Ridge regression: Biased estimation for nonorthogonal problems. *Technometrics* **1970**, *12*, 55–67. [CrossRef]

28. Hoerl, A.; Kannard, R.; Baldwin, K. Ridge regression: Some simulations. *Commun. Stat. Theory Methods* **1975**, *4*, 105–123. [CrossRef]

29. Marquardt, D. Generalized inverses, ridge regression, biased linear estimation, and nonlinear estimation. *Technometrics* **1970**, *12*, 591–612. [CrossRef]

30. Tibshirani, R. Regression shrinkage and selection via the lasso. *J. R. Stat. Soc. Ser. B (Methodol.)* **1996**, *58*, 267–288. [CrossRef]

31. García, C.G.; Pérez, J.G.; Liria, J.S. The raise method. An alternative procedure to estimate the parameters in presence of collinearity. *Qual. Quant.* **2011**, *45*, 403–423. [CrossRef]

32. Salmerón, R.; García, C.; García, J.; López, M.d.M. The raise estimator estimation, inference, and properties. *Commun. Stat. Theory Methods* **2017**, *46*, 6446–6462. [CrossRef]

33. García, J.; Ramírez, D. The successive raising estimator and its relation with the ridge estimator. *Commun. Stat. Theory Methods* **2017**, *46*, 11123–11142. [CrossRef]

34. Salmerón, R.; Rodríguez, A.; García, C.; García, J. The VIF and MSE in Raise Regression. *Mathematics* **2020**, *8*, 605. [CrossRef]

35. York, R. Residualization is not the answer: Rethinking how to address multicollinearity. *Soc. Sci. Res.* **2012**, *41*, 1379–1386. [CrossRef]

36. García, C.; Salmerón, R.; García, C.; García, J. Residualization: Justification, properties and application. *J. Appl. Stat.* **2017**. [CrossRef]

37. Zou, H.; Hastie, T. Regularization and variable selection via the elastic net. *J. R. Stat. Soc. Ser. B (Stat. Methodol.)* **2005**, *67*, 301–320. [CrossRef]

38. Spanos, A. Near-collinearity in linear regression revisited: The numerical vs. the statistical perspective. *Commun. Stat. Theory Methods* **2019**, 48, 5492–5516. [CrossRef]

39. R Core Team. *R: A Language and Environment for Statistical Computing*; R Foundation for Statistical Computing: Vienna, Austria, 2019.

7

Do Trade and Investment Agreements Promote Foreign Direct Investment within Latin America? Evidence from a Structural Gravity Model

Marta Bengoa [1,2,*], Blanca Sanchez-Robles [3] and Yochanan Shachmurove [4,5]

[1] Colin Powell School, City University of New York (CUNY-CCNY), New York, NY 10031, USA
[2] SARChI College of Business and Economics, University of Johannesburg South Africa, Senior Fellow at CIRANO, Montreal, QC H2Y1C6, Canada
[3] Department of Economic Analysis at UNED University, 28040 Madrid, Spain; bsanchez-robles@cee.uned.es
[4] The City College and Graduate Center of the City University of New York (CUNY-CCNY), New York, NY 10031, USA; yshachmurove@ccny.cuny.edu
[5] Faculty of Management at The University of Warsaw, 00-927 Warsaw, Poland
*   Correspondence: mbengoa@ccny.cuny.edu

Abstract: Latin America has experienced a surge in foreign direct investment (FDI) in the last two decades, in parallel with the ratification of major regional trade agreements (RTAs) and bilateral investment treaties (BITs). This paper uses the latest developments in the structural gravity model theory to study if the co-existence of BITs and two major regional agreements, Mercosur and the Latin American Integration Association (ALADI), exerts enhancing or overlapping effects on FDI for eleven countries in Latin America over the period 1995–2018. The study is novel as it accounts for variations in the degree of investment protection across BITs within Latin America by computing a quality index of BITs. It also explores the nature of interactions (enhancing/overlapping effects) between RTAs and BITs. The findings reveal that belonging to a well-established regional trade agreement, such as Mercosur, is significantly more effective than BITs in fostering intra-regional FDI. Phasing-in effects are large and significant and there is evidence of enhancing effects. Results within the bloc are heterogeneous: BITs exert a positive, but small effect, for middle income countries. However, BITs are not effective in attracting FDI in the case of middle to low income countries, unless these countries ratify BITs with a high degree of investment protection.

Keywords: foreign direct investment; bilateral investment treaties; regional trade agreements; structural gravity model

1. Introduction

Foreign Direct Investment (FDI) into and across Latin America has experienced a dynamic performance in the last few decades. In parallel, many countries in the area have taken part in regional trade agreements (RTAs) and bilateral investment treaties (BITs). RTAs foster trade by facilitating access to foreign markets. Sometimes they contain provisions about FDI which enhance these flows. BITs specify conditions under which foreign investment operates in the host country. This paper addresses the following questions: What is the relative importance of RTAs versus BITs as a way of attracting FDI? Do effects differ depending on the nature of the BITs and the presence of other agreements? Do they complement or substitute for economic and political institutions? There is substantial controversy in the empirical literature about these matters.

Some contributions have argued that host countries should exhibit a certain minimum level of income or other forms of social capacity in order to profit from FDI [1,2]. Nevertheless, it is frequent for developing countries to lack, at least partially, the necessary environment (human capital, rule of law, institutions, etc.) for efficient activity of multinational enterprises (MNEs). This raises the question of whether the impact of RTAs and BITs on FDI might be contingent on the institutional framework of the host country.

Specifically, this paper addresses three questions:

(i)   What is the impact of regional agreements and BITs on intraregional FDI in Latin America? In particular, the paper focuses on the FDI creation and diversion effects of the two main RTAs in the region, Mercosur (Southern Common Market) and ALADI (The Latin American Integration Association).   The study explores the relative effectiveness—interaction and complementarity—of trade and investment treaties regarding their impact on FDI.

(ii) Do the qualitative aspects of BITs, as measured by a new index, matter for their efficacy?

(iii) Do the specific institutional characteristics of recipient countries determine or condition the effectiveness of major RTAs and BITs?

The framework of a structural gravity model for FDI is used for this purpose (see [3], for a thorough exposition). The structural gravity model in economics, inspired by its physic counterpart, has recently acquired popularity as an appropriate tool for analyzing international trade and investment. According to this model, bilateral flows/stocks among countries are directly related to their sizes (usually captured by their Gross Domestic Product or GDPs) and inversely related to the distance between them. This framework combines an intuitive appeal, which can be rigorously founded on theoretical propositions, with strong predicting capabilities.

The study constructs a panel data detailing intra-regional bilateral FDI stocks among eleven Latin American countries over the period 1995–2018. It takes into account BITs' quality in terms of the degree of investment protection they warrant, cross-country differences in endowments, and level of developed institutions. The paper employs the Poisson pseudo-maximum likelihood estimator (PPML), as recommended by [4]. It addresses the potential endogeneity derived from the establishment of RTAs and BITs as well as the robustness of the results to alternative estimations. The main findings suggest that Mercosur exerts a larger impact than either ALADI or the presence of BITs on intra-bloc foreign direct investment. This is also true when controlling for investment protection strength. However, BITs are effective in fostering intra-regional FDI in Latin America when there is a sizeable degree of institutional development in the host country or a high degree of investment protection entailed by the treaty. Furthermore, the interaction of Mercosur, ALADI and BITs positively impacts FDI. The effects of BITs are larger for middle income than in low-middle income economies. The results are consistent with those obtained for other areas of the world [5–7].

This paper focuses on Latin America since the subcontinent is composed of developing and middle-income countries, whose population have the potential to substantially improve their living conditions. Therefore, it is of the utmost importance from a development viewpoint. Furthermore, the area is in the midst of undergoing an active and complex integration process, in which countries have engaged historically in different, often conflicting, approaches to trade liberalization and FDI. In addition, the empirical literature exploring FDI in the area is scarce as well as reaching ambiguous results. More generally, South-South empirical studies of the impact of RTAs and BITs on FDI for developing countries are still sparse. Finally, the area comprises countries which exhibit a substantial degree of heterogeneity, while sharing common aspects. It is, therefore, an appropriate sample for an empirical investigation.

This paper lies at the intersection of several strands of the literature. On one hand, it is closely related to contributions exploring FDI from a theoretical and empirical viewpoint [8–11]. On the other hand, it builds upon analyses conducted within the structural gravity model see [3,12–15]. Additionally, it is similar in spirit to papers which examine the impact of BITs on FDI [7,16–18]. Finally, Dixon and Haslam's work [17] analyze the impact of BITs on FDI in several samples, one of them of intraregional Latin American flows. Their results for this subsample are somewhat puzzling, since they suggest that the interaction of weak BITs and RTAs has a negative impact on FDI for this area. This study extends and complements these previous studies.

This paper contributes to the literature in four dimensions. First, and in terms of methodology, we work with a fully specified structural gravity model expressly accounting for multilateral resistance terms among countries. Second, and as a consequence of methodological differences, the results are more in accordance with the underlying theoretical framework than other contributions, and very robust to alternative specifications. Third, the study accounts for variations in the quality of BITs through computing a quality index. Refs [7,18] analyze the effects of BITs by means of an index capturing dispute settlement mechanisms. This study extends and complements these analyses by designing a more thorough index of BITs, encompassing a wider set of BIT clauses potentially important for investors. The samples are also different, since they work with a large number of developed and developing countries, while the focus of this study is Latin America. Additionally, this paper explores the possibility of enhancing or overlapping effects when there are major RTAs in place coexisting with BITs. Finally, the analysis here covers the largest temporal horizon possible by working with bilateral data over 1995–2018.

In particular, the paper suggests that the interaction of Mercosur and BITs has a positive and significant impact on FDI whereas the combination of ALADI and BITs also displays a positive effect, although smaller in size and less significant. The study also explores the heterogeneity within the country sample according to their income levels.

The structure of the paper is as follows: Section 2 provides insights about the main RTAs and BITs in Latin America and discusses the links between RTAs, BITs, and foreign direct investment, summarizing the relevant literature. Section 3 describes the theoretical model that underlies our empirical work. Section 4 presents the data and develops the empirical methodology. Section 5, presents the results. Section 6 concludes.

2. An Overview of Integration Agreements in Latin America and the Links between RTAs, BITs and FDI

Mercosur was signed in 1991 by Argentina, Brazil, Paraguay and Uruguay. Mercosur was designed to be a customs union, with a free intra-zone trade and a common trade policy. Bolivia entered in 2006 but has not been recognized as a full member by the other members. Venezuela joined in 2015 and has since been suspended from the Treaty. Chile, Colombia, Ecuador, Peru, Guyana and Suriname are associated members. Mexico signed a deep FTA in 2006 and it has the status of observer. Members started to lower their tariffs in 1991 and the tariff schedule varies in the range 0%–20%. Approximately 90% of trade was liberalized by 1997. Mercosur included protocols for BIT protection and investor-state dispute settlement (ISDS) mechanisms; however, they have never been enforced. Mercosur engaged in negotiations with other Latin American countries to establish free trade agreements (FTAs). The FTAs provide substantial levels of integration between Mercosur and third countries, named associated members. The associated members are Chile, Colombia, Ecuador, Peru, Guyana, and Suriname. FTAs aimed to reduce tariffs to the same levels as Mercosur and diminish non-tariff barriers, facilitating trade and investment. The online Appendix A exhibits the sequence of the signatories of the FTAs.

The Latin America Free Trade Association was created in 1962 as the first component of an intended large integration project. It was superseded by ALADI in 1980. ALADI provides a general framework which intends to foster integration in the region and guarantee its economic and social development. It is not a deep integration mechanism per se. From that starting point, individual countries have strengthened their integration process by gradually engaging in bilateral or multilateral treaties with other ALADI members. De facto, ALADI now encompasses various free trade agreements within its framework. Not all countries within ALADI have yet established substantial/deep trade agreements among themselves. The countries under the ALADI umbrella are: Argentina, Bolivia,

Brazil, Chile, Colombia, Cuba, Ecuador, Mexico, Paraguay, Panama, Peru, Uruguay, and Venezuela. Hence the gradual integration that ALADI envisaged is still in process. Table A1 of the online Appendix A summarizes the pairs of countries, under the general ALADI scheme, involved over time in FTA agreements.

Latin American countries have signed an increasing number of BITs between 1995 and 2007, although the attitude of countries towards these agreements is not uniform. Chile has been very active and takes part in seven BITs, which include clauses with a high degree of protection to foreign investors. Colombia and Mexico, instead, have only signed one and two BITs respectively, with a lower degree of investment protection. During our period of analysis Brazil has not ratified any BIT, but since 2015 the country has negotiated, but not concluded, BITs with Mexico, Chile, Colombia and Peru (for a more detailed account see the United Nations Commission for Trade and Development (UNCTAD), 2017). Table A2 of the online Appendix A offers the list of BITs and their dates of entry into force.

2.1. The Relationship between Regional Trade Agreements and Foreign Direct Investment

The literature has traditionally focused on the distinction between horizontal and vertical types of foreign investment. Horizontal (or proximity concentration) FDI undertakes all production in the country whose market it intends to serve, thus substituting trade between the parent firm and affiliates Refs [8,19]. High trade barriers incentivize the setup of proximity-concentration FDI and therefore RTAs do not necessarily impact horizontal FDI positively [10].

Vertical FDI, instead, carries out each step of the production process in a different location, in order to minimize costs through scale economies and/or benefit from the low cost of inputs [20]. This implies an active exchange of intermediate and final goods between parents and affiliates. Vertical MNEs benefit from the trade liberalization which an agreement entails; hence RTAs exert a positive impact on vertical FDI.

On the other hand, US multinationals abroad seem to be organized in a horizontal pattern, although frequently MNE parent firms own vertically linked affiliates [11]. The combination between horizontal and vertical features follows what has been named a hybrid-knowledge capital model [9]. A particular case is the export-platform strategy [21]: companies set up a plant in a country belonging to a trade bloc in order to improve their access to other markets in the bloc. In these instances, net effects of trade integration are more nuanced and non-predictable a priori, since they depend on the relative importance and complex relationships between horizontal and vertical integration patterns within the firms.

Additionally, RTAs may also alter the macroeconomic environment where firms operate by strengthening fiscal discipline, macroeconomic stability and the rule of law in the host country [22–24]. Therefore, they might provide a more favourable setting to attract FDI.

Since the net impact of RTAs on aggregate FDI is a priori ambiguous, due to the intertwining of different forces described previously, the connection between RTAs and FDI is an empirical issue. Related evidence is not unanimous, though. A number of contributions report a positive impact of RTAs on FDI. With respect to the case of Mexico and NAFTA, ref [24] find a non-significant effect. For the European Union [25] documents a similar result (although the effect gradually decays). Ref [13] asserts that trade liberalization favoured the relocation of FDI from West to East Europe in the 90s, partly based upon export platform motives. Finally, these studies document a positive impact of trade agreements on FDI for a sample of OECD and non-OECD countries (see [10,26]).

In the case of the Canada–US Free Trade Agreement (CUSFTA) on FDI flows [24], no significant effect was found. For Latin America, Ref [22] identify pro-market and stable macroeconomic policies as the main factors attracting FDI, but an important role for Mercosur was not found. Finally, there are contributions suggesting that the impact of RTAs on FDI is contingent on other factors, such as skill differences in the home and host country [27], the institutional, financial, and macroeconomic framework of the host country [28], and the features of the agreement itself [16].

The lack of consensus in the literature might be due to the use of different identification strategies and econometric methods, such as the set of control variables included in the equations, the specification of fixed effects, and the estimation procedures. This paper contributes to shedding light on these issues.

2.2. Bilateral Investment Treaties and Foreign Direct Investment

The literature has identified three main theoretical reasons why BITs may impact FDI: they *signal* that signatory governments are willing to create an adequate institutional and economic environment for FDI [29,30]; they provide an *insurance* for foreign investors by establishing compensation schemes and conflict resolution procedures; they *deter* non-compliance because of the potential reputation costs for countries breaching the treaties [7]. When BITs are considered as signals, they may attract FDI from both partner and non-partner countries. If BITs are considered as insurers or deterrents, though, the attraction of FDI from partners will be higher than from non-partners, albeit both will be positive.

The first wave of empirical contributions about the impact of BITs on FDI addressed the link between the presence of a BIT and FDI, while more recent research focuses on the association between the nature of the BIT (as summarized by a set of characteristics) and the attraction of flows. In general, results from both cases are mixed. These studies [6,29,31–33] report a positive impact of investment treaties on FDI. In addition, Ref [12] found that the (positive) long-run effect of BITs on FDI is larger than the short-run impact because of phasing in effects. Following refs [30,33], BITs act as substitutes for weak legal and regulatory institutions in the host country.

Other studies, refs [34–37], instead, do not find a link between BITs and FDI. Tobin and Rose-Ackerman [38] suggest that BITs do not impact FDI when considered in isolation, but that they exert a positive effect when interacting with institutional or fundamental variables, thus concluding that BITs complement institutions in the host country.

The strand of the literature which deals with the nature of BITs is more recent in time and sparser. These contributions consider not only the number of BITs in place but also their key qualitative aspects. They usually work with bilateral data (as opposed to aggregate), which allows an investigation the link between a particular BIT signed by a pair of countries and the inflows between that same pair of countries.

A key feature of BITs is the treatment of dispute settlement procedures but results here are not uniform either. The impact of BITs on North-South and South-South FDI flows over the period 1990–2008 is the focus of the study by Dixon and Haslam [17]. They construct an index to capture more thoroughly the degree of FDI protection entailed by each BIT, including, but not restrained to, dispute settlement procedures (see their online Appendix A for classification). Their empirical results suggest that only treaties providing a strong degree of protection to investment impact FDI.

Frenkel and Walter's work [18] focuses on dispute settlement procedures. In the spirit of [17], they construct an indicator for each BIT by adding the assigned scores to various features. They show that the strength of the dispute settlement mechanisms is positively correlated with FDI. A recent study [7] concentrates on the effects of dispute settlement mechanisms on both partner and non-partner countries. They suggest that BITs have a positive impact on FDI from partner countries if a dispute with an investor has not affected the host country.

This paper builds partially on these contributions. Alternatively to the Dixon and Haslam study [17], it uses a gravity model with bilateral data which enables us to identify the impact of particular BITs on their own signatories. The analysis is not restricted uniquely to the quality of BITs dispute settlement mechanisms, as in previous studies [7,18].

It follows from the above that results regarding the connection between the existence and/or characteristics of BITs and FDI are mixed so far. As in the case of RTAs, some of the discrepancies may relate to econometric aspects such as the definition of the variable capturing the BITs, the strategy of controlling for endogeneity and phasing-in effects, the estimation techniques, and the use of aggregate versus bilateral data. Moreover, there is no consensus about the key characteristics of a BIT and how to measure them. Finally, it is not clear either if BITs have a differential impact in countries with weak versus strong institutions. On the one hand, they may substitute for institutions by giving credibility to governments, (as claimed by [30–33]). On the other, they act as complements since strong institutions lend support to treaties [38]. Ultimately, this is a multifaceted issue related to geography, the quality of institutions, the nature of the agreements, the rule of law, and other idiosyncratic aspects of the country itself.

3. Theoretical Framework: The Gravity Model for FDI

The gravity model has been extensively used to study international trade flows. Further theoretical and empirical advances allow its use as a framework to study FDI [39]. The gravity model is compatible with a theoretical model of heterogeneous multinational firms. Moreover, it conveniently allows us to capitalize on the rich information embedded in databases organized around dyads of countries (home/parent country origin of FDI flows and host/receptor of FDI flows); this feature is especially relevant for this paper because we study how RTAs and bilateral BITs signed across Latin American countries impact intra-bloc bilateral FDI.

In addition, the disaggregation by country pairs over time increases the number of observations available to explore the panel dimension. Finally, recent contributions have been actived in designing adequate techniques to circumvent econometric issues associated with the gravity equation, such as the inclusion of fixed effects [40], or the presence of many zeros in the data [4].

While the gravity equation for trade now has a solid theoretical background, the development of theoretical gravity FDI models is more recent. The Head and Ries' model [41] serves as baseline for this paper, but we consider technology as non-rival as in [9]. This analysis follows, as well, Anderson and Yotov's model [42] in developing an intuitive FDI gravity equation, similar to the structural gravity system for trade, which is possible to estimate directly.

The FDI structural system is also similar in spirit to the trade structural gravity model [43,44]. It departs from a definition of bilateral FDI:

$$FDI_{ij,t}^{stock} \equiv \omega_{ij,t}^{\varepsilon} M_{i,t} \tag{1}$$

where $FDI_{ij,t}$ represents FDI stocks between countries i and j at a time t, $M_{i,t}$ is the non-rival aggregate technology capital stock in a particular time, ω_{ijt} represents openness (or barriers to FDI) for foreign technology coming from country i to country j, and ε is the elasticity of FDI with respect to openness. To transform FDI stocks into values we multiply Equation (1) by its marginal product:

$$FDI_{ij,t}^{stock,value} \equiv \omega_{ij,t}^{\varepsilon} M_{i,t} \frac{\partial Y_{j,t}}{\partial M_{i,t}} \tag{2}$$

in which $M_i = \phi_i \frac{E_i}{P_i}$, where E_i represents total expenditures of country i which equal the country's output plus net rents from foreign investment, P_i stands for consumer prices (which can be considered as a multilateral resistance since higher prices for goods and inputs can affect FDI), and Y is nominal output. The production function is Cobb Douglas. Therefore $\frac{\partial Y_j}{\partial M_i} = \phi_j \frac{Y_j}{M_i}$; Y_j equals $Y_t = \sum_j Y_{j,t}$. Solving the representative agent's problem delivers a structural system for the steady-state. The gravity system of equations is given by:

$$FDI_{ij} = \phi_i \phi_j \omega_{ij}^{\varepsilon} \frac{E_i}{P_i} \frac{Y_j}{M_i} \tag{3}$$

$$P_i = \left[\sum_{j=1}^{N} \left(\frac{\tau_{ji}}{\Pi_j} \right)^{1-\sigma} \frac{Y_j}{Y} \right]^{\frac{1}{1-\sigma}}, \tag{4}$$

$$\Pi_j = \left[\sum_{i=1}^{N} \left(\frac{\tau_{ji}}{P_i} \right)^{1-\sigma} \frac{E_i}{Y} \right]^{\frac{1}{1-\sigma}}. \tag{5}$$

where P_i denotes the aggregate price index or the multilateral resistance, as defined in [43], and τ_{ji} represents standard iceberg trade costs. Equation (3) establishes that FDI between two countries depends positively on the home country size E_i and the size of the host economy Y_j. According to Equation (3), FDI depends negatively on FDI barriers $\phi_i\phi_j$. Higher multilateral resistances (MR) in the country of origin or higher opportunity cost of investing in technology should lead to lower FDI. ω_{ij} takes the form:

$$\omega_{ij,t} = d_{ij}^{\beta_1} \cdot \exp\left(\beta_2 X_{ij,t}\right) \tag{6}$$

where d_{ij} stands for the bilateral distance between the countries and $X_{ij,t}$ is a set of variables that capture both deterrents and incentives for FDI. This includes the variables Mercosur, ALADI, and BITs, as well as the BIT investment protection index (details are included below). The analysis adds control for other common institutional characteristics, differences in factor endowments, and labor costs. It also includes time-invariant covariates such as distance and adjacency. It is possible to transform Equation (3) into a baseline specification that includes time-varying bilateral determinants, factors that are specific to the country of origin or destination, and time-invariant variables affecting FDI:

$$X_{ij,t} = \sum_{h=1}^{H} \alpha_h Z_{i,t}^h + \sum_{r=1}^{R} \alpha_r Z_{j,t}^r + \sum_{m=1}^{M} \alpha_m Z_{ij}^m + \sum_{k=1}^{K} \alpha_k Z_{ij,t}^k + \varepsilon_{ij,t} \tag{7}$$

where $X_{ij,t}$ represents FDI stocks from country i to country j in year t, $Z_{i,t}$ is a set of H variables which are specific for the country I, $Z_{j,t}$ is a set of R variables specific for the country j, Z_{ij} stands for the M time invariant variables, $Z_{ij,t}$ is a set of K time-varying variables for both countries, and $\varepsilon_{ij,t}$ is the error component. The structure of fixed effects (FE) determines which variables could be included in the regression to avoid collinearity. There are N cross sections units observed for T periods (1995–2018). An estimation caveat in Equation (7) is that the MRs are not directly observable. The following section discusses this further.

4. Data and Empirical Strategy

4.1. Descriptive Analysis

This analysis focuses on a panel dataset of 11 Latin American countries over the period 1995–2018. The countries in our sample are: Argentina, Bolivia, Brazil, Chile, Colombia, Costa Rica, Ecuador, Mexico, Paraguay, Peru, and Uruguay. Data on FDI stocks come from the United Nations Commission for Trade and Development (UNCTAD). Our panel is organized in dyads of countries. If country i does not invest in country j in time t, the correspondent observation is zero. This structure entails that a number of observations are zero. The World Trade Organization (WTO) provides extensive data on RTAs, and BIT data comes from UNCTAD. The rest of the gravity variables come from CEPII (Centre d'Etudes Prospectives et d'Informations Internationals), Penn World Tables 8.0, World Bank, and UNCTAD (see Table A3 in the online Appendix A for definition of variables and sources). The countries in the sample account for more than 90% of GDP and FDI within the region.

Figure 1 compares the countries in our sample in terms of their FDI within Latin America. The main investor in the area is Chile, followed by Mexico, Brazil and Argentina, while the main recipients of FDI are Brazil, Argentina, and Chile. Economies with high GDP have greater capacity of attracting FDI, in accord with the gravity model.

Figure 2 displays a slight negative correlation between the total numbers of BITs in force in a country and the total FDI (R-square = 0.0987). This suggests that the link between FDI and number of BITs is more complex than expected. Therefore, the use of number of BITs per country to capture the relationship between BITs and FDI presents shortcomings and, as established in the literature review, might reflect only a signaling effect. In the empirical approach the focus turns to an analysis of the impact of a BIT signed by a pair of countries (instead of the total number of BITs a country has signed over the period) and the evolution of FDI among that pair over time. In this way it is possible to capture more thoroughly the effectiveness of establishing a particular BIT between two countries.

Do Trade and Investment Agreements Promote Foreign Direct Investment within Latin...

123

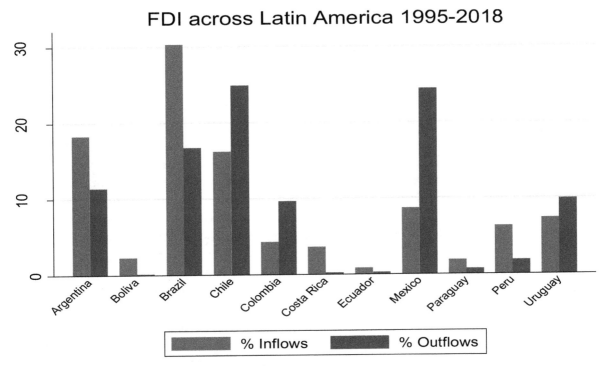

Figure 1. Intra-regional foreign direct investment (FDI) inflows/outflows in Latin America. Source: own elaboration. Vertical axis represents inflows/outflows by country over total FDI inflows/outflows in the area.

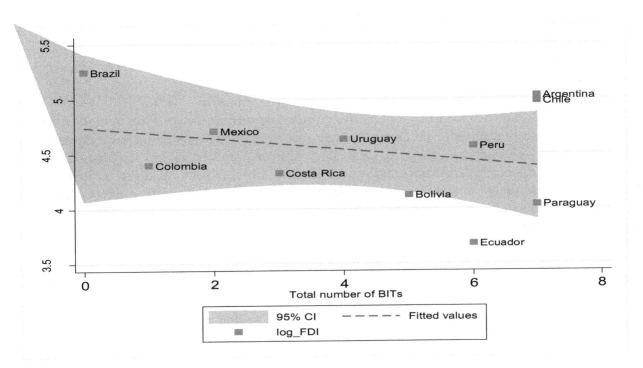

Figure 2. Intra-regional FDI vs number of bilateral investment treaties (BITs) in force (1995–2018). Source: Authors' calculations based on the United Nations Commission for Trade and Development (UNCTAD). Horizontal axis: total number of BITs in force in country j over the period 1995–2018. Vertical axis: sum of the stocks (constant dollars of 2012) received by each country j from the rest of countries in the sample.

The descriptive analysis offers some useful insights: it conveys the idea of differential patterns of intraregional FDI, a non-perfect matching between origin and destination countries across Latin America, and the need to control for size and other country characteristics.

4.2. Empirical Strategy: Estimation of the Gravity Equation for FDI

The general specification in Equation (7) raises the question about the appropriate estimation technique. One possible approach is to estimate the log-linearized gravity model by ordinary least squares (OLS). However, estimating using OLS presents several issues. First, the OLS estimation introduces bias associated with the presence of zero-FDI bilateral observations, due to the nonexistence of the natural log of zero. Therefore, estimating the model without taking into account zero observations generates biased estimated coefficients. Our FDI stock presents zeros since there are years and pair of countries that do not have FDI. Second, the log-linearization of the gravity equation changes the properties of the error term, leading to inefficient estimations in the presence of heteroscedasticity. FDI data are subject to heteroscedasticity, thus, estimating by OLS will give a log-linear residual that depends on the vector of covariates, generating inconsistent estimators.

Given the limitations that FDI presents regarding the existence of observations with zero values and the presence of heteroscedasticity, the seminal paper of Santos-Silva and Tenreyro [4] proposes to use the Poisson pseudo-maximum likelihood estimator (PPML). The PPML estimator circumvents the shortcomings of a linear model and estimates the gravity equation in its multiplicative form. Their study conveys that even when controlling for fixed effects, the presence of heteroscedasticity can generate strikingly different estimates when the gravity equation is log-linearized, rather than estimated in levels. The PPML is a special case of the Generalized Nonlinear Linear Model (GNLM) in which the variance is proportional to the mean. The authors show that this method is robust to different patterns of heteroscedasticity and resolves the inefficiency problem since it changes the distribution of the error term.

Despite the proven robustness of the PPML estimator, there are still some limitations, as heteroscedasticity might persist. The PPML estimator relies on the assumption that the variance is proportional to the mean ($\exp(x\beta)$), which may pose questions about its optimality. Additionally, PPML may present limited-dependent variable bias when a significant part of the observations is censored (which is not the case in this study).

Figure 3 sums up the main aspects of our empirical investigation.

Alternatively, and for robustness, in this study the structural gravity model is estimated using two alternative methods: Hausman-Taylor and the inverse hyperbolic sine transformation. The Hausman-Taylor method allows for the estimation of parameters of variables such as GDP, which vary only in a single dimension, and for the selection of variables considered endogenous in the model without uniquely controlling for heterogeneity by the structure of fixed effects. The inverse hyperbolic sine transformation is also adequate for estimating bilateral FDI across countries because its distribution is defined at zero.

To estimate the structural gravity model, the empirical analysis follows the methodology exposed in [3,40,45]. Therefore, this analysis includes fixed effects (FE), as opposed to random effects, since FE provide a better fit with samples encompassed by countries selected on a priori grounds [46]. It is also an appropriate technique to handle the unobservable heterogeneity potentially remaining among country pairs [47]. The variable BITs refers to those agreements that are in force, in line with the works of [13,23]. For the gravity variables, the study follows [39], who conclude that the variables more robustly correlated with FDI are the home and host country GDPs, RTAs, BITs, distance, and differences in endowments.

One of the problems when estimating Equation (7) is how to control for multilateral resistances. One natural way is to include fixed effects. Including time fixed effects and home and host fixed effects [45] is sufficiently adequate. Time fixed effects capture the business cycle, whereas country fixed effects control for all time invariant country characteristics. However, the omission of specific effects capturing the bilateral interaction between countries could bias the estimation [40]. It is proposed to complement the main effects (time, home country and host country) with interaction effects, defined for country pairs and characterized for being time invariant, together with other country specific characteristics such as distance, contiguity, or common language.

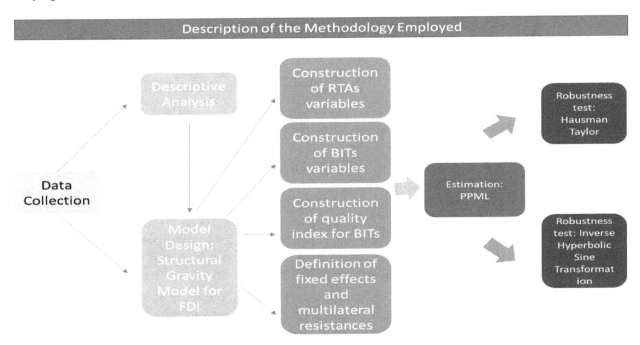

Figure 3. Empirical Model Description. Source: own elaboration. Notes: this figure displays some relevant features of our empirical investigation. Its starting point has been the collection of data from the sources detailed in Table A3. At first, descriptive analysis of the data has been carried out and discussed to inform the empirical model. The structural gravity model has been chosen as the most appropriate theoretical framework for the data. The next step has been the design and construction of different variables intended to capture the effects of regional trade agreements (RTAs) and BITs and the fixed effects. To design, code and compute these variables it was necessary to map all the agreements within Mercosur, The Latin American Integration Association (ALADI) and all the BITs, together with the design and computation of a quality index for BITs. The Poisson Pseudo-Likelihood Estimator (PPML) has been identified as the most convenient method of estimation for the model and it has been complemented with two additional robustness tests.

With respect to multilateral resistances, refs [3,48,49] suggest the inclusion of exporter time and importer time FE, taking into account that these will already capture the national output or expenditure of both countries.

In this setting, estimations may present endogeneity due to unobserved heterogeneity and reverse causality. The problem is tractable by alternative methods; this is how this study addresses this issue:

1. The analysis uses time invariant country pair fixed effects to correct for endogeneity due to unobserved heterogeneity in country pairs. In cross sections of country-pairs observed repeatedly over time, previous empirical studies suggest the inclusion of country-pair fixed effects in order to absorb the potential correlation between one or several regressors and the error term [13,47]. This way of controlling for country-pair and multilateral resistances with country-time fixed effects leads to estimates that can be interpreted as a difference-in-difference direct effect of the Mercosur, ALADI and BIT agreements on bilateral FDI.

2. If a group of countries interchange vast amounts of FDI, it is possible that they may be prompted to set up a RTA or a BIT. In this case, refs [3,47] recommend testing for endogeneity associated with reverse causation by including future leads of the RTA and BIT variables in the estimation. The empirical analysis also incorporates this approach in the estimations.

3.   Additionally, the Hausman-Taylor method is used to control for endogeneity. Thus, it explicitly considers the Mercosur, ALADI and BITs variables as endogenous. Previous studies [46,50–52] apply this methodology to gravity models.

Therefore, Equation (7) can be estimated by PPML as:

$$X_{ij,t} = exp\left[\sum_{h=1}^{H} \alpha_h Z_{i,t}^h + \sum_{r=1}^{R} \alpha_r Z_{j,t}^r + \sum_{m=1}^{M} \alpha_m Z_{ij}^m + \sum_{k=1}^{K} \alpha_k Z_{ij,t}^k + v_i + v_j + v_t\right] + \varepsilon_{ij,t} \quad (8)$$

$$X_{ij,t} = exp\left[\sum_{h=1}^{H} \alpha_h Z_{i,t}^h + \sum_{r=1}^{R} \alpha_r Z_{j,t}^r + \sum_{m=1}^{M} \alpha_m Z_{ij}^m + \sum_{k=1}^{K} \alpha_k Z_{ij,t}^k + v_{i,t} + v_{j,t} + v_{ij}\right] + \varepsilon_{ij,t} \quad (9)$$

The difference between Equations (8) and (9) lies in the structure of the fixed effects. The analysis accounts for MR in Equation (9) with origin country-time (annual) and destination country-time (annual) FE. When we use country-year FE, the variables which proxy for the size of the countries drop out from the equation to avoid collinearity. The same effect applies for time invariant variables that are collinear with the country-pair FE structure.

$X_{ij,t}$ is the bilateral FDI stock in year t from country i to country j. The set of H observable variables $Z_{i,t}^h$ includes gross domestic product (GDP) in origin, and political risk in origin (we use this as control variable). The set of R observable variables $Z_{j,t}^r$ includes GDP in the recipient country, the sum of the GDP of the countries linked to the recipient by a trade agreement, and the political risk index of the recipient. The set of M observable variables Z_{ij}^m includes distance between the two countries, and adjacency (if both countries share a common border). Finally, the set of K observable variables $Z_{ij,t}^k$ includes our variables of main interest, capturing RTAs, Mercosur and ALADI, bilateral investment agreements, diversion effects, factor endowment differentials and labor cost differentials for each dyad of countries. Factor endowment differentials are computed as $\left|ln\left(\frac{K_{i,t}}{L_{i,t}}\right) - ln\left(\frac{K_{j,t}}{L_{j,t}}\right)\right|$, K being capital stock and L labor. The labor cost differential between pairs of countries is computed as: $\left|ln\left(\frac{Y_{i,t}}{L_{i,t}}\right) - ln\left(\frac{Y_{j,t}}{L_{j,t}}\right)\right|$, Y being gross domestic product.

The economic intuitions for the observable variables are as follows:

1.   The GDP of the home and host country are expected to have a positive impact on FDI. In the case of the destination country, a larger level of income is tantamount to a more dynamic market.

2.   The variable, $\left(\sum_j GDP_{j,t}^{RIA}\right)$, which is the sum of the GDP of the countries linked to the recipient by a trade agreement, is intended to capture the extended market effect [10]. Note that the gravity equation is an expenditure function and we must use variables in nominal terms, to avoid what is called the bronze medal mistake (see [3]).

3.   The analysis uses two dyad variables, one to capture the FDI creation and the other the FDI diversion effect of Mercosur, in the spirit of [10,53]. The variables are Mercosur and One Mercosur, respectively. The Mercosur variable reflects the original treaty and the subsequent creation of free trade agreements with the associate members. Mercosur is a dummy which takes the value one when both countries, i and j, are part of Mercosur (either as original signatories, as an associated member or as signing a FTA with full scope, as described in the Appendix A) in a particular year t, and 0 otherwise. Since associated members incorporated in Mercosur in different years, it follows that the variable Mercosur exhibits time and country-pair variation.

The variable One Mercosur takes the value one when the recipient country j—the host country—belongs to Mercosur in the way defined above, while the country of origin of the flows, i, does not; it takes the value zero otherwise. Note that in this case the dummy equals one when the recipient country in the dyad belongs in the RTA as an original signatory, as an associated member (Chile, Colombia, Ecuador and Peru) or as a signatory of a non-partial scope FTA agreement within the Mercosur framework (Mexico from 2006 onwards) at a particular time. This captures the FDI diversion effect (see [54]). FDI diversion occurs when investment flows from a Mercosur non-member country to a Mercosur member decline after that host country joined the RTA.

The variable ALADI follows the same construction as Mercosur. The variable ALADI reflects the FTAs (free trade zones) established over time across the countries within the ALADI framework. It takes value one for a pair of countries i, j —that were original signatories of ALADI—when the two countries entered into a free trade zone in time t (t being the year when the agreement entered into force) and zero otherwise. Therefore, the variable ALADI exhibits time and country-pair variation. The variable One ALADI is similar to One Mercosur.

4. The empirical analysis captures the effect *of* BITs in two ways. The variable BIT takes the value 1 if a ratified agreement is in place between the pair of countries at time t, and 0 otherwise. This variable captures the signaling effect. Second, the variable BIT-index is a continuous variable in the interval (0,1) which captures the degree of investment protection conferred by the said BIT. It is constructed in the spirit of [17,18].

To create the BIT investor protection index, it is necessary first to map all the BITs signed among the countries in our sample. BITs are classified according to 14 different clauses (see online Appendix A). We agree with the assessment of Berger et al. [55] in the sense that investors worry not only about dispute settlement arrangements but also about other aspects, such as policies on transfers of funds, treatment before and after the establishment, and performance requirements.

Ultimately, a sound dispute settlement mechanism is non-effective if the foreign firm in the host country is not profitable enough in the first place, because the treatment it receives prevents the consolidation of earnings and/or the contention of operational costs. In the sample, all BITs include ISDS provisions as well as State-State Dispute Settlement (SSDS) and similar clauses; focusing only on variations within these two clauses, therefore, would have given us less variability across BITs (for a complete definition of all clauses mapped see Appendix A).

Next, each indicator has a score associated with it. The score reflects how each particular aspect is covered in each BIT: 1 meaning maximum protection for investors and 0 non-protection. All individual scores add up (assuming equal weights, following [17,18,56]), to be normalized. Figure 4 displays the relationship between the BITs' pro-investment index and FDI.

The bulk of the treaties have a score of around 0.64–0.72, although there are a few values in the neighbourhood of 0.8. The median BIT protection index score is 0.68 and we use this value as a cut-off point (the average is 0.69). The assumption of equal weights could be problematic, but any other method of weighing individual indicators could also be contested.

5. To capture the enhancing or overlapping effects between trade agreements and BITs, the empirical analysis includes interactions in the model, i.e., Mercosur and ALADI are multiplied by the BIT investor protection index.
6. The relative availability and costs of inputs, which may have an important role in location decisions are FactorEndow and laborCost [9]. Following [57], FactorEndow measures the difference in the capital/labor ratio between the two countries. LaborCost captures the gap between countries in the price of labor. Because of the absence of good data on this issue, the analysis uses official data from the International Labor Organization (ILO). ILO assumes that real wages are equal to productivity, defined as the ratio GDP/number of workers.
7. The Political Risk variable accounts for the degree of consolidation of the rule of law, social, economic and political institutions and political stability. It has been constructed from the World Bank Aggregate Governance Indicator 1995–2018, complemented with the International Country Risk Indexes from Princeton University.

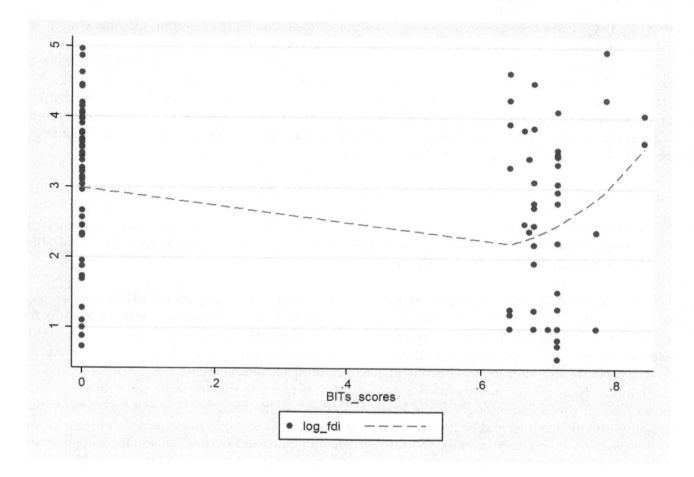

Figure 4. FDI intra-regional inflows per country (as percentage of total intra-regional inflows in Latin America) vs BITs pro-investor index (1995–2018). Source: Author's calculations using data from UNCTAD and WTO.

5. Empirical Results

Table 1 displays the results of the PPML estimation of the baseline gravity model described in Equation (8). In these regressions, the main focus lies on the impact of Mercosur, ALADI, and BIT related agreements. Regressions include fixed effects and time fixed effects to control for national heterogeneity and business cycles, respectively. The fixed effects absorb all observable and unobservable characteristics that are country-specific.

The variables which capture the purchasing power or market power of the host and home country are positive and significant, as expected. Their signs and magnitudes are similar to those reported by [39,58] in their meta-analyses of robust FDI determinants. The empirical studies analogous to ours use a large variety of samples, methodologies, and specifications. This implies some degree of heterogeneity in the size of the point estimates of the main variables, albeit results are typically the same in spirit. Therefore, both the market size of the investor and, more importantly, according to the point estimate, the market of the host country exerts a large influence on the decision to invest in the countries in our sample. This result makes economic sense: a big market represents a dynamic expected demand by potential consumers which, in turn, entails a higher level of revenues for firms offering that particular good or service. In addition, in this kind of setting, fixed costs related to the establishment of a firm in a foreign market can be supported by a larger number of products, hence reducing total costs per unit.

The market potential is captured by the sum of the GDPs of the countries belonging to the same RTA as the host country. This variable exhibits a positive and significant point estimate, in the neighborhood of 0.9, which is similar or even slightly higher than the coefficient of the host country GDP. The analysis of Yeyati et al. [10] also finds a positive and significant impact of the extended market on FDI. The results regarding this variable suggests that foreign firms choose their location in Latin America not only to satisfy the local market of the destination country but also to access their neighbors more easily via an export platform strategy, as in [13,21]. Furthermore, these findings provide preliminary evidence about the effectiveness of the trade agreements in attracting FDI from third countries.

Distance is negative and significant while adjacency is positive and significant, as expected, with magnitudes similar to those reported by [23,58,59]. The latter find a lower point estimate for distance, between −0.38 and −0.46, but the impact of contiguity is quite akin to ours. A recent paper [60] reports distance estimates between −0.68 and −1.5. Although their level of analysis is slightly different, since they work with disaggregated data by industries and with a sample of 243 countries, it is reassuring that our distance coefficients are closer to theirs than those reported by [23]. Our results of magnitude and signs of traditional variables included in gravity models are thus comparable to those displayed in the literature.

The variable Mercosur is positive, significant and quite stable, with point estimates that vary around 0.136–0.147. We can recover the impact of this dummy from the expression $\left[e^{\beta}-1\right]$. A point estimate of 0.147 (column 4), means that, since Mercosur entered into force, FDI flows to its members have increased on average by 15.83% per year. Thus, the effect of Mercosur ranges between 14.56% and 15.83% per year. This is similar to the result reported by [23] for Economic Integration Agreements and Custom Unions (0.11), and also to [7] when they perform their estimation using PPML. It is also in line with the results reported by [3] but is smaller than the 0.41–0.5 point estimate documented by [13] for European agreements. The difference in the estimates found by [13] and by this paper can be attributed to two reasons: firstly, European countries have been traditionally very connected; secondly, European agreements bring about very strong ties among their members, implying ultimately free movement of goods, services and resources, to an extent not reached yet by Latin American treaties.

The variable One Mercosur displays a negative and significant coefficient. The joint consideration of the Mercosur and One-Mercosur variables indicates that, when the host country enters Mercosur, FDI within the members of the blocs increase, but FDI between a member and a third country declines. This sort of FDI diversion is not negligible since it amounts to 8.43–6.60%. Empirical evidence for this phenomenon can be found in [10]. The dummy capturing the ALADI agreements is positive, although less significant than Mercosur. The point estimate of ALADI is also considerably smaller, around 0.049–0.062. Thus, the effect of ALADI on FDI is between 5.02 to 6.39%. The diversion effect of ALADI is only significant at the 10% level (column 4) and amounts approximately to 3%. In the rest of the estimations the coefficient of ONE_ALADI is non-significant.

The different degrees of integration provided by the agreements can explain the dissimilar creation and diversion effects of Mercosur and ALADI. Mercosur is a consolidated, common market RTA that has promoted a certain degree of stability within the region. The FTAs within ALADI, (in contrast to the Mercosur type agreement) do not necessarily exert a significant impact on the macroeconomic environment of the host country, nor contribute to the harmonization of legislation and standards between them. Their impact on FDI, therefore, while relevant, is more subdued than that of Mercosur. As mentioned above, ref [13] estimate this effect to be around 0.4–0.5 for European agreements, thus lending countenance to our claim that the impact of a trade agreement is positively correlated with the degree of integration it provides.

Table 1. Estimates of RTAs and BITs on FDI stocks. Gravity-PPML with country and time fixed effects.

	(1)	(2)	(3)	(4)	(5)	(6)	(7)	(8)	(9)
$Y_{i,t}$ (log)	0.726 (0.000)***		0.764 (0.003)***	0.701 (0.006)***		0.693 (0.007)***	0.752 (0.003)***		0.628 (0.005)***
$Y_{j,t}$ (log)	0.815 (0.002)***		0.804 (0.003)***	0.831 (0.003)***		0.809 (0.004)***	0.802 (0.002)***		0.813 (0.003)***
$\left(SumGDP_{ij,t}^{RIA}\right)(log)$		0.935 (0.490)**	0.947 (0.486)**		0.895 (0.488)*	0.906 (0.475)*		0.926 (0.468)**	0.985 (0.506)**
Distance$_{ij}$ (log)	−0.702 (0.104)***	−0.713 (0.096)***	−0.724 (0.109)***	−0.743 (0.113)***	−0.782 (0.095)***	−0.736 (0.079)**	−0.801 (0.108)***	−0.751 (0.123)***	−0.762 (0.114)***
Adjacency$_{ij}$	0.216 (0.065)***	0.261 (0.053)***	0.272 (0.048)***	0.260 (0.047)***	0.206 (0.052)***	0.214 (0.050)***	0.236 (0.044)***	0.221 (0.039)***	0.274 (0.049)***
Mercosur$_{ij,t}$	0.143 (0.033)***	0.146 (0.031)***	0.138 (0.029)***	0.147 (0.026)***	0.136 (0.027)***	0.142 (0.022)***	0.136 (0.019)***	0.138 (0.017)***	0.140 (0.021)***
ALADI$_{ij,t}$	0.061 (0.024)**	0.049 (0.026)*	0.055 (0.029)*	0.062 (0.030)*	0.056 (0.031)*	0.053 (0.026)**	0.054 (0.024)**	0.060 (0.026)**	0.049 (0.027)**
BITs$_{ij,t}$	0.086 (0.046)*		0.082 (0.044)*	0.074 (0.039)**	0.069 (0.036)*	0.065 (0.035)*	0.063 (0.033)*		0.052 (0.028)*
BIT index$_{ij,t}$		0.045 (0.024)*	0.043 (0.023)*			0.042 (0.022)*		0.039 (0.021)*	
ONE_Mercosur$_{ij,t}$				−0.081 (0.022)***	−0.076 (0.032)**	−0.074 (0.026)***	−0.070 (0.024)***	−0.065 (0.028)**	−0.064 (0.031)**
ONE_ALADI$_{ij,t}$				−0.026 (0.025)	−0.023 (0.023)	−0.028 (0.032)	−0.025 (0.037)	−0.018 (0.042)	−0.021 (0.041)
Factor Endow$_{ij,t}$							0.104 (0.031)***	0.113 (0.039)***	0.107 (0.042)***
Political Risk$_{j,t}$							−0.043 (0.010)***	−0.052 (0.009)***	−0.053 (0.014)***
Labor Cost dif$_{ij,t}$							0.037 (0.020)*	0.042 (0.0321)*	0.045 (0.022)*
No. Observations	2230	2230	2230	2230	2230	2230	2230	2230	2230
Adj. R^2	0.537	0.521	0.546	0.557	0.560	0.529	0.587	0.579	0.601
Individual Country Fixed Effect	Yes	Yes	Yes	Yes	Yes	Yes	Yes	Yes	Yes
Time Fixed effect	Yes	Yes	Yes	Yes	Yes	Yes	Yes	Yes	Yes

Note: This table reports panel gravity estimates for FDI stocks from country i to country j for 1995–2018. It reports Poisson pseudo-maximum likelihood estimation with individual country effects and time FE. Robust standard errors are in parenthesis and clustered by country pair. *** $p < 0.01$, ** $p < 0.05$, * $p < 0.10$.

The variable capturing BITs is positive and significant at least at the 10% level in all specifications. The point estimate ranges between 0.052 and 0.086, indicating a yearly effect between 5.3% and 8.5%, consistent with results of previous studies employing a similar methodology [6]. Qualitative results are similar in spirit to those of [7]. The main message here is that BITs also enhance FDI inflows to host countries; The differences in the point estimates of the BIT indicator in their contribution and ours can be attributed to alternative econometric specifications, since we use PPML as our baseline technique and they do not. Interestingly, the point estimate is smaller than the coefficients obtained for Mercosur, but larger than that of ALADI. The variable that captures the impact of the quality of BITs (the BIT index) on FDI is significant and ranges between 0.039 and 0.045. The economic interpretation of this result is straightforward. Those treaties granting a higher level of protection to foreign investments, in the form of less stringent establishment prerequisites, assurance of fair and equitable treatment, allowance for transfer of funds, and design of sound dispute settlements mechanisms, among others, facilitate the smooth operation of foreign firms and hence help attract new investment.

The effect of the variable capturing differences in factor endowments is positive and highly significant. Intuitively, if labor is relatively more abundant in the host country than in the home country, it will also be cheaper, thus creating incentives for foreign firms intending to rationalize their employee costs. Labor cost differentials are only marginally significant. The economic interpretation of this variable is the same as for differences in factor endowments but its effect is captured with less precision. This variable is constructed as the difference in GDP over total employment in the home and the host countries. In other words, it captures differences in productivities, which should be closely linked to dissimilarities in labor costs, under the hypothesis of efficient labor markets. This assumption, however, may not hold in some developing countries, thus negatively affecting the accuracy of the indicator.

The political risk variable exerts a significant and negative impact on FDI stocks. Since it proxies for the institutional environment, our results suggest that more stable countries attract higher amounts of FDI, while political unrest acts as a deterrent. Countries with larger degrees of macroeconomic and political stability and well-established political institutions provide more predictable environments and reduce the uncertainty associated with new investments, thus fostering the attraction of FDI. The size of effect is akin to that reported by [28,58], in this last case for Middle East and North African countries, respectively.

These results support the hypothesis of an intra-regional FDI in Latin America driven both by considerations about market size and relative endowments. These findings suggest, therefore, that the pattern of FDI within Latin America can be represented by a hybrid, knowledge capital model in the particular case of the export-platform strategy [13,21]. Intuitively, according to this analytical framework, firms make decisions taking into account the opportunities provided by a potentially dynamic demand for the goods they offer (as proxied by market size), and by differentials in input costs (captured by relative endowments), which translate into more efficient production processes.

Table 2 summarizes the results obtained from the estimation of Equation (9). Now the structure of the fixed effects has changed and includes country-time fixed effects to account for multilateral resistances. This specification [47,48,61] addresses the potential endogeneity in the model by using country-pair fixed effects (or first-differencing) in panel data structures. This structure of fixed effects (country-year and country-pair) absorbs the host-home GDPs, the market purchasing power, and the distance and adjacency variables.

The estimated coefficient for the BIT index is positive and significant at the 90% level. The point estimate is around 0.042. Both the coefficients of the dummy for the BIT and the degree of protection index are quite similar to the results obtained by [18] when they work with bilateral FDI flows. We have estimated the model specified in Table 2 including diversion effect variables and the results are similar to those in Table 1. The magnitude of the coefficients slightly changes but the interpretation remains. Since we are working now with a continuous function over an interval, instead of using a dummy, the index allows the testing of several interesting hypotheses. It is possible, as ref [17] show, that the relationship between BIT–FDI varies for different values of the index (notice that the score attributed to each BIT does not change once the BIT enters into force unless withdrawal occurs; in this framework, BIT index is equivalent to BIT index t-5). In order to test this hypothesis, we have considered two scenarios and introduced them separately in the equations: a value of the index smaller than 0.68 (meaning that the corresponding BIT is less pro-investor) and an index larger than 0.68 (which represents a treaty with a more pro-investor orientation).

Results suggest that the impact of the index does change with its value: those BITs whose indexes show a less favorable stance for the investor are non-significant whereas those which are more pro-investor are positive and significant at 90% (see column 3 and 5). Notice, however, that the impact of BITs (as captured either by the variable BITs or BIT index) is still lower than that of Mercosur but larger than ALADI's, as in the previous specifications.

In order to further explore the heterogeneity suggested by the index, the model includes interactions of the BIT index with the proxies for the RTAs. When interacted with Mercosur, the pro-investor index is positive and significant at 99%, with a point estimate of 0.068. The result carries over to the subset of BITs with higher index values (with an impact of 7%). Instead, the interaction of ALADI with the index, although showing the expected signs, is not significant. A higher value of the index combined with participation in Mercosur is, hence, more effective in attracting FDI than just a higher index score (columns 4 and 5). The interaction term, both positive and significant, indicates that the effect of Mercosur is enhanced for higher values of the BIT investment protection variable.

Table 2. Impact of RTA and BIT investor protection index on FDI. Gravity-PPML estimation with country-year and country-pair FE.

	Stock FDI$_{ij,t}$				
	(1)	(2)	(3)	(4)	(5)
Mercosur	0.129 (0.018) ***	0.122 (0.023) ***	0.115 (0.019) ***	0.103 (0.013) ***	0.096 (0.010) ***
ALADI	0.030 (0.016) *	0.032 (0.017) *	0.027 (0.016) *	0.025 (0.014) *	0.031 (0.013) *
BITs	0.042 (0.021) **			0.039 (0.019) **	0.034 (0.019) **
BIT index		0.034 (0.018) *		0.039 (0.019) *	
BIT Index < 0.68 (less pro−investor)			0.026 (0.029)		0.018 (0.036)
BIT Index ≥ 0.68 (pro−investor)			0.037 (0.020) *		0.042 (0.019) *
Mercosur * BIT Index				0.062 (0.013) ***	
Mercosur * BIT Index ≥ 0.68					0.068 (0.020) ***
Aladi*BIT Index				0.023 (0.017)	
ISDS concluded				−0.008 (0.023)	−0.007 (0.029)
Controls	Yes	Yes	Yes	Yes	Yes
No. Observations	2230	2230	2230	2230	2230
Individual country−year fixed effect	Yes	Yes	Yes	Yes	Yes
Country−pair fixed effect	Yes	Yes	Yes	Yes	Yes

Note: This table reports panel gravity estimates for FDI stocks from country i to country j for the period 1995–2018. It reports Poisson pseudo-maximum likelihood estimation with country time FE (η_{it}, η_{jt}) and pair country FE (η_{ij}). We control for the effect of country outliers as part of FE. We control for labor cost differentials, endowment differences, and political risks. Country pair fixed effects are used to address the issue of endogeneity in RTAs and BITs [47]. Robust standard errors are in parenthesis, clustered by country pair. *** $p < 0.01$, ** $p < 0.05$, * $p < 0.10$.

Panel A of Table 3 presents two additional specifications of the basic estimation in order to test for the impact of the policy variables. The first column includes a country-pair fixed effects structure and estimates coefficients for the leads of the policy variables to test for endogeneity due to reverse causation [3,47]. In other words, this specification aims to assess whether abundant FDI among some countries prompts the constitution of a trade agreement among them, so investment at time t translates into RTAs or BITs at time t + h. If RTAs/BITs are exogenous to FDI, then the estimated coefficient for the lead variables should not be significantly different from zero. Indeed, the results show a non-significant effect of the lead variables.

The lags of the Mercosur, ALADI and BITs capture the impact of phasing-in effects. Now the question is whether trade and investment agreements take some time to fully display their effects. It is reasonable to think that firms need a period of adaptation to changing circumstances in order to consider alternatives and make location decisions. The lagged coefficients, also positive and significant, display a significant impact on FDI, meaning that their effect comes about gradually. We have worked with five lags for several reasons. First, effects of trade and investment agreements seem to peak in four–five years. Second, we want to capture the heterogeneous effects of implementation processes across countries. These results are consistent with [12]. In general, the impact of (lagged) Mercosur lies at around 13.42%. The effect of (lagged) BITs is, again, smaller than that of Mercosur but larger than that of ALADI. These results are in accord with the reported pattern in [3]: the lagged impact of Mercosur, ALADI and BITs is larger than the contemporaneous impact. In other words, medium- and long-term effects of these treaties exceed short-term effects.

Panel B of Table 3's estimations presents the results using the Hausman-Taylor method to further address the possible endogeneity of the policy variables. This method uses the deviations from the mean of the exogenous time-varying variables for each country pair as instruments [62]. This procedure removes the part of the error term correlated with the endogenous time-varying variables. Since the deviations from the group means are by definition uncorrelated with the error term, they do not alter the estimation of the exogenous time varying variables when estimating the coefficient of the rest of the variables.

The main policy variables are treated as endogenous. The estimated coefficients are slightly higher in magnitude than those obtained by PPML with country-time and country-pair fixed effects. These results are consistent with the larger coefficients obtained by [3,47] when estimating the effects of RTAs on exports for a different set of countries. The Hausman test gives us a chi-square tests with a probability below 0.05. Therefore, we reject the null hypothesis of random effects. The instruments pass a conventional test for overidentifying restrictions. As a robustness check the online Appendix A presents estimations using an inverse hyperbolic sine transformation of the FDI dependent variable.

It is plausible that BITs exert heterogeneous effects not only because of their own characteristics but also due to the nature of the signatories in terms of economic and institutional development. To test this hypothesis, a further analysis first classifies the countries in our sample in two categories, according to their income level, and works with subsamples.

Table 4 reports very suggestive results. The impact of BITs per se is large in the subsample encompassed by medium income countries, and non-significant for middle-low income countries. The BIT index is positive and significant in the first subsample, but only marginally significant in the second.

Similarly, a BIT index above 0.68 is significant for middle income countries; it is only marginally significant, however, for middle-low income countries. When the BIT index is below 0.68, it is only significant at the 90% confidence level for the first subsample and non-significant for the second. The interaction between Mercosur and BITs displays results consistent with previous estimations (Table 2). Notice that the interaction term is also positive and significant for middle-low income countries. This model specification seems to confirm the hypothesis of complementarity between BITs and institutions. BITs are primarily effective in reducing the perceived risk by investors, and thus help attract FDI, when the host country has sounder and more stable institutions. From an economic point of view, a more developed institutional framework in a particular country provides credibility to the agreements signed by that country, enhancing their efficacy. In [10], the authors find that the effect of RTA is higher in those countries which are more attractive for FDI.

Table 3. Impact of RTAs and BITs on FDI. PPML and Hausman-Taylor Estimations.

	Panel A: PPML		Panel B: Hausman−Taylor		
	(1)	(2)	(1)	(2)	(3)
$Y_{i,t}$ (log)			0.564 (0.062) ***		0.537 (0.071 ***
$Y_{j,t}$ (log)			0.792 (0.069) ***		0.805 (0.042 ***
$\left(SumGDP_{j,t}^{RIA}\right)$(log)				0.901 (0.489) **	0.875 (0.425) **
Distance (log)			−0.503 (0.257) **	−0.498 (0.250) **	−0.485 (0.248) **
Adjacency			0.273 (0.081) ***	0.253 (0.073) ***	0.261 (0.062) ***
Mercosur	0.123 (0.032) ***	0.118 (0.026) ***	0.153 (0.070) ***	0.145 (0.062) ***	0.169 (0.073) ***
ALADI	0.031 (0.016) *	0.026 (0.014) *	0.056 (0.028) *	0.048 (0.025) **	0.052 (0.026) **
BITs	0.047 (0.024) **	0.039 (0.020) **	0.063 (0.032) **		0.072 (0.035) **
BIT index				0.041 (0.022) *	0.046 (0.021) *
Mercosur_LEAD5	0.072 (0.048)				
ALADI_ LEAD5	0.015 (0.032)				
BITs_ LEAD5	0.029 (0.054)				
Mercosur_LAG5		0.126 (0.011) ***			
ALADI_ LAG5		0.038 (0.020) *			
BITs_ LAG5		0.046 (0.021) **			
Controls	Yes	Yes	Yes	Yes	Yes
No. Observations	1896	1896	1670	1670	1670
Adj. R^2			0.426	0.443	0.521
Sigma_u			0.729	0.931	0.834
Sigma_e			1.317	1.320	1.320
Rho (fraction of variance due to u_i)			0.234	0.332	0.285
F−stat overidentification restriction			1.345 (0.426)	1.421 (0.432)	1.415 (0.447)

Note: Panel A represents Poisson pseudo-maximum likelihood estimation with country time FE (η_{it}, η_{jt}) and pair country FE (η_{ij}). Country pair fixed effects are used to address endogeneity in RTAs and BITs (see [47]). As control variables we include labor cost differentials, endowment differences, and political risk. Panel B reports Hausman-Taylor estimates for bilateral FDI in logs. GDPs and sum GDP are considered as time-varying and exogenous. Distance is considered as endogenous, time-invariant (proxy for trade costs). Adjacency is considered exogenous, time-invariant. Mercosur, ALADI, and BITs are considered as endogenous, time-varying. The F-statistic should not be different from zero, and refers to the test for over-identifying restrictions in the corresponding log-linear instrumental variable (IV) model (p-value of over-identifying restrictions in parenthesis). Robust standard errors in parenthesis, clustered by country pair *** $p < 0.01$, ** $p < 0.05$, * $p < 0.10$.

Table 4. Impact of RTA and BIT pro-investor index for country subsets. Gravity-PPML, with country-time and country-pair fixed effects.

	Middle Income Countries				Middle-Low Income Countries			
	(1)	(2)	(3)	(4)	(1)	(2)	(3)	(4)
Mercosur	0.106 (0.016)***	0.097 (0.023)***	0.115 (0.020)***	0.119 (0.016)***	0.092 (0.024)***	0.101 (0.013)***	0.095 (0.021)***	0.087 (0.025)***
Aladi	0.036 (0.020)*	0.042 (0.021)*	0.031 (0.025)	0.028 (0.015)*	0.030 (0.016)*	0.019 (0.011)*	0.022 (0.012)*	0.015 (0.018)
BITs	0.039 (0.022)*	0.036 (0.020)*		0.041 (0.022)*	0.032 (0.045)	0.027 (0.038)		0.037 (0.042)
BIT Index		0.043 (0.020)**				0.029 (0.015)*		
BIT Index < 0.68	0.023 (0.011)*		0.028 (0.012)*	0.019 (0.011)*	0.021 (0.018)		0.025 (0.029)	0.018 (0.027)
BIT Index ≥ 0.68	0.042 (0.021)**		0.045 (0.020)**	0.047 (0.021)**	0.036 (0.019)*		0.039 (0.021)*	0.042 (0.019)**
Mercosur * BIT Index		0.055 (0.027)**				0.057 (0.025)**		
Mercosur * BIT Index ≥ 0.68	0.057 (0.019)***		0.059 (0.012)***	0.055 (0.010)***	0.042 (0.011)***		0.040 (0.013)***	0.036 (0.015)***
Aladi*BIT Index		0.017 (0.030)	0.018 (0.037)	0.014 (0.026)		0.021 (0.010)*	0.019 (0.009)*	0.023 (0.011)*
ISDS concluded		−0.018 (0.047)	−0.012 (0.052)	-0.015 (0.061)		−0.006 (0.039)	−0.009 (0.042)	−0.011 (0.058)
Mercosur_LAG5			0.084 (0.012)***	0.093 (0.024)***			0.090 (0.022)***	0.092 (0.031)***
Aladi_LAG5			0.023 (0.008)*	0.016 (0.009)*			0.014 (0.007)*	0.012 (0.006)*
BITs_LAG5				0.039 (0.020)**				0.030 (0.014)**
Controls	Yes	Yes	Yes	Yes	Yes	Yes	Yes	Yes
Adj-R^2	0.439	0.520	0.561	0.536	0.410	0.421	0.438	0.446
Wald Test	32.15	31.29	31.42	27.31	28.22	31..05	27.31	32.91
Observations	1160	1160	1042	1042	960	960	852	852

Source: Own elaboration. Notes: Middle income countries division according to GDP per capita in constant dollars using the World Bank's approach. First group of countries includes: Argentina, Brazil, Chile, Costa Rica, Mexico, and Uruguay. Middle-low income countries include: Bolivia, Colombia, Ecuador, Peru, and Paraguay. Dependent variable accounts for bilateral FDI stocks received in country j (subset) from all 11 economies. All models include origin and destination time fixed effects to control for MR and country-pair FE to control for endogeneity. We control for labor cost differentials, endowment differences, and political risk. Country-pair clustered robust standard errors in parentheses. *** $p < 0.01$, ** $p < 0.05$, * $p < 0.1$. Wald test p-value for the difference of coefficients in both samples is 0.00.

6. Concluding Remarks

When it comes to institutional strategies promoting trade agreements and bilateral investment treaties to attract FDI to areas in development, there are still empirical questions that remain unclear. This study is novel in addressing the following questions: (i) Does the effect on FDI depend on key characteristics (clauses) of the BITs? (ii) If there is co-existence of BITs in force with major trade agreements, which ones are more effective in attracting foreign investment? Are there overlapping or enhancing effects? (iii) Finally, it is not clear if BITs have a differential impact in countries with weak versus strong institutions. This paper uses a flexible econometric specification derived from a structural gravity model of FDI to assess the impact of RTAs and BITs on intra-regional FDI stocks in Latin America over the years 1995–2018.

The analysis shows that the participation in deep integration agreements, such as Mercosur, has the strongest impact on intra-regional FDI inflows, of between 14.56% and 15.83%. Taking part in less ambitious trade agreements as ALADI does help attract FDI inflows but the effect is more modest and amounts to 3–5% on average. Finally, BITs enhance the attraction of foreign investment, with an average effect of 3.7% and 4.6%, which lies in between those estimated for Mercosur and ALADI.

To disentangle the mere presence of a BIT between two countries from that associated with the quality of the BIT, we have constructed an index in order to capture the level of protection provided to foreign investors by a BIT. The estimations suggest that higher levels of protection are associated with greater capacities of attraction of FDI in Latin America, when the index is above a certain threshold. Additionally, the analysis shows that when RTAs are combined with investment agreements offering a high degree of protection, they help attract foreign investment within Latin America.

Not only the features of the BIT influence the capacity to attract foreign investment. The institutional characteristics of the host country are crucial as well. According to estimations, BITs are associated with larger FDI inflows in a subsample made up of the countries with the highest income. For middle-low income countries (Bolivia, Colombia, Ecuador, Paraguay, and Peru), however, the mere presence of BITs per se is not associated with an increase in FDI. Furthermore, the impact of higher quality BITs is smaller and statistically less significant for middle-low income countries than for more developed nations. Thus, BITs appear as complements of a sound institutional environment in the host country.

These findings have implications for policy making. First, belonging to solid, consolidated trade agreements which imply high levels of integration is beneficial not only from the point of view of external trade but also because it helps attract FDI inflows. Countries seeking higher levels of foreign investment might want to consider membership in these types of accords, together with a reinforcement of the treaties they have already signed.

Second, empirical analysis has shown that BIT exerts a signal effect but its impact is conditional upon the degree of integration and consolidation of the RTA, the level of development—or institutional advancement—of the host country, and the extent to which a particular BIT protects foreign investment. Policy makers interested in attracting FDI should engage in investment treaties that warrant a reasonable degree of protection to foreign investors. The signing of these agreements may entail a costs, in the form of restrictions to the autonomy of the host country, for example. In line with other contributions our results imply that policymakers should weigh carefully the trade-offs associated with entry into a BIT. Otherwise, the political costs associated with the signing of these agreements may not be worthwhile. Finally, Latin American economies striving to attract foreign investment should keep in mind that the combined effect of belonging to consolidated RTAs together with BITs enhances FDI.

The main limitation of this paper is the use of aggregate data instead of disaggregated FDI by sector. It would be interesting to ascertain whether the impact of Mercosur, ALADI and BITs varies across different industries. Further research is necessary to gauge in more detail the potentially different effect of treaties according to their sectoral distribution, but unfortunately sectoral/industry data are not yet available on a bilateral basis at a cross-country level for Latin America.

Author Contributions: M.B.: conceptualization, data curation, formal analysis, methodology, writing, review and editing. B.S.-R.: conceptualization, investigation, methodology, writing, review and editing. Y.S.: conceptualization, investigation, writing, review and editing. All authors have read and agreed to the published version of the manuscript.

Acknowledgments: We thank the CIRANO data lab, Thierry Warin, Joseph Pelzman, Zadia Feliciano, Mona Pinchis-Paulsen, Federico Ortino, Thilo Huning, and Kevin Foster for helpful comments. David Dam provided excellent research assistance. We are grateful to participants in the VIII La Laguna Workshop on International Economics 2019, the Global Research on Emerging Economies Conference 2018, the Lipsey Panel at the Western Economic Association 2017, the International Panel Data Conference 2016, the Workshop of Economic Integration, the European Trade Study Group 2016, the International Trade and Finance Association meeting 2016 and seminar participants at Department of Economics at University of Cape Town, SARChI and Dept. of Economics at University of Johannesburg, CIRANO, and the Institute of Economics at University of

Do Trade and Investment Agreements Promote Foreign Direct Investment within Latin...

137

Republic (Uruguay) for the comments received during presentations of previous versions of this work. All errors are our own.

Abbreviations

ALADI	The Latin American Integration Association/Asociación Latinoamericana de Integración
ASEAN	Association of Southeast Asian Nations
BITs	Bilateral investment treaties
CEPII	French Centre d'Etudes Prospectives et d'Informations Internationales
CUSFTA	The Canada-United States Free Trade Agreement
FDI	Foreign direct investment
FE	Fixed effects
FET	Fair and equitable treatment
GDP	Gross Domestic Product
GNLM	Generalized Nonlinear Linear Model
IHS	Inverse hyperbolic sine transformation
ILO	International Labor Organization
IMF	International Monetary Fund
ISDS	Investor-state dispute settlement
Mercosur	Mercado comun del sur
MFN	Most-favored-nation clause
MNEs	Multinational enterprises
MRs	Multilateral resistances
NAFTA	North American Free Trade Agreement
NT	National treatment
OECD	The Organisation for Economic Co-operation and Development
OLS	Ordinary least square
PPML	Poisson pseudo-maximum likelihood
RTAs	Regional trade agreements
SSDS	State-State dispute settlement
UNCTAD	United Nations Commission for Trade and Development
WTO	World Trade Organization

Appendix A

Appendix A.1. Clauses Mapped in the BIT Investment Protection Index

Individual provisions are coded for all the BITs between the 11 Latin American countries in our sample, i.e., 14 provisions that UNCTAD and the American Bar Association consider of substance to protect any investment to which a developing host country is a signatory. Low scores indicate less investment protection. Values of 0.5 are assigned to medium level investor protection [17,18].

1. National treatment (NT) pre-establishment: Ensures that requirements for foreign firms upon entry in the host country, such as establishment and participation in existing enterprises, are no greater than those for domestic firms. If the clause is present, the index in this section sums 1 in this category, 0 otherwise.
2. National treatment post establishment: The same as 1 but associated with "the treatment of the investment after its entry". If present, the index in this category takes value 1, 0 otherwise.
3. Most-favored-nation (MFN) treatment pre-establishment: MFN treatment of the foreign firm regarding entry, establishment and participation in existing enterprises. If present, the index in this category takes value 1, 0 otherwise.
4. Most-favored-nation (MFN) treatment post-establishment: The same as 3, after the entry of the foreign firm. If the clause is present it takes value 1.

5. Fair and equitable treatment (FET): Can be qualified either by reference to International Law (General International Law, Principles of International Law or Customary International Law) or "by listing the elements of the FET obligation". In the last case, the FET obligation may "include an indicative or exhaustive list of more specific elements" to avoid.

6. Full protection and security: This commitment, in turn, may be:

    • Standard "if the treaty contains an unqualified obligation to provide full protection and security" (with formulations such as most constant protection, legal protection and security, and so forth).

    • Referenced to domestic law of the host country

7. No general security exception: Ensures that the host country does not prevent investment in a particular sector for security reasons.

8. Indirect expropriation: Treaties may refer to this issue under two approaches: the scope of measures covered, and/or refining expropriation clauses.

    On the scope of measures covered: The options under this classification are the following:
    Indirect expropriation not mentioned "if the treaty's expropriation clause does not contain an explicit reference to indirect expropriation".

    • Indirect expropriation mentioned, whatever the formulae it employs ("measures having effect equivalent to nationalization or expropriation", measures tantamount to expropriation, de facto expropriation).

    • No expropriation clause "if the treaty does not include a provision that protects foreign investors against non-compensated dispossession of their investments".

9. Transfer of funds: A "provision regarding the free transfer of funds relating to investments (covering outward and/or inward transfers". If present, the index in this category takes a value of 1.

10. Performance requirements: If the treaty includes a provision that restricts the use of performance requirements, the measure in these clause takes value 1.

11. Umbrella clause: requiring the signatories "to respect or observe any obligation assumed by it with regard to a specific investment", hence protecting it de facto under its umbrella. The measure in these clause takes value 1.

12. State-State Dispute Settlement (SSDS): If the treaty provides for a dispute settlement procedure (e.g., arbitration) between States, the measure in this clause takes value 1.

13. Investor-State Dispute Settlement (ISDS): If the treaty establishes a mechanism for the settlement of disputes between covered investors and the host State (arbitration and/or domestic courts of the host State) the measure in these clause takes value 1.

14. Alternatives to arbitration: The more options at investors' disposal the better, although we assign a value of 0.5 to a treaty that establishes that the investor needs to go first through a local court before international arbitration.

    • "Voluntary Alternative Dispute Resolution (conciliation/mediation)" "If the treaty mentions the possibility of such procedures (e.g., non-binding, third-party procedures) but does not prescribe them as a necessary step".

    • "Compulsory Alternative Dispute Resolution (conciliation/mediation) If the treaty prescribes the use of compulsory conciliation or mediation.

    • "None" if the treaty does not refer to alternative means of settling investor–State disputes (conciliation/mediation or similar non-binding procedures).

Appendix A.2. Construction of the Mercosur and ALADI Variables

The sequence of the signature of the FTAs within Mercosur, considered deep integration agreements, and the incorporation of associated members is as follows:

1. All Mercosur original countries (Argentina, Brazil, Paraguay and Uruguay) and Chile entered into a FTA (Free Trade Agreement named AAP.CE number 35) in 1996.
2. All Mercosur original countries and Bolivia entered into a FTA (Free Trade Agreement AAP.CE number 36) in 1997.
3. All Mercosur original countries and Colombia and Ecuador entered into a FTA (Free Trade Agreement named AAP.CE number 59) in 2005.
4. All Mercosur original countries and Mexico entered into a FTA (Free Trade Agreement named AAP.CE number 54 and 55) in 2006.
5. All Mercosur original countries and Peru entered into a FTA (Free Trade Agreement, named AAP.CE number 58) in 2006.
6. Paraguay was suspended as a member during 2012.

Every FTA within ALADI are mapped. Table A2 shows the FTAs within the ALADI framework together with the year in which the FTA entered into force.

Table A1. Free Trade Zones across the signatories of original ALADI treaty.

	Argentina	Bolivia	Brazil	Chile	Colombia	Ecuador	Mexico	Paraguay	Peru	Uruguay
Argentina			1995							
Bolivia				2006						
Brazil	1995									
Chile		2006			2007		1999		2007	
Colombia				2007			1995			
Costa Rica										
Ecuador				2010						
Mexico				1999	1995					2004
Paraguay										
Peru				2007						
Uruguay							2004			

Source: own elaboration based on ALADI records. See http://www.aladi.org/nsfaladi/textacdos.nsf/vACEWEB?OpenView&Start=1&Count=800&Expand=7#7.

1. Argentina and Brazil signed the RTA called AAP.CE number 14 in 1999.
2. Bolivia and Chile signed the RTA called AAP.CE number 22 in 2006.
3. Chile and Mexico signed the RTA called AAP.CE number 41 in 1999.
4. Chile and Bolivia signed the RTA called AAP.CE number 22 in 2006.
5. Chile and Colombia signed the RTA called AAP.CE number 22 in 2007 (they had a previous partial agreement since 1995).
6. Chile and Mexico signed the RTA called AAP.CE number 41 in 1999.
7. Chile and Peru signed the RTA called AAP.CE number 38 in 2007 (they had a previous partial scope agreement since 1998).
8. Colombia and Mexico signed the RTA called AAP.CE number 33 in 1995.
9. Ecuador has not engaged in any free trade zone with other Latin American countries. It has a partial scope agreement with Chile since 2010.
10. Mexico and Uruguay signed the RTA called AAP.CE number 60 in 2004.

Table A2. BITs in force across Latin American countries.

	Argentina	Bolivia	Brazil	Chile	Colombia	Costa Rica	Ecuador	Mexico	Paraguay	Peru	Uruguay
Argentina		2005		1995		2001	1996	1998	1995	1996	
Bolivia	2005			1999			1997		2003	1995	
Brazil											
Chile	1995	1999				2000	1996		1998	2001	2010
Colombia										2004	
Costa Rica	2001			2000					2001		
Ecuador	1996	1997		1996					1995–2008	2000	1985–2008
Mexico	1998										2002
Paraguay	1995	2003		1998		2001	1995–2008			1995	1994
Peru	1996	1995		2001	2004		2000		1995		
Uruguay				2010			1985-2008	2002	1994		

Source: own elaboration based on UNCTAD (2017). The years reflects when the agreement entered in force and if terminated before 2018.

Appendix A.3. Gravity Model for FDI

The gravity model for FDI departs from a definition of bilateral FDI:

$$FDI_{ij,t}^{stock} \equiv \omega_{ij,t}^{\varepsilon} M_{i,t} \tag{A1}$$

where $FDI_{ij,t}$ represents FDI stocks between countries i and j at a time t. $M_{i,t}$ is the non-rival aggregate technology capital stock in a particular time. ω_{ijt} represents openness (or barriers to FDI) for foreign technology coming from country i to country j. ε is the elasticity of FDI with respect to openness. To transform FDI stocks into values we multiply Equation (A1) by its marginal product:

$$FDI_{ij,t}^{stock,value} \equiv \omega_{ij,t}^{\varepsilon} M_{i,t} \frac{\partial Y_{j,t}}{\partial M_{i,t}} \tag{A2}$$

in which $M_i = \phi_i \frac{E_i}{P_i}$, where E_i represents total expenditures of country i which equals the country output plus net rents from foreign investment. P_i stands for consumer prices (which can be considered as a multilateral resistance since higher prices for goods and inputs can affect FDI). Y is nominal output. Solving the representative agent's problem delivers a structural system for the steady-state. Then, the gravity structural system is given by:

$$FDI_{ij} = \phi_i \phi_j \omega_{ij}^{\varepsilon} \frac{E_i}{P_i} \frac{Y_j}{M_i} \tag{A3}$$

$$P_i = \left[\sum_{j=1}^{N} \left(\frac{\tau_{ji}}{\Pi_j} \right)^{1-\sigma} \frac{Y_j}{Y} \right]^{\frac{1}{1-\sigma}}, \tag{A4}$$

$$\Pi_j = \left[\sum_{i=1}^{N} \left(\frac{\tau_{ji}}{P_i} \right)^{1-\sigma} \frac{E_i}{Y} \right]^{\frac{1}{1-\sigma}}. \tag{A5}$$

where P_i denotes the aggregate price index or the multilateral resistance, as defined by Anderson and van Wincoop [43]. τ_{ji} represents standard iceberg trade costs. Equation (A3) can be transformed to estimate the parameters of interest empirically (see Section 4.2 of the manuscript).

Appendix A.4. Data and Robustness Tests

Table A3. Variables and sources.

Variable	Description	Source
FDI_{ij}	Bilateral Foreign Direct Investment stocks	UNCTAD (proprietary data from 1990–2008 and 2012–2018). Foreign Direct Investment Statistics database.
$Y_{i/j,t}$	GDP home/host country (dollars 2010) Bilateral distance between two countries	Balance of Payments, IMF CEPII dataset available http://www.cepii.fr/CEPII/en/
D_{ij}	based on distances between their biggest cities	bdd_modele/presentation.asp?id=6
$\left(\Delta GDP_{ij,t}^{RIA}\right)$	Sum of GDP to which the host country has tariff-free access.	Own elaboration from IMF http://www.imf.org/external/ns/cs.aspx?id=28
Adjacency	Dummy, takes value 1 when countries share border, 0 otherwise.	Own elaboration
Mercosur	Dummy, 1 when both countries belong to Mercosur, including associated members and deep FTA within Mercosur framework, 0 otherwise.	Own elaboration
ONE Mercosur	Dummy: 1 if recipient country belongs to Mercosur, and sender country does not, 0 otherwise.	Own elaboration
ALADI	Dummy: 1 when both countries belong to a FTA within the *ALADI framework*, 0 otherwise.	Own elaboration
BITs	Dummy: 1 when there is a BIT in force among the two countries, 0 otherwise	World Trade Organization database (WTO)
BIT index	Continuous variable in the interval (0,1). See text for details and Appendix A below	Own elaboration with data from UNCTAD (2017)
FactEndow	Difference between home and host country ratio of gross fixed capital formation over labor force	World Development Indicators; labor force from ILO, UN
LaborCost Dif	Difference in the Relative Cost of Labor among the home and host country	International Labor Organization http://www.ilo.org/global/statistics-and-databases/lang--en/index.htm
PolitRisk	Role of Institutions, law enforcement and government stability. Complemented with International Country Risk	World Bank and Princeton University

Source: own elaboration.

Estimations with the Inverse Hyperbolic Sine (IHS) Transformation Method

This method is also adequate for zeros and negative values. The inverse hyperbolic sine transformation for FDI is defined as: $log\left(FDI_{ij,t} + \left(FDI_{ij,t}^2 + 1\right)^{\frac{1}{2}}\right)$. Except for very small values of FDI, the IHS is approximately equal to $log(2FDI_{ij,t})$ or $log(2) + log(FDI_{ij,t})$ and it can be interpreted in exactly the same way as a standard logarithmic dependent variable (see Aisbett et al., 2018 for discussion).

Table A4. Impact of RTAs and BITs investor protection index on FDI. Inverse hyperbolic sine transformation, two-way fixed effects.

	(1)	(2)	(3)	(4)	(5)	(6)	(7)
Mercosur	0.132 (0.028) ***	0.127 (0.031) ***	0.122 (0.028) ***	0.112 (0.036) ***	0.117 (0.029) ***	0.119 (0.027) ***	0.121 (0.031) ***
ALADI	0.025 (0.011) *	0.021 (0.009) *	0.017 (0.008) *	0.023 (0.012) *	0.018 (0.008) *	0.015 (0.007) *	0.019 (0.012)
BITs	0.047	0.045	0.038	0.032	0.036	0.035	0.039
ONE_Mercosur	-0.064 (0.015) **	-0.061 (0.022) **	-0.066 (0.019) **	-0.058 (0.014) **	-0.052 (0.018) **	-0.054 (0.018) *	-0.056 (0.020) *
ONE_ALADI	-0.012 (0.005) *	-0.014 (0.007) *	-0.016 (0.008) *	-0.015 (0.006) *	-0.011 (0.015)	-0.010 (0.015)	-0.009 (0.019)
BIT index	0.044 (0.020) *	0.044 (0.020) *		0.039 (0.019) *			0.043 (0.021) *
BIT Index < 0.68 (less pro-investor)			0.016 (0.022)		0.018 (0.026)	0.014 (0.029)	
BIT Index $\geq$ 0.68 (pro-investor)			0.032 (0.017) *		0.030 (0.015) *	0.028 (0.013) *	
Mercosur * BIT Index				0.042 (0.012) ***			0.036 (0.009) ***
Mercosur * BIT Index $\geq$ 0.68					0.048 (0.010) ***	0.052 (0.006) ***	
Aladi*BIT Index				0.016 (0.023)		0.014 (0.028)	0.011 (0.031)
ISDS concluded				-0.015 (0.048)	-0.012 (0.052)	-0.006 (0.043)	-0.009 (0.039)
Mercosur_LAG5						0.096 (0.033) ***	0.102 (0.038) ***
ALADI_LAG5						0.008 (0.003) *	0.010 (0.005) *
BITs_LAG5							0.036 (0.018) **
Controls	Yes	Yes	Yes	Yes	Yes	Yes	Yes
No. Observations	1962	1962	1962	1962	1962	1632	1632
Individual country–year fixed effect	Yes	Yes	Yes	Yes	Yes	Yes	Yes
Country–pair fixed effect	Yes	Yes	Yes	Yes	Yes	Yes	Yes

Note: This table reports estimates for FDI flows from country i to country j at the aggregate level for the period 1995–2018. Estimation with host year FE and pair-country FE (η_{ij}). We control for labor cost differentials, endowment difference, political risk, and GDP in the home economy. Robust standard errors in parenthesis, clustered by country pair. *** $p < 0.01$, ** $p < 0.05$, * $p < 0.10$.

Do Trade and Investment Agreements Promote Foreign Direct Investment within Latin...

143

Table A5. Correlation Matrix.

	fdi stock	gdp_d	gdp_o	Distance	Adjacency	Mercosur	ONE_Mercosur
fdistock	1						
gdp_d	0.1534 *	1					
gdp_o	0.1921 *	0.0109	1				
distance	-0.0300	0.1615 *	0.1615 *	1			
adjacency	0.0687 *	0.1115 *	0.0541 *	-0.5483 *	1		
Mercosur	0.2109 *	0.1511 *	0.1511 *	-0.0853 *	0.1681 *	1	
ONE_Mercosur	-0.1201 *	0.2538 *	0.0334	-0.0191	0.1101 *	0.4601 *	1
Aladi	0.1389 *	0.1356 *	0.1356 *	0.1188 *	0.0679 *	0.1637	0.0902
ONE_Aladi	-0.1370 *	0.5079 *	0.0292	0.1104 *	0.0775 *	0.2341	0.357
l5_Mercosur	0.2194 *	0.1190 *	0.1190 *	-0.2246 *	0.2270 *	0.3857 *	0.2604
l5_Aladi	0.1133 *	0.1598 *	0.1598 *	0.0942 *	0.0441	0.1682	0.0843
Mercosur_LEAD5	0.1743	0.1386 *	0.1386 *	-0.0069	0.1322 *	0.4438	0.3889
Aladi_LEAD5	0.1006	0.1261	0.1261	0.1569	0.069	0.0838	0.0496
bit_enforced	0.0251 *	0.2224 *	0.2138 *	0.0235	0.0481 *	0.1113	0.0974
bit_index	0.0151 *	0.2066 *	0.2061 *	0.0527 *	0.1042 *	0.0244	-0.0164
BIT_LAG5	0.0307 *	0.2202 *	0.2113 *	0.0164	0.0165	0.1657	0.1119
BIT_LEAD5	0.0119	0.2506	0.2422	0.0558	0.0674	0.0211	0.0677
sum_gdp_partner	0.2215 *	0.0832 *	0.0927 *	0.1982	0.0408	0.1879 *	0.0264
factendow	0.0828 *	0.2192 *	0.1093 *	0.0000	-0.0203	0.0000	0.2208
laborcostdif	0.0495 *	0.1286 *	0.1014 *	0.0000	-0.0122	0.0000	-0.2745 *
politrisk	-0.1233 *	-0.0046 *	-0.0273	0.0890 *	-0.1127	0.0451	-0.0245
	Aladi	ONE_Aladi	Mercosur_LAG5	Aladi_LAG5	Mercosur_LEAD5	Aladi_LEAD5	bit_enforced

Table A5. *Cont.*

	fdi stock	gdp_d	gdp_o	Distance	Adjacency	Mercosur	ONE_Mercosur
Aladi	1						
ONE_Aladi	0.2386 *	1					
Mercosur_LAG5	0.0838 *	0.1541 *	1				
Aladi_LAG5	0.4325 *	0.1784 *	0.1251 *	1			
Mercosur_LEAD5	0.1706 *	0.2052 *	0.3531 *	0.1647 *	1		
Aladi_LEAD5	0.4713 *	0.2274 *	-0.0018	0.6186 *	0.1637 *	1	
bit_enforced	0.004	-0.0921	0.0211	-0.0816 *	0.1657 *	0.0185	1
bit_index	0.0265	-0.0457	-0.1609 *	-0.0879 *	0.0393	0.0561 *	0.4251 *
BIT_LAG5	0.0185	-0.0935	0.1145 *	-0.0530 *	0.1620 *	-0.0581	0.4461 *
BIT_LEAD5	-0.0816 *	-0.1800	0.0242	-0.1479 *	0.0663 *	0.0067	0.3105 *
sum_gdp_partner	0.1561 *	-0.0068	0.1460 *	0.1762 *	0.1507 *	0.1419 *	-0.1323 *
factendow	0.000	-0.0562	0.0000	0.0000	0.0000	0.000	0.0210
laborcostdif	0.000	-0.0095	0.0000	0.0000	0.0000	0.000	0.0311
politrisk	0.1008 *	-0.0283	-0.0202 *	0.0478	-0.0204	0.1297	-0.0032

	bit_index	BIT_LAG5	BIT_LEAD5	sum_gdp_partner	factendow	laborcostdif	politrisk
bit_index	1						
BIT_LAG5	0.3493 *	1					
BIT_LEAD5	0.3778 *	0.3466 *	1				
sum_gdp_partner	0.2232	0.2205	0.2735	1			
factendow	0.0121	0.0193	0.0166	0.1268 *	1		
laborcostdif	-0.0116	0.0332	0.0274	0.1217 *	0.2015 *	1	
politrisk	-0.0612 *	-0.0302	0.0380	0.0270	0.2530 *	0.1381 *	1

Source: own elaboration. Variables gdp_o and gdp_d stand for origin and destination. The rest of variables are self-explanatory. * $p < 0.05$.

References

1. Borensztein, E.; De Gregorio, J.; Lee, J. How does FDI affect economic growth? *J. Int. Econ.* **1998**, *45*, 115–135. [CrossRef]
2. Alvarado, R.; Iñiguez, M.; Ponce, P. FDI and economic growth in Latin America. *Econ. Anal. Policy* **2017**, *56*, 176–187. [CrossRef]
3. Yotov, Y.; Piermartini, R.; Monteiro, J.A.; Larch, M. *An Advanced Guide to Trade Policy Analysis: The Structural Gravity Model*; World Trade Organization: Geneva, Switzerland, 2016.
4. Santos-Silva, J.; Tenreyro, S. The Log of gravity. *Rev. Econ. Stat.* **2006**, *88*, 641–658. [CrossRef]
5. Jang, Y. The Impact of bilateral FTA on bilateral FDI among developed countries. *World Econ.* **2011**, *34*, 1628–1651. [CrossRef]
6. Egger, P.; Merlo, V. BITs bite: An anatomy of the impact of BITs on multinational firms. *Scand. J. Econ.* **2012**, *114*, 1240–1266. [CrossRef]
7. Aisbett, E.; Busse, M.; Nunnenkamp, P. BITs as deterrents of host-country discretion: The impact of investor-state disputes on FDI in developing countries. *Rev. World Econ.* **2018**, *154*, 119–155. [CrossRef]
8. Markusen, J.R.; Venables, A. The theory of endowment, intra-industry and multi-national trade. *J. Int. Econ.* **2000**, *52*, 209–234. [CrossRef]
9. Markusen, J.R.; Maskus, K. Discriminating among alternative theories of the multinational enterprise. *Rev. Int. Econ.* **2002**, *104*, 694–707. [CrossRef]
10. Levy-Yeyati, E.; Stein, E.; Daude, C. *Regional Integration and the Location of FDI. Working Paper 492*; Inter-American Development Bank, Research Department: Washington, DC, USA, 2003.
11. Ramondo, N.; Rappoport, V.; Ruhl, K. Intra-firm trade and vertical fragmentation in U.S. multinational corporations. *J. Int. Econ.* **2016**, *98*, 51–59. [CrossRef]
12. Egger, P.; Merlo, V. The impact of BITs on FDI dynamics. *World Econ.* **2007**, *30*, 1536–1549. [CrossRef]
13. Baltagi, B.H.; Egger, P.; Pfaffermayr, M. Estimating Regional Trade Agreement effects on FDI in an interdependent world. *J. Econom.* **2008**, *145*, 194–208. [CrossRef]
14. Chenaf-Nicet, D.; Rougier, E. The effect of macroeconomic instability on FDI flows: A gravity estimation of the impact of regional integration in the case of Euro-Mediterranean agreements. *Int. Econ.* **2016**, *145*, 66–91. [CrossRef]
15. Felbermayr, G.; Toubal, F. Cultural Proximity and Trade. *Eur. Econ. Rev.* **2010**, *54*, 279–293. [CrossRef]
16. Büthe, T.; Milner, H. FDI and institutional diversity in trade agreements: Credibility, commitment and economic flows in the developing world, 1971–2007. *World Politics* **2014**, *66*, 88–122. [CrossRef]
17. Dixon, J.; Haslam, P.A. Does the quality of investment protection affect FDI flows to Developing Countries? Evidence from Latin America. *World Econ.* **2016**, *39*, 1080–1108. [CrossRef]
18. Frenkel, M.; Walter, B. Do bilateral investment treaties attract FDI? The role of international dispute settlement provisions. *World Econ.* **2019**, *42*, 1316–1342. [CrossRef]
19. Markusen, J.R. Multinationals, multiplant economies and the gains from trade. *J. Int. Econ.* **1984**, *16*, 205–226. [CrossRef]
20. Helpman, E. A simple theory of international trade with multinational corporations. *J. Political Econ.* **1984**, *92*, 451–471. [CrossRef]
21. Neary, J.P. FDI and the single market. *Manch. Sch.* **2002**, *70*, 291–314. [CrossRef]
22. Castilho, M.; Zignago, S. Trade, FDI and regional integration in Mercosur. *Revue Econ.* **2000**, *51*, 761–774.
23. Anderson, J.E.; Larch, M.; Yotov, Y. Trade liberalization, growth and FDI: A structural estimation framework. *ETSG Work. Pap.* 2017. Available online: http://www.etsg.org/ETSG2016/Papers/052.pdf (accessed on 1 November 2018).
24. Blomström, M.; Kokko, A. *Regional Integration and FDI*; NBER Working Paper 1997; NBER: Cambridge, MA, USA, 1997.
25. Egger, P.; Pfaffermayr, M. FDI and European integration in the 1990s. *World Econ.* **2004**, *27*, 99–110. [CrossRef]
26. Büge, M. *Do PTA Increase Their Members' FDI?* German Development Institute Discussion Paper; DIE-GDI: Bonn, Germany, 2014.
27. Carr, D.L.; Markusen, J.R.; Maskus, K.E. Estimating the knowledge-capital model of the multinational enterprise. *Am. Econ. Rev.* **2001**, *91*, 693–708. [CrossRef]

28. Cherif, M.; Dreger, C. Institutional determinants of financial development in MENA countries. *Rev. Dev. Econ.* **2016**, *20*, 670–680. [CrossRef]

29. Kerner, A. Why should I believe you? Costs and consequences of BITs. *Int. Stud. Q.* **2009**, *53*, 73–102. [CrossRef]

30. Busse, M.; Königer, J.; Nunnenkamp, P. FDI promotion through bilateral investment treaties: More than a bit? *Rev. World Econ.* **2010**, *146*, 147–177. [CrossRef]

31. Neumayer, E.; Spess, L. Do BITs increase FDI to developing countries? *World Dev.* **2005**, *33*, 1567–1585. [CrossRef]

32. Salacuse, J.W.; Sullivan, N. Do BITs really work? An evaluation of BITs and their grand bargain. *Harv. Int. Law J.* **2005**, *46*, 67–130.

33. Sirr, G.; Garvey, J.; Gallagher, L. BITs and FDI: Evidence of asymmetric effects on vertical and horizontal investments. *Dev. Policy Rev.* **2017**, *35*, 93–113. [CrossRef]

34. Hallward-Driemeier, M. *Do Bilateral Investment Treaties Attract FDI? Only a Bit ... and They Could Bite*; Policy Research Working Paper WPS3121 2003; World Bank: Washington, DC, USA, 2003.

35. Rose-Ackerman, S.; Tobin, J. FDI and the business environment in developing countries: The impact of BITs. *Yale Law Econ. Res. Paper* **2005**, *293*. Available online: http://ssrn.com/abstract=557121 (accessed on 1 November 2018).

36. Gallagher, K.P.; Birch, M.B. Do investment agreements attract investment? Evidence from Latin America. *J. World Investig. Trade* **2006**, *7*, 961–974. [CrossRef]

37. Yackee, J.W. BITs, credible commitment, and the rule of (International) Law: Do BITs promote foreign direct investment? *Law Soc. Rev.* **2008**, *42*, 805–832. [CrossRef]

38. Tobin, J.L.; Rose-Ackerman, S. When BITs have some bite: The political-economic environment for bilateral investment treaties. *Rev. Int. Organ.* **2011**, *6*, 1–32. [CrossRef]

39. Blonigen, B.A.; Piger, J. Determinants of FDI. *Can. J. Econ.* **2014**, *47*, 775–812. [CrossRef]

40. Egger, P.; Pfaffermayr, M. The proper panel econometric specification of the gravity equation: A three-way model with bilateral interaction effects. *Empir. Econ.* **2003**, *28*, 571–580. [CrossRef]

41. Head, K.; Ries, J. FDI as an outcome of the market for corporate control: Theory and evidence. *J. Int. Econ.* **2008**, *74*, 2–20. [CrossRef]

42. Anderson, J.E.; Yotov, Y. Terms of trade and global efficiency effects of free trade agreements, 1990–2002. *J. Int. Econ.* **2016**, *99*, 279–298. [CrossRef]

43. Anderson, J.E.; van Wincoop, E. Gravity with gravitas: A solution to the border puzzle. *Am. Econ. Review* **2003**, *93*, 170–192. [CrossRef]

44. Head, K.; Mayer, T. Gravity equations: Workhorse, toolkit, and cookbook. In *Handbook of International Economics*; Gopinath, G., Helpman, E., Rogoff, K., Eds.; Elsevier: Amsterdam, The Netherlands, 2014; Volume 4, pp. 131–195.

45. Mátyás, L. Proper econometric specification of the gravity model. *World Econ.* **1997**, *20*, 363–368. [CrossRef]

46. Egger, P. A note on the proper econometric specification of the gravity equation. *Econ. Lett.* **2000**, *66*, 25–31. [CrossRef]

47. Baier, S.L.; Bergstrand, J.H. Do free trade agreements actually increase members' international trade? *J. Int. Econ.* **2007**, *71*, 72–95. [CrossRef]

48. Olivero, M.P.; Yotov, Y. Dynamic gravity: Endogenous country size and asset accumulation. *Can. J. Econ.* **2012**, *45*, 64–92. [CrossRef]

49. Feenstra, R. *Advanced International Trade: Theory and Evidence*; Princeton University Press: Princeton, NJ, USA, 2016.

50. Egger, P.; Pfaffermayr, M. Distance, trade and FDI: A Hausman–Taylor SUR approach. *J. Appl. Econom.* **2004**, *19*, 227–246. [CrossRef]

51. Babetskaia-Kukharchuk, O.; Maurel, M. Russia's accession on to the WTO: The potential for trade increase. *J. Comp. Econ.* **2004**, *32*, 680–699. [CrossRef]

52. McPherson, M.; Trumbull, W. Rescuing observed fixed effects: Using the Hausman-Taylor method for out-of-sample trade projections. *Int. Trade J.* **2008**, *22*, 315–340. [CrossRef]

53. Frankel, M.; Funke, K.; Stadtmann, G. A panel Analysis of bilateral FDI flows to emerging economies. *Econ. Syst.* **2004**, *28*, 281–300. [CrossRef]

54. Yang, S.; Martinez-Zarzoso, I. A panel data analysis of trade creation and trade diversion effects: The case of ASEAN-China Free Trade Area. *China Econ. Rev.* **2014**, *29*, 138–151. [CrossRef]

55. Berger, A.; Busse, M.; Nunnenkamp, P.; Roy, M. Do trade and investment agreements lead to more FDI? Accounting for key provisions inside the black box. *Int. Econ. Econ. Policy* **2013**, *10*, 247–275. [CrossRef]

56. Kohl, T.; Brakman, S.; Garretsen, H. Do trade agreements stimulate international trade differently? Evidence from 296 trade agreements. *World Econ.* **2016**, *39*, 97–131. [CrossRef]

57. Janicki, H.P.; Warin, T.; Wunnava, P. Endogenous OCA theory: Using the gravity model to test Mundell's intuition. *CES Work. Pap.* **2005**, 125.

58. Eicher, T.S.; Papageorgiou, C.; Raftery, A.E. Default priors and predictive performance in Bayesian model averaging, with application to growth determinants. *J. Appl. Econom.* **2011**, *26*, 30–55. [CrossRef]

59. Bergstrand, J.; Egger, P. A knowledge-and-physical-capital model of international trade flows, FDI and multinational enterprises. *J. Int. Econ.* **2007**, *73*, 278–308. [CrossRef]

60. Borchert, I.; Larch, M.; Shikher, S.; Yotov, Y. *Disaggregated Gravity: Benchmark Estimates and Stylized Facts from a New Database*; School of Economics Working Paper Series 2020-8; LeBow College of Business, Drexel University: Philadelphia, PA, USA, 2020.

61. Egger, P.; Nigai, S. Structural gravity with dummies only: Constrained ANOVA-type estimation of gravity models. *J. Int. Econ.* **2015**, *97*, 86–99. [CrossRef]

62. Hausman, J.A.; Taylor, W.E. Panel data and unobservable individual effects. *Econometrica* **1981**, *49*, 1377–1398. [CrossRef]

8

The VIF and MSE in Raise Regression

Román Salmerón Gómez [1], Ainara Rodríguez Sánchez [2], Catalina García García [1,*] and José García Pérez [3]

[1] Department of Quantitative Methods for Economics and Business, University of Granada, 18010 Granada, Spain; romansg@ugr.es

[2] Department of Economic Theory and History, University of Granada, 18010 Granada, Spain; arsanchez@ugr.es

[3] Department of Economy and Company, University of Almería, 04120 Almería, Spain; jgarcia@ual.es

* Correspondence: cbgarcia@ugr.es

Abstract: The raise regression has been proposed as an alternative to ordinary least squares estimation when a model presents collinearity. In order to analyze whether the problem has been mitigated, it is necessary to develop measures to detect collinearity after the application of the raise regression. This paper extends the concept of the variance inflation factor to be applied in a raise regression. The relevance of this extension is that it can be applied to determine the raising factor which allows an optimal application of this technique. The mean square error is also calculated since the raise regression provides a biased estimator. The results are illustrated by two empirical examples where the application of the raise estimator is compared to the application of the ridge and Lasso estimators that are commonly applied to estimate models with multicollinearity as an alternative to ordinary least squares.

Keywords: detection; mean square error; multicollinearity; raise regression; variance inflation factor

1. Introduction

In the last fifty years, different methods have been developed to avoid the instability of estimates derived from collinearity (see, for example, Kiers and Smilde [1]). Some of these methods can be grouped within a general denomination known as penalized regression.

In general terms, the penalized regression parts from the linear model (with p variables and n observations), $\mathbf{Y} = \mathbf{X}\boldsymbol{\beta} + \mathbf{u}$, and obtains the regularization of the estimated parameters, minimizing the following objective function:

$$(\mathbf{Y} - \mathbf{X}\boldsymbol{\beta})^t(\mathbf{Y} - \mathbf{X}\boldsymbol{\beta}) + P(\boldsymbol{\beta}),$$

where $P(\boldsymbol{\beta})$ is a penalty term that can take different forms. One of the most common penalty terms is the bridge penalty term ([2,3]) is given by

$$P(\boldsymbol{\beta}) = \lambda \sum_{j=1}^{p} |\beta_j|^{\alpha}, \ \alpha > 0,$$

where λ is a tuning parameter. Note that the ridge ([4]) and the Lasso ([5]) regressions are obtained when $\alpha = 2$ and $\alpha = 1$, respectively. Penalties have also been called soft thresholding ([6,7]).

These methods are applied not only for the treatment of multicollinearity but also for the selection of variables (see, for example, Dupuis and Victoria-Feser [8], Li and Yang [9] Liu et al. [10], or Uematsu and Tanaka [11]), which is a crucial issue in many areas of science when the number of variables exceeds the sample size. Zou and Hastie [12] proposed elastic net regularization by using the penalty terms λ_1 and λ_2 that combine the Lasso and ridge regressions:

$$P(\boldsymbol{\beta}) = \lambda_1 \sum_{j=1}^{p} |\beta_j| + \lambda_2 \sum_{j=1}^{p} \beta_j^2.$$

Thus, the Lasso regression usually selects one of the regressors from among all those that are highly correlated, while the elastic net regression selects several of them. In the words of Tutz and Ulbricht [13] "the elastic net catches all the big fish", meaning that it selects the whole group.

From a different point of view, other authors have also presented different techniques and methods well suited for dealing with the collinearity problems: continuum regression ([14]), least angle regression ([15]), generalized maximum entropy ([16–18]), the principal component analysis (PCA) regression ([19,20]), the principal correlation components estimator ([21]), penalized splines ([22]), partial least squares (PLS) regression ([23,24]), or the surrogate estimator focused on the solution of the normal equations presented by Jensen and Ramirez [25].

Focusing on collinearity, the ridge regression is one of the more commonly applied methodologies and it is estimated by the following expression:

$$\widehat{\boldsymbol{\beta}}(K) = \left(\mathbf{X}^t\mathbf{X} + K \cdot \mathbf{I}\right)^{-1}\mathbf{X}^t\mathbf{Y} \tag{1}$$

where $\mathbf{I}$ is the identity matrix with adequate dimensions and K is the ridge factor (ordinary least squares (OLS) estimators are obtained when $K = 0$). Although ridge regression has been widely applied, it presents some problems with current practice in the presence of multicollinearity and the estimators derived from the penalty come into these same problems whenever $n > p$:

- In relation to the calculation of the variance inflation factors (VIF), measures that quantify the degree of multicollinearity existing in a model from the coefficient of determination of the regression between the independent variables (for more details, see Section 2), García et al. [26] showed that the application of the original data when working with the ridge estimate leads to non-monotone VIF values by considering the VIF as a function of the penalty term. Logically, the Lasso and the elastic net regression inherit this property.
- By following Marquardt [27]: "The least squares objective function is mathematically independent of the scaling of the predictor variables (while the objective function in ridge regression is mathematically dependent on the scaling of the predictor variables)". That is to say, the penalized objective function will bring problems derived from the standardization of the variables. This fact has to be taken into account both for obtaining the estimators of the regressors and for the application of measures that detect if the collinearity has been mitigated. Other penalized regressions (such as Lasso and elastic net regressions) are not scale invariant and hence yield different results depending on the predictor scaling used.
- Some of the properties of the OLS estimator that are deduced from the normal equations are not verified by the ridge estimator and, among others, the estimated values for the endogenous variable are not orthogonal to the residuals. As a result, the following decomposition is verified

$$\sum_{i=1}^{n} (Y_i - \bar{Y})^2 = \sum_{i=1}^{n} (\hat{Y}_i(K) - \bar{Y})^2 + \sum_{i=1}^{n} e_i(K)^2 + 2\sum_{i=1}^{n} (\hat{Y}_i(K) - \bar{Y}) \cdot e_i(K).$$

When the OLS estimators are obtained ($K = 0$), the third term is null. However, this term is not null when K is not zero. Consequently, the relationship $TSS(K) = ESS(K) + RSS(K)$ is not satisfied in ridge regression, and the definition of the coefficient of determination may not be suitable. This fact not only limits the analysis of the goodness of fit but also affects the global significance since the critical coefficient of determination is also questioned. Rodríguez et al. [28]

showed that the estimators obtained from the penalties mentioned above inherit the problem of the ridge regression in relation to the goodness of fit.

In order to overcome these problems, this paper is focused on the raise regression (García et al. [29] and Salmerón et al. [30]) based on the treatment of collinearity from a geometrical point of view. It consists in separating the independent variables by using the residuals (weighted by the raising factor) of the auxiliary regression traditionally used to obtain the VIF. Salmerón et al. [30] showed that the raise regression presents better conditions than ridge regression and, more recently, García et al. [31] showed, among other questions, that the ridge regression is a particular case of the raise regression.

This paper presents the extension of the VIF to the raise regression showing that, although García et al. [31] showed that the application of the raise regression guarantees a diminishing of the VIF, it is not guaranteed that its value is lower the threshold traditionally established as troubling. Thus, it will be concluded that an unique application of the raise regression does not guarantee the mitigation of the multicollinearity. Consequently, this extension complements the results presented by García et al. [31] and determines, on the one hand, whether it is necessary to apply a successive raise regression (see García et al. [31] for more details) and, on the other hand, the most adequate variable for raising and the most optimal value for the raising factor in order to guarantee the mitigation of the multicollinearity.

On the other hand, the transformation of variables is common when strong collinearity exists in a linear model. The transformation to unit length (see Belsley et al. [32]) or standardization (see Marquardt [27]) is typical. Although the VIF is invariant to these transformations when it is calculated after estimation by OLS (see García et al. [26]), it is not guaranteed either in the case of the raise regression or in ridge regression as showed by García et al. [26]. The analysis of this fact is one of the goals of this paper.

Finally, since the raise estimator is biased, it is interesting to calculate its mean square error (MSE). It is studied whether the MSE of the raise regression is less than the one obtained by OLS. In this case, this study could be used to select an adequate raising factor similar to what is proposed by Hoerl et al. [33] in the case of the ridge regression. Note that estimators with MSE less than the one from OLS estimators are traditionally preferred (see, for example, Stein [34], James and Stein [35], Hoerl and Kennard [4], Ohtani [36], or Hubert et al. [37]). In addition, this measure allows us to conclude whether the raise regression is preferable, in terms of MSE, to other alternative techniques.

The structure of the paper is as follows: Section 2 briefly describes the VIF and the raise regression, and Section 3 extends the VIF to this methodology. Some desirable properties of the VIF are analyzed, and its asymptotic behavior is studied. It is also concluded that the VIF is invariant to data transformation. Section 4 calculates the MSE of the raise estimator, showing that there is a minimum value that is less than the MSE of the OLS estimator. Section 5 illustrates the contribution of this paper with two numerical examples. Finally, Section 6 summarizes the main conclusions of this paper.

2. Preliminaries

2.1. Variance Inflation Factor

The following model for p independent variables and n observations is considered:

$$\mathbf{Y} = \beta_1 + \beta_2 \mathbf{X}_2 + \cdots + \beta_i \mathbf{X}_i + \cdots + \beta_p \mathbf{X}_p + \mathbf{u} = \mathbf{X}\beta + \mathbf{u}, \tag{2}$$

where $\mathbf{Y}$ is a vector $n \times 1$ that contains the observations of the dependent variable, $\mathbf{X} = [\mathbf{1} \, \mathbf{X}_2 \ldots \mathbf{X}_i \ldots \mathbf{X}_p]$ (with $\mathbf{1}$ being a vector of ones with dimension $n \times 1$) is a matrix with order $n \times p$ that contains (by columns) the observations of the independent variables, β is a vector $p \times 1$ that contains the coefficients of the independent variables, and $\mathbf{u}$ is a vector $n \times 1$ that represents the random disturbance that is supposed to be spherical ($E[\mathbf{u}] = \mathbf{0}$ and $Var(\mathbf{u}) = \sigma^2 \mathbf{I}$, where $\mathbf{0}$ is a vector with zeros with dimension $n \times 1$ and $\mathbf{I}$ the identity matrix with adequate dimensions, in this case $p \times p$).

Given the model in Equation (2), the variance inflation factor (VIF) is obtained as follows:

$$VIF(k) = \frac{1}{1 - R_k^2}, \quad k = 2, \ldots, p, \tag{3}$$

where R_k^2 is the coefficient of determination of the regression of the variable $\mathbf{X}_k$ as a function of the rest of the independent variables of the model in Equation (2):

$$\mathbf{X}_k = \alpha_1 + \alpha_2 \mathbf{X}_2 + \cdots + \alpha_{k-1} \mathbf{X}_{k-1} + \alpha_{k+1} \mathbf{X}_{k+1} + \cdots + \alpha_p \mathbf{X}_p + \mathbf{v} = \mathbf{X}_{-k} \boldsymbol{\alpha} + \mathbf{v}, \tag{4}$$

where $\mathbf{X}_{-k}$ corresponds to the matrix $\mathbf{X}$ after the elimination of the column k (variable $\mathbf{X}_k$).

If the variable $\mathbf{X}_k$ has no linear relationship (i.e., is orthogonal) with the rest of the independent variables, the coefficient of determination will be zero ($R_k^2 = 0$) and the $VIF(k) = 1$. As the linear relationship increases, the coefficient of determination (R_k^2) and consequently $VIF(k)$ will also increase. Thus, the higher the VIF associated with the variable $\mathbf{X}_k$, the greater the linear relationship between this variable and the rest of the independent variables in the model in Equation (2). It is considered that the collinearity is troubling for values of VIF higher than 10. Note that the VIF ignores the role of the constant term (see, for example, Salmerón et al. [38] or Salmerón et al. [39]), and consequently, this extension will be useful when the multicollinearity is essential; that is to say, when there is a linear relationship between at least two independent variables of the model of regression without considering the constant term (see, for example, Marquandt and Snee [40] for the definitions of essential and nonessential multicollinearity).

2.2. Raise Regression

Raise regression, presented by García et al. [29] and more developed further by Salmerón et al. [30], uses the residuals of the model in Equation (4), $\mathbf{e}_k$, to raise the variable k as $\widetilde{\mathbf{X}}_k = \mathbf{X}_k + \lambda \mathbf{e}_k$ with $\lambda \geq 0$ (called the raising factor) and to verify that $\mathbf{e}_k^t \mathbf{X}_{-k} = \mathbf{0}$, where $\mathbf{0}$ is a vector of zeros with adequate dimensions. In that case, the raise regression consists in the estimation by OLS of the following model:

$$\mathbf{Y} = \beta_1(\lambda) + \beta_2(\lambda) \mathbf{X}_2 + \cdots + \beta_k(\lambda) \widetilde{\mathbf{X}}_k + \cdots + \beta_p(\lambda) \mathbf{X}_p + \widetilde{\mathbf{u}} = \widetilde{\mathbf{X}} \boldsymbol{\beta}(\lambda) + \widetilde{\mathbf{u}}, \tag{5}$$

where $\widetilde{\mathbf{X}} = [\mathbf{1} \ \mathbf{X}_2 \ldots \widetilde{\mathbf{X}}_k \ldots \mathbf{X}_p] = [\mathbf{X}_{-k} \ \widetilde{\mathbf{X}}_k]$. García et al. [29] showed (Theorem 3.3) that this technique does not alter the global characteristics of the initial model. That is to say, the models in Equations (2) and (5) have the same coefficient of determination and experimental statistics for the global significance test.

Figure 1 illustrates the raise regression for two independent variables being geometrically separated by using the residuals weighted by the raising factor λ. Thus, the selection of an adequate value for λ is essential, analogously to what occurs with the ridge factor K. A preliminary proposal about how to select the raising factor in a model with two independent standardized variables can be found in García et al. [41]. Other recently published papers introduce and highlight the various advantages of raise estimators for statistical analysis: Salmerón et al. [30] presented the raise regression for $p = 3$ standardized variables and showed that it presents better properties than the ridge regression and that the individual inference of the raised variable is not altered, García et al. [31] showed that it is guaranteed that all the VIFs associated with the model in Equation (5) diminish but that it is not possible to quantify the decrease, García and Ramírez [42] presented the successive raise regression, and García et al. [31] showed, among other questions, that ridge regression is a particular case of raise regression.

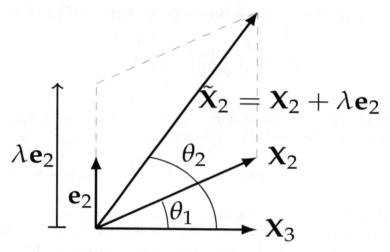

Figure 1. Representation of the raise method.

The following section presents the extension of the VIF to be applied after the estimation by raise regression since it will be interesting whether, after the raising of one independent variable, the VIF falls below 10. It will be also analyzed when a successive raise regression can be recommendable (see García and Ramírez [42]).

3. VIF in Raise Regression

To calculate the VIF in the raise regression, two cases have to be differentiated depending on the dependent variable, X_k, of the auxiliary regression:

1. If it is the raised variable, $\tilde{X}_i$ with $i = 2, \ldots, p$, the coefficient of determination, $R_i^2(\lambda)$, of the following auxiliary regression has to be calculated:

$$
\begin{aligned}
\tilde{X}_i &= \alpha_1(\lambda) + \alpha_2(\lambda)X_2 + \cdots + \alpha_{i-1}(\lambda)X_{i-1} + \alpha_{i+1}(\lambda)X_{i+1} + \cdots + \alpha_p(\lambda)X_p + \tilde{v} \\
&= X_{-i}\alpha(\lambda) + \tilde{v}.
\end{aligned}
\tag{6}
$$

2. If it is not the raised variable, X_j with $j = 2, \ldots, p$ being $j \neq i$, the coefficient of determination, $R_j^2(\lambda)$, of the following auxiliary regression has to be calculated:

$$
\begin{aligned}
X_j &= \alpha_1(\lambda) + \alpha_2(\lambda)X_2 + \cdots + \alpha_i(\lambda)\tilde{X}_i + \cdots + \alpha_{j-1}(\lambda)X_{j-1} + \alpha_{j+1}(\lambda)X_{j+1} \\
&\quad + \cdots + \alpha_p(\lambda)X_p + \tilde{v} \\
&= \left(X_{-i,-j} \ \tilde{X}_i\right) \begin{pmatrix} \alpha_{-i,-j}(\lambda) \\ \alpha_i(\lambda) \end{pmatrix} + \tilde{v},
\end{aligned}
\tag{7}
$$

where $X_{-i,-j}$ corresponding to the matrix X after the elimination of columns i and j (variables X_i and X_j). The same notation is used for $\alpha_{-i,-j}(\lambda)$.

Once these coefficients of determination are obtained (as indicated in the following subsections), the VIF of the raise regression will be given by the following:

$$
VIF(k, \lambda) = \frac{1}{1 - R_k^2(\lambda)}, \quad k = 2, \ldots, p.
\tag{8}
$$

3.1. VIF Associated with Raise Variable

In this case, for $i = 2, \ldots, p$, the coefficient of determination of the regression in Equation (6) is given by

$$
\begin{aligned}
R_i^2(\lambda) &= 1 - \frac{(1+2\lambda+\lambda^2)RSS_i^{-i}}{TSS_i^{-i}+(\lambda^2+2\lambda)RSS_i^{-i}} = \frac{ESS_i^{-i}}{TSS_i^{-i}+(\lambda^2+2\lambda)RSS_i^{-i}} \\
&= \frac{R_i^2}{1+(\lambda^2+2\lambda)(1-R_i^2)},
\end{aligned}
\tag{9}
$$

since:

$$
\begin{aligned}
TSS_i^{-i}(\lambda) &= \widetilde{\mathbf{X}}_i^t\widetilde{\mathbf{X}}_i - n \cdot \overline{\widetilde{\mathbf{X}}}_i^2 = \mathbf{X}_i^t\mathbf{X}_i + (\lambda^2+2\lambda)\mathbf{e}_i^t\mathbf{e}_i - n \cdot \overline{\mathbf{X}}_i^2 \\
&= TSS_i^{-i} + (\lambda^2+2\lambda)RSS_i^{-i}, \\
RSS_i^{-i}(\lambda) &= \widetilde{\mathbf{X}}_i^t\widetilde{\mathbf{X}}_i - \widehat{\boldsymbol{\alpha}}(\lambda)^t\mathbf{X}_{-i}^t\widetilde{\mathbf{X}}_i = \mathbf{X}_i^t\mathbf{X}_i + (\lambda^2+2\lambda)\mathbf{e}_i^t\mathbf{e}_i - \widehat{\boldsymbol{\alpha}}^t\mathbf{X}_{-i}^t\mathbf{X}_i \\
&= (\lambda^2+2\lambda+1)RSS_i^{-i},
\end{aligned}
$$

where TSS_i^{-i}, ESS_i^{-i} and RSS_i^{-i} are the total sum of squares, explained sum of squares, and residual sum of squares of the model in Equation (4). Note that it has been taken into account that

$$
\widetilde{\mathbf{X}}_i^t\widetilde{\mathbf{X}}_i = (\mathbf{X}_i + \lambda\mathbf{e}_i)^t (\mathbf{X}_i + \lambda\mathbf{e}_i) = \mathbf{X}_i^t\mathbf{X}_i + (\lambda^2 + 2\lambda)\mathbf{e}_i^t\mathbf{e}_i,
$$

since $\mathbf{e}_i^t\mathbf{X}_i = \mathbf{e}_i^t\mathbf{e}_i = RSS_i^{-i}$ and

$$
\widehat{\boldsymbol{\alpha}}(\lambda) = \left(\mathbf{X}_{-i}^t\mathbf{X}_{-i}\right)^{-1}\mathbf{X}_{-i}^t\widetilde{\mathbf{X}}_i = \widehat{\boldsymbol{\alpha}},
$$

due to $\mathbf{X}_{-i}^t\widetilde{\mathbf{X}}_i = \mathbf{X}_{-i}^t\mathbf{X}_i$.

Indeed, from Equation (9), it is evident that

1. $R_i^2(\lambda)$ decreases as λ increases.
2. $\lim\limits_{\lambda \to +\infty} R_i^2(\lambda) = 0$.
3. $R_i^2(\lambda)$ is continuous in zero; that is to say, $R_i^2(0) = R_i^2$.

Finally, from properties 1) and 3), it is deduced that $R_i^2(\lambda) \leq R_i^2$ for all λ.

3.2. VIF Associated with Non-Raised Variables

In this case, for $j = 2, \ldots, p$, with $j \neq i$, the coefficient of determination of regression in Equation (7) is given by

$$
\begin{aligned}
R_j^2(\lambda) &= 1 - \frac{RSS_j^{-j}(\lambda)}{TSS_j^{-j}(\lambda)} \\
&= \frac{1}{TSS_j^{-j}}\left(TSS_j^{-j} - RSS_j^{-i,-j} + \frac{RSS_i^{-i,-j} \cdot \left(RSS_j^{-i,-j} - RSS_j^{-j}\right)}{RSS_i^{-i,-j}+(\lambda^2+2\lambda)\cdot RSS_i^{-i}}\right),
\end{aligned}
\tag{10}
$$

Taking into account that $\widetilde{\mathbf{X}}_i^t\mathbf{X}_j = (\mathbf{X}_i + \lambda\mathbf{e}_i)^t\mathbf{X}_j = \mathbf{X}_i^t\mathbf{X}_j$ since $\mathbf{e}_i^t\mathbf{X}_j = 0$, it is verified that

$$
TSS_j^{-j}(\lambda) = \mathbf{X}_j^t\mathbf{X}_j - n \cdot \overline{\mathbf{X}}_j^2 = TSS_j^{-j},
$$

and, from Appendices A and B,

$$RSS_j^{-j}(\lambda) = \mathbf{X}_j^t\mathbf{X}_j - \widehat{\boldsymbol{\alpha}}(\lambda)^t \begin{pmatrix} \mathbf{X}_{-i,-j}^t\mathbf{X}_j \\ \widetilde{\mathbf{X}}_i^t\mathbf{X}_j \end{pmatrix}$$

$$= \mathbf{X}_j^t\mathbf{X}_j - \widehat{\boldsymbol{\alpha}}_{-i,-j}(\lambda)^t\mathbf{X}_{-i,-j}^t\mathbf{X}_j - \widehat{\alpha}_i(\lambda)^t\mathbf{X}_i^t\mathbf{X}_j$$

$$\underbrace{=}\ \mathbf{X}_j^t\mathbf{X}_j - \mathbf{X}_j^t\mathbf{X}_{-i,-j}\left(\mathbf{X}_{-i,-j}^t\mathbf{X}_{-i,-j}\right)^{-1}\mathbf{X}_{-i,-j}^t\mathbf{X}_j$$

Appendix A

$$-\frac{RSS_i^{-i,-j}}{RSS_i^{-i,-j} + (\lambda^2 + 2\lambda)\cdot RSS_i^{-i}}\cdot$$

$$\cdot\left(RSS_i^{-i,-j}\mathbf{X}_j^t\mathbf{X}_{-i,-j}\cdot B\cdot B^t\cdot \mathbf{X}_{-i,-j}^t\mathbf{X}_j\right.$$

$$\left.+\mathbf{X}_j^t\mathbf{X}_i\cdot B^t\cdot\mathbf{X}_{-i,-j}^t\mathbf{X}_j\right)$$

$$-\frac{RSS_i^{-i,-j}}{RSS_i^{-i,-j} + (\lambda^2 + 2\lambda)\cdot RSS_i^{-i}}\cdot\widehat{\alpha}_i^t\mathbf{X}_i^t\mathbf{X}_j$$

$$= \mathbf{X}_j^t\left(\mathbf{I} - \mathbf{X}_{-i,-j}\left(\mathbf{X}_{-i,-j}^t\mathbf{X}_{-i,-j}\right)^{-1}\mathbf{X}_{-i,-j}^t\right)\mathbf{X}_j$$

$$-\frac{RSS_i^{-i,-j}}{RSS_i^{-i,-j} + (\lambda^2 + 2\lambda)\cdot RSS_i^{-i}}\cdot$$

$$\cdot\left(RSS_i^{-i,-j}\mathbf{X}_j^t\mathbf{X}_{-i,-j}\cdot B\cdot B^t\cdot\mathbf{X}_{-i,-j}^t\mathbf{X}_j\right.$$

$$\left.+\mathbf{X}_j^t\mathbf{X}_i\cdot B^t\cdot\mathbf{X}_{-i,-j}^t\mathbf{X}_j + \widehat{\alpha}_i^t\mathbf{X}_i^t\mathbf{X}_j\right)$$

$$\underbrace{=}\ RSS_j^{-i,-j}$$

Appendix B

$$-\frac{RSS_i^{-i,-j}}{RSS_i^{-i,-j} + (\lambda^2 + 2\lambda)\cdot RSS_i^{-i}}\cdot\left(RSS_j^{-i,-j} - RSS_j^{-j}\right),$$

where TSS_j^{-j} and RSS_j^{-j} are the total sum of squares and residual sum of squares of the model in Equation (4) and where $RSS_i^{-i,-j}$ and $RSS_j^{-i,-j}$ are the residual sums of squares of models:

$$\mathbf{X}_i = \mathbf{X}_{-i,-j}\gamma + \eta, \tag{11}$$

$$\mathbf{X}_j = \mathbf{X}_{-i,-j}\delta + \nu. \tag{12}$$

Indeed, from Equation (10), it is evident that

1. $R_j^2(\lambda)$ decreases as λ increases.

2. $\displaystyle\lim_{\lambda\to+\infty} R_j^2(\lambda) = \frac{TSS_j^{-j} - RSS_j^{-i,-j}}{TSS_j^{-j}}.$

3. $R_j^2(\lambda)$ is continuous in zero. That is to say, $R_j^2(0) = \frac{TSS_j^{-j} - RSS_j^{-j}}{TSS_j^{-j}} = R_j^2.$

Finally, from properties 1) and 3), it is deduced that $R_j^2(\lambda) \le R_j^2$ for all λ.

3.3. Properties of $VIF(k, \lambda)$

From conditions verified by the coefficient of determination in Equations (9) and (10), it is concluded that $VIF(k, \lambda)$ (see expression Equation (8)), verifies that

1. The VIF associated with the raise regression is continuous in zero because the coefficients of determination of the auxiliary regressions in Equations (6) and (7) are also continuous in zero. That is to say, for $\lambda = 0$, it coincides with the VIF obtained for the model in Equation (2) when it is estimated by OLS:

$$VIF(k, 0) = \frac{1}{1 - R_k^2(0)} = \frac{1}{1 - R_k^2} = VIF(k), \quad k = 2, \ldots, p.$$

2. The VIF associated with the raise regression decreases as λ increases since this is the behavior of the coefficient of determination of the auxiliary regressions in Equations (6) and (7). Consequently,

$$VIF(k, \lambda) = \frac{1}{1 - R_k^2(\lambda)} \leq \frac{1}{1 - R_k^2} = VIF(k), \quad k = 2, \ldots, p, \quad \forall \lambda \geq 0.$$

3. The VIF associated with the raised variable is always higher than one since

$$\lim_{\lambda \to +\infty} VIF(i, \lambda) = \lim_{\lambda \to +\infty} \frac{1}{1 - R_i^2(\lambda)} = \frac{1}{1 - 0} = 1, \quad i = 2, \ldots, p.$$

4. The VIF associated with the non-raised variables has a horizontal asymptote since

$$\lim_{\lambda \to +\infty} VIF(j, \lambda) = \lim_{\lambda \to +\infty} \frac{1}{1 - R_j^2(\lambda)} = \frac{1}{1 - \frac{TSS_j^{-j} - RSS_j^{-i,-j}}{TSS_j^{-j}}}$$

$$= \frac{TSS_j^{-j}}{RSS_j^{-i,-j}} = \frac{TSS_j^{-i,-j}}{RSS_j^{-i,-j}} = \frac{1}{1 - R_{ij}^2} = VIF_{-i}(j),$$

where R_{ij}^2 is the coefficient of determination of the regression in Equation (12) for $j = 2, \ldots, p$ and $j \neq i$. Indeed, this asymptote corresponds to the VIF, $VIF_{-i}(j)$, of the regression $\mathbf{Y} = \mathbf{X}_{-i}\boldsymbol{\xi} + \mathbf{w}$ and, consequently, will also always be equal to or higher than one.

Thus, from properties (1) to (4), $VIF(k, \lambda)$ has the very desirable properties of being continuous, monotone in the raise parameter, and higher than one, as presented in García et al. [26].

In addition, the property (4) can be applied to determine the variable to be raised only considering the one with a lower horizontal asymptote. If the asymptote is lower than 10 (the threshold established traditionally as worrying), the extension could be applied to determine the raising factor by selecting, for example, the first λ that verifies $VIF(k, \lambda) < 10$ for $k = 2, \ldots, p$. If none of the $p - 1$ asymptotes is lower than the established threshold, it will not be enough to raise one independent variable and a successive raise regression will be recommended (see García and Ramírez [42] and García et al. [31] for more details). Note that, if it were necessary to raise more than one variable, it is guaranteed that there will be values of the raising parameter that mitigate multicollinearity since, in the extreme case where all the variables of the model are raised, all the VIFs associated with the raised variables tend to one.

3.4. Transformation of Variables

The transformation of data is very common when working with models where strong collinearity exists. For this reason, this section analyzes whether the transformation of the data affects the VIF obtained in the previous section.

Since the expression given by Equation (9) can be expressed with $i = 2, \ldots, p$ in the function of R_i^2:

$$R_i^2(\lambda) = \frac{R_i^2}{1 + (\lambda^2 + 2\lambda) \cdot (1 - R_i^2)},$$

it is concluded that it is invariant to origin and scale changes and, consequently, the VIF calculated from it will also be invariant.

On the other hand, the expression given by Equation (10) can be expressed for $j = 2, \ldots, p$, with $j \neq i$ as

$$
\begin{aligned}
R_j^2(\lambda) &= 1 - \frac{RSS_j^{-i,-j}}{TSS_j^{-j}} + \frac{1}{TSS_j^{-j}} \cdot \frac{RSS_i^{-i,-j} \cdot (RSS_j^{-i,-j} - RSS_j^{-j})}{RSS_i^{-i,-j} + (\lambda^2 + 2\lambda) \cdot RSS_i^{-i}} \\
&= R_{ij}^2 + \frac{RSS_i^{-i,-j}}{RSS_i^{-i,-j} + (\lambda^2 + 2\lambda) \cdot RSS_i^{-i}} \cdot \left(\frac{RSS_j^{-i,-j}}{TSS_j^{-i,-j}} - \frac{RSS_j^{-j}}{TSS_j^{-j}} \right) \\
&= R_{ij}^2 + \frac{R_j^2 - R_{ij}^2}{1 + (\lambda^2 + 2\lambda) \cdot \frac{RSS_i^{-i}}{RSS_i^{-i,-j}}},
\end{aligned}
\tag{13}
$$

where it was applied that $TSS_j^{-j} = TSS_j^{-i,-j}$.

In this case, by following García et al. [26], transforming the variable $\mathbf{X}_i$ as

$$\mathbf{x}_i = \frac{\mathbf{X}_i - a_i}{b_i}, \quad a_i \in \mathbb{R}, \ b_i \in \mathbb{R} - \{0\}, \quad i = 2, \ldots, p,$$

it is obtained that $RSS_i^{-i}(T) = \frac{1}{b_i^2} RSS_i^{-i}$ and $RSS_i^{-i,-j}(T) = \frac{1}{b_i^2} RSS_i^{-i,-j}$ where $RSS_i^{-i}(T)$ and $RSS_i^{-i,-j}(T)$ are the residual sum of squares of the transformed variables.

Taking into account that $\mathbf{X}_i$ is the dependent variables in the regressions of RSS_i^{-i} and $RSS_i^{-i,-j}$, the following is obtained:

$$\frac{RSS_i^{-i}}{RSS_i^{-i,-j}} = \frac{RSS_i^{-i}(T)}{RSS_i^{-i,-j}(T)}.$$

Then, the expression given by Equation (13) is invariant to data transformations (As long as the dependent variables are transformed from the regressions of RSS_i^{-i} and $RSS_i^{-i,-j}$ in the same form. For example, (a) for considering that a_i is its mean and b_i is its standard deviation (typification), (b) for considering that a_i is its mean and b_i is its standard deviation multiplied by the square root of the number of observations (standardization), or (c) for considering that a_i is zero and b_i is the square root of the squares sum of observations (unit length).) and, consequently, the VIF calculated from it will also be invariant.

4. MSE for Raise Regression

Since the estimator β obtained from Equation (5) is biased, it is interesting to study its Mean Square Error (MSE).

Taking into account that, for $k = 2, \ldots, p$,

$$
\begin{aligned}
\widetilde{\mathbf{X}}_k &= \mathbf{X}_k + \lambda \mathbf{e}_k \\
&= (1 + \lambda)\mathbf{X}_k - \lambda \left(\widehat{\alpha}_0 + \widehat{\alpha}_1 \mathbf{X}_1 + \cdots + \widehat{\alpha}_{k-1}\mathbf{X}_{k-1} + \widehat{\alpha}_{k+1}\mathbf{X}_{k+1} + \cdots + \widehat{\alpha}_p \mathbf{X}_p \right),
\end{aligned}
$$

it is obtained that matrix $\widetilde{\mathbf{X}}$ of the expression in Equation (5) can be rewritten as $\widetilde{\mathbf{X}} = \mathbf{X} \cdot \mathbf{M}_\lambda$, where

$$
\mathbf{M}_\lambda = \begin{pmatrix}
1 & 0 & \cdots & 0 & -\lambda\widehat{\alpha}_0 & 0 & \cdots & 0 \\
0 & 1 & \cdots & 0 & -\lambda\widehat{\alpha}_1 & 0 & \cdots & 0 \\
\vdots & \vdots & & \vdots & \vdots & \vdots & & \vdots \\
0 & 0 & \cdots & 1 & -\lambda\widehat{\alpha}_{k-1} & 0 & \cdots & 0 \\
0 & 0 & \cdots & 0 & 1+\lambda & 0 & \cdots & 0 \\
0 & 0 & \cdots & 0 & -\lambda\widehat{\alpha}_{k+1} & 1 & \cdots & 0 \\
\vdots & \vdots & & \vdots & \vdots & \vdots & & \vdots \\
0 & 0 & \cdots & 0 & -\lambda\widehat{\alpha}_p & 0 & \cdots & 1
\end{pmatrix}.
\tag{14}
$$

Thus, we have $\widehat{\beta}(\lambda) = (\widetilde{\mathbf{X}}^t \cdot \widetilde{\mathbf{X}})^{-1}\widetilde{\mathbf{X}}^t \cdot \mathbf{Y} = \mathbf{M}_\lambda^{-1} \cdot \widehat{\beta}$, and then, the estimator of β obtained from Equation (5) is biased unless $\mathbf{M}_\lambda = \mathbf{I}$, which only occurs when $\lambda = 0$, that is to say, when the raise regression coincides with OLS. Moreover,

$$
\begin{aligned}
tr\left(Var\left(\widehat{\beta}(\lambda) \right) \right) &= tr(\mathbf{M}_\lambda^{-1} \cdot Var(\widehat{\beta}) \cdot (\mathbf{M}_\lambda^{-1})^t) = \sigma^2 tr((\widetilde{\mathbf{X}}^t\widetilde{\mathbf{X}})^{-1}), \\
(E[\widehat{\beta}(\lambda)] - \beta)^t(E[\widehat{\beta}(\lambda)] - \beta) &= \beta^t(\mathbf{M}_\lambda^{-1} - \mathbf{I})^t(\mathbf{M}_\lambda^{-1} - \mathbf{I})\beta,
\end{aligned}
$$

where tr denotes the trace of a matrix.

In that case, the MSE for raise regression is

$$
\begin{aligned}
\text{MSE}\left(\widehat{\beta}(\lambda) \right) &= tr\left(Var\left(\widehat{\beta}(\lambda) \right) \right) + (E[\widehat{\beta}(\lambda)] - \beta)^t(E[\widehat{\beta}(\lambda)] - \beta) \\
&= \sigma^2 tr((\widetilde{\mathbf{X}}^t\widetilde{\mathbf{X}})^{-1}) + \beta^t(\mathbf{M}_\lambda^{-1} - \mathbf{I})^t(\mathbf{M}_\lambda^{-1} - \mathbf{I})\beta \\
&\underset{\text{Appendix C}}{=} \sigma^2 tr\left((\mathbf{X}_{-k}^t\mathbf{X}_{-k})^{-1} \right) + \left(1 + \sum_{j=0, j\neq k}^{p} \widehat{\alpha}_j^2 \right) \cdot \beta_k^2 \cdot \frac{\lambda^2 + h}{(1+\lambda)^2},
\end{aligned}
$$

where $h = \frac{\sigma^2}{\beta_k^2 \cdot RSS_k^{-k}}$.

We can obtain the MSE from the estimated values of σ^2 and β_k from the model in Equation (2).

On the other hand, once the estimations are obtained and taking into account the Appendix C, $\lambda_{min} = \frac{\widehat{\sigma}^2}{\widehat{\beta}_k^2 \cdot RSS_k^{-k}}$ minimizes MSE $\left(\widehat{\beta}(\lambda) \right)$. Indeed, it is verified that MSE $\left(\widehat{\beta}(\lambda_{min}) \right) <$ MSE $\left(\widehat{\beta}(0) \right)$; that is to say, if the goal is exclusively to minimize the MSE (as in the work presented by Hoerl et al. [33]), λ_{min} should be selected as the raising factor.

Finally, note that, if $\lambda_{min} > 1$, then MSE $\left(\widehat{\beta}(\lambda) \right) <$ MSE $\left(\widehat{\beta}(0) \right)$ for all $\lambda > 0$.

5. Numerical Examples

To illustrate the results of previous sections, two different set of data will be used that collect the two situations shown in the graphs of Figures A1 and A2. The second example also compares results obtained by the raise regression to results obtained by the application of ridge and Lasso regression.

5.1. Example 1: $h < 1$

The data set includes different financial variables for 15 Spanish companies for the year 2016 (consolidated account and results between €800,000 and €9,000,000) obtained from the dabase Sistema de Análisis de Balances Ibéricos (SABI) database. The relationship is studied between the number of employees, E, and the fixed assets (€), FA; operating income (€), OI; and sales (€), S. The model is expressed as

$$E = \beta_1 + \beta_2 FA + \beta_3 OI + \beta_4 S + u. \tag{15}$$

Table 1 displays the results of the estimation by OLS of the model in Equation (15). The presence of essential collinearity in the model in Equation (15) is indicated by the determinant close to zero (0.0000919) of the correlation matrix of independent variables

$$R = \begin{pmatrix} 1 & 0.7264656 & 0.7225473 \\ 0.7264656 & 1 & 0.9998871 \\ 0.7225473 & 0.9998871 & 1 \end{pmatrix},$$

and the VIFs (2.45664, 5200.315, and 5138.535) higher than 10. Note that the collinearity is provoked fundamentally by the relationship between OI and S.

In contrast, due to the fact that the coefficients of variation of the independent variables (1.015027, 0.7469496, and 0.7452014) are higher than 0.1002506, the threshold established as troubling by Salmerón et al. [39], it is possible to conclude that the nonessential multicollinearity is not troubling. Thus, the extension of the VIF seems appropriate to check if the application of the raise regression has mitigated the multicollinearity.

Remark 1. $\lambda^{(1)}$ and $\lambda^{(2)}$ will be the raising factor of the first and second raising, respectively.

Table 1. Estimations of the models in Equations (15)–(18): Standard deviation is inside the parenthesis, R^2 is the coefficient of determination, $F_{3,11}$ is the experimental value of the joint significance contrast, and $\hat{\sigma}^2$ is the variance estimate of the random perturbation.

	Model (15)	p-Value	Model (16) for $\lambda_{vif}^{(1)}=24.5$	p-Value	Model (17) for $\lambda_{min}^{(1)}=0.42$ and $\lambda_{vif}^{(2)}=17.5$	p-Value	Model (18) for $\lambda_{mse}^{(1)}=1.43$ and $\lambda_{vif}^{(2)}=10$	p-Value
Intercept	994.21 (17940)	0.957	4588.68 (17,773.22)	0.801	5257.84 (1744.26)	0.772	5582.29 (17740.18)	0.759
FA	−1.28 (0.55)	0.039	−1.59 (0.50)	0.009	−1.59 (0.51)	0.009	−1.58 (0.51)	0.009
OI	−81.79 (52.86)	0.150						
$\widetilde{OI}_{\lambda_{vif}^{(1)}}$			−3.21 (2.07)	0.150				
$\widetilde{OI}_{\lambda_{min}^{(1)}}$					1.67 (2.28)	0.478		
$\widetilde{OI}_{\lambda_{mse}^{(1)}}$							1.51 (2.24)	0.517
S	87.58 (53.29)	0.129	8.38 (2.35)	0.004				
$\widetilde{S}_{\lambda_{vif}^{(2)}}$					3.42 (2.03)	0.120	3.55 (1.99)	0.103
R^2	0.70		0.70		0.70		0.70	
$F_{3,11}$	8.50		8.50		8.50		8.50	
$\hat{\sigma}^2$	1,617,171,931		1,617,171,931		1,617,171,931		1,617,171,931	
MSE	321,730,738		321,790,581		336,915,567		325,478,516	

5.1.1. First Raising

A possible solution could be to apply the raise regression to try to mitigate the collinearity. To decide which variable is raised, the thresholds for the VIFs associated with the raise regression are calculated with the goal of raising the variable that the smaller horizontal asymptotes present. In addition to raising the variable that presents the lowest VIF, it would be interesting to obtain a lower mean squared error (MSE) after raising. For this, the $\lambda_{min}^{(1)}$ is calculated for each case. Results are shown in Table 2. Note that the variable to be raised should be the second or third since their asymptotes are lower than 10, although in both cases $\lambda_{min}^{(1)}$ is lower than 1 and it is not guaranteed that the MSE of the raise regression will be less than the one obtained from the estimation by the OLS of the model in Equation (15). For this reason, this table also shows the values of $\lambda^{(1)}$ that make the MSE of the raise regression coincide with the MSE of the OLS regression, $\lambda_{mse}^{(1)}$, and the minimum value of $\lambda^{(1)}$ that leads to values of VIF less than 10, $\lambda_{vif}^{(1)}$.

Table 2. Horizontal asymptotes for variance inflation factors (VIF) after raising each variable and $\lambda_{min}^{(1)}$, $\lambda_{mse}^{(1)}$, and $\lambda_{vif}^{(1)}$.

Raised	$\lim\limits_{\lambda^{(1)}\to+\infty} VIF(FA,\lambda^{(1)})$	$\lim\limits_{\lambda^{(1)}\to+\infty} VIF(OI,\lambda^{(1)})$	$\lim\limits_{\lambda^{(1)}\to+\infty} VIF(S,\lambda^{(1)})$
Variable 1	1	4429.22	4429.22
Variable 2	2.09	1	2.09
Variable 3	2.12	2.12	1
Raised	$\lambda_{min}^{(1)}$	$\lambda_{mse}^{(1)}$	$\lambda_{vif}^{(1)}$
Variable 1	0.18	0.45	∄
Variable 2	0.42	1.43	24.5
Variable 3	0.37	1.18	24.7

Figure 2 displays the VIF associated with the raise regression for $0 \leq \lambda^{(1)} \leq 900$ after raising the second variable. It is observed that VIFs are always higher than its corresponding horizontal asymptotes.

The model after raising the second variable will be given by

$$E = \beta_1(\lambda) + \beta_2(\lambda)\mathbf{FA} + \beta_3(\lambda)\widetilde{\mathbf{OI}} + \beta_4(\lambda)\mathbf{S} + \widetilde{\boldsymbol{u}}, \tag{16}$$

where $\widetilde{\mathbf{OI}} = \mathbf{OI} + \lambda^{(1)} \cdot \mathbf{e_{OI}}$ with $\mathbf{e_{OI}}$ the residual of regression:

$$\mathbf{OI} = \alpha_1 + \alpha_2\mathbf{FA} + \alpha_3\mathbf{S} + \boldsymbol{v}.$$

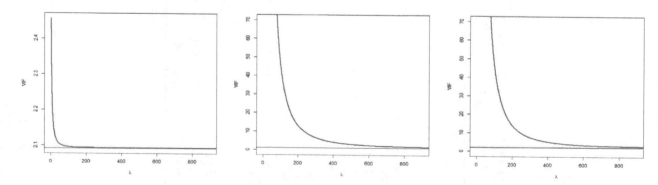

Figure 2. VIF of the variables after raising **OI**.

Remark 2. *The coefficient of variation of* $\widetilde{\mathbf{OI}}$ *for* $\lambda^{(1)} = 24.5$ *is equal to 0.7922063; that is to say, it was lightly increased.*

As can be observed from Table 3, in Equation (16), the collinearity is not mitigated by considering $\lambda^{(1)}$ equal to $\lambda^{(1)}_{min}$ and $\lambda^{(1)}_{mse}$. For this reason, Table 1 only shows the values of the model in Equation (16) for the value of $\lambda^{(1)}$ that leads to VIF lower than 10.

Table 3. VIF of regression Equation (16) for $\lambda^{(1)}$ equal to $\lambda^{(1)}_{min}$, $\lambda^{(1)}_{mse}$, and $\lambda^{(1)}_{vif}$.

	$VIF(\mathbf{FA}, \lambda^{(1)})$	$VIF(\widetilde{\mathbf{OI}}, \lambda^{(1)})$	$VIF(\mathbf{S}, \lambda^{(1)})$
$\lambda^{(1)}_{min}$	2.27	2587.84	2557.66
$\lambda^{(1)}_{mse}$	2.15	878.10	868.58
$\lambda^{(1)}_{vif}$	2.09	9.00	9.99

5.1.2. Transformation of Variables

After the first raising, it is interesting to verify that the VIF associated with the raise regression is invariant to data transformation. With this goal, the second variable has been raised, obtaining the $VIF(\mathbf{FA}, \lambda^{(1)})$, $VIF(\widetilde{\mathbf{OI}}, \lambda^{(1)})$, and $VIF(\mathbf{S}, \lambda^{(1)})$ for $\lambda^{(1)} \in \{0, 0.5, 1, 1.5, 2, \ldots, 9.5, 10\}$, supposing original, unit length, and standardized data. Next, the three possible differences and the average of the VIF associated with each variable are obtained. Table 4 displays the results from which it is possible to conclude that differences are almost null and that, consequently, the VIF associated with the raise regression is invariant to the most common data transformation.

Table 4. Effect of data transformations on VIF associated with raise regression.

	$VIF(\mathbf{FA}, \lambda^{(1)})$	$VIF(\widetilde{\mathbf{OE}}, \lambda^{(1)})$	$VIF(\mathbf{S}, \lambda^{(1)})$
Original–Unit length	$9.83 \cdot 10^{-16}$	$1.55 \cdot 10^{-11}$	$1.83 \cdot 10^{-10}$
Original–Standardized	$-1.80 \cdot 10^{-16}$	$-3.10 \cdot 10^{-10}$	$2.98 \cdot 10^{-10}$
Unit length–Standardized	$-1.16 \cdot 10^{-15}$	$-3.26 \cdot 10^{-10}$	$1.15 \cdot 10^{-10}$

5.1.3. Second Raising

After the first raising, we can use the results obtained from the value of λ that obtains all VIFs less than 10 or consider the results obtained for λ_{min} or λ_{mse} and continue the procedure with a second raising. By following the second option, we part from the value of $\lambda^{(1)} = \lambda^{(1)}_{min} = 0.42$ obtained after the first raising. From Table 5, the third variable is selected to be raised. Table 6 shows the VIF associated with the following model for $\lambda^{(2)}_{min}$, $\lambda^{(2)}_{mse}$, and $\lambda^{(2)}_{vif}$:

$$E = \beta_1(\lambda) + \beta_2(\lambda)\mathbf{FA} + \beta_3(\lambda)\widetilde{\mathbf{OI}} + \beta_4(\lambda)\widetilde{\mathbf{S}} + \widetilde{u}, \qquad (17)$$

where $\widetilde{\mathbf{S}} = \mathbf{S} + \lambda^{(2)} \cdot \mathbf{e_S}$ with $\mathbf{e_S}$ the residuals or regression:

$$\mathbf{S} = \alpha_1(\lambda) + \alpha_2(\lambda)\mathbf{FA} + \alpha_3(\lambda)\widetilde{\mathbf{OI}} + \widetilde{v}.$$

Remark 3. *The coefficient of variation of* $\widetilde{\mathbf{OI}}$ *for* $\lambda^{(1)} = 0.42$ *is equal to 0.7470222, and the coefficient of variation of* $\widetilde{\mathbf{S}}$ *for* $\lambda^{(2)} = 17.5$ *is equal to 0.7473472. In both cases, they were slightly increased.*

Note than it is only possible to state that collinearity has been mitigated when $\lambda^{(2)} = \lambda^{(2)}_{vif} = 17.5$. Results of this estimation are displayed in Table 1.

Table 5. Horizontal asymptote for VIFs after raising each variable in the second raising for $\lambda_{min}^{(2)}$, $\lambda_{mse}^{(2)}$ and $\lambda_{vif}^{(2)}$.

Raised	$\lim\limits_{\lambda^{(2)} \to +\infty} VIF(\mathbf{FA}, \lambda^{(2)})$	$\lim\limits_{\lambda^{(2)} \to +\infty} VIF(\widetilde{\mathbf{OI}}, \lambda^{(2)})$	$\lim\limits_{\lambda^{(2)} \to +\infty} VIF(\mathbf{S}, \lambda^{(2)})$
Variable 1	1	2381.56	2381.56
Variable 3	2.12	2.12	1
Raised	$\lambda_{min}^{(2)}$	$\lambda_{mse}^{(2)}$	$\lambda_{vif}^{(2)}$
Variable 1	0.15	0.34	$\nexists$
Variable 3	0.35	1.09	17.5

Table 6. VIFs of regression Equation (16) for $\lambda^{(2)}$ equal to $\lambda_{min}^{(2)}$, $\lambda_{mse}^{(2)}$, and $\lambda_{vif}^{(2)}$.

	$VIF(\mathbf{FA}, \lambda^{(2)})$	$VIF(\widetilde{\mathbf{OI}}, \lambda^{(2)})$	$VIF(\widetilde{\mathbf{S}}, \lambda^{(2)})$
$\lambda_{min}^{(2)}$	2.20	1415.06	1398.05
$\lambda_{mse}^{(2)}$	2.15	593.98	586.20
$\lambda_{vif}^{(2)}$	2.12	9.67	8.47

Considering that, after the first raising, it is obtained that $\lambda^{(1)} = \lambda_{mse}^{(1)} = 1.43$, from Table 7, the third variable is selected to be raised. Table 8 shows the VIF associated with the following model for $\lambda_{min}^{(2)}$, $\lambda_{mse}^{(2)}$, and $\lambda_{vif}^{(2)}$:

$$E = \beta_1(\lambda) + \beta_2(\lambda)\mathbf{FA} + \beta_3(\lambda)\widetilde{\mathbf{OI}} + \beta_4(\lambda)\widetilde{\mathbf{S}} + \widetilde{u}, \tag{18}$$

where $\widetilde{\mathbf{S}} = \mathbf{S} + \lambda \cdot \mathbf{e_S}$.

Remark 4. *The coefficient of variation of $\widetilde{\mathbf{OI}}$ for $\lambda^{(1)} = 1.43$ is equal to 0.7473033, and the coefficient of variation of $\widetilde{\mathbf{S}}$ for $\lambda^{(2)} = 10$ is equal to 0.7651473. In both cases, they were lightly increased.*

Remark 5. *Observing the coefficients of variation of $\widetilde{\mathbf{OI}}$ for different raising factor. it is concluded that the coefficient of variation increases as the raising factor increases: 0.7470222 ($\lambda = 0.42$), 0.7473033 ($\lambda = 1.43$), and 0.7922063 ($\lambda = 24.5$).*

Note that it is only possible to state that collinearity has been mitigated when $\lambda^{(2)} = \lambda_{vif}^{(2)} = 10$. Results of the estimations of this model are shown in Table 1.

Table 7. Horizontal asymptote for VIFs after raising each variables in the second raising for $\lambda_{min}^{(2)}$, $\lambda_{mse}^{(2)}$, and $\lambda_{vif}^{(2)}$.

Raised	$\lim\limits_{\lambda^{(2)} \to +\infty} VIF(\mathbf{FA}, \lambda^{(2)})$	$\lim\limits_{\lambda^{(2)} \to +\infty} VIF(\widetilde{\mathbf{OI}}, \lambda^{(2)})$	$\lim\limits_{\lambda^{(2)} \to +\infty} VIF(\mathbf{S}, \lambda^{(2)})$
Variable 1	1	853.40	853.40
Variable 3	2.12	2.12	1
Raised	$\lambda_{min}^{(2)}$	$\lambda_{mse}^{(2)}$	$\lambda_{vif}^{(2)}$
Variable 1	0.12	0.27	$\nexists$
Variable 3	0.32	0.92	10

Table 8. VIFs of regression Equation (16) for $\lambda^{(2)}$ equal to $\lambda_{min}^{(2)}$, $\lambda_{mse}^{(2)}$, and $\lambda_{vif}^{(2)}$.

	$VIF(\mathbf{FA}, \lambda^{(2)})$	$VIF(\widetilde{\mathbf{OI}}, \lambda^{(2)})$	$VIF(\widetilde{\mathbf{S}}, \lambda^{(2)})$
$\lambda_{min}^{(2)}$	2.14	508.54	502.58
$\lambda_{mse}^{(2)}$	2.13	239.42	236.03
$\lambda_{vif}^{(2)}$	2.12	9.36	8.17

5.1.4. Interpretation of Results

Analyzing the results of Table 1, it is possible to conclude that

1. In the model in Equation (16) (in which the second variable is raised considering the smallest λ that makes all the VIFs less than 10, $\lambda^{(1)} = 24.5$), the variable sales have a coefficient significantly different from zero, where in the original model this was not the case. In this case, the MSE is superior to the one obtained by OLS.
2. In the model in Equation (17) (in which the second variable is raised considering the value of λ that minimizes the MSE, $\lambda^{(1)} = 0.42$, and after that, the third variable is raised considering the smallest λ that makes all the VIFs less than 10, $\lambda^{(2)} = 17.5$), there is no difference in the individual significance of the coefficient.
3. In the model in Equation (18) (in which the second variable is raised considering the value of λ that makes the MSE of the raise regression coincide with that of OLS, $\lambda^{(1)} = 1.43$, and next, the third variable is raised considering the smallest λ that makes all the VIFs less than 10, $\lambda^{(2)} = 10$), there is no difference in the individual significance of the coefficient.
4. Although the coefficient of variable **OI** is not significantly different from zero in any case, the not expected negative sign obtained in model in Equation (15) is corrected in models Equations (17) and (18).
5. In the models with one or two raisings, all the global characteristics coincide with that of the model in Equation (15). Furthermore, there is a relevant decrease in the estimation of the standard deviation for the second and third variable.
6. In models with one or two raisings, the MSE increases, with the model in Equation (16) being the one that presents the smallest MSE among the biased models.

Thus, in conclusion, the model in Equation (16) is selected as it presents the smallest MSE and there is an improvement in the individual significance of the variables.

5.2. Example 2: $h > 1$

This example uses the following model previously applied by Klein and Goldberger [43] about consumption and salaries in the United States from 1936 to 1952 (1942 to 1944 were war years, and data are not available):

$$\mathbf{C} = \beta_1 + \beta_2\mathbf{WI} + \beta_3\mathbf{NWI} + \beta_4\mathbf{FI} + \mathbf{u}, \tag{19}$$

where **C** is consumption, **WI** is wage income, **NWI** is non-wage, non-farm income, and **FI** is the farm income. Its estimation by OLS is shown in Table 9.

However, this estimation is questionable since no estimated coefficient is significantly different to zero while the model is globally significant (with 5% significance level), and the VIFs associated with each variable (12.296, 9.23, and 2.97) indicate the presence of severe essential collinearity. In addition, the determinant of the matrix of correlation

$$\mathbf{R} = \begin{pmatrix} 1 & 0.9431118 & 0.8106989 \\ 0.9431118 & 1 & 0.7371272 \\ 0.8106989 & 0.7371272 & 1 \end{pmatrix},$$

is equal to 0.03713592 and, consequently, lower than the threshold recommended by García et al. [44] ($1.013 \cdot 0.1 + 0.00008626 \cdot n - 0.01384 \cdot p = 0.04714764$ being $n = 14$ and $p = 4$); it is maintained the conclusion that the near multicollinearity existing in this model is troubling.

Once again, the values of the coefficients of variation (0.2761369, 0.2597991, and 0.2976122) indicate that the nonessential multicollinearity is not troubling (see Salmerón et al. [39]). Thus, the extension of the VIF seems appropriate to check if the application of the raise regression has mitigated the near multicollinearity.

Next, it is presented the estimation of the model by raise regression and the results are compared to the estimation by ridge and Lasso regression.

5.2.1. Raise Regression

When calculating the thresholds that would be obtained for VIFs by raising each variable (see Table 10), it is observed that, in all cases, they are less than 10. However, when calculating λ_{min} in each case, a value higher than one is only obtained when raising the third variable. Figure 3 displays the MSE for $\lambda \in [0, 37)$. Note that $MSE(\widehat{\boldsymbol{\beta}}(\lambda))$ is always less than the one obtained by OLS, 49.434, and presents an asymptote in $\lim_{\lambda \to +\infty} MSE(\widehat{\boldsymbol{\beta}}(\lambda)) = 45.69422$.

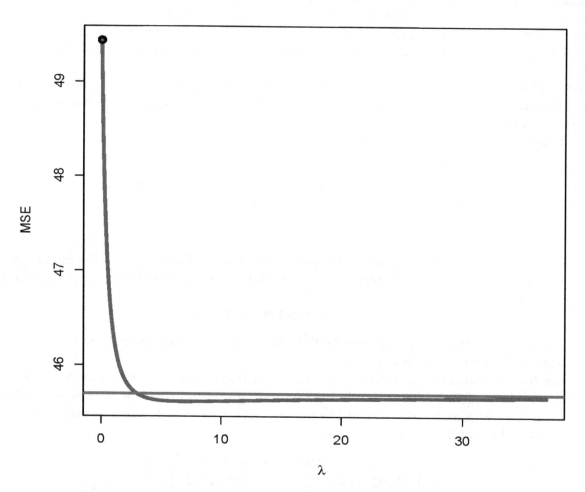

Figure 3. Mean square error (MSE) for the model in Equation (19) after raising third variable.

Table 9. Estimation of the original and raised models: Standard deviation is inside the parentheses, R^2 is the coefficient of determination, $F_{3,10}$ is the experimental value of the joint significance contrast, and $\hat{\sigma}^2$ is the variance estimate of the random perturbation.

	Model (19)	p-Value	Model (20) for $\lambda_{min} = 6.895$	p-Value	Model (21) for $\lambda_{min} = 0.673$	p-Value
Intercept	18.7021 (6.8454)	0.021	19.21507 (6.67216)	0.016	18.2948 (6.8129)	0.023
WI	0.3803 (0.3121)	0.251	0.43365 (0.26849)	0.137		
$\widetilde{WI}$					0.2273 (0.1866)	0.251
NWI	1.4186 (0.7204)	0.077	1.38479 (0.71329)	0.081	1.7269 (0.5143)	0.007
FI	0.5331 (1.3998)	0.711			0.8858 (1.2754)	0.503
$\widetilde{FI}$			0.06752 (0.17730)	0.711		
R^2	0.9187		0.9187		0.9187	
$\hat{\sigma}$	6.06		6.06		6.06	
$F_{3,10}$	37.68		37.68		37.68	
MSE	49.43469		45.61387		48.7497	

Table 10. Horizontal asymptote for VIFs after raising each variable and λ_{min}.

Raised	$\lim\limits_{\lambda \to +\infty} VIF(WI, \lambda)$	$\lim\limits_{\lambda \to +\infty} VIF(NWI, \lambda)$	$\lim\limits_{\lambda \to +\infty} VIF(FI, \lambda)$	λ_{min}
Variable 1	1	2.19	2.19	0.673
Variable 2	2.92	1	2.92	0.257
Variable 3	9.05	9.05	1	6.895

The following model is obtained by raising the third variable:

$$\mathbf{C} = \beta_1(\lambda) + \beta_2(\lambda)\mathbf{WI} + \beta_3(\lambda)\mathbf{NWI} + \beta_4(\lambda)\widetilde{\mathbf{FI}} + \widetilde{\mathbf{u}}, \tag{20}$$

where $\widetilde{\mathbf{FI}} = \mathbf{FI} + \lambda \cdot \mathbf{e_{FI}}$ being $\mathbf{e_{FI}}$ the residuals of regression:

$$\mathbf{FI} = \alpha_1 + \alpha_2\mathbf{WI} + \alpha_3\mathbf{NWI} + \mathbf{v}.$$

Remark 6. *The coefficient of variation* $\widetilde{\mathbf{FI}}$ *for* $\lambda^{(1)} = 6.895$ *is 1.383309. Thus, the application of the raise regression has mitigated the nonessential multicollinearity in this variable.*

Table 9 shows the results for the model in Equation (20), being $\lambda = 6.895$. In this case, the MSE is the lowest possible for every possible value of λ and lower than the one obtained by OLS for the model in Equation (19). Furthermore, in this case, the collinearity is not strong once all the VIF are lower than 10 (9.098, 9.049, and 1.031, respectively). However, the individual significance in the variable was not improved.

With the purpose of improving this situation, another variable is raised. If the first variable is selected to be raised, the following model is obtained:

$$\mathbf{C} = \beta_1(\lambda) + \beta_2(\lambda)\widetilde{\mathbf{WI}} + \beta_3(\lambda)\mathbf{NWI} + \beta_4(\lambda)\mathbf{FI} + \widetilde{\mathbf{u}}, \tag{21}$$

where $\widetilde{\mathbf{WI}} = \mathbf{WI} + \lambda \cdot \mathbf{e_{WI}}$ being $\mathbf{e_{WI}}$ the residuals of regression:

$$\mathbf{WI} = \alpha_1 + \alpha_2\mathbf{NWI} + \alpha_3\mathbf{FI} + \mathbf{v}.$$

Remark 7. *The coefficient of variation of* $\widetilde{\mathbf{WI}}$ *for* $\lambda^{(1)} = 0.673$ *is 0.2956465. Thus, it is noted that the raise regression has lightly mitigated the nonessential mutlicollinearity of this variable.*

Table 9 shows the results for the model in Equation (21), being $\lambda = 0.673$. In this case, the MSE is lower than the one obtained by OLS for the model in Equation (19). Furthermore, in this case, the collinearity is not strong once all the VIF are lower than 10 (5.036024, 4.705204, and 2.470980, respectively). Note that raising this variable, the values of VIFs are lower than raising the first variable but the MSE is higher. However, this model is selected as preferable due to the individual significance being better in this model and the MSE being lower than the one obtained by OLS.

5.2.2. Ridge Regression

This subsection presents the estimation of the model in Equation (19) by ridge regression (see Hoerl and Kennard [4] or Marquardt [45]). The first step is the selection of the appropriate value of K.

The following suggestions are addressed:

- Hoerl et al. [33] proposed the value of $K_{HKB} = p \cdot \frac{\widehat{\sigma}^2}{\widehat{\beta}'\widehat{\beta}}$ since probability higher than 50% leads to a MSE lower than the one from OLS.
- García et al. [26] proposed the value of K, denoted as K_{VIF}, that leads to values of VIF lower than 10 (threshold traditionally established as troubling).

- García et al. [44] proposed the following values:

$$
\begin{aligned}
K_{exp} &= 0.006639 \cdot e^{1-det(\mathbf{R})} - 0.00001241 \cdot n + 0.005745 \cdot p, \\
K_{linear} &= 0.01837 \cdot (1 - det(\mathbf{R})) - 0.00001262 \cdot n + 0.005678 \cdot p, \\
K_{sq} &= 0.7922 \cdot (1 - det(\mathbf{R}))^2 - 0.6901 \cdot (1 - det(\mathbf{R})) - 0.000007567 \cdot n \\
&\quad -0.01081 \cdot p,
\end{aligned}
$$

where $det(\mathbf{R})$ denotes the determinant of the matrix of correlation, $\mathbf{R}$.

The following values are obtained $K_{HKB} = 0.417083$, $K_{VIF} = 0.013$, $K_{exp} = 0.04020704$, $K_{linear} = 0.04022313$, and $K_{sq} = 0.02663591$.

Tables 11 and 12 show (The results for K_{linear} are not considered as they are very similar to results obtained by K_{exp}.) the estimations obtained from ridge estimators (expression (1)) and the individual significance intervals obtained by bootstrap considering percentiles 5 and 95 for 5000 repeats. It is also calculated the goodness of the fit by following the results shown by Rodríguez et al. [28] and the MSE.

Note that only the constant term can be considered significatively different to zero and that, curiously, the value of K proposed by Hoerl et al. [33] leads to a value of MSE higher than the one from OLS while the values proposed by García et al. [26] and García et al. [44] lead to a value of MSE lower than the one obtained by OLS. All cases lead to values of VIF lower than 10; see García et al. [26] for its calculation:

$$
\begin{aligned}
2.0529, 1.8933 \text{ and } 1.5678 &\quad \text{for} \quad K_{HKB}, \\
9.8856, 7.5541 \text{ and } 2.7991 &\quad \text{for} \quad K_{VIF}, \\
7.1255, 5.6191 \text{ and } 2.5473 &\quad \text{for} \quad K_{exp}, \\
8.2528, 6.4123 \text{ and } 2.65903 &\quad \text{for} \quad K_{sq}.
\end{aligned}
$$

In any case, the lack of individual significance justifies the selection of the raise regression as preferable in comparison to the models obtained by ridge regression.

Table 11. Estimation of the ridge models for $K_{HKB} = 0.417083$ and $K_{VIF} = 0.013$. Confidence interval, at 10% confidence, is obtained from bootstrap inside the parentheses, and R^2 is the coefficient of determination obtained from Rodríguez et al. [28].

	Model (19) for $K_{HKB} = 0.417083$	Model (19) for $K_{VIF} = 0.013$
Intercept	12.2395 (6.5394, 15.9444)	18.3981 (12.1725, 24.1816)
WI	0.3495 (−0.4376, 1.2481)	0.3787 (−0.4593, 1.216)
NWI	1.6474 (−0.1453, 3.4272)	1.4295 (−0.2405, 3.2544)
FI	0.8133 (−1.5584, 3.028)	0.5467 (−1.827, 2.9238)
R^2	0.8957	0.9353
MSE	64.20028	47.99713

Table 12. Estimation of the ridge models for $K_{exp} = 0.04020704$ and $K_{sq} = 0.02663591$. Confidence interval, at 10% confidence, is obtained from bootstrap inside the parentheses, and R^2 is the coefficient of determination obtained from Rodríguez et al. [28].

	Model (19) for $K_{exp} = 0.04020704$	Model (19) for $K_{sq} = 0.02663591$
Intercept	17.7932 (11.4986, 22.9815)	18.0898 (11.8745, 23.8594)
WI	0.3756 (−0.4752, 1.2254)	0.3771 (−0.4653, 1.2401)
NWI	1.4512 (−0.2249, 3.288)	1.4406 (−0.2551, 3.2519)
FI	0.5737 (−1.798, 2.9337)	0.5605 (−1.6999, 2.9505)
R^2	0.918034	0.9183955
MSE	45.76226	46.75402

5.2.3. Lasso Regression

The Lasso regression (see Tibshirani [5]) is a method initially designed to select variables constraining the coefficient to zero, being specially useful in models with a high number of independent variables. However, this estimation methodology has been widely applied in situation where the model presents worrying near multicollinearity.

Table 13 shows results obtained by the application of the Lasso regression to the model in Equation (19) by using the package *glmnet* of the programming environment R Core Team [46]. Note that these estimations are obtained for the optimal value of $\lambda = 0.1258925$ obtained after a k-fold cross-validation.

Table 13. Estimation of the Lasso model for $\lambda = 0.1258925$: Confidence interval at 10% confidence (obtained from bootstrap inside the parentheses).

	Model (19) for $\lambda = 0.1258925$
Intercept	19.1444 (13.5814489, 24.586207)
WI	0.4198 (−0.2013491, 1.052905)
NWI	1.3253 (0.0000000, 2.752345)
FI	0.4675 (−1.1574169, 2.151648)

The inference obtained by bootstrap methodology (with 5000 repeats) allows us to conclude that in, at least, the 5% of the cases, the coefficient of **NWI** is constrained to zero. Thus, this variable should be eliminated from the model.

However, we consider that this situation should be avoided, and as an alternative to the elimination of variable, that is, as an alternative from the following model, the estimation by raise or ridge regression is proposed.

$$\mathbf{C} = \pi_1 + \pi_2\mathbf{WI} + \pi_3\mathbf{FI} + \epsilon, \tag{22}$$

It could be also appropriate to apply the residualization method (see, for example, York [47], Salmerón et al. [48], and García et al. [44]), which consists in the estimation of the following model:

$$\mathbf{C} = \tau_1 + \tau_2\mathbf{WI} + \tau_3\mathbf{FI} + \tau_4\mathbf{res}_{\mathbf{NWI}} + \varepsilon, \tag{23}$$

where, for example, $\mathbf{res}_{\mathbf{NWI}}$ represents the residuals of the regression of **NWI** as a function of **WI** that will be interpreted as the part of **NWI** not related to **WI**. In this case (see García et al. [44]), it is verified that $\widehat{\pi}_i = \widehat{\tau}_i$ for $i = 1, 2, 3$. That is to say, the model in Equation (23) estimates the same relationship between **WI** and **FI** with **C** as in the model in Equation (22) with the benefit that the variable **NWI** is not eliminated due to a part of it being considered..

6. Conclusions

The Variance Inflation Factor (VIF) is one of the most applied measures to diagnose collinearity together with the Condition Number (CN). Once the collinearity is detected, different methodologies can be applied as, for example, the raise regression, but it will be required to check if the methodology has mitigated the collinearity effectively. This paper extends the concept of VIF to be applied after the raise regression and presents an expression of the VIF that verifies the following desirable properties (see García et al. [26]):

1. continuous in zero. That is to say, when the raising factor (λ) is zero, the VIF obtained in the raise regression coincides with the one obtained by OLS;
2. decreasing as a function of the raising factor (λ). That is to say, the degree of collinearity diminishes as λ increases, and
3. always equal or higher than 1.

The paper also shows that the VIF in the raise regression is scale invariant, which is a very common transformation when working with models with collinearity. Thus, it yields identical results regardless of whether predictions are based on unstandardized or standardized predictors. Contrarily, the VIFs obtained from other penalized regressions (ridge regression, Lasso, and Elastic Net) are not scale invariant and hence yield different results depending on the predictor scaling used.

Another contribution of this paper is the analysis of the asymptotic behavior of the VIF associated with the raised variable (verifying that its limit is equal to 1) and associated with the rest of the variables (presenting an horizontal asymptote). This analysis allows to conclude that

- It is possible to know a priori how far each of the VIFs can decrease simply by calculating their horizontal asymptote. This could be used as a criterion to select the variable to be raised, the one with the lowest horizontal asymptote being chosen.

- If there is asymptote under the threshold established as worrying, the extension of the VIF can be applied to select the raising factor considering the value of λ that verifies $VIF(k, \lambda) < 10$ for $k = 2, \ldots, p$.

- It is possible that the collinearity is not mitigated with any value of λ. This can happen when at least one horizontal asymptote is greater than the threshold. In that case, a second variable has to be raised. García and Ramírez [42] and García et al. [31] show the successive raising procedure.

On the other hand, since the raise estimator is biased, the paper analyzes its Mean Square Error (MSE), showing that there is a value of λ that minimizes the possibility of the MSE being lower than the one obtained by OLS. However, it is not guaranteed that the VIF for this value of λ presents a value less than the established thresholds. The results are illustrated with two numerical examples, and in the second one, the results obtained by OLS are compared to the results obtained with the raise, ridge, and Lasso regressions that are widely applied to estimated models with worrying multicollinearity. It is showed that the raise regression can compete and even overcome these methodologies.

Finally, we propose as future lines of research the following questions:

- The examples showed that the coefficients of variation increase after raising the variables. This fact is associated with an increase in the variability of the variable and, consequently, with a decrease of the near nonessential multicollinearity. Although a deeper analysis is required, it seems that raise regression mitigates this kind of near multicollinearity.

- The value of the ridge factor traditionally applied, K_{HKB}, leads to estimators with smaller MSEs than the OLS estimators with probability greater than 0.5. In contrast, the value of the raising factor λ_{min} always leads to estimators with smaller MSEs than OLS estimators. Thus, it is deduced that the ridge regression provides estimators with MSEs higher than the MSEs of OLS estimators with probability lower than 0.5. These questions seem to indicate that, in terms of MSE, the raise regression can present better behaviour than the ridge regression. However, the confirmation of this judgment will require a more complete analysis, including other aspects such as interpretability and inference.

Author Contributions: conceptualization, J.G.P., C.G.G. and R.S.G. and A.R.S.; methodology, R.S.G. and A.R.S.; software, A.R.S.; validation, J.G.P., R.S.G. and C.G.G.; formal analysis, R.S.G. and C.G.G.; investigation, R.S.G. and A.R.S.; writing—original draft preparation, A.R.S. and C.G.G.; writing—review and editing, C.G.G.; supervision, J.G.P. All authors have read and agreed to the published version of the manuscript.

Acknowledgments: We thank the anonymous referees for their useful suggestions.

Appendix A

Given the linear model in Equation (7), it is obtained that

$$
\begin{aligned}
\widehat{\boldsymbol{\alpha}}(\lambda) &= \begin{pmatrix} \mathbf{X}^t_{-i,-j}\mathbf{X}_{-i,-j} & \mathbf{X}^t_{-i,-j}\widetilde{\mathbf{X}}_i \\ \widetilde{\mathbf{X}}^t_i\mathbf{X}_{-i,-j} & \widetilde{\mathbf{X}}^t_i\widetilde{\mathbf{X}}_i \end{pmatrix}^{-1} \cdot \begin{pmatrix} \mathbf{X}^t_{-i,-j}\mathbf{X}_j \\ \widetilde{\mathbf{X}}^t_i\mathbf{X}_j \end{pmatrix} \\
&= \begin{pmatrix} \mathbf{X}^t_{-i,-j}\mathbf{X}_{-i,-j} & \mathbf{X}^t_{-i,-j}\mathbf{X}_i \\ \mathbf{X}^t_i\mathbf{X}_{-i,-j} & \mathbf{X}^t_i\mathbf{X}_i + (\lambda^2+2\lambda)RSS^{-i}_i \end{pmatrix}^{-1} \cdot \begin{pmatrix} \mathbf{X}^t_{-i,-j}\mathbf{X}_j \\ \mathbf{X}^t_i\mathbf{X}_j \end{pmatrix} \\
&= \begin{pmatrix} A(\lambda) & B(\lambda) \\ B(\lambda)^t & C(\lambda) \end{pmatrix} \cdot \begin{pmatrix} \mathbf{X}^t_{-i,-j}\mathbf{X}_j \\ \mathbf{X}^t_i\mathbf{X}_j \end{pmatrix} \\
&= \begin{pmatrix} A(\lambda)\cdot\mathbf{X}^t_{-i,-j}\mathbf{X}_j + B(\lambda)\cdot\mathbf{X}^t_i\mathbf{X}_j \\ B(\lambda)^t\cdot\mathbf{X}^t_{-i,-j}\mathbf{X}_j + C(\lambda)\cdot\mathbf{X}^t_i\mathbf{X}_j \end{pmatrix} = \begin{pmatrix} \widehat{\boldsymbol{\alpha}}_{-i,-j}(\lambda) \\ \widehat{\alpha}_i(\lambda) \end{pmatrix},
\end{aligned}
$$

Since it is verified that $\mathbf{e}^t_i\mathbf{X}_{-i,-j} = \mathbf{0}$, then $\widetilde{\mathbf{X}}^t_i\mathbf{X}_{-i,-j} = (\mathbf{X}_i + \lambda\mathbf{e}_i)^t\mathbf{X}_{-i,-j} = \mathbf{X}^t_i\mathbf{X}_{-i,-j}$, where

$$
\begin{aligned}
C(\lambda) &= \left(\mathbf{X}^t_i\mathbf{X}_i + (\lambda^2+2\lambda)RSS^{-i}_i - \mathbf{X}^t_i\mathbf{X}_{-i,-j}\left(\mathbf{X}^t_{-i,-j}\mathbf{X}_{-i,-j}\right)^{-1}\mathbf{X}^t_{-i,-j}\mathbf{X}_i \right)^{-1} \\
&= \left(\mathbf{X}^t_i\left(\mathbf{I} - \mathbf{X}_{-i,-j}\left(\mathbf{X}^t_{-i,-j}\mathbf{X}_{-i,-j}\right)^{-1}\mathbf{X}^t_{-i,-j}\right)\mathbf{X}_i + (\lambda^2+2\lambda)RSS^{-i}_i \right)^{-1} \\
&= \left(RSS^{-i,-j}_i + (\lambda^2+2\lambda)RSS^{-i}_i \right)^{-1}, \\
B(\lambda) &= -\left(\mathbf{X}^t_{-i,-j}\mathbf{X}_{-i,-j}\right)^{-1}\mathbf{X}^t_{-i,-j}\mathbf{X}_i \cdot C(\lambda) = \frac{RSS^{-i,-j}_i}{RSS^{-i,-j}_i + (\lambda^2+2\lambda)RSS^{-i}_i} \cdot B, \\
A(\lambda) &= \left(\mathbf{X}^t_{-i,-j}\mathbf{X}_{-i,-j}\right)^{-1} + \left(\mathbf{X}^t_{-i,-j}\mathbf{X}_{-i,-j}\right)^{-1}\mathbf{X}^t_{-i,-j}\mathbf{X}_i \cdot C(\lambda)\cdot\mathbf{X}^t_i\mathbf{X}_{-i,-j}\left(\mathbf{X}^t_{-i,-j}\mathbf{X}_{-i,-j}\right)^{-1} \\
&= \left(\mathbf{X}^t_{-i,-j}\mathbf{X}_{-i,-j}\right)^{-1} + \frac{(RSS^{-i,-j}_i)^2}{RSS^{-i,-j}_i + (\lambda^2+2\lambda)RSS^{-i}_i} \cdot B\cdot B^t.
\end{aligned}
$$

Then,

$$
\begin{aligned}
\widehat{\boldsymbol{\alpha}}_{-i,-j}(\lambda) &= \left(\mathbf{X}^t_{-i,-j}\mathbf{X}_{-i,-j}\right)^{-1}\mathbf{X}^t_{-i,-j}\mathbf{X}_j + \frac{(RSS^{-i,-j}_i)^2}{RSS^{-i,-j}_i + (\lambda^2+2\lambda)RSS^{-i}_i} \cdot B\cdot B^t\cdot\mathbf{X}^t_{-i,-j}\mathbf{X}_j \\
&\quad + \frac{RSS^{-i,-j}_i}{RSS^{-i,-j}_i + (\lambda^2+2\lambda)RSS^{-i}_i} \cdot B\cdot\mathbf{X}^t_i\mathbf{X}_j \\
&= \left(\mathbf{X}^t_{-i,-j}\mathbf{X}_{-i,-j}\right)^{-1}\mathbf{X}^t_{-i,-j}\mathbf{X}_j \\
&\quad + \frac{RSS^{-i,-j}_i\left(RSS^{-i,-j}_i\cdot B\cdot B^t\cdot\mathbf{X}^t_{-i,-j}\mathbf{X}_j + B\cdot\mathbf{X}^t_i\mathbf{X}_j\right)}{RSS^{-i,-j}_i + (\lambda^2+2\lambda)RSS^{-i}_i}, \\
\widehat{\alpha}_i(\lambda) &= \frac{RSS^{-i,-j}_i}{RSS^{-i,-j}_i + (\lambda^2+2\lambda)RSS^{-i}_i} \cdot B^t\cdot\mathbf{X}^t_{-i,-j}\mathbf{X}_j \\
&\quad + \frac{1}{RSS^{-i,-j}_i + (\lambda^2+2\lambda)RSS^{-i}_i} \cdot \mathbf{X}^t_i\mathbf{X}_j \\
&= \frac{RSS^{-i,-j}_i}{RSS^{-i,-j}_i + (\lambda^2+2\lambda)RSS^{-i}_i} \cdot \left(B^t\cdot\mathbf{X}^t_{-i,-j}\mathbf{X}_j + (RSS^{-i,-j}_i)^{-1}\mathbf{X}^t_i\mathbf{X}_j \right) \\
&= \frac{RSS^{-i,-j}_i}{RSS^{-i,-j}_i + (\lambda^2+2\lambda)RSS^{-i}_i} \cdot \widehat{\alpha}_i.
\end{aligned}
$$

Appendix B

Given the linear model

$$
\mathbf{X}_j = \mathbf{X}_{-j}\boldsymbol{\alpha} + \mathbf{v} = (\mathbf{X}_{-i,-j}\ \mathbf{X}_i)\begin{pmatrix} \boldsymbol{\alpha}_{-i,-j} \\ \alpha_i \end{pmatrix} + \mathbf{v},
$$

it is obtained that

$$
\widehat{\boldsymbol{\alpha}} = \begin{pmatrix} \mathbf{X}^t_{-i,-j}\mathbf{X}_{-i,-j} & \mathbf{X}^t_{-i,-j}\mathbf{X}_i \\ \mathbf{X}^t_i\mathbf{X}_{-i,-j} & \mathbf{X}^t_i\mathbf{X}_i \end{pmatrix}^{-1} \cdot \begin{pmatrix} \mathbf{X}^t_{-i,-j}\mathbf{X}_j \\ \mathbf{X}^t_i\mathbf{X}_j \end{pmatrix} = \begin{pmatrix} A & B \\ B^t & C \end{pmatrix} \cdot \begin{pmatrix} \mathbf{X}^t_{-i,-j}\mathbf{X}_j \\ \mathbf{X}^t_i\mathbf{X}_j \end{pmatrix}
$$

$$
= \begin{pmatrix} A \cdot \mathbf{X}^t_{-i,-j}\mathbf{X}_j + B \cdot \mathbf{X}^t_i\mathbf{X}_j \\ B^t \cdot \mathbf{X}^t_{-i,-j}\mathbf{X}_j + C \cdot \mathbf{X}^t_i\mathbf{X}_j \end{pmatrix} = \begin{pmatrix} \widehat{\boldsymbol{\alpha}}_{-i,-j} \\ \widehat{\alpha}_i \end{pmatrix},
$$

where

$$
C = \left(\mathbf{X}^t_i\mathbf{X}_i - \mathbf{X}^t_i\mathbf{X}_{-i,-j} \left(\mathbf{X}^t_{-i,-j}\mathbf{X}_{-i,-j} \right)^{-1} \mathbf{X}^t_{-i,-j}\mathbf{X}_i \right)^{-1}
$$

$$
= \left(\mathbf{X}^t_i \left(\mathbf{I} - \mathbf{X}_{-i,-j} \left(\mathbf{X}^t_{-i,-j}\mathbf{X}_{-i,-j} \right)^{-1} \mathbf{X}^t_{-i,-j} \right) \mathbf{X}_i \right)^{-1} = \left(RSS_i^{-i,-j} \right)^{-1},
$$

$$
B = -\left(\mathbf{X}^t_{-i,-j}\mathbf{X}_{-i,-j} \right)^{-1} \mathbf{X}^t_{-i,-j}\mathbf{X}_i \cdot C,
$$

$$
A = \left(\mathbf{X}^t_{-i,-j}\mathbf{X}_{-i,-j} \right)^{-1} \cdot \left(\mathbf{I} + \mathbf{X}^t_{-i,-j}\mathbf{X}_i \cdot C \cdot \mathbf{X}^t_i\mathbf{X}_{-i,-j} \left(\mathbf{X}^t_{-i,-j}\mathbf{X}_{-i,-j} \right)^{-1} \right)
$$

$$
= \left(\mathbf{X}^t_{-i,-j}\mathbf{X}_{-i,-j} \right)^{-1} + \frac{1}{C} \cdot B \cdot B^t.
$$

In that case, the residual sum of squares is given by

$$
RSS_j^{-j} = \mathbf{X}^t_j\mathbf{X}_j - \begin{pmatrix} A \cdot \mathbf{X}^t_{-i,-j}\mathbf{X}_j + B \cdot \mathbf{X}^t_i\mathbf{X}_j \\ B^t \cdot \mathbf{X}^t_{-i,-j}\mathbf{X}_j + C \cdot \mathbf{X}^t_i\mathbf{X}_j \end{pmatrix}^t \begin{pmatrix} \mathbf{X}^t_{-i,-j}\mathbf{X}_j \\ \mathbf{X}^t_i\mathbf{X}_j \end{pmatrix}
$$

$$
= \mathbf{X}^t_j\mathbf{X}_j - \mathbf{X}^t_j\mathbf{X}_{-i,-j} \cdot A^t \cdot \mathbf{X}^t_{-i,-j}\mathbf{X}_j - \mathbf{X}^t_j\mathbf{X}_i \cdot B^t \cdot \mathbf{X}^t_{-i,-j}\mathbf{X}_j - \widehat{\alpha}_i^t\mathbf{X}^t_i\mathbf{X}_j
$$

$$
= \left(\mathbf{X}^t_j\mathbf{X}_j - \mathbf{X}^t_j\mathbf{X}_{-i,-j} \left(\mathbf{X}^t_{-i,-j}\mathbf{X}_{-i,-j} \right)^{-1} \mathbf{X}^t_{-i,-j}\mathbf{X}_j \right)
$$

$$
- RSS_i^{-i,-j}\mathbf{X}^t_j\mathbf{X}_{-i,-j} \cdot B \cdot B^t \cdot \mathbf{X}^t_{-i,-j}\mathbf{X}_j - \mathbf{X}^t_j\mathbf{X}_i \cdot B^t \cdot \mathbf{X}^t_{-i,-j}\mathbf{X}_j - \widehat{\alpha}_i^t\mathbf{X}^t_i\mathbf{X}_j
$$

$$
= RSS_j^{-i,-j} - \left(RSS_i^{-i,-j}\mathbf{X}^t_j\mathbf{X}_{-i,-j} \cdot B \cdot B^t \cdot \mathbf{X}^t_{-i,-j}\mathbf{X}_j + \mathbf{X}^t_j\mathbf{X}_i \cdot B^t \cdot \mathbf{X}^t_{-i,-j}\mathbf{X}_j \right.
$$

$$
\left. + \widehat{\alpha}_i^t\mathbf{X}^t_i\mathbf{X}_j \right),
$$

and consequently

$$
RSS_j^{-i,-j} - RSS_j^{-j} = RSS_i^{-i,-j}\mathbf{X}^t_j\mathbf{X}_{-i,-j} \cdot B \cdot B^t \cdot \mathbf{X}^t_{-i,-j}\mathbf{X}_j + \mathbf{X}^t_j\mathbf{X}_i \cdot B^t \cdot \mathbf{X}^t_{-i,-j}\mathbf{X}_j + \widehat{\alpha}_i^t\mathbf{X}^t_i\mathbf{X}_j.
$$

Appendix C

First, parting from the expression Equation (14), it is obtained that

$$
\mathbf{M}_\lambda^{-1} = \begin{pmatrix}
1 & 0 & \cdots & 0 & -\frac{\lambda}{1+\lambda}\widehat{\alpha}_0 & 0 & \cdots & 0 \\
0 & 1 & \cdots & 0 & \frac{\lambda}{1+\lambda}\widehat{\alpha}_1 & 0 & \cdots & 0 \\
\vdots & \vdots & & \vdots & \vdots & \vdots & & \vdots \\
0 & 0 & \cdots & 1 & (-1)^{k-1}\frac{\lambda}{1+\lambda}\widehat{\alpha}_{k-1} & 0 & \cdots & 0 \\
0 & 0 & \cdots & 0 & \frac{1}{1+\lambda} & 0 & \cdots & 0 \\
0 & 0 & \cdots & 0 & (-1)^{k+1}\frac{\lambda}{1+\lambda}\widehat{\alpha}_{k+1} & 1 & \cdots & 0 \\
\vdots & \vdots & & \vdots & \vdots & \vdots & & \vdots \\
0 & 0 & \cdots & 0 & (-1)^p\frac{\lambda}{1+\lambda}\widehat{\alpha}_p & 0 & \cdots & 1
\end{pmatrix},
$$

and then,

$$(\mathbf{M}_\lambda^{-1} - \mathbf{I})^t (\mathbf{M}_\lambda^{-1} - \mathbf{I}) = \begin{pmatrix} 0 & 0 & \cdots & 0 & 0 & 0 & \cdots & 0 \\ 0 & 0 & \cdots & 0 & 0 & 0 & \cdots & 0 \\ \vdots & \vdots & & \vdots & \vdots & \vdots & & \vdots \\ 0 & 0 & \cdots & 0 & 0 & 0 & \cdots & 0 \\ 0 & 0 & \cdots & 0 & a(\lambda) & 0 & \cdots & 0 \\ 0 & 0 & \cdots & 0 & 0 & 0 & \cdots & 0 \\ \vdots & \vdots & & \vdots & \vdots & \vdots & & \vdots \\ 0 & 0 & \cdots & 0 & 0 & 0 & \cdots & 0 \end{pmatrix},$$

where $a(\lambda) = \frac{\lambda^2}{(1+\lambda)^2} \cdot \left(\widehat{\alpha}_0 + \widehat{\alpha}_1 + \cdots + \widehat{\alpha}_{k-1}^2 + 1 + \widehat{\alpha}_{k+1}^2 + \cdots + \widehat{\alpha}_p^2 \right)$. In that case,

$$\boldsymbol{\beta}^t (\mathbf{M}_\lambda^{-1} - \mathbf{I})^t (\mathbf{M}_\lambda^{-1} - \mathbf{I}) \boldsymbol{\beta} = a(\lambda) \cdot \beta_k^2.$$

Second, partitioning $\widetilde{\mathbf{X}}$ in the form $\widetilde{\mathbf{X}} = \left[\mathbf{X}_{-k} \ \widetilde{\mathbf{X}}_k \right]$, it is obtained that

$$\left(\widetilde{\mathbf{X}}^t \widetilde{\mathbf{X}} \right)^{-1} = \begin{pmatrix} \left(\mathbf{X}_{-k}^t \mathbf{X}_{-k} \right)^{-1} + \frac{\widehat{\alpha}\widehat{\alpha}^t}{(1+\lambda)^2 \cdot \mathbf{e}_k^t \mathbf{e}_k} & -\frac{\widehat{\alpha}}{(1+\lambda)^2 \cdot \mathbf{e}_k^t \mathbf{e}_k} \\ -\frac{\widehat{\alpha}^t}{(1+\lambda)^2 \cdot \mathbf{e}_k^t \mathbf{e}_k} & \frac{1}{(1+\lambda)^2 \cdot \mathbf{e}_k^t \mathbf{e}_k} \end{pmatrix},$$

and then,

$$tr((\widetilde{\mathbf{X}}^t \widetilde{\mathbf{X}})^{-1}) = tr \left(\left(\mathbf{X}_{-k}^t \mathbf{X}_{-k} \right)^{-1} \right) + \frac{1}{(1+\lambda)^2 \cdot \mathbf{e}_k^t \mathbf{e}_k} \cdot \left(tr \left(\widehat{\alpha}\widehat{\alpha}^t \right) + 1 \right).$$

Consequently, it is obtained that

$$\text{MSE} \left(\widehat{\boldsymbol{\beta}}(\lambda) \right) = \sigma^2 tr \left(\left(\mathbf{X}_{-k}^t \mathbf{X}_{-k} \right)^{-1} \right) + \left(1 + \sum_{j=0, j\neq k}^{p} \widehat{\alpha}_j^2 \right) \cdot \beta_k^2 \cdot \frac{\lambda^2 + h}{(1+\lambda)^2}, \tag{A1}$$

where $h = \frac{\sigma^2}{\beta_k^2 \cdot RSS_{-k}}$.

Third, taking into account that the first and second derivatives of expression Equation (A1) are, respectively,

$$\frac{\partial}{\partial \lambda} \text{MSE} \left(\widehat{\boldsymbol{\beta}}(\lambda) \right) = \left(1 + \sum_{j=0, j\neq k}^{p} \widehat{\alpha}_j^2 \right) \cdot \beta_k^2 \cdot \frac{2(\lambda - h)}{(1+\lambda)^3},$$

$$\frac{\partial^2}{\partial \lambda^2} \text{MSE} \left(\widehat{\boldsymbol{\beta}}(\lambda) \right) = -2 \left(1 + \sum_{j=0, j\neq k}^{p} \widehat{\alpha}_j^2 \right) \cdot \beta_k^2 \cdot \frac{2\lambda - (1+3h)}{(1+\lambda)^4}.$$

Since $\lambda \geq 0$, it is obtained that $\text{MSE} \left(\widehat{\boldsymbol{\beta}}(\lambda) \right)$ is decreasing if $\lambda < h$ and increasing if $\lambda > h$, and it is concave if $\lambda > \frac{1+3h}{2}$ and convex if $\lambda < \frac{1+3h}{2}$.

Indeed, given that

$$\lim_{\lambda \to +\infty} \text{MSE} \left(\widehat{\boldsymbol{\beta}}(\lambda) \right) = \sigma^2 tr \left(\left(\mathbf{X}_{-k}^t \mathbf{X}_{-k} \right)^{-1} \right) + \left(1 + \sum_{j=0, j\neq k}^{p} \widehat{\alpha}_j^2 \right) \cdot \beta_k^2,$$

$$\text{MSE} \left(\widehat{\boldsymbol{\beta}}(0) \right) = \sigma^2 tr \left(\left(\mathbf{X}_{-k}^t \mathbf{X}_{-k} \right)^{-1} \right) + \left(1 + \sum_{j=0, j\neq k}^{p} \widehat{\alpha}_j^2 \right) \cdot \beta_k^2 \cdot h, \tag{A2}$$

if $h > 1$, then $\text{MSE}\left(\widehat{\beta}(0)\right) > \lim_{\lambda \to +\infty} \text{MSE}\left(\widehat{\beta}(\lambda)\right)$, and if $h < 1$, then $\text{MSE}\left(\widehat{\beta}(0)\right) <$ $\lim_{\lambda \to +\infty} \text{MSE}\left(\widehat{\beta}(\lambda)\right)$. That is to say, if $h > 1$, then the raise estimator presents always a lower MSE than the one obtained by OLS for all λ, and comparing expressions Equations (A1) and (A2) when $h < 1$, $\text{MSE}\left(\widehat{\beta}(\lambda)\right) \leq \text{MSE}\left(\widehat{\beta}(0)\right)$ if $\lambda \leq \frac{2 \cdot h}{1-h}$.

From this information, the behavior of the MSE is represented in Figures A1 and A2. Note that the MSE presents a minimum value for $\lambda = h$.

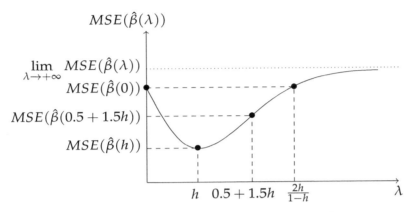

Figure A1. $MSE(\hat{\beta}(\lambda))$ representation for $h = \frac{\sigma^2}{(e_k^t e_k) \cdot \beta_k^2} < 1$.

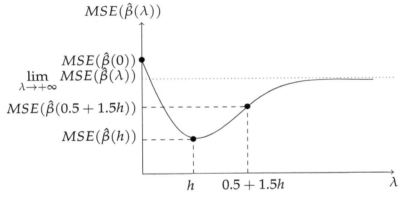

Figure A2. $MSE(\hat{\beta}(\lambda))$ representation for $h = \frac{\sigma^2}{(e_k^t e_k) \cdot \beta_k^2} > 1$.

References

1. Kiers, H.; Smilde, A. A comparison of various methods for multivariate regression with highly collinear variables. *Stat. Methods Appl.* **2007**, *16*, 193–228. [CrossRef]

2. Frank, L.E.; Friedman, J.H. A statistical view of some chemometrics regression tools. *Technometrics* **1993**, *35*, 109–135. [CrossRef]

3. Fu, W.J. Penalized regressions: the bridge versus the lasso. *J. Comput. Graph. Stat.* **1998**, *7*, 397–416.

4. Hoerl, A.E.; Kennard, R.W. Ridge regression: Biased estimation for nonorthogonal problems. *Technometrics* **1970**, *12*, 55–67. [CrossRef]

5. Tibshirani, R. Regression shrinkage and selection via the lasso. *J. R. Stat. Soc. Ser. B (Methodol.)* **1996**, *58*, 267–288. [CrossRef]

6. Donoho, D.L.; Johnstone, I.M. Adapting to unknown smoothness via wavelet shrinkage. *J. Am. Stat. Assoc.* **1995**, *90*, 1200–1224. [CrossRef]

7. Klinger, A. Inference in high dimensional generalized linear models based on soft thresholding. *J. R. Stat. Soc. Ser. B (Stat. Methodol.)* **2001**, *63*, 377–392. [CrossRef]

8. Dupuis, D.; Victoria-Feser, M. Robust VIF regression with application to variable selection in large data sets. *Ann. Appl. Stat.* **2013**, *7*, 319–341. [CrossRef]

9.   Li, Y.; Yang, H. A new Liu-type estimator in linear regression model. *Stat. Pap.* **2012**, *53*, 427–437. [CrossRef]

10. Liu, Y.; Wang, Y.; Feng, Y.; Wall, M. Variable selection and prediction with incomplete high-dimensional data. *Ann. Appl. Stat.* **2016**, *10*, 418–450. [CrossRef]

11. Uematsu, Y.; Tanaka, S. High-dimensional macroeconomic forecasting and variable selection via penalized regression. *Econom. J.* **2019**, *22*, 34–56. [CrossRef]

12. Zou, H.; Hastie, T. Regularization and variable selection via the elastic net. *J. R. Stat. Soc. Ser. B (Stat. Methodol.)* **2005**, *67*, 301–320. [CrossRef]

13. Tutz, G.; Ulbricht, J. Penalized regression with correlation-based penalty. *Stat. Comput.* **2009**, *19*, 239–253. [CrossRef]

14. Stone, M.; Brooks, R.J. Continuum regression: Cross-validated sequentially constructed prediction embracing ordinary least squares, partial least squares and principal components regression. *J. R. Stat. Soc. Ser. B (Methodol.)* **1990**, *52*, 237–269. [CrossRef]

15. Efron, B.; Hastie, T.; Johnstone, I.; Tibshirani, R. Least angle regression. *Ann. Stat.* **2004**, *32*, 407–499.

16. Golan, A.; Judge, G.; Miller, D. *Maximum Entropy Econometrics: Robust Estimation With Limited Data*; John Wiley and Sons: Chichester, UK, 1997.

17. Golan, A. Information and entropy econometrics review and synthesis. *Found. Trends Econom.* **2008**, *2*, 1–145. [CrossRef]

18. Macedo, P. Ridge Regression and Generalized Maximum Entropy: An improved version of the Ridge–GME parameter estimator. *Commun. Stat.-Simul. Comput.* **2017**, *46*, 3527–3539. [CrossRef]

19. Batah, F.S.M.; Özkale, M.R.; Gore, S. Combining unbiased ridge and principal component regression estimators. *Commun. Stat. Theory Methods* **2009**, *38*, 2201–2209. [CrossRef]

20. Massy, W.F. Principal components regression in exploratory statistical research. *J. Am. Stat. Assoc.* **1965**, *60*, 234–256. [CrossRef]

21. Guo, W.; Liu, X.; Zhang, S. The principal correlation components estimator and its optimality. *Stat. Pap.* **2016**, *57*, 755–779. [CrossRef]

22. Aguilera-Morillo, M.; Aguilera, A.; Escabias, M.; Valderrama, M. Penalized spline approaches for functional logit regression. *Test* **2013**, *22*, 251–277. [CrossRef]

23. Wold, S.; Sjöström, M.; Eriksson, L. PLS-regression: A basic tool of chemometrics. *Chemom. Intell. Lab. Syst.* **2001**, *58*, 109–130. [CrossRef]

24. De Jong, S. SIMPLS: An alternative approach to partial least squares regression. *Chemom. Intell. Lab. Syst.* **1993**, *18*, 251–263. [CrossRef]

25. Jensen, D.; Ramirez, D. Surrogate models in ill-conditioned systems. *J. Stat. Plan. Inference* **2010**, *140*, 2069–2077. [CrossRef]

26. García, J.; Salmerón, R.; García, C.; López Martín, M.D.M. Standardization of variables and collinearity diagnostic in ridge regression. *Int. Stat. Rev.* **2016**, *84*, 245–266. [CrossRef]

27. Marquardt, D. You should standardize the predictor variables in your regression models. Discussion of: A critique of some ridge regression methods. *J. Am. Stat. Assoc.* **1980**, *75*, 87–91.

28. Rodríguez, A.; Salmerón, R.; García, C. The coefficient of determination in the ridge regression. *Commun. Stat. Simul. Comput.* **2019**. [CrossRef]

29. García, C.G.; Pérez, J.G.; Liria, J.S. The raise method. An alternative procedure to estimate the parameters in presence of collinearity. *Qual. Quant.* **2011**, *45*, 403–423. [CrossRef]

30. Salmerón, R.; García, C.; García, J.; López, M.D.M. The raise estimator estimation, inference, and properties. *Commun. Stat. Theory Methods* **2017**, *46*, 6446–6462. [CrossRef]

31. García, J.; López-Martín, M.; García, C.; Salmerón, R. A geometrical interpretation of collinearity: A natural way to justify ridge regression and its anomalies. *Int. Stat. Rev.* **2020**. [CrossRef]

32. Belsley, D.A.; Kuh, E.; Welsch, R.E. *Regression Diagnostics: Identifying Influential Data and Sources of Collinearity*; John Wiley & Sons: Hoboken, NJ, USA, 2005; Volume 571.

33. Hoerl, A.; Kannard, R.; Baldwin, K. Ridge regression: some simulations. *Commun. Stat. Theory Methods* **1975**, *4*, 105–123. [CrossRef]

34. Stein, C. Inadmissibility of the Usual Estimator for the Mean of a Multivariate Normal Distribution. In *Proceedings of the Third Berkeley Symposium on Mathematical Statistics and Probability, Volume 1: Contributions to the Theory of Statistics*; University of California Press: Berkeley, CA, USA, 1956; pp. 197–206.

35. James, W.; Stein, C. Estimation with Quadratic Loss. In *Proceedings of the Fourth Berkeley Symposium on Mathematical Statistics and Probability, Volume 1: Contributions to the Theory of Statistics*; University of California Press: Berkeley, CA, USA, 1961; pp. 361–379.

36. Ohtani, K. An MSE comparison of the restricted Stein-rule and minimum mean squared error estimators in regression. *Test* **1998**, *7*, 361–376. [CrossRef]

37. Hubert, M.; Gijbels, I.; Vanpaemel, D. Reducing the mean squared error of quantile-based estimators by smoothing. *Test* **2013**, *22*, 448–465. [CrossRef]

38. Salmerón, R.; García, C.; García, J. Variance Inflation Factor and Condition Number in multiple linear regression. *J. Stat. Comput. Simul.* **2018**, *88*, 2365–2384. [CrossRef]

39. Salmerón, R.; Rodríguez, A.; García, C. Diagnosis and quantification of the non-essential collinearity. *Comput. Stat.* **2019**. [CrossRef]

40. Marquandt, D.; Snee, R. Ridge regression in practice. *Am. Stat.* **1975**, *29*, 3–20.

41. García, C.B.; Garcí, J.; Salmerón, R.; López, M.M. Raise regression: Selection of the raise parameter. In Proceedings of the International Conference on Data Mining, Vancouver, BC, Canada, 30 April–2 May 2015.

42. García, J.; Ramírez, D. The successive raising estimator and its relation with the ridge estimator. *Commun. Stat. Simul. Comput.* **2016**, *46*, 11123–11142. [CrossRef]

43. Klein, L.; Goldberger, A. *An Economic Model of the United States, 1929–1952*; North Holland Publishing Company: Amsterdan, The Netherlands, 1964.

44. García, C.; Salmerón, R.; García, C.; García, J. Residualization: Justification, properties and application. *J. Appl. Stat.* **2019**. [CrossRef]

45. Marquardt, D. Generalized inverses, ridge regression, biased linear estimation, and nonlinear estimation. *Technometrics* **1970**, *12*, 591–612. [CrossRef]

46. R Core Team. *R: A Language and Environment for Statistical Computing*; R Foundation for Statistical Computing: Vienna, Austria, 2017.

47. York, R. Residualization is not the answer: Rethinking how to address multicollinearity. *Soc. Sci. Res.* **2012**, *41*, 1379–1386. [CrossRef]

48. Salmerón, R.; García, J.; García, C.; García, C. Treatment of collinearity through orthogonal regression: An economic application. *Boletín Estadística Investig. Oper.* **2016**, *32*, 184–202.

9

Deep Learning Methods for Modeling Bitcoin Price

Prosper Lamothe-Fernández [1], David Alaminos [2,*], Prosper Lamothe-López [3]
and Manuel A. Fernández-Gámez [4]

[1]   Department of Financing and Commercial Research, UDI of Financing, Calle Francisco Tomás y Valiente, 5, Universidad Autónoma de Madrid, 28049 Madrid, Spain; prosper.lamothe@uam.es
[2]   Department of Economic Theory and Economic History, Campus El Ejido s/n, University of Malaga, 29071 Malaga, Spain; mangel@uma.es
[3]   Rho Finanzas Partner, Calle de Zorrilla, 21, 28014 Madrid, Spain; pll@rhofinanzas.com
[4]   Department of Finance and Accounting, Campus El Ejido s/n, University of Malaga, 29071 Malaga, Spain
*   Correspondence: alaminos@uma.es

Abstract: A precise prediction of Bitcoin price is an important aspect of digital financial markets because it improves the valuation of an asset belonging to a decentralized control market. Numerous studies have studied the accuracy of models from a set of factors. Hence, previous literature shows how models for the prediction of Bitcoin suffer from poor performance capacity and, therefore, more progress is needed on predictive models, and they do not select the most significant variables. This paper presents a comparison of deep learning methodologies for forecasting Bitcoin price and, therefore, a new prediction model with the ability to estimate accurately. A sample of 29 initial factors was used, which has made possible the application of explanatory factors of different aspects related to the formation of the price of Bitcoin. To the sample under study, different methods have been applied to achieve a robust model, namely, deep recurrent convolutional neural networks, which have shown the importance of transaction costs and difficulty in Bitcoin price, among others. Our results have a great potential impact on the adequacy of asset pricing against the uncertainties derived from digital currencies, providing tools that help to achieve stability in cryptocurrency markets. Our models offer high and stable success results for a future prediction horizon, something useful for asset valuation of cryptocurrencies like Bitcoin.

Keywords: bitcoin; deep learning; deep recurrent convolutional neural networks; forecasting; asset pricing

1. Introduction

Bitcoin is a cryptocurrency built by free software based on peer-to-peer networks as an irreversible private payment platform. Bitcoin lacks a physical form, is not backed by any public body, and therefore any intervention by a government agency or other agent is not necessary to transact [1]. These transactions are made from the blockchain system. Blockchain is an open accounting book, which records transactions between two parties efficiently, leaving such a mark permanently and impossible to erase, making this tool a decentralized validation protocol that is difficult to manipulate, and with low risk of fraud. The blockchain system is not subject to any individual entity [2].

For Bitcoin, the concept originated from the concept of cryptocurrency, or virtual currency [3]. Cryptocurrencies are a monetary medium that is not affected by public regulation, nor is it subject to a regulatory body. It only affects the activity and rules developed by the developers. Cryptocurrencies are virtual currencies that can be created and stored only electronically [4]. The cryptocurrency is designed to serve as a medium of exchange and for this, it uses cryptography systems to secure the transaction and control the subsequent creation of the cryptocurrency. Cryptocurrency is a subset of a digital currency designed to function as a medium of exchange and cryptography is used to secure the transaction and control the future creation of the cryptocurrency.

Forecasting Bitcoin price is vitally important for both asset managers and independent investors. Although Bitcoin is a currency, it cannot be studied as another traditional currency where economic theories about uncovered interest rate parity, future cash-flows model, and purchasing power parity matter, since different standard factors of the relationship between supply and demand cannot be applied in the digital currency market like Bitcoin [5]. On the one hand, Bitcoin has different characteristics that make it useful for those agents who invest in Bitcoin, such as transaction speed, dissemination, decentrality, and the large virtual community of people interested in talking and providing relevant information about digital currencies, mainly Bitcoin [6].

Velankar and colleagues [7] attempted to predict the daily price change sign as accurately as possible using Bayesian regression and generalized linear model. To do this, they considered the daily trends of the Bitcoin market and focused on the characteristics of Bitcoin transactions, reaching an accuracy of 51% with the generalized linear model. McNally and co-workers [8] studied the precision with which the direction of the Bitcoin price in United States Dollar (USD) can be predicted. They used a recurrent neural network (RNN), a long short-term memory (LSTM) network, and the autoregressive integrated moving average (ARIMA) method. The LSTM network obtains the highest classification accuracy of 52% and a root mean square error (RMSE) of 8%. As expected, non-linear deep learning methods exceeded the ARIMA method's prognosis. For their part, Yogeshwaran and co-workers [9] applied convolutional and recurrent neural networks to predict the price of Bitcoin using data from a time interval of 5 min to 2 h, with convolutional neural networks showing a lower level of error, at around 5%. Demir and colleagues [10] predicted the price of Bitcoin using methods such as long short-term memory networks, naïve Bayes, and the nearest neighbor algorithm. These methods achieved accuracy rates between 97.2% and 81.2%. Rizwan, Narejo, and Javed [11] continued with the application of deep learning methods with the techniques of RNN and LSTM. Their results showed an accuracy of 52% and an 8% RMSE by the LSTM. Linardatos and Kotsiantis [12] had the same results, after using eXtreme Gradient Boosting (XGBoost) and LSTM; they concluded that this last technique yielded a lower RMSE of 0.999. Despite the superiority of computational techniques, Felizardo and colleagues [13] showed that ARIMA had a lower error rate than methods, such as random forest (RF), support vector machine (SVM), LSTM, and WaveNets, to predict the future price of Bitcoin. Finally, other works showed new deep learning methods, such as Dutta, Kumar, and Basu [14], who applied both LSTM and the gated recurring unit (GRU) model; the latter showed the best error result, with an RMSE of 0.019. Ji and co-workers [15] predicted the price of Bitcoin with different methodologies such as deep neural network (DNN), the LSTM model, and convolutional neural network. They obtained a precision of 60%, leaving the improvement of precision with deep learning techniques and a greater definition of significant variables as a future line of research. These authors show the need for stable prediction models, not only with data in and out of the sample, but also in forecasts of future results.

To contribute to the robustness of the Bitcoin price prediction models, in the present study a comparison of deep learning methodologies to predict and model the Bitcoin price is developed and, as a consequence, a new model that generates better forecasts of the Bitcoin price and its behavior in the future. This model can predict achieving accuracy levels above 95%. This model was constructed from a sample of 29 variables. Different methods were applied in the construction of the Bitcoin price prediction model to build a reliable model, which is contrasted with various methodologies used in previous works to check with which technique a high predictive capacity is achieved; specifically, the methods of deep recurrent neural networks, deep neural decision trees, and deep support vector machines, were used. Furthermore, this work attempts to obtain high accuracy, but it is also robust and stable in the future horizon to predict new observations, something that has not yet been reported by previous works [7–15], but which some authors demand for the development of these models and their real contribution [9,12].

We make two main contributions to the literature. First, we consider new explanatory variables for modeling the Bitcoin price, testing the importance of these variables which have not been considered so far. It has important implications for investors, who will know which indicators provide reliable, accurate, and potential forecasts of the Bitcoin price. Second, we improve the prediction accuracy concerning that obtained in previous studies with innovative methodologies.

This study is structured as follows: Section 2 explains the theory of methods applied. Section 3 offers details of the data and the variables used in this study. Section 4 develops the results obtained. Section 5 provides conclusions of the study and the purposes of the models obtained.

2. Deep Learning Methods

As previously stated, different deep learning methods have been applied for the development of Bitcoin price prediction models. We use this type of methodology thanks to its high predictive capacity obtained in the previous literature on asset pricing to meet one of the objectives of this study, which is to achieve a robust model. Specifically, deep recurrent convolution neural network, deep neural decision trees, and deep learning linear support vector machines have been used. The characteristics of each classification technique used are detailed below. In addition, the method of analysis of the sensitivity of variables used in the present study, in particular, the method of Sobol [16], which is necessary to determine the level of significance of the variables used in the prediction of Bitcoin price is recorded, fulfilling the need presented by the previous literature in the realization of the task of feature selection [15].

2.1. Deep Recurrent Convolution Neural Network (DRCNN)

Recurrent neural networks (RNN) have been applied in different fields for prediction due to its huge prediction performance. The previous calculations made are those that form the result within the structure of the RNN [17]. Having an input sequence vector x, the hidden nodes of a layer s, and the output of a hidden layer y, can be estimated as explained in Equations (1) and (2).

$$s_t = \sigma(W_{xs}x_t + W_{ss}s_{t-1} + b_s) \tag{1}$$

$$y_t = o(W_{so}s_t + b_y) \tag{2}$$

where W_{xs}, W_{ss}, and W_{so} define the weights from the input layer x to the hidden layer s, by the biases of the hidden layer and output layer. Equation (3) points out σ and o as the activation functions.

$$STFT\{z(t)\}(\tau,\omega) \equiv T(\tau,\omega) = \int_{-\infty}^{+\infty} z(t)\omega(t-\tau)e^{-j\omega t}\,dt \tag{3}$$

where $z(t)$ is the vibration signals, and $\omega(t)$ is the Gaussian window function focused around 0. $T(\tau,\omega)$ is the function that expresses the vibration signals. To calculate the hidden layers with the convolutional operation, Equations (4) and (5) are applied.

$$S_t = \sigma(W_{TS} * T_t + W_{ss} * S_{t-1} + B_s) \tag{4}$$

$$Y_t = o(W_{YS} * S_t + B_y) \tag{5}$$

where W indicates the convolution kernels.

Recurrent convolutional neural network (RCNN) can be heaped to establish a deep architecture, called the deep recurrent convolutional neural network (DRCNN) [18,19]. To use the DRCNN method in the predictive task, Equation (6) determines how the last phase of the model serves as a supervised learning layer.

$$\hat{r} = \sigma(W_h * h + b_h) \tag{6}$$

where W_h is the weight and b_h is the bias. The model calculates the residuals caused by the difference between the predicted and the actual observations in the training stage [20]. Stochastic gradient descent is applied for optimization to learn the parameters. Considering that the data at time t is r, the loss function is determined as shown in Equation (7).

$$L(\mathbf{r}, \hat{\mathbf{r}}) = \frac{1}{2}\|\mathbf{r} - \hat{\mathbf{r}}\|_2^2 \tag{7}$$

2.2. Deep Neural Decision Trees (DNDT)

Deep neural decision trees are decision tree (DT) models performed by deep learning neural networks, where a weight division corresponding to the DNDT belongs to a specific decision tree and, therefore, it is possible to interpret its information [21]. Stochastic gradient descent (SGD) is used to optimize the parameters at the same time; this partitions the learning processing in mini-batches and can be attached to a larger standard neural network (NN) model for end-to-end learning with backward propagation. In addition, standard DTs gain experience through a greedy and recursive factor division. This can make a selection of functions more efficient [22]. The method starts by performing a soft binning function to compute the residual rate for each node, making it possible to make decisions divided into DNDTs [23]. The input of a binning function is a real scalar x which makes an index of the containers to which x belongs.

The activation function of the DNDT algorithm is carried out based on the NN represented in Equation (8).

$$\pi = fw,b,\tau \ (x) = softmax((wx + b)/\tau) \tag{8}$$

where w is a constant with value w = [1, 2, ..., n + 1], $\tau > 0$ is a temperature factor, and b is defined in Equation (9).

$$b = [0, -\beta1, -\beta1, -\beta2, ..., -\beta1 - \beta2 - \cdots - \beta n] \tag{9}$$

The coding of the binning function x is given by the NN according the expression of Equation (9) [24]. The key idea is to build the DT with the applied Kronecker product from the binning function defined above. Connecting every feature x_d with its NN $f_d\ (x_d)$, we can determine all the final nodes of the DT as appears in Equation (10).

$$z = f1(x1) \otimes f2(x2) \otimes \cdots \otimes fD(xD) \tag{10}$$

where z expresses the leaf node index obtained by instance x in vector form. The complexity parameter of the model is determined by the number of cut points of each node. There may be inactive points since the values of the cut points are usually not limited.

2.3. Deep Learning Linear Support Vector Machines (DSVR)

Support vector machines (SVMs) were created for binary classification. Training data are denoted by its labels $(x_n, y_n), n = 1, \ldots, N, x_n \in \mathbb{R}^D, t_n \in \{-1, +1\}$; SVMs are optimized according to Equation (11).

$$\min_{w\xi_n}\tfrac{1}{2}W^T W + C\sum_{n=1}^N \xi_n$$
$$s.t.\ W^T x_n t_n \geq 1 - \xi_n > \forall n \tag{11}$$
$$\xi_n \geq 0 \ \forall n$$

where ξ_n are features that punish observations that do not meet the margin requirements [25]. The optimization problem is defined as appears in Equation (12).

$$\min_{w}\frac{1}{2}W^T W + C\sum_{n=1}^{N} max(1 - W^T x_n t_n, 0) \tag{12}$$

Usually the Softmax or 1-of-K encoding method is applied in the classification task of deep learning algorithms. In the case of working with 10 classes, the Softmax layer is composed of 10 nodes and expressed by p_i, where $i = 1, ..., 10$; p_i specifies a discrete probability distribution, $\sum_i^{10} p_i = 1$.

Equation (13) is defined by h as the activation of the penultimate layer nodes, W as the weight linked by the penultimate layer to the Softmax layer, and the total input into a Softmax layer. The next expression is the result.

$$a_i = \sum_k h_k W_{ki} \tag{13}$$

$$p_i = \frac{exp(a_i)}{\sum_j^{10} exp(a_j)} \tag{14}$$

The predicted class $\hat{\imath}$ would be as follows in Equation (15).

$$\hat{\imath} = \underset{i}{argmax}\, p_i = \underset{i}{argmax}\, a_i \tag{15}$$

Since linear-SVM is not differentiable, a popular variation is known as the DSVR, which minimizes the squared hinge loss as indicated in Equation (16).

$$\min_w \frac{1}{2} W^T W + C \sum_{n=1}^{N} max(1 - W^T x_n t_n, 0)^2 \tag{16}$$

The target of the DSVR is to train deep neural networks for prediction [24,25]. Equation (17) expresses the differentiation of the activation concerning the penultimate layer, where $l\,(w)$ is said differentiation, changing the input x for the activation h.

$$\frac{\partial l(w)}{\partial h_n} = -C t_n w(\mathbb{I}\{1 > w^T h_t t_n\}) \tag{17}$$

where $\mathbb{I}\{\cdot\}$ is the indicator function. Likewise, for the DSVR, we have Equation (18).

$$\frac{\partial l(w)}{\partial h_n} = -2 C t_n w(max(1 - W^T h_n t_n, 0)) \tag{18}$$

2.4. Sensitivity Analysis

Data mining methods have the virtue of offering a great amount of explanation to the authors' studied problem. To know what the degree is, sensitivity analysis is performed. This analysis tries to quantify the relative importance of the independent variables concerning the dependent variable [26,27]. To do this, the search for the reduction of the set of initial variables continues, leaving only the most significant ones. The variance limit follows, where one variable is significant if its variance increases concerning the rest of the variables as a whole. The Sobol method [16] is applied to decompose the variance of the total output V (Y) offered by the set of equations expressed in Equation (19).

$$V(Y) = \sum_i V_i + \sum_i \sum_{j>1} V_{ij} + \ldots + V_{1,2,\ldots k} \tag{19}$$

where $V_i = VE(Y|X_i)$ and $V_{ij} = VE(Y|X_i, X_j)) - V_i - V_j$.

$S_i = V_i/V$ and $S_{ij} = V_{ij}/V$ define the sensitivity indexes, with S_{ij} being the effect of interaction between two variables. The Sobol decomposition allows the estimation of a total sensitivity index, STi, which measures the sum of all the sensitivity effects involved in the independent variables.

3. Data and Variables

The sample period selected is from 2011 to 2019, with a quarterly frequency of data. To obtain the information of the independent variables, data from the IMF's International Financial Statistics (IFS), the World Bank, FRED Sant Louis, Google Trends, Quandl, and Blockchain.info were used.

The dependent variable used in this study is the Bitcoin price and is defined as the value of Bitcoin in USD. In addition, we used 29 independent variables, classified into demand and supply variables, attractiveness, and macroeconomic and financial variables, as possible predictors of the Bitcoin future price (Table 1). These variables were used throughout the previous literature [1,3,4,14].

Table 1. Independent variables.

Variables	Description
(a) Demand and Supply	
Transaction value	Value of daily transactions
Number of Bitcoins	Number of mined Bitcoins currently circulating on the network
Bitcoins addresses	Number of unique Bitcoin addresses used per day
Transaction volume	Number of transactions per day
Unspent transactions	Number of valid unspent transactions
Blockchain transactions	Number of transactions on blockchain
Blockchain addresses	Number of unique addresses used in blockchain
Block size	Average block size expressed in megabytes
Miners reward	Block rewards paid to miners
Mining commissions	Average transaction fees (in USD)
Cost per transaction	Miners' income divided by the number of transactions
Difficulty	Difficulty mining a new blockchain block
Hash	Times a hash function can be calculated per second
Halving	Process of reducing the emission rate of new units
(b) Attractive	
Forum posts	Number of new members in online Bitcoin forums
Forum members	New posts in online Bitcoin forums
(c) Macroeconomic and Financial	
Texas oil	Oil Price (West Texas)
Brent oil	Oil Price (Brent, London)
Dollar exchange rate	Exchange rate between the US dollar and the euro
Dow Jones	Dow Jones Index of the New York Stock Exchange
Gold	Gold price in US dollars per troy ounce

The sample is fragmented into three mutually exclusive parts, one for training (70% of the data), one for validation (10% of the data), and the third group for testing (20% of the data). The training data are used to build the intended models, while the validation data attempt to assess whether there is overtraining of those models. As for the test data, they serve to evaluate the built model and measure the predictive capacity. The percentage of correctly classified cases is the precision results and RMSE measures the level of errors made. Furthermore, for the distribution of the sample data in these three phases, cross-validation 10 times with 500 iterations was used [28,29].

4. Results

4.1. Descriptive Statistics

Table 2 shows a statistical summary of the independent variables for predicting Bitcoin price. It is observed that all the variables obtain a standard deviation not higher than each value of the mean. Therefore, the data show initial stability. On the other hand, there is a greater difference between the minimum and maximum values. Variables like mining commissions and cost per transaction show a small minimum value compared to their mean value. The same fact happens with the hash variable. Despite these extremes, they do not affect the values of the standard deviations of the respective variables.

Table 2. Summary statistics.

Variables	Obs	Mean	SD	Min	Max
Transaction value	112	342,460,106,866,711.0000	143,084,554,727,531.0000	59,238,547,391,199.6000	735,905,260,141,564.0000
Number of bitcoins	112	13,634,297.4824	3,709,010.0736	5,235,454.5455	18,311,982.5000
Bitcoins addresses	112	285,034.2515	219,406.3874	1576.8333	849,668.1000
Transaction volume	112	154,548.8041	117,104.3686	1105.5000	373,845.6000
Unspent transactions	112	28,581,914.9054	22,987,595.3012	78,469.7273	66,688,779.9000
Blockchain transactions	112	156,444,312.9120	161,252,448.1997	237,174.8889	520,792,976.5000
Blockchain addresses	112	4,812,692.05	13,735,245.35	−14,437,299.03	117,863,226.2
Block size	112	0.4956	0.3638	0.0022	0.9875
Miners reward	112	420,160,582,581,028.0000	174,396,895,338,462.0000	101,244,436,734,897.0000	796,533,076,376,536.0000
Mining commissions	112	9,581,973,325,205.4400	42,699,799,790,392.8000	0.2591	315,387,506,596,395.0000
Cost per transaction	112	155,354,364,458,705.0000	156,696,788,525,225.0000	0.1179	757,049,771,708,905.0000
Difficulty	112	187,513,499,336,866.0000	195,421,886,528,251.0000	212,295,141,771.2000	836,728,509,520,663.0000
Hash	112	110,434,372.2765	154,717,725.3881	0.5705	516,395,703.4338
Halving	112	279,853,454,485,387.0000	162,806,469,642,875.0000	6,473,142,955,255.1700	804,437,327,302,638.0000
Forum posts	112	9279.8844	8585.0583	455.0000	53132.0000
Forum members	112	2432.2545	3394.4635	30.6364	14,833.3409
Texas Oil	112	72.4878	23.7311	21.1230	135.6700
Brent Oil	112	78.4964	26.5819	19.1900	139.3800
Dollar exchange rate	112	1.3767	0.9604	1.0494	8.7912
Dow Jones	112	15,926.7161	3324.8875	11,602.5212	22,044.8627
Gold	112	1329.400847	244.4099259	739.15	1846.75

4.2. Empirical Results

Table 3 and Figures 1–3 show the level of accuracy, the root mean square error (RMSE), and the mean absolute percentage error (MAPE). In all models, the level of accuracy always exceeds 92.61% for testing data. For its part, the RMSE and MAPE levels are adequate. The model with the highest accuracy is that of deep recurrent convolution neural network (DRCNN) with 97.34%, followed by the model of deep neural decision trees (DNDT) method with 96.94% on average by regions. Taken together, these results provide a level of accuracy far superior to that of previous studies. Thus, in the work of Ji and co-workers [15], an accuracy of around 60% is revealed; in the case of McNally and co-workers [8], it is close to 52%; and in the study of Rizwan, Narejo, and Javed [11], it approaches 52%. Finally, Table 4 shows the most significative variables by methods after applying the Sobol method for the sensitivity analysis.

Table 3. Results of accuracy evaluation: classification (%).

Sample	DRCNN			DNDT			DSVR		
	Acc. (%)	RMSE	MAPE	Acc. (%)	RMSE	MAPE	Acc. (%)	RMSE	MAPE
Training	97.34	0.66	0.29	95.86	0.70	0.33	94.49	0.75	0.38
Validation	96.18	0.71	0.34	95.07	0.74	0.37	93.18	0.81	0.43
Testing	95.27	0.77	0.40	94.42	0.79	0.42	92.61	0.84	0.47

DRCNN: deep recurrent convolution neural network; DNDT: deep neural decision trees; DSVR: deep learning linear support vector machines; Acc: accuracy; RMSE: root mean square error; MAPE: mean absolute percentage error.

Table 4. Results of accuracy evaluation: greater sensitivity variables.

DRCNN	DNDT	DSVR
Transaction value	Transaction volume	Transaction value
Transaction volume	Block size	Block size
Block size	Blockchain transactions	Blockchain transactions
Cost per transaction	Cost per transaction	Cost per transaction
Difficulty	Difficulty	Difficulty
Dollar exchange rate	Forum posts	Forum posts
Dow Jones	Dow Jones	Dollar exchange rate
Gold	Gold	Dow Jones
		Gold

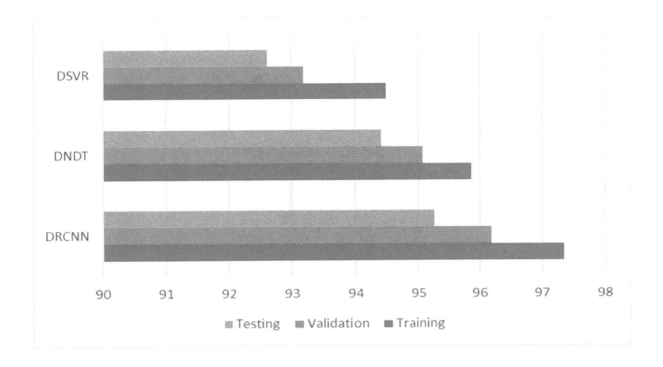

Figure 1. Results of accuracy evaluation: classification (%).

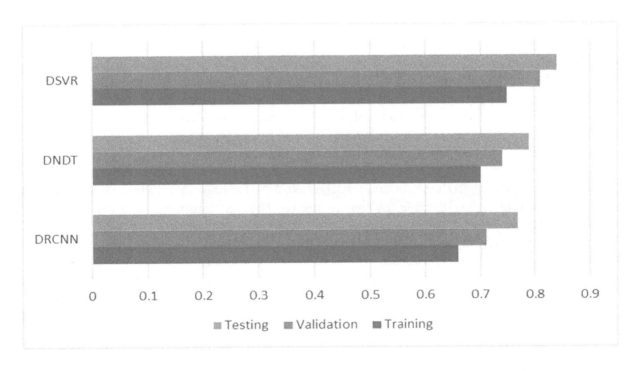

Figure 2. Results of accuracy evaluation: RMSE.

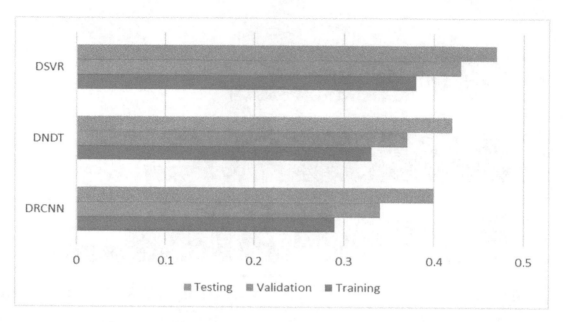

Figure 3. Results of accuracy evaluation: MAPE.

Table 4 shows additional information on the significant variables. Block size, cost per transaction, and difficulty were significant in the three models for each method applied. This demonstrates the importance of the cost to carry out the Bitcoin transaction, of the block of Bitcoins to buy, as well as the difficulty of the miners to find new Bitcoins, as the main factors in the task of determining the price of Bitcoin. This contrasts with the results shown in previous studies, where these variables are not significant or are not used by the initial set of variables [5,7,8]. The best results were obtained by the DRCNN method, where in addition to the aforementioned variables, the transaction value, transaction volume, block size, dollar exchange rate, Dow Jones, and gold were also significant. This shows that the demand and supply variables of the Bitcoin market are essential to predict its price, something that has been shown by some previous works [1,30]. Yet significant macroeconomic and financial variables have not been observed as important factors by other recent works [30,31], since they were shown as variables that did not influence Bitcoin price fluctuations. In our results, the macroeconomic variables of Dow Jones and gold have been significant in all methods.

On the other hand, the models built by the DNDT and DSVR methods show high levels of precision, although lower than those obtained by the DRCNN. Furthermore, these methods show some different significant variables. Such is the case of the variables of forum posts, a variable popularly used as a proxy for the level of future demand that Bitcoin could have, although with divergences in previous works regarding its significance to predict the price of Bitcoin, where some works show that this variable is not significant [11,14]. Finally, these methods show another macroeconomic variable that is more significant, in the case of the dollar exchange rate. This represents the importance that changes in the price of the USD with Bitcoin can be decisive in estimating the possible demand and, therefore, a change in price. This variable, like the rest of the macroeconomic variables, has not been shown as a significant variable [5,31].

This set of variables observed as significant represents a group of novel factors that determine the price of Bitcoin and therefore, is different from that shown in the previous literature.

4.3. Post-Estimations

In this section, we try to perform estimations of models to generate forecasts in a future horizon. For this, we used the framework of multiple-step ahead prediction, applying the iterative strategy and models built to predict one step forward are trained [32]. At time t, a prediction is made for moment $t + 1$, and this prediction is used to predict for moment $t + 2$ and so on. This means that the predicted data for $t + 1$ are considered real data and are added to the end of the available data [33]. Table 5 and Figures 4–6 show the accuracy and error results for $t + 1$ and $t + 2$ forecasting horizons. For $t + 1$, the range of precision for the three methods is 88.34–94.19% on average, where the percentage of accuracy is higher in the DRCNN (94.19%). For $t + 2$, this range of precision is 85.76–91.37%, where the percentage of accuracy is once again higher in the DRCNN (91.37%). These results show the high precision and great robustness of the models.

Table 5. Multiple-step ahead forecasts in forecast horizon = $t + 1$ and $t + 2$.

Horizon	DRCNN			DNDT			DSVR		
	Acc. (%)	RMSE	MAPE	Acc. (%)	RMSE	MAPE	Acc. (%)	RMSE	MAPE
$t + 1$	94.19	0.81	0.52	92.35	0.87	0.59	88.34	0.97	0.65
$t + 2$	91.37	0.92	0.63	89.41	1.03	0.67	85.76	1.10	0.78

Acc: accuracy.

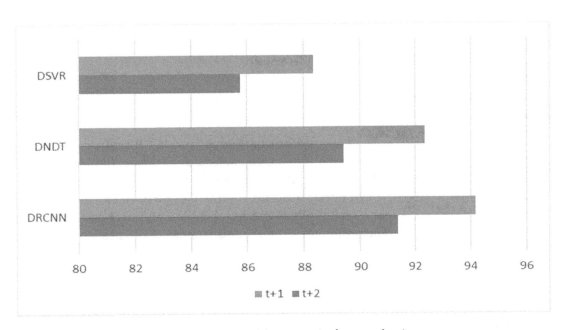

Figure 4. Multiple-step ahead forecasts in forecast horizon: accuracy.

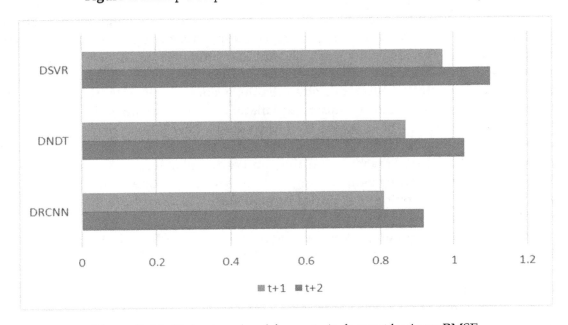

Figure 5. Multiple-step ahead forecasts in forecast horizon: RMSE.

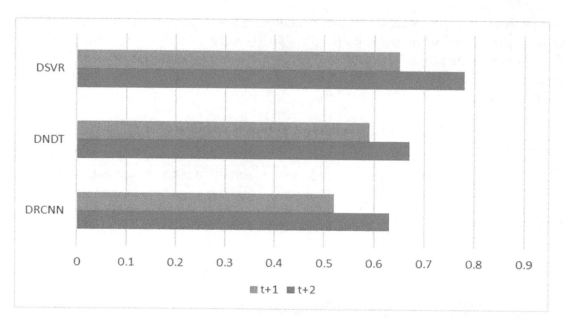

Figure 6. Multiple-step ahead forecasts in forecast horizon: MAPE.

5. Conclusions

This study developed a comparison of methodologies to predict Bitcoin price and, therefore, a new model was created to forecast this price. The period selected was from 2011 to 2019. We applied different deep learning methods in the construction of the Bitcoin price prediction model to achieve a robust model, such as deep recurrent convolutional neural network, deep neural decision trees and deep support vector machines. The DRCNN model obtained the highest levels of precision. We propose to increase the level of performance of the models to predict the price of Bitcoin compared to previous literature. This research has shown significantly higher precision results than those shown in previous works, achieving a precision hit range of 92.61–95.27%. Likewise, it was possible to identify a new set of significant variables for the prediction of the price of Bitcoin, offering great stability in the models developed predicting in the future horizons of one and two years.

This research allows us to increase the results and conclusions on the price of Bitcoin concerning previous works, both in matters of precision and error, but also on significant variables. A set of significant variables for each methodology applied has been selected analyzing our results, but some of these variables are recurrent in the three methods. This supposes an important addition to the field of cryptocurrency pricing. The conclusions are relevant to central bankers, investors, asset managers, private forecasters, and business professionals for the cryptocurrencies market, who are generally interested in knowing which indicators provide reliable, accurate, and potential forecasts of price changes. Our study suggests new and significant explanatory variables to allow these agents to predict the Bitcoin price phenomenon. These results have provided a new Bitcoin price forecasting model developed using three methods, with the DCRNN model as the most accurate, thus contributing to existing knowledge in the field of machine learning, and especially, deep learning. This new model can be used as a reference for setting asset pricing and improved investment decision-making.

In summary, this study provides a significant opportunity to contribute to the field of finance, since the results obtained have significant implications for the future decisions of asset managers, making it possible to avoid big change events of the price and the potential associated costs. It also helps these agents send warning signals to financial markets and avoid massive losses derived from an increase of volatility in the price.

Opportunities for further research in this field include developing predictive models considering volatility correlation of the other new alternative assets and also safe-haven assets such as gold or stable currencies, that evaluate the different scenarios of portfolio choice and optimization.

Author Contributions: Conceptualization, P.L.-F., D.A., P.L.-L. and M.A.F.-G.; Data curation, D.A. and M.A.F.-G.; Formal analysis, P.L.-F., D.A. and P.L.-L.; Funding acquisition, P.L.-F., P.L.-L. and M.A.F.-G.; Investigation, D.A. and M.A.F.-G.; Methodology, D.A.; Project administration, P.L.-F. and M.A.F.-G.; Resources, P.L.-F. and M.A.F.-G.; Software, D.A.; Supervision, D.A.; Validation, D.A. and P.L.-L.; Visualization, P.L.-F. and D.A.; Writing—original draft, P.L.-F. and D.A.; Writing—review & editing, P.L.-F., D.A., P.L.-L. and M.A.F.-G. All authors have read and agreed to the published version of the manuscript.

References

1. Kristoufek, L. What Are the Main Drivers of the Bitcoin Price? Evidence from Wavelet Coherence Analysis. *PLoS ONE* **2015**, *10*, e0123923. [CrossRef]

2. Wamba, S.F.; Kamdjoug, J.R.K.; Bawack, R.E.; Keogh, J.G. Bitcoin, Blockchain and Fintech: A systematic review and case studies in the supply chain. *Prod. Plan. Control Manag. Oper.* **2019**, *31*, 115–142. [CrossRef]

3. Chen, W.; Zheng, Z.; Ma, M.; Wu, J.; Zhou, Y.; Yao, J. Dependence structure between bitcoin price and its influence factors. *Int. J. Comput. Sci. Eng.* **2020**, *21*, 334–345. [CrossRef]

4. Balcilar, M.; Bouri, E.; Gupta, R.; Roubaud, D. Can volume predict bitcoin returns and volatility? A quantiles-based approach. *Econ. Model.* **2017**, *64*, 74–81. [CrossRef]

5. Ciaian, P.; Rajcaniova, M.; Artis Kancs, D. The economics of BitCoin price formation. *Appl. Econ.* **2016**, *48*, 1799–1815. [CrossRef]

6. Schmidt, R.; Möhring, M.; Glück, D.; Haerting, R.; Keller, B.; Reichstein, C. Benefits from Using Bitcoin: Empirical Evidence from a European Country. *Int. J. Serv. Sci. Manag. Eng. Technol.* **2016**, *7*, 48–62. [CrossRef]

7. Velankar, S.; Valecha, S.; Maji, S. Bitcoin Price Prediction using Machine Learning. In Proceedings of the 20th International Conference on Advanced Communications Technology (ICACT), Chuncheon-si, Korea, 11–14 February 2018.

8. McNally, S.; Roche, J.; Caton, S. Predicting the Price of Bitcoin Using Machine Learning. In Proceedings of the 26th Euromicro International Conference on Parallel, Distributed, and Network-Based Processing, Cambridge, UK, 21–23 March 2018.

9. Yogeshwaran, S.; Kaur, M.J.; Maheshwari, P. Project Based Learning: Predicting Bitcoin Prices using Deep Learning. In Proceedings of the 2019 IEEE Global Engineering Education Conference (EDUCON), Dubai, UAE, 9–11 April 2019.

10. Demir, A.; Akılotu, B.N.; Kadiroğlu, Z.; Şengür, A. Bitcoin Price Prediction Using Machine Learning Methods. In Proceedings of the 2019 1st International Informatics and Software Engineering Conference (UBMYK), Ankara, Turkey, 6–7 November 2019.

11. Rizwan, M.; Narejo, S.; Javed, M. Bitcoin price prediction using Deep Learning Algorithm. In Proceedings of the 13th International Conference on Mathematics, Actuarial Science, Computer Science and Statistics (MACS), Karachi, Pakistan, 14–15 December 2019.

12. Linardatos, P.; Kotsiantis, S. Bitcoin Price Prediction Combining Data and Text Mining. In *Advances in Integrations of Intelligent Methods. Smart Innovation, Systems and Technologies*; Hatzilygeroudis, I., Perikos, I., Grivokostopoulou, F., Eds.; Springer: Singapore, 2020.

13. Felizardo, L.; Oliveira, R.; Del-Moral-Hernández, E.; Cozman, F. Comparative study of Bitcoin price prediction using WaveNets, Recurrent Neural Networks and other Machine Learning Methods. In Proceedings of the 6th International Conference on Behavioral, Economic and Socio-Cultural Computing (BESC), Beijing, China, 28–30 October 2019.

14. Dutta, A.; Kumar, S.; Basu, M. A Gated Recurrent Unit Approach to Bitcoin Price Prediction. *J. Risk Financ. Manag.* **2020**, *13*, 23. [CrossRef]

15. Ji, S.; Kim, J.; Im, H. A Comparative Study of Bitcoin Price Prediction Using Deep Learning. *Mathematics* **2019**, *7*, 898. [CrossRef]

16. Saltelli, A. Making best use of model evaluations to compute sensitivity indices. *Comput. Phys. Commun.* **2002**, *145*, 280–297. [CrossRef]

17. Wang, S.; Chen, X.; Tong, C.; Zhao, Z. Matching Synchrosqueezing Wavelet Transform and Application to Aeroengine Vibration Monitoring. *IEEE Trans. Instrum. Meas.* **2017**, *66*, 360–372. [CrossRef]

18. Huang, C.-W.; Narayanan, S.S. Deep convolutional recurrent neural network with attention mechanism for robust speech emotion recognition. In Proceedings of the 2017 IEEE International Conference on Multimedia and Expo, Hong Kong, China, 10–14 July 2017; pp. 583–588.

19. Ran, X.; Xue, L.; Zhang, Y.; Liu, Z.; Sang, X.; Xe, J. Rock Classification from Field Image Patches Analyzed Using a Deep Convolutional Neural Network. *Mathematics* **2019**, *7*, 755. [CrossRef]

20. Ma, M.; Mao, Z. Deep Recurrent Convolutional Neural Network for Remaining Useful Life Prediction. In Proceedings of the 2019 IEEE International Conference on Prognostics and Health Management (ICPHM), San Francisco, CA, USA, 17–20 June 2019; pp. 1–4.

21. Yang, Y.; Garcia-Morillo, I.; Hospedales, T.M. Deep Neural Decision Trees. In Proceedings of the 2018 ICML Workshop on Human Interpretability in Machine Learning (WHI 2018), Stockholm, Sweden, 14 July 2018.

22. Norouzi, M.; Collins, M.D.; Johnson, M.; Fleet, D.J.; Kohli, P. Efficient non-greedy optimization of decision trees. In Proceedings of the 28th International Conference on Neural Information Processing Systems, Montreal, QC, Canada, 8–13 December 2015; pp. 1729–1737.

23. Dougherty, J.; Kohavi, R.; Sahami, M. Supervised and unsupervised discretization of continuous features. In Proceedings of the 12th International Conference on Machine Learning (ICML), Tahoe City, CA, USA, 9–12 July 1995.

24. Jang, E.; Gu, S.; Poole, B. Categorical reparameterization with Gumbel-Softmax. *arXiv* **2017**, arXiv:1611.01144.

25. Tang, Y. Categorical reparameterization with Gumbel-Softmax. *arXiv* **2013**, arXiv:1306.0239.

26. Delen, D.; Kuzey, C.; Uyar, A. Measuring firm performance using financial ratios: A decision tree approach. *Expert Syst. Appl.* **2013**, *40*, 3970–3983. [CrossRef]

27. Efimov, D.; Sulieman, H. Sobol Sensitivity: A Strategy for Feature Selection. In *Mathematics Across Contemporary Sciences. AUS-ICMS 2015*; Springer Proceedings in Mathematics & Statistics: Cham, Switzerland, 2017; Volume 190.

28. Alaminos, D.; Fernández, S.M.; García, F.; Fernández, M.A. Data Mining for Municipal Financial Distress Prediction, Advances in Data Mining, Applications and Theoretical Aspects. *Lect. Notes Comput. Sci.* **2018**, *10933*, 296–308.

29. Zhang, G.P.; Qi, M. Neural network forecasting for seasonal and trend time series. *Eur. J. Oper. Res.* **2005**, *160*, 501–514. [CrossRef]

30. Polasik, M.; Piotrowska, A.I.; Wisniewski, T.P.; Kotkowski, R.; Lightfoot, G. Price fluctuations and the use of Bitcoin: An empirical inquiry. *Int. J. Electron. Commer.* **2015**, *20*, 9–49. [CrossRef]

31. Al-Khazali, O.; Bouri, E.; Roubaud, D. The impact of positive and negative macroeconomic news surprises: Gold versus Bitcoin. *Econ. Bull.* **2018**, *38*, 373–382.

32. Koprinska, I.; Rana, M.; Rahman, A. Dynamic ensemble using previous and predicted future performance for Multi-step-ahead solar power forecasting. In Proceedings of the ICANN 2019: Artificial Neural Networks and Machine Learning, Munich, Germany, 17–19 September 2019; pp. 436–449.

33. Makridakis, S.; Spiliotis, E.; Assimakopoulos, V. Statistical and Machine Learning forecasting methods: Concerns and ways forward. *PLoS ONE* **2018**, *13*, e0194889. [CrossRef] [PubMed]

10

Market Volatility of the Three Most Powerful Military Countries during their Intervention in the Syrian War

Viviane Naimy [1], José-María Montero [2], Rim El Khoury [1,*] and Nisrine Maalouf [3]

[1] Faculty of Business Administration and Economics, Notre Dame University—Louaize, Zouk Mikayel, Zouk Mosbeh 72, Lebanon; vnaimy@ndu.edu.lb

[2] Department of Political Economy and Public Finance, Economic and Business Statistics, and Economic Policy, Faculty of Law and Social Sciences, University of Castilla-La Mancha, 45071 Toledo, Spain; Jose.mlorenzo@uclm.es

[3] Financial Risk Management—Faculty of Business Administration and Economics, Notre Dame University—Louaize, Zouk Mikayel, Zouk Mosbeh 72, Lebanon; nisrinemaalouf1@gmail.com

* Correspondence: rkhoury@ndu.edu.lb

Abstract: This paper analyzes the volatility dynamics in the financial markets of the (three) most powerful countries from a military perspective, namely, the U.S., Russia, and China, during the period 2015–2018 that corresponds to their intervention in the Syrian war. As far as we know, there is no literature studying this topic during such an important distress period, which has had very serious economic, social, and humanitarian consequences. The Generalized Autoregressive Conditional Heteroscedasticity (GARCH (1, 1)) model yielded the best volatility results for the in-sample period. The weighted historical simulation produced an accurate value at risk (VaR) for a period of one month at the three considered confidence levels. For the out-of-sample period, the Monte Carlo simulation method, based on student t-copula and peaks-over-threshold (POT) extreme value theory (EVT) under the Gaussian kernel and the generalized Pareto (GP) distribution, overstated the risk for the three countries. The comparison of the POT-EVT VaR of the three countries to a portfolio of stock indices pertaining to non-military countries, namely Finland, Sweden, and Ecuador, for the same out-of-sample period, revealed that the intervention in the Syrian war may be one of the pertinent reasons that significantly affected the volatility of the stock markets of the three most powerful military countries. This paper is of great interest for policy makers, central bank leaders, participants involved in these markets, and all practitioners given the economic and financial consequences derived from such dynamics.

Keywords: GARCH; EGARCH; VaR; historical simulation approach; peaks-over-threshold; EVT; student t-copula; generalized Pareto distribution

1. Introduction

Political uncertainty occurs due to many factors like elections and changes in the government or parliament, changes in policies, strikes, minority disdain, foreign intervention in national affairs, and others. In many cases, these uncertainties lead to further complications affecting the economy and the financial market of the concerned country. Accordingly, the currency could devaluate, prices of assets, commodities, and stocks could fluctuate, and the growth of the economy could be hindered. From this perspective, countries strive to keep political risks controlled to be able to endure the cost or consequence of any sudden political unrest. This is one of the main reasons behind the intervention of powerful countries in the political and military affairs of less powerful countries, which is usually done at a high cost. This paper studies the impact of the intervention of the three most powerful military countries in the world, namely, the United States, Russia, and China (Figure 1), in the Syrian war on their market volatility.

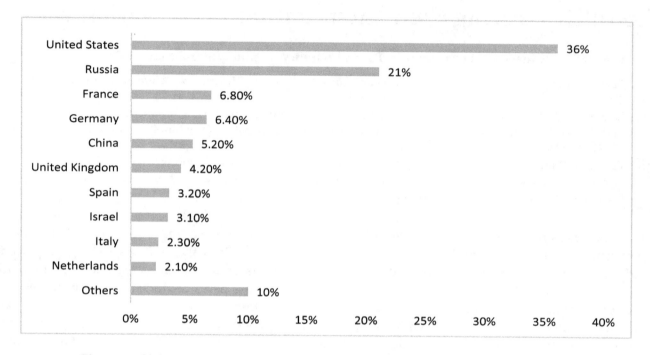

Figure 1. Global share of major arms exports by the 10 largest exporters, 2014–2018.

In March 2011, large peaceful protests broke in Syria to call for economic and political reforms with few armed protesters, leading to man arrests. Events evolved into violent acts using artillery and aircrafts, antigovernment rebels, terrorist and extremist attacks, suicide attacks, explosive operations, the intervention of foreign countries, chemical weapons, and others leading to a humanitarian crisis. In 2015, Russia started supporting the Syrian president through financial aid and military support [1]. In the meantime, the United States was providing support for the local Syrians. Later on, the United States and Russia increased their intervention in the war mainly through arms and aircrafts, each supporting their own political interests and allies. By the same token, China's involvement was shifting from humanitarian assistance and weapon exports [2] to armed forces and increased weapon exports to support its allies' objectives during this war [3].

Table 1 shows countries with the highest military spending in the world for 2016, 2017, and 2018. The U.S. spends the highest budget in the world on defense forces. This expenditure rounded up to USD 649 billion during 2018 based on information from the Stockholm International Peace Research Institute [4]. In fact, the defense spending of the United States alone is higher than the sum of that of the next eight countries in the ranking. These countries include China, Russia, Saudi Arabia, India, France, UK, Japan, and Germany. The country with the second highest defense expenditure is China with USD 250 billion in 2018 compared to USD 228 billion in 2017. As for Russia, its expenditure reached USD 61.4 billion in 2018 compared to USD 66.5 billion in 2017. Figure 1 represents the 10 largest arms exporters in the world between 2013 and 2017 [5]. Besides having the highest budgets for defense, the U.S. and Russia are also the top exporters of weapons, and China is among the top five worldwide countries. Based on these facts, the importance of the U.S., China, and Russia among military countries is highly reinforced. For this reason, we opted to study the dynamics of their financial markets to comprehend the risks and opportunities they might face, which would affect their worldwide exposure.

Table 1. Countries with the highest military spending worldwide in 2016–2018 (In Billion USD).

In USD Billion	2016	2017	2018
USA	600.1	605.8	648.8
China	216.0	227.8	250.0
Russia	69.2	66.5	61.4
Saudi Arabia	63.7	70.4	67.6
India	56.6	64.6	66.5
France	57.4	60.4	63.8

Source: Stockholm International Peace Research Institute (SIPRI), 2019.

To this end, measuring the effect of their intervention in the Syrian war on their financial market volatility is of great importance for policy makers, central bank leaders, analysts, and practitioners because there is a complete absence in the literature of studies that involve the volatility of the financial markets of the U.S., China, and Russia together. Many studies, however, explored the volatility of these countries during different periods and using different volatility models.

In his paper, Wei [6] forecasted the Chinese stock market volatility using non-linear Generalized Autoregressive Conditional Heteroscedasticity (GARCH) models such as the quadratic GARCH (QGARCH) and the Glosten, Jagannathan, and Runkle GARCH (GJR GRACH) models. The author studied seven-year data for the Shanghai Stock Exchange Composite (HSEC) and the Shenzhen Stock Exchange Component (ZSEC). The QGARCH outperformed the linear GARCH model. Furthermore, Lin and Fei [7] concluded that the nonlinear asymmetric power GARCH (APGARCH) model outperformed other GARCH models on different time scales in estimation of the "long memory property of the Shanghai and Shenzhen stock markets". Recently, Lin [8] studied the volatility of the SSE Composite Index using GARCH models during the period 2013–2017. The asymmetric exponential GARCH (EGARCH (1, 1)) model outperformed the symmetric ones in the forecasting results.

Value at risk (VaR), extreme value theory (EVT), and expected shortfall (ES) models were also used by Wang et al. [9], who implemented an EVT based VaR and ES to estimate the exchange rate risk of the Chinese currency (CNY). They found that the EVT-based VaR estimation produces accurate results for the currency exchange rate risks of EUR/CNY and JPY/CNY. However, EVT underestimated this risk for both exchange rates. Chen et al. [10] estimated VaR and ES by applying EVT on 13 worldwide stock indices. They concluded that China ranks first for VaR and ES with negative returns and ranks third for positive returns with high levels of risk.

A new strategy to estimate daily VaR based on the autoregressive fractionally integrated moving average model (ARFIMA), the multifractal volatility (MFV) model, and EVT was implemented by Wei et al. [11] for the Chinese stock market using high-frequency intraday quotes of the Shanghai Stock Exchange Component (SSEC). This hybrid ARFIMA-MFV-EVT strategy was compared to a number of popular linear and nonlinear GARCH-type-EVT models, i.e., the RiskMetrics, GARCH, IGARCH, and EGARCH models. Although GARCH-type models showed a good performance, VaR results obtained from the ARFIMA-MFV-EVT method outperformed several of them widely used in the literature. Furthermore, Hussain and Li [12] focused on the effect of extreme returns in stock markets on risk management by studying the SSEC index and by using the block maxima (Minima) method (BMM), instead of the popular peaks-over-threshold (POT) method, with various time intervals of extreme daily returns. Three well-known distributions in extreme value theory, i.e., generalized extreme value (GEV), generalized logistic (GL), and generalized Pareto distributions (GP), were employed to model the SSEC index returns. Results showed that GEV and GL distributions are found to be appropriate for the modeling of the extreme upward and downward market movements for China.

Another comparative study, conducted by Hou and Li [13], investigated the transmission of information between the U.S. and China's index futures markets using an asymmetric dynamic conditional correlation GARCH (DCC GARCH) approach. They found that the correlation between U.S. and Chinese index futures markets increases with the rise of negative shocks in these markets, and that the U.S. index futures market is more efficient in terms of price adjustment, since it is older and more mature. On the other hand, Awartani and Corradi [14] focused on the role of asymmetries in the prediction of the volatility of the S&P 500 Composite Price Index. They examined the relative out-of-sample predictive ability of different GARCH-type models. First, they performed pairwise comparisons of various models against GARCH (1, 1). Then, they carried out a joint comparison of all models. They found that for the case of the one-step ahead pairwise comparison, GARCH (1, 1) is beaten by the asymmetric GARCH models. A similar finding applies to different longer forecast horizons. In the multiple comparison case, GARCH (1, 1) is only beaten when compared against the class of asymmetric GARCH. Another interesting finding is that the RiskMetrics exponential smoothing seems to be the worst model in terms of predictive ability. Furio and Climent [15] studied extreme movements in the return of S&P 500, FTSE 100, and NIKKEI 225 using GARCH-type models and EVT estimates. Results pointed out that more accurate estimates are derived from EVT calculations in both the in-sample and out-of-sample, when compared to less accurate estimates using the GARCH models.

As can be deduced from the review of the above literature, the question of how devastating wars, with indirect consequences all around the world, affect the volatility of financial markets of countries supporting them (and others, of course) might be of core importance for those directly or indirectly involved in such markets. Therefore, the main research question is the following: are the volatility dynamics of those countries affected by an event of the importance of the Syrian war? This paper fills this gap through evaluating the results of a number of traditional volatility models of the GARCH-type family and using EVT and historical simulation (HS) to estimate the VaR of these markets during the Syrian war period.

S&P 500 (Standard & Poor's), SSEC (Shanghai Stock Exchange Composite) and MICEX (Moscow Interbank Currency Exchange) are used to assess the financial markets' volatility of the U.S., China, and Russia, respectively. The period of study extends from 2015 to 2018. The in-sample period extends from 5 January 2015 until 30 December 2016 as it refers to the beginning of the direct and indirect intervention of the chosen countries in the war in Syria [1]; the out-of-sample interval is 3 January 2017–31 May 2018.

The paper is structured as follows: Section 2 reviews the methodology and the specificities of the applied econometric models, and Section 3 shows the estimated GARCH-type models considered and the selection process. This section also depicts the results related to the calculation of VaR using HS volatility and the "peaks-over-threshold" (POT) EVT model under the GP distribution. Section 4 concludes and discusses the empirical findings.

2. Econometric Models

As previously outlined, we use the GARCH (1, 1) and EGARCH (1, 1) as competing models to measure the volatility of the financial markets of the U.S., Russia, and China. GARCH models are commonly used by financial institutions to obtain volatility and correlation forecasts of asset and risk factor return. We use the symmetric normal GARCH given its strength to provide short- and medium-term volatility forecasts. We also use EGARCH, the asymmetric GARCH model, which is widely recognized in providing a better in-sample fit than other types of GARCH processes and avoids the need for any parameter constraints (see [16,17] for details on other GARCH-type models). The exponentially weighted moving average (EWMA) model is not used because it does not account for mean reversion and overvalue volatility after severe price fluctuation [18]. As said in the introductory section, for VaR estimation with high confidence intervals, we apply EVT [19], and more specifically GEV, GL, and GP distributions. We decided to use EVT because of its ability to provide good estimates and serve of help in situations where high confidence levels are needed, since EVT has proven to be a robust way of smoothing and extrapolating the tails of an empirical distribution [20]. The EVT implementation in this paper is based on a multivariate analysis to accurately measure the VaR of the portfolio composed of the U.S., Russia, and China stock markets. We also estimate the VaR of the portfolio using HS for comparison.

2.1. GARCH Model

The pioneering work of Engle [21], where the Autoregressive Conditional Heteroscedasticity (ARCH) model (that relates the current level of volatility to p past squared error terms) was introduced, constitutes the main pillar of modern financial econometrics. However, the ARCH strategy has some limitations, including the typically required 5–8 lagged error terms to adequately model conditional variance. That was the reason for this model to be generalized by Bollerslev [22], giving rise to the generalized ARCH (GARCH) model, by adding lagged conditional variance, which acts as a smoothing term. In practical terms, the GARCH (p, q) model builds on the ARCH (p) by including q lags of the conditional variance. Therefore, a GARCH specification uses the weighted average of long-run variance, the predicted variance for the current period, and any new information in this period, as captured by the squared residuals, to forecast a future variance. More specifically, the general GARCH (p, q) model is as shown in Equation (1):

$$\sigma_t^2 = \gamma V_L + \sum_{i=1}^{p} \alpha_i u_{t-i}^2 + \sum_{j=1}^{q} \beta_j \sigma_{t-j}^2 \tag{1}$$

where σ_t^2 is the time $t-1$ conditional variance, V_L is the long run average variance, σ_{t-j}^2 are the lags of the conditional variance, and u_{t-i}^2 are the lagged squared error terms. $u_t = \sigma_t e_t$ with e_t i.i.d. $N(0, 1)$. Coefficients γ, α_i and β_j are the weights for V_L and the lags of the conditional variance and the squared error terms, respectively, and their estimates are obtained by Maximum Likelihood.

GARCH (1, 1) is the most used model of all GARCH models. It can be written as follows:

$$\sigma_t^2 = \gamma V_L + \alpha_1 u_{t-1}^2 + \beta_1 \sigma_{t-1}^2 \tag{2}$$

or, alternatively,

$$\sigma_t^2 = \omega + \alpha_1 u_{t-1}^2 + \beta_1 \sigma_{t-1}^2 \tag{3}$$

where $\omega = \gamma V_L$. Coefficients in the GARCH specification sum up to the unity and have to be restricted for the conditional variances to be uniformly positive. In the case of the GARCH (1, 1) such restrictions are: $\omega > 0$, $\alpha_1 \geq 0$ and $\beta_1 \geq 0$. In addition, the requirement for stationarity is $1 - \alpha_1 - \beta_1 > 0$. The unconditional variance can be shown to be $E(\sigma_t^2) = \omega / (1 - \alpha_1 - \beta_1)$.

2.2. EGARCH Model

The EGARCH model was proposed by Nelson [23] to capture the leverage effects observed in financial series and represents a major shift from the ARCH and GARCH models. The EGARCH specification does not model the variance directly, but its natural logarithm. This way, there is no need to impose sign restrictions on the model parameters to guarantee that the conditional variance is positive. In addition, EGARCH is an asymmetric model in the sense that the conditional variance depends not only on the magnitude of the lagged innovations but also on their sign. This is how the model accounts for the different response of volatility to the upwards and downwards movement of the series of the same magnitude. More specifically, EGARCH implements a function $g(e_t)$ of the innovations e_t, which are i.i.d. variables with zero mean, so that the innovation values are captured by the expression $|e_t| - E|e_t|$.

An EGARCH (p, q) is defined as:

$$\log \sigma_t^2 = \omega + \sum_{j=1}^{q} \beta_j \log \sigma_{t-j}^2 + \sum_{j=1}^{p} \theta_i g(e_{t-j}) \tag{4}$$

where $g(e_t) = \delta e_t + \alpha(|e_t| - E|e_t|)$ are variables i.i.d. with zero mean and constant variance. It is through this function that depends on both the sign and magnitude of e_t, that the EGARCH model captures the asymmetric response of the volatility to innovations of different sign, thus allowing the modeling of a stylized fact of the financial series: negative returns provoke a greater increase in volatility than positive returns do.

The innovation (standardized error divided by the conditional standard deviation) is normally used in this formulation. In such a case, $E|e| = \sqrt{2/\pi}$ and the sequence $g(e_t)$ is time independent with zero mean and constant variance, if finite. In the case of Gaussianity, the equation for the variance in the model EGARCH (1, 1) is:

$$\log \sigma_t^2 = \omega + \beta \log \sigma_{t-1}^2 + \delta e_{t-1} + \alpha \left(|e_{t-1}| - \sqrt{\frac{2}{\pi}} \right). \tag{5}$$

Stationarity requires $|\beta| < 1$, the persistence in volatility is indicated by β, and δ indicates the magnitude of the leverage effect. δ is expected to be negative, which implies that negative innovations have a greater effect on volatility than positive innovations of the same magnitude. As in the case of the standard GARCH specification, maximum likelihood is used for the estimation of the model.

2.3. EVT

EVT deals with the stochastic behavior of extreme events found in the tails of probability distributions, and, in practice, it has two approaches. The first one relies on deriving block maxima (minima) series as a preliminary step and is linked to the GEV distribution. The second, referred to as the peaks over threshold (POT) approach, relies on extracting, from a continuous record, the peak values reached for any period during which values exceed a certain threshold and is linked to the GP distribution [24]. The latter is the approach used in this paper.

The generalized Pareto distribution was developed as a distribution that can model tails of a wide variety of distributions. It is based on the POT method which consists in the modelling of the extreme values that exceed a particular threshold. Obviously, in such a framework there are some important decisions to take: (i) the threshold, μ; (ii) the cumulative function that best fits the exceedances over the threshold; and (iii) the survival function, that is, the complementary of the cumulative function.

The choice of the threshold implies a trade-off bias-variance. A low threshold means more observations, which probably diminishes the fitting variance but probably increases the fitting bias, because observations that do not belong to the tail could be included. On the other hand, a high threshold means a fewer number of observations and, maybe, an increment in the fitting variance and a decrement in the fitting bias.

As for the distribution function that best fits the exceedances over the threshold, let us suppose that $F(x)$ is the distribution function for a random variable X, and that threshold μ is a value of X in the right tail of the distribution; let y denote the value of the exceedance over the threshold μ. Therefore, the probability that X lies between μ and $\mu + y$ ($y > 0$) is $F(\mu + y) - F(\mu)$ and the probability for X greater than μ is $1 - F(\mu)$. Writing the exceedances (over a threshold μ) distribution function $F^\mu(y)$ as the probability that X lies between μ and $\mu + y$ conditional on $X > \mu$, and taking into account the identity linking the extreme and the exceedance: $X = Y + \mu$, it follows that:

$$F^\mu(y) = P(Y \leq y | X > \mu) = P(\mu < X \leq \mu + y | X > \mu) = \frac{F(x) - F(\mu)}{1 - F(\mu)} \tag{6}$$

and that

$$1 - F^\mu(y) = 1 - \frac{F(x) - F(\mu)}{1 - F(\mu)} = \frac{1 - F(x)}{1 - F(\mu)} \tag{7}$$

In the case that the parent distribution F is known, the distribution of threshold exceedances also would be known. However, this is not the practical situation, and approximations that are broadly applicable for high values of the threshold are sough. Here is where Pickands–Balkema–de Haan theorem ([25,26]) comes into play. Once the threshold has been estimated, the conditional distribution $F^\mu(y)$ converges to the GP distribution. It is known that $F^\mu(y) \to G_{\xi,\sigma}(y)$ as $\mu \to \infty$, with

$$G_{\xi,\sigma}(y) = \begin{cases} 1 - \left(1 + \xi\frac{y}{\sigma}\right)^{-\frac{1}{\xi}} & \text{if } \xi \neq 0 \\ 1 - e^{-\frac{y}{\sigma}} & \text{if } \xi = 0 \end{cases} \tag{8}$$

where $\sigma > 0$ and $y \geq 0$ if $\xi \geq 0$ and $0 \leq y \leq -\sigma/\xi$ if $\xi < 0$. ξ is a shape parameter that determines the heaviness of the tail of the distribution, and σ is a scale parameter. When $\xi = 0$, $G_{\xi,\sigma}(y)$ reduces to the exponential distribution with expectation $\exp(\sigma)$; in the case that $\xi < 0$, it becomes a Uniform $(0,\sigma)$; finally, $\xi > 0$ leads to the Pareto distribution of the second kind [27]. In general, ξ has a positive value between 0.1 and 0.4. The GP distribution parameters are estimated via maximum likelihood.

Once the maximum likelihood estimates are available, a specific GP distribution function is selected, and an analytical expression for *VaR* with a confidence level q can be defined as a function of the GP distribution parameters:

$$VaR_{\hat{q}} = \mu + \frac{\hat{\sigma}(\mu)}{\hat{\xi}}\left(\frac{N}{N_\mu}(1-q)^{-\hat{\xi}} - 1\right) \tag{9}$$

where N is the number of observations in the left tail and N_μ is the number of excesses beyond the threshold μ.

$$VaR_{\hat{q}} = \mu + \frac{\hat{\sigma}(\mu)}{\hat{\xi}}\left(\frac{N}{N_\mu}(1-q)^{-\hat{\xi}} - 1\right) \tag{10}$$

3. Results

3.1. Descriptive Statistics

Data for 3 years were extracted from the Bloomberg platform for the three selected stock market indices and were manipulated to derive the return from the closing prices corresponding to each index. For the in-sample period, 458 daily observations were studied compared to 315 for the out-of-sample forecast period. It is important to note that in November 2017, the name of the MICEX index (composed of Russian stocks of the top 50 largest issues in the Moscow Exchange) was officially changed to the MOEX Russia Index, representing the "Russian stock market benchmark" [28]. Table 2 lists the descriptive statistics of S&P 500, SSEC, and MICEX for the in- and out-of-sample periods. Surprisingly, S&P 500 and the MICEX behaved similarly in terms of return during the in-sample and out-of-sample periods.

Table 2. Descriptive Statistics of S&P 500, SSEC, and MICEX: 5 January 2015–30 December 2016 and 3 January 2017–31 May 2018.

Stock Markets	S&P 500 (In-Sample)	SSEC (In-Sample)	MICEX (In-Sample)	S&P 500 (Out-of-Sample)	SSEC (Out-of-Sample)	MICEX (Out-of-Sample)
Mean	0.022%	−0.017%	0.017%	0.060%	−0.001%	0.054%
Standard Deviation	1.0%	2.10%	1.2%	0.711%	0.774%	1.025%
Skewness	1.0%	2.10%	1.2%	0.711%	0.774%	1.025%
Kurtosis	3.33	4.62	0.97	7.93	4.83	12.45
Median	0.01%	0.10%	0.04%	0.06%	0.08%	−0.05%
Minimum	−4.0%	−10.8%	−4.4%	−4.18%	−4.14%	−8.03%
Maximum	4.7%	6.0%	4.4%	2.76%	2.15%	3.89%
1st Quartile	−0.41%	−0.66%	−0.65%	−0.18%	−0.35%	−0.51%
3rd Quartile	0.49%	0.87%	0.85%	0.34%	0.40%	0.54%

In reference to the two chosen time periods, the skewness of the returns of the three indices is close to 0 and the returns display excess in kurtosis. This implies that the distributions of returns are not normal as confirmed by Jarque-Bera normality tests (Table 3). The distributions of returns are stationary according to the augmented Dicky–Fuller (ADF) test applied to the three indices (Table 4).

Table 3. Jarque-Bera Normality Test of S&P 500, SSEC, and MICEX.

Stock Markets	In-Sample		Out-of-Sample	
	Score	p-Value	Score	p-Value
S&P 500	198.66	0.000	865.78	0.000
SSEC	483.75	0.000	352.63	0.000
MICEX	18.12	0.000	2027.03	0.000

Note: p-value refers to Jarque–Bera normality test, Ho: the index return is normally distributed.

Table 4. ADF Stationarity Test.

	Critical Values at 5%	STAT	p-Value	STAT	p-Value	STAT	p-Value
		S&P 500		SSEC		MICEX	
No Constant	−1.9	−28.4	0.001	−12.8	0.001	−26.9	0.001
Constant Only	−2.9	−28.4	0.001	−12.8	0.001	−11.6	0.001
Constant and Trend	−1.6	−28.4	0.000	−12.7	0.000	−11.6	0.000
Constant, Trend, and Trend^2	−1.6	−28.4	0.000	−12.7	0.000	−11.6	0.000

Note: ADF p-value refers to the augmented Dickey–Fuller unit root test, Ho: the index return has a unit root.

3.2. GARCH (1, 1) and EGARCH (1, 1) Results

GARCH (1, 1) and EGARCH (1, 1) parameters were estimated using the daily returns of each index. Results from the normal distribution, the student's t-distribution and the Generalized Error Distribution (GED) were derived. The goodness of fit test and residual analysis were then performed to ensure that the assumptions of the applied models were all met. The model parameters were estimated by maximum likelihood. Table 5 presents a summary of such estimates for GARCH (1, 1) and EGARCH (1,1).

Table 5. Estimates of the Parameters of GARCH (1,1) and EGARCH (1,1) (with GED).

	S&P 500	SSEC	MICEX
	GARCH (1, 1)		
Long-run mean (μ)	0.000249	−0.00009	0.00080
Omega (ω)	8.5218×10^{-6}	1.1035×10^{-6}	2.9655×10^{-6}
ARCH component (α)	0.1972	0.0569	0.0653
GARCH component (β)	0.7105	0.9331	0.9065
	EGARCH (1, 1)		
Long-run mean (μ)	0.00030	−0.00009	0.00142
Omega (ω)	−0.72879	−0.08598	−0.87318
ARCH component (α)	0.04766	0.20530	0.30477
Leverage coefficient (δ)	−0.29149	−0.01362	0.05345
GARCH component (β)	0.92471	0.98689	0.90237

Note: The GED was selected after checking the average, standard deviation, skewness, kurtosis, the noise, and ARCH tests corresponding to the three distributions.

3.3. Best Volatility Model Selection for the In- and Out-of-Sample Periods

The root mean square error (RMSE), the mean absolute error (MAE), and the mean absolute percentage error (MAPE) are implemented to choose the best volatility model. For S&P 500, we compared the estimated volatility to the implied volatility. However, this was not possible for SSEC and MICEX due the absence of data. Results depicted in Table 6 reveal the superiority of GARCH (1, 1) in estimating the volatility of the three countries in the in-sample period, which coincides with the peak period of the Syrian war. As for the out-of-sample period, while GARCH (1, 1) ranks first for S&P 500, EGARCH (1, 1) ranks first for the SSEC and MICEX with a difference in RMSE of around 0.002 and 0.01 units respectively as compared to GARCH (1, 1). Volatilities estimated with the superior volatility models in comparison to the realized volatilities for the out-of-sample period are depicted in Figure 2.

Table 6. In-Sample Period Error Statistics.

	RMSE	Rating	MAE	Rating	MAPE	Rating
S&P 500 during In-Sample Period (from 5 January 2015 till 30 December 2016)						
Implied Vol.	0.047694	2	0.039028	2	0.00377	3
GARCH (1, 1)	0.040995	1	0.028954	1	0.002376	1
EGARCH (1, 1)	0.049947	3	0.039066	3	0.003261	2
SSEC during In-Sample Period (from 5 January 2015 till 30 December 2016)						
GARCH (1, 1)	0.09567	1	0.080424	1	0.002879	1
EGARCH (1, 1)	0.11588	2	0.090075	2	0.003134	2
MICEX during In-Sample Period (from 5 January 2015 till 30 December 2016)						
GARCH (1, 1)	0.184631	1	0.173261	1	0.004775	1
EGARCH (1, 1)	0.188566	2	0.179723	2	0.004997	2
S&P 500 during Out-of-Sample (from 3 January 2017 till 31 May 2018)						
Implied Vol.	0.04809	3	0.04325	3	0.006092	3
GARCH (1, 1)	0.040024	1	0.035135	1	0.004896	1
EGARCH (1, 1)	0.047078	2	0.041034	2	0.005689	2
SSEC during Out-of-Sample (from 3 January 2017 till 31 May 2018)						
GARCH (1, 1)	0.08478	2	0.080437	2	0.004033	2
EGARCH (1, 1)	0.07113	1	0.063535	1	0.00322	1
MICEX during Out-of-Sample (from 3 January 2017 till 31 May 2018)						
GARCH (1, 1)	0.071894	2	0.064616	2	0.002909	2
EGARCH (1, 1)	0.069381	1	0.061135	1	0.00271	1

Note: $RME = \sqrt{\sum_{t=1}^{n} (f - Y)^2 / n}$; $MAE = \sum_{t=1}^{n} |f - Y| / n$; $MAPE = 100 \sum_{t=1}^{n} \left|\frac{f-Y}{Y}\right| / n$, where n is the number of periods, Y is the true value and f is the prediction value. The best model is the one that has a minimum value of $RMSE$, MAE and $MAPE$.

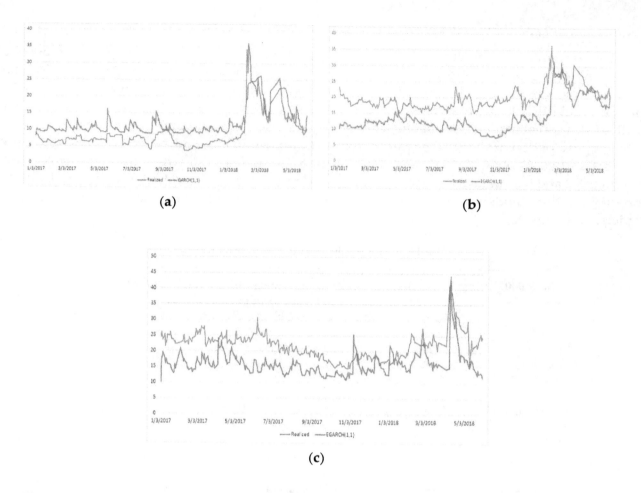

(a)   **(b)**

(c)

Figure 2. Realized Volatility vs. Volatilities Estimated with the Superior Volatility Models–Out-of-Sample Period: **(a)** for S&P 500. **(b)** for SSEC. **(c)** for MICEX.

3.4. VaR Output

Based on the superior model corresponding to each index, a portfolio of volatility updates was established for each sample period. First, the historical simulation approach was implemented. It involved incorporating volatility in updating the historical return. Because the volatility of a market variable may vary over time, we modified the historical data to reflect the variation in volatility. This approach uses the variation in volatility in a spontaneous way to estimate VaR by including more recent information. Second, a Monte Carlo simulation method including student t-copula and EVT was applied to the created portfolio composed of the three markets to estimate VaR with different confidence levels. The filtered residuals of each return series were extracted using EGARCH. The Gaussian kernel estimate was used for the interior marginal cumulative distribution function (CDF) and the generalized Pareto distribution (GP) was applied to estimate the upper and lower tails. The student t-copula was also applied to the portfolio's data in order to reveal the correlation among the residuals of each index. This process led to the estimation of the portfolio's VaR over a horizon of one month and confidence levels of 90%, 95%, and 99%. Table 7 summarizes all the VaR estimates calculated for the in-sample and out-of-sample periods using HS and EVT compared to the Real VaR. The visual illustrations of the relevant outcomes related to the logarithmic returns of the selected stock indices, the auto-correlation function (ACF) of returns and of the squared returns, the filtered residuals and the filtered conditional standard deviation, the ACF of standardized residuals, and the upper tail of standardized residuals for both periods, are presented in Appendix A (Figures A1 and A2).

Table 7. VaR Summary Results.

Outcome	HS (Volatility Weighted)	EVT	Real VaR
In-Sample			
90% VaR	0.68%	2.93%	1.31%
95% VaR	1.03%	4.83%	1.68%
99% VaR	2.31%	8.39%	2.38%
Out-of-Sample			
90% VaR	0.48%	3.76%	0.73%
95% VaR	0.71%	5.47%	0.94%
99% VaR	1.65%	9.60%	1.33%

It is apparent that VaR with a confidence level of 99%, using HS and EVT, overrates the risk for the three countries during both periods. Furthermore, the HS VaR results are closer to the Real VaR results compared to those of the EVT VaR. This is not altogether surprising since the EVT method is concerned with studying the behavior of extremes within these markets rather than simply fitting the curve. Therefore, the above output represents a benchmark that can be extrapolated beyond the data during stress periods.

4. Discussion

This paper revealed original common points among the most powerful military countries in the world regarding the behavior of their financial markets during the period 2015–2018, which corresponds to their intervention in the Syrian war. First, the returns of S&P 500 and MICEX were quite similar during the in-sample and out-of-sample periods. Second, the GARCH (1, 1) was found to be the best volatility model for the in-sample period for S&P 500, MICEX, and SSEC, outperforming EGARCH (1, 1). The incorporation of the GARCH (1, 1) specification to the HS produced an accurate VaR for a period of one month, at the three confidence levels, compared to the real VaR.

EVT VaR results are consistent with those found by Furio and Climent [15] and Wang et al. [9], who highlighted the accuracy of studying the tails of loss severity distribution of several stock markets. Furthermore, part of our results corroborates the work of Peng et al. [29], who showed that EVT GP distribution is superior to certain GARCH models implemented on the Shanghai Stock Exchange Index.

The GP distribution highlighted the behavior of "extremes" for the U.S., Russian, and Chinese financial markets, which is of great importance since it emphasizes the risks and opportunities inherent to the dynamics of their markets and also underlines the uncertainty corresponding to their worldwide exposure.

Expected EVT VaR values of 3.76%, 5.47%, and 9.60%, at 90%, 95%, and 99% confidence levels, respectively (for the out-of-sample period), might appear overstated. However, uncertainty layers are all the way inherent and our results are, naturally, subject to standard error. For comparison purposes, and in order to make a relevant interpretation of the tail distribution of returns corresponding to these markets, we opted to derive the EVT VaR of a portfolio of stock indices pertaining to non-military countries, namely Finland, Sweden, and Ecuador, for the same out-of-sample period of study (January 2017 to May 2018). These countries were chosen randomly based on the similarities in income groups when compared to the selected military countries. While Finland and Sweden are both classified as high income like the U.S., Ecuador is classified as upper middle income like Russia and China [30]. Also, the selection of these non-military countries follows the same structure of the capital market development found at the military countries which, when combined, find their average ratio of stock market capitalization to GDP is 77.23%, compared to 76.46% for Finland, Sweden, and Ecuador [30,31]. Finally, when comparing the ratio of private credit ratio to the stock market capitalization ratio corresponding to each country, we notice that the former is higher than the latter for Ecuador, Sweden, Finland, Russia, and China [32]. Only the U.S. depends mostly on its stock market to finance its economy. The portfolio is composed of the OMX Helsinki index, the ECU Ecuador General index, and the OMX 30 Sweden index. The GP distribution was used to estimate the upper and lower tails. Remarkably, EVT VaR results were 2.23%, 3.49%, and 6.45% at the 90%, 95%, and 99% confidence levels, respectively, well below the estimates found for the U.S., Russian, and Chinese stock markets. Consequently, it can be concluded that the intervention in the Syrian war may have been one of the latent and relevant factors that affected the volatility of the stock markets of the selected military countries. This conclusion is reinforced by the fact that the EVT VaR was higher by 40%, 26%, and 32%, at the 90%, 95%, and 99% confidence levels, respectively, compared to the VaR of the portfolio constituted of the selected non-military countries. However, it can neither be deduced nor confirmed that the intervention in the Syrian war is the sole source, and more specifically, the trigger of the significant increase in the volatility of the American, Russian, and Chinese stock markets. Answering this question requires further lines of future research that involves incorporating a number of control covariates and using a different modeling methodology.

Although we covered a significant number of observations, our results are subject to errors; it is never possible to have enough data when implementing the extreme value analysis, since the tail distribution inference remains less certain. Introducing hypothetical losses to our historical data to generate stress scenarios is of no interest to this study and falls outside its main objective. It would be interesting to repeat the same study with the same selected three military countries during the period 2018–2020, which is expected to be the last phase of the Syrian war given that the Syrian army reached back to the border frontier with Turkey and that the Syrian Constitutional Committee Delegates launched meetings in Geneva to hold talks on the amendment of Syria's constitution.

Author Contributions: Conceptualization, V.N.; methodology, V.N., N.M., and J.-M.M.; formal analysis, J.-M.M.; resources, N.M.; writing—original draft preparation, V.N., N.M., and J.-M.M.; writing—review and editing, V.N., J.-M.M., and R.E.K.; visualization, R.E.K.; supervision, V.N.; project administration, J.-M.M. and V.N.; funding acquisition, J.-M.M. All authors have read and agreed to the published version of the manuscript.

Appendix A

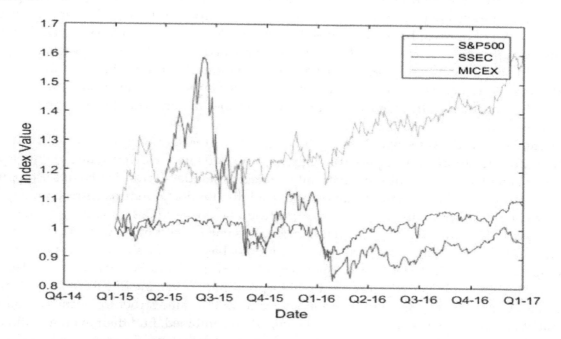

Relative Daily Index Closings of the In-Sample Portfolio

Figure A1. *Cont.*

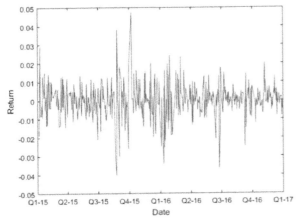

Daily Logarithmic Returns of S&P 500

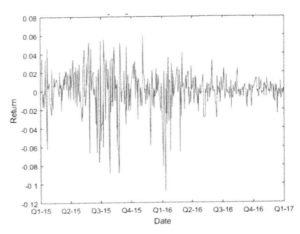

Daily Logarithmic Returns of SSEC

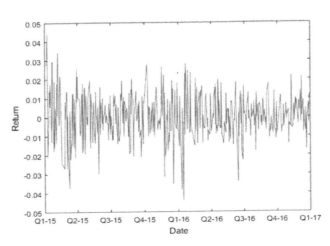

Daily Logarithmic Returns of MICEX

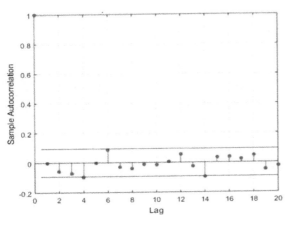

ACF of Returns of S&P 500

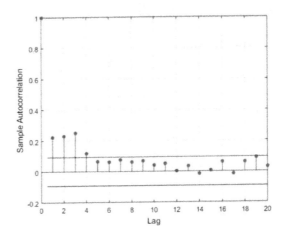

ACF of Squared Returns of S&P 500

Figure A1. *Cont.*

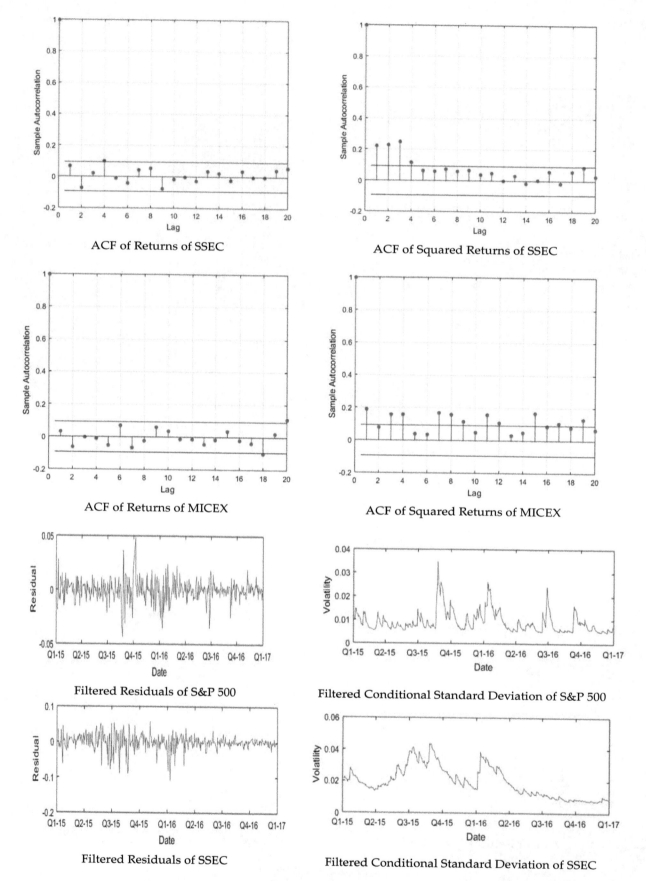

Figure A1. *Cont.*

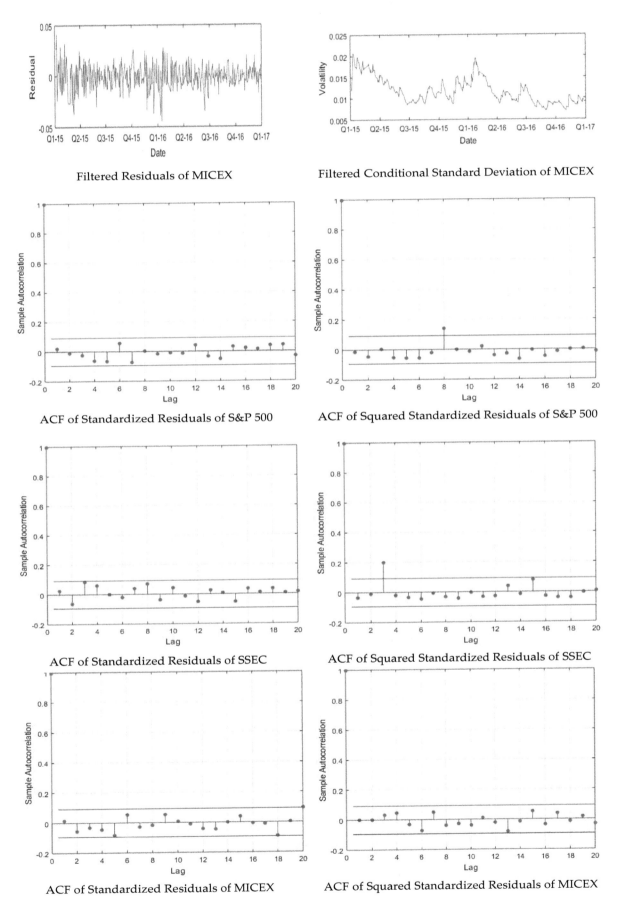

Figure A1. *Cont.*

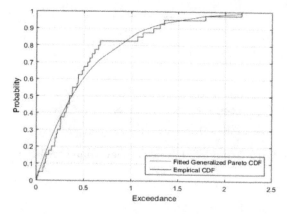

S&P 500 Upper Tail of Standardized Residuals   SSEC Upper Tail of Standardized Residuals

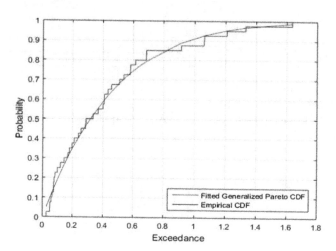

MICEX Upper Tail of Standardized Residuals

Figure A1. In-Sample VaR Figures.

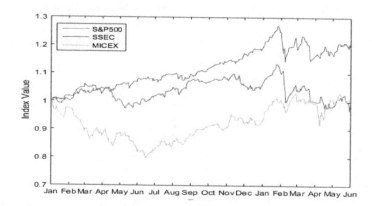

Relative Daily Index Closings of the Out-of-Sample Portfolio

Figure A2. *Cont.*

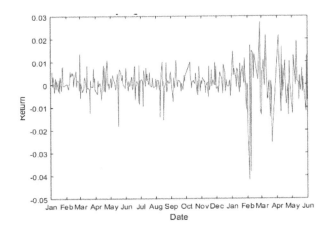

Daily Logarithmic Returns of S&P 500

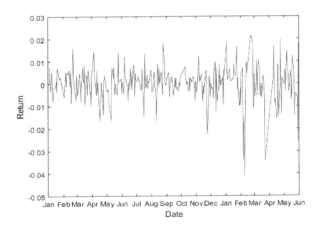

Daily Logarithmic Returns of SSEC

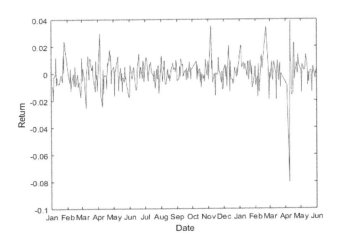

Daily Logarithmic Returns of MICEX

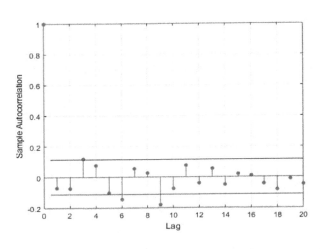

ACF of Returns of S&P 500

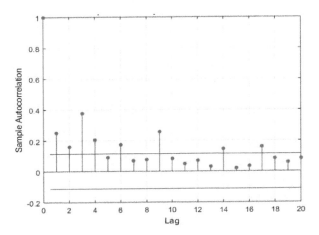

ACF of Squared Returns of S&P 500

Figure A2. *Cont.*

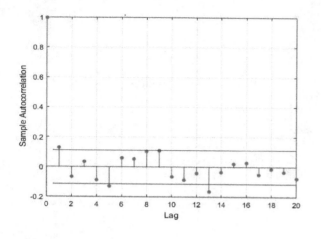

ACF of Returns of SSEC

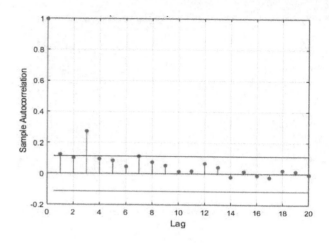

ACF of Squared Returns of SSE

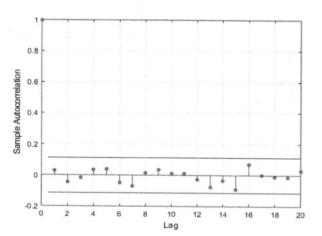

ACF of Returns of MICEX

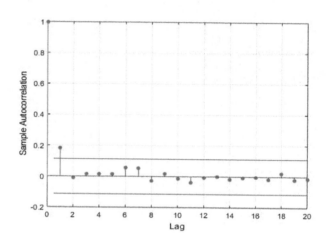

ACF of Squared Returns of MICEX

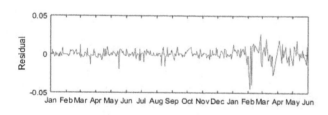

Filtered Residuals of S&P 500

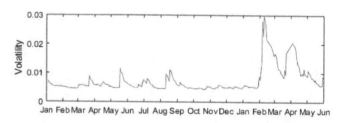

Filtered Conditional Standard Deviation of S&P 500

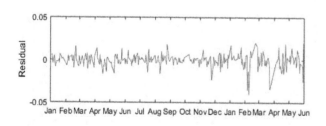

Filtered Residuals of SSEC

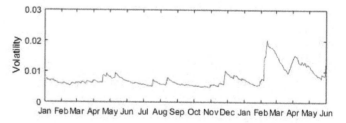

Filtered Conditional Standard Deviation of SSEC

Figure A2. *Cont.*

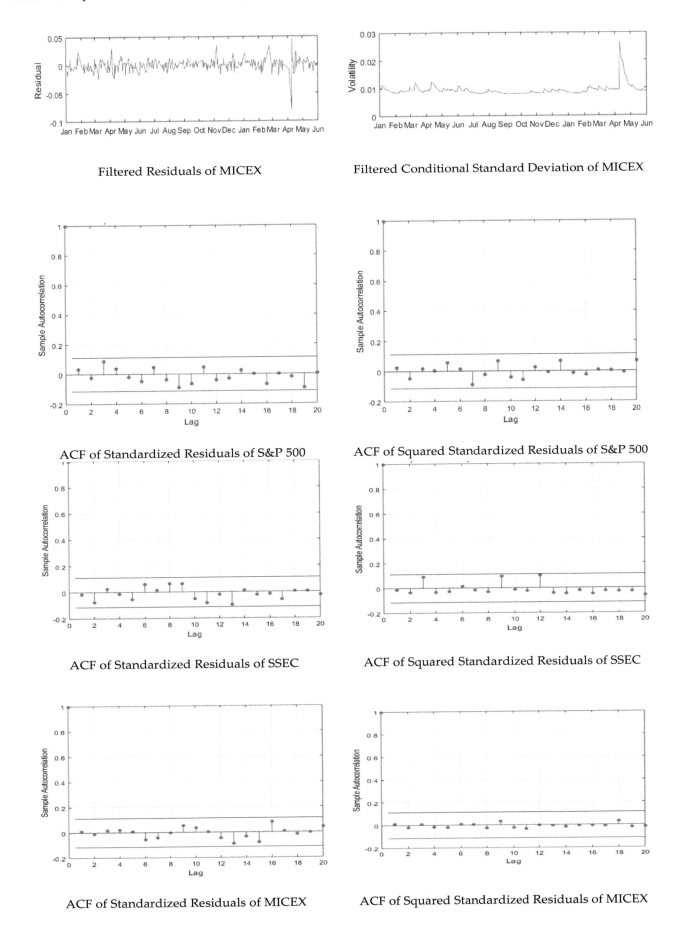

Filtered Residuals of MICEX

Filtered Conditional Standard Deviation of MICEX

ACF of Standardized Residuals of S&P 500

ACF of Squared Standardized Residuals of S&P 500

ACF of Standardized Residuals of SSEC

ACF of Squared Standardized Residuals of SSEC

ACF of Standardized Residuals of MICEX

ACF of Squared Standardized Residuals of MICEX

Figure A2. *Cont.*

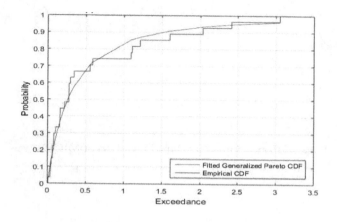

S&P 500 Upper Tail of Standardized Residuals

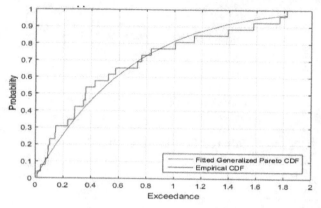

SSEC Upper Tail of Standardized Residuals

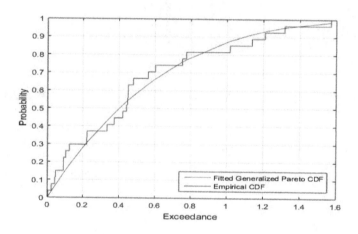

MICEX Upper Tail of Standardized Residuals

Figure A2. Out-of-Sample VaR Figures.

References

1.   Humud, C.E.; Blanchar, C.M.; Nikitin, M.B.D. *Armed Conflict in Syria: Overview and U.S. Response*; CRS: Washington, DC, USA, 2017.

2.   Swaine, M. *Chinese Views of the Syrian Conflict*; Carnegie Endowment for International Peace: Washington, DC, USA, 2012.

3.   O'Conor, T. China May Be the Biggest Winner of All If Assad Takes over Syria. *Newsweek*, 19 January 2018.

4.   SIPRI. *Trends in Military Expenditures, 2018*; SIPRI: Solna, Sweden; Stockholm, Sweden, 2019.

5.   SIPRI. *Trends in International Arms Transfers, 2018*; SIPRI: Solna, Sweden; Stockholm, Sweden, 2019.

6.   Wei, W. Forecasting Stock Market Volatility with Non-Linear GARCH Models: A Case for China. *Appl. Econ. Lett.* **2002**, *9*, 163–166. [CrossRef]

7.   Lin, X.; Fei, F. Long Memory Revisit in Chinese Stock Markets: Based on GARCH-Class Models and Multiscale Analysis. *Econ. Model.* **2013**, *31*, 265–275. [CrossRef]

8.   Lin, Z. Modelling and Forecasting the Stock Market Volatility of SSE Composite Index Using GARCH Models. *Future Gener. Comput. Syst.* **2018**, *79*, 960–972. [CrossRef]

9.   Wang, Z.; Wu, W.; Chen, C.; Zhou, Y. The Exchange Rate Risk of Chinese Yuan: Using VaR and ES Based on Extreme Value Theory. *J. Appl. Stat.* **2010**, *37*, 265–282. [CrossRef]

10.   Chen, Q.; Giles, D.E.; Feng, H. The Extreme-Value Dependence between the Chinese and Other International Stock Markets. *Appl. Financ. Econ.* **2012**, *22*, 1147–1160. [CrossRef]

11.   Wei, Y.; Chen, W.; Lin, Y. Measuring Daily Value-at-Risk of SSEC Index: A New Approach Based on Multifractal Analysis and Extreme Value Theory. *Phys. A Stat. Mech. Appl.* **2013**, *392*, 2163–2174. [CrossRef]

12. Hussain, S.I.; Li, S. Modeling the Distribution of Extreme Returns in the Chinese Stock Market. *J. Int. Financ. Mark. Inst. Money* **2015**, *34*, 263–276. [CrossRef]
13. Hou, Y.; Li, S. Information Transmission between U.S. and China Index Futures Markets: An Asymmetric DCC GARCH Approach. *Econ. Model.* **2016**, *52*, 884–897. [CrossRef]
14. Awartani, B.M.A.; Corradi, V. Predicting the Volatility of the S&P-500 Stock Index via GARCH Models: The Role of Asymmetries. *Int. J. Forecast.* **2005**, *21*, 167–183. [CrossRef]
15. Furió, D.; Climent, F.J. Extreme Value Theory versus Traditional GARCH Approaches Applied to Financial Data: A Comparative Evaluation. *Quant. Financ.* **2013**, *13*, 45–63. [CrossRef]
16. Trinidad Segovia, J.E.; Fernández-Martínez, M.; Sánchez-Granero, M.A. A Novel Approach to Detect Volatility Clusters in Financial Time Series. *Phys. A Stat. Mech. Appl.* **2019**, *535*, 122452. [CrossRef]
17. Ramos-requena, J.P.; Trinidad-segovia, J.E.; Sánchez-granero, M.Á. An Alternative Approach to Measure Co-Movement between Two Time Series. *Mathematics* **2020**, *8*, 261. [CrossRef]
18. Naimy, V.Y.; Hayek, M.R. Modelling and Predicting the Bitcoin Volatility Using GARCH Models. *Int. J. Math. Model. Numer. Optim.* **2018**, *8*, 197–215. [CrossRef]
19. Embrechts, P.; Resnick, S.I.; Samorodnitsky, G. Extreme Value Theory as a Risk Management Tool. *N. Am. Actuar. J.* **1999**, *3*, 30–41. [CrossRef]
20. Jorion, P. *Value at Risk: The New Benchmark for Managing Financial Risk*, 3rd ed.; McGraw-Hill: New York, NY, USA, 2007. [CrossRef]
21. Engle, R.F. Autoregressive Conditional Heteroscedasticity with Estimates of the Variance of United Kingdom Inflation. *Econometrica* **1982**, *50*, 987–1007. [CrossRef]
22. Bollerslev, T. Generalized Autoregressive Conditional Heteroskedasticity. *J. Econom.* **1986**, *31*, 307–327. [CrossRef]
23. Nelson, D. Conditional Heteroskedasticity in Asset Returns: A New Approach. *Econometrica* **1991**, *59*, 347–370. [CrossRef]
24. McNeil, A. Extreme Value Theory for Risk Managers. In *Internal Modelling and CAD II*; Risk Waters Books: London, UK, 1999; pp. 93–113.
25. Pickands, J. Statistical Inference Using Extreme Order Statistics. *Ann. Stat.* **1975**, *3*, 119–131.
26. Balkema, A.A.; de Haan, L. Residual Life Time at Great Age. *Ann. Probab.* **1974**, *2*, 792–804. [CrossRef]
27. Lee, W. *Applying Generalized Pareto Distribution to the Risk Management of Commerce Fire Insurance*; Working Paper; Tamkang University: New Taipei, Taiwan, 2009.
28. Russian Benchmark Officially Renamed the MOEX Russia Index. Available online: https://www.moex.com/n17810 (accessed on 3 April 2020).
29. Peng, Z.X.; Li, S.; Pang, H. *Comparison of Extreme Value Theory and GARCH Models on Estimating and Predicting of Value-at-Risk*; Working Paper; Wang Yanan Institute for Studies in Economics, Xiamen University: Xiamen, China, 2006.
30. Beck, T.; Demirguc-Kunt, A.; Levine, R.E.; Cihak, M.; Feyen, E. *Financial Development and Structure Dataset*. (updated September 2014). Available online: https://www.worldbank.org/en/publication/gfdr/data/financial-structure-database (accessed on 2 April 2020).
31. Market Capitalziation: % of GDP. Available online: https://www.ceicdata.com/en/indicator/market-capitalization-nominal-gdp (accessed on 2 April 2020).
32. Beck, T.; Demirguc-Kunt, A.; Levine, R.E.; Cihak, M.; Feyen, E. *Financial Development and Structure Dataset*. (updated September 2019). Available online: https://www.worldbank.org/en/publication/gfdr/data/financial-structure-database (accessed on 2 April 2020).

Dispersion Trading Based on the Explanatory Power of S&P 500 Stock Returns

Lucas Schneider * and Johannes Stübinger

Department of Statistics and Econometrics, University of Erlangen-Nürnberg, Lange Gasse 20,
90403 Nürnberg, Germany; johannes.stuebinger@fau.de
* Correspondence: lucas.schneider@fau.de

Abstract: This paper develops a dispersion trading strategy based on a statistical index subsetting procedure and applies it to the S&P 500 constituents from January 2000 to December 2017. In particular, our selection process determines appropriate subset weights by exploiting a principal component analysis to specify the individual index explanatory power of each stock. In the following out-of-sample trading period, we trade the most suitable stocks using a hedged and unhedged approach. Within the large-scale back-testing study, the trading frameworks achieve statistically and economically significant returns of 14.52 and 26.51 percent p.a. after transaction costs, as well as a Sharpe ratio of 0.40 and 0.34, respectively. Furthermore, the trading performance is robust across varying market conditions. By benchmarking our strategies against a naive subsetting scheme and a buy-and-hold approach, we find that our statistical trading systems possess superior risk-return characteristics. Finally, a deep dive analysis shows synchronous developments between the chosen number of principal components and the S&P 500 index.

Keywords: dispersion trading; option arbitrage; volatility trading; correlation risk premium; econometrics; computational finance

---

1. Introduction

Relative value trading strategies, often referred to as statistical arbitrage, were developed by Morgan Stanley's quantitative group in the mid-1980s and describe a market neutral trading approach [1]. Those strategies attempt to generate profits from the mean reversion of two closely related securities that diverge temporarily. Pairs trading, which in its plain form tries to exploit mispricing between two co-moving assets, is probably the most popular delta-one trading approach amongst relative value strategies. Several studies show that those procedures generate significant and robust returns (see [2–6]).

In the non-linear space, relative value strategies are also prominent. Dispersion approaches are one of the most common trading algorithms and attempt to profit from implied volatility spreads of related assets and changes in correlations. Since index options usually incorporate higher implied volatility and correlation than an index replicating basket of single stock options, returns are generated by selling index options and buying the basket. Ultimately, the trader goes long volatility and short correlation [7]. As shown by [8,9], volatility based strategies generate meaningful and reliable returns. Dispersion trades are normally conducted by sophisticated investors such as hedge funds [10]. In 2011, the Financial Times speculated that Och-Ziff Capital Management (renamed to Sculptor Capital Management, Inc. New York, NY, USA in 2019 with headquarter in New York City, United States), an alternative asset manager with $34.5bn total assets under management [11], set up a dispersion trade worth around $8.8bn on the S&P 100 index [12]. In academia, References [13–15] examined the profitability of dispersion trades and delivered evidence of substantial returns across markets.

However, Reference [16] reported that returns declined after the year 2000 due to structural changes in options markets. References [14–16] enhanced their returns by trading dispersion based on an index subset. All of those studies try to replicate the index with as few securities as possible, but neglect the individual explanatory power of stocks in their weighting schemes. This provides a clear opportunity for further improvements of the subsetting procedure.

This manuscript contributes to the existing literature in several aspects. First, we introduce a novel statistical approach to select an appropriate index subset by determining weights based on the individual index explanatory power of each stock. Second, we provide a large-scale empirical study on a highly liquid market that covers the period from January 2000 to December 2017 and therefore includes major financial events such as 9/11 and the global financial crisis. Third, we benchmark our statistical trading approaches against baseline dispersion trading algorithms and a buy-and-hold strategy. Fourth, we conduct a deep dive analysis, including robustness, risk factor, and sub-period analysis, that reports economically and statistically significant annual returns of 14.51 percent after transaction costs. Our robustness analysis suggests that our approach produces reliable results independent of transaction costs, reinvestment rate, and portfolio size. Fifth, we evaluate in depth our innovative selection process and report the number of required principal components and selected sector exposures over the study period. We find a synchronous relationship between the number of principal components that are necessary to describe 90 percent of the stock variance and the S&P 500 index performance, i.e., if the market performs well, more components are required. Finally, we formulate policy recommendations for regulators and investors that could utilize our approach for risk management purposes and cost-efficient dispersion trade executions.

The remainder of this paper is structured as follows. Section 2 provides the underlying theoretical framework. In Section 3, we describe the empirical back-testing framework followed by a comprehensive result analysis in Section 4. Finally, Section 5 concludes our work, provides practical policy recommendations, and gives an outlook of future research areas.

2. Theoretical Framework

This section provides an overview of the theoretical framework of our trading strategy. Section 2.1 describes the underlying methodology and the drivers of dispersion trades. Different dispersion trading structures and enhancement methods are elaborated in Section 2.2.

2.1. Dispersion Foundation and Trading Rational

The continuous process of stock price S is defined as [17]:

$$\frac{dS_t}{S_t} = \mu(t)dt + \sigma(t)dZ_t, \tag{1}$$

where the dt term represents the drift and the second term denotes the diffusion component. In one of its simplest forms, continuous processes follow a constant drift μ and incorporate a constant volatility σ. In various financial models, for example in the well-known Black–Scholes model (see [18]), it is assumed that the underlying asset follows a geometric Brownian motion (GBM):

$$dS_t = \mu S_t dt + \sigma S_t dW_t. \tag{2}$$

Following [19,20], we define return dispersion for an equity index at time t as:

$$RD_t = \sqrt{\sum_{i=1}^{N} w_i \left(R_{i,t} - R_{I,t}\right)^2} = \sqrt{\sum_{i=1}^{N} w_i R_{i,t}^2 - R_{I,t}^2}, \tag{3}$$

where N represents the number of index members, w_i the index weight, and $R_{i,t}$ the return of stock i at time t. Moreover, $R_{I,t}$ denotes the index return with $R_{I,t} = \sum_{i=1}^{N} w_i R_{i,t}$. Return dispersion statistically describes the spread of returns in an index. References [21–23] showed in their seminal works that the realized variance (RV) is an accurate estimator of the actual variance (σ^2) as RV converges against the quadratic variation. Therefore, RV and σ^2 are used interchangeably in the following. Applying the definition of realized variance of the last J returns $RV_{i,t} = \sum_{k=1}^{J} R_{i,t-k}^2$, Equation (3) can be rewritten as:

$$RD_t^2 = \sum_{i=1}^{N} w_i RV_{i,t} - RV_{I,t}. \tag{4}$$

Expanding Equation (4) by the index variance of perfectly correlated index constituents yields:

$$RD_t^2 = \left(\sum_{i=1}^{N} w_i RV_{i,t} - \left(\sum_{i=1}^{N} w_i \sqrt{RV_{i,t}} \right)^2 \right) + \left(\left(\sum_{i=1}^{N} w_i \sqrt{RV_{i,t}} \right)^2 - RV_{I,t} \right). \tag{5}$$

The first term represents the variance dispersion of the single index constituents. This component is independent of the individual correlations. However, the second expression depends on realized correlations and describes the spread between the index variance under perfectly positively correlated index members and the realized correlations. Therefore, dispersion trades are exposed to volatility and correlation. This is reasonable as the variance of the index is eventually a function of the realized correlations between index members and their variances. Reference [24] already quantified this relationship in 1952:

$$\sigma_I^2 = \sum_{i=1}^{N} w_i^2 \sigma_i^2 + \sum_{i=1}^{N} \sum_{j \neq i}^{N} w_i w_j \sigma_i \sigma_j \rho_{i,j}, \tag{6}$$

where σ_i (σ_j) represents the volatility of stock i (j) and $\rho_{i,j}$ denotes the correlation coefficient between shares i and j.

Figure 1 illustrates the dispersion drivers graphically. Dispersion consists of volatility and correlation dispersion, i.e., the deviation of the realized correlation from perfectly positively correlated index members. The missing diversification benefits of the index compared to uncorrelated constituents decrease the profit of a dispersion trade, highlighting the short correlation characteristic of a long dispersion trade. Hence, a long dispersion trade profits from an increase in individual stock volatility and a decrease in index volatility, which itself implies a decline in correlation. Shorting dispersion leads to a gain when index volatility rises while the constituent's volatility remains unchanged or falls. In practice, multiple ways exist to structure dispersion trades that possess distinct merits. In our empirical study in Section 3, we develop a cost-efficient way to trade dispersion. Within the scope of this work, we focus on two trading approaches, namely at-the-money (ATM) straddles with and without delta hedging. Both strategies rely on options to trade volatility. When expressing a view on dispersion using non-linear products, one has to consider the implied volatility (IV), which essentially reflects the costs of an option. Profits from owning plain vanilla options are generally achieved when the realized volatility exceeds the implied one due to the payoff convexity. The contrary applies to short positions since these exhibit a concave payoff structure. Thus, a long dispersion trade would only be established if the expected realized volatility exceeds the implied one.

Two essential metrics exist for measuring the implied costs of dispersion trades. First, the costs can be expressed as implied volatility. To assess the attractiveness of a trade, the IV of the index has to be compared with that of the index replicating basket. This method has to assume an average correlation coefficient in order to calculate the IV of the basket. To estimate the average correlation, historical realizations are often used. Second, implied costs can also be directly expressed as average implied correlation, which is computed based on the IVs of the index and its constituents. This measurement simply backs out the average implied correlation so that the IV of the basket equals the index IV. Through modification of the Markowitz portfolio variance equation (see Equation (6)) and assuming

$\rho = \rho_{i,j}$ for $i \neq j$ and $i, j = 1, ..., N$, the implied volatility can be expressed as average implied correlation (see [16]):

$$\overline{\rho} = \frac{\sigma_I^2 - \sum_{i=1}^N w_i^2 \sigma_i^2}{\sum_{i=1}^N \sum_{j \neq i}^N w_i w_j \sigma_i \sigma_j}. \tag{7}$$

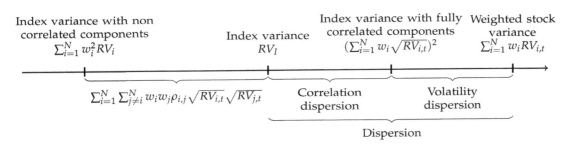

For a better understanding, we give the following example: Assume an equal weighted portfolio of two stocks with a pairwise correlation of 0.5 and RV of 0.04 and 0.08, respectively. The arisen dispersion of 0.0159 can be split as followed:

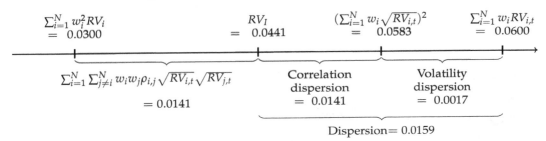

Figure 1. Visualization of dispersion trade performance drivers. Source: authors' calculations.

Figure 2 reports the effect of correlation on index volatility in a simple two stock portfolio case. It is easily perceivable that the index variance decreases with a lower correlation of the two stocks. If the two assets are perfectly negatively correlated, the index variance is virtually zero. This represents the best case for a long dispersion trade as the single index constituents variance is unaffected at 0.0064%, while the index is exposed to 0% variance. This state generates in the simulation a return dispersion of 0.0800%. Nevertheless, this extreme case is not realistic as indices normally incorporate more than two securities. Adding an additional stock leads inevitably to a positive linear relationship with one or the other constituent. Moreover, stocks are typically positively correlated as they exhibit similar risk factors.

The representation of implied costs as average implied correlation is a useful concept as it enables us to assess deviations of index and basket IV by solely computing one figure that is independent of the index size. Hence, this metric is always one-dimensional. Typically, the implied average correlation is compared with historical or forecasted correlations to identify profitable trading opportunities [13,16]. We included this trading filter in our robustness check in Section 4.4 to examine if it is economically beneficial to trade conditional on correlation. Overall, investors would rather sell dispersion in an environment of exceptionally low implied correlation than to build a long position since correlation is expected to normalize in the long run.

However, most of the time investors engage in long dispersion trades. This has mainly two reasons. First, a historical overpricing of implied volatility of index options compared to that of its constituents is persisting. Thus, selling index options is more attractive than buying them. Second, index option sellers can generate profits from the embedded correlation risk premium. Buying index options is ultimately an insurance against decreasing diversification as correlations tend to rise in market downturns. An increase in correlation negatively affects any portfolio diversification. Therefore, many investors are willing to pay a premium to hedge against rising correlations, making long dispersion trades more attractive [25,26]. Nonetheless, Reference [16] showed that the correlation risk premium seems to play only a minor role in explaining the performance of dispersion trades and concluded that returns depend mainly on mispricing and market inefficiency.

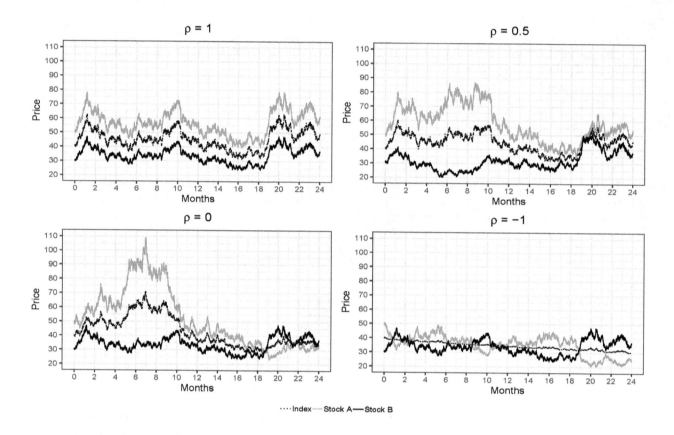

Figure 2. Illustration of the effect of different correlation levels on the variance of an equally weighted index of two stocks. Source: authors' calculations.

Over the years, several explanations for the overpricing of index options have emerged. The most prominent argument is related to the supply and demand of index and stock options. Changes in implied volatility are rooted in net buying and selling pressure. Amongst institutional investors, there is usually high demand for index options, especially puts, to hedge their portfolios. This creates net buying pressure, resulting in a higher implied volatility for index options [27–29]. Hedge funds and other sophisticated investors engage in call and put underwriting on single stock options to earn the negatively embedded volatility premium [30]. Due to consistent overpricing, selling both insurance (puts) and lottery tickets (calls) generates positive net returns in the long run, despite a substantial crash risk [31]. Hence, sophisticated market participants would sell volatility especially when the implied volatility is high. This was for example the case after the bankruptcy of Long-Term Capital Management in 1998 when several investors sold the high implied volatility [32]. The net buying pressure for index options and net selling pressure for stock options create the typical mispricing between index IV and the IV of a replicating portfolio. Dispersion trades therefore help balance the supply and demand of index and single name options as the strategy involves buying the oversupplied single stock options and selling the strongly demanded index options. In a long dispersion trade, investors ultimately act as the liquidity provider to balance single stock and index volatility.

2.2. Dispersion Trading Strategies

In the market, a variety of structures to capture dispersion are well established. In this subsection, we give an overview of the two most common variations, namely at-the-money straddles (Section 2.2.1) and at-the-money straddles with delta hedging (Section 2.2.2).

2.2.1. At-The-Money Straddle

One of the traditional and most transparent, as well as liquid ways to trade volatility is by buying and selling ATM straddles. A long straddle involves a long position in a call and put with the same strike price (K) and maturity (T). Selling both options results in a short straddle. The payoff of a long straddle position at T with respect to the share price (S_T) is given by:

$$P_T = \underbrace{[S_T - K]^+}_{\text{Call}} + \underbrace{[K - S_T]^+}_{\text{Put}}, \tag{8}$$

where $[x]^+$ represents $\max(x, 0)$. Translating an ATM straddle into the context of a long dispersion trade, the payoff equals:

$$P_{T,Dispersion} = \sum_i^N w_i \left([S_{i,T} - K_i]^+ + [K_i - S_{i,T}]^+ \right) - \left([S_{I,T} - K_I]^+ + [K_I - S_{I,T}]^+ \right). \tag{9}$$

The first part denotes the single stock option portfolio while the second term corresponds to the index leg. When setting up an at-the-money straddle, the initial delta of the position is approximately zero as the put and call delta offset each other [7]. Despite the low delta at inception, this structure is exposed to directional movements and is therefore not a pure volatility play. This is rooted in changes of the position's overall delta as the underlying moves or the time to maturity decreases.

2.2.2. At-the-Money Straddle with Delta Hedging

Delta hedging eliminates the directional exposure of ATM straddles. Through directional hedging, profits from an increase in volatility are locked in. Therefore, this structure generates income even in the case that the underlying ends up at expiry exactly at-the-money. The volatility profits are generated through gamma scalping. A long gamma position implies buying shares of the asset on the way down and selling them on the way up [7]. This represents every long investor's goal: buying low and selling high. A net profit is generated when the realized volatility is higher than the implied volatility at inception as more gamma gains are earned as from the market priced in. Hence, ATM straddles with frequent delta hedging are better suited to trade volatility than a plain option.

Assuming the underlying time series follows a GBM (Equation (2)) and the Black–Scholes assumptions hold, it can be shown that the gamma scalping gains are exactly offset by the theta bleeding when the risk-free rate equals zero [18,33]. Taking the Black–Scholes PDE:

$$\frac{\partial \Pi}{\partial t} + rS \frac{\partial \Pi}{\partial S} + \frac{1}{2} \sigma^2 S^2 \frac{\partial^2 \Pi}{\partial S^2} = r\Pi \tag{10}$$

and substituting the partial derivatives with the Greeks yields:

$$\Theta + rS\Delta + \frac{1}{2} \sigma^2 S^2 \Gamma = r\Pi. \tag{11}$$

Invoking Itô's lemma, this can be expressed for an infinitesimal small time change dt as:

$$\Theta dt = -\frac{1}{2} \sigma^2 S^2 \Gamma dt. \tag{12}$$

In the above-mentioned equations, Π describes the delta neutral portfolio, S represents the asset price, r illustrates the risk-free interest rate, and Θ and Γ denote the option's price sensitivities with respect to the passage of time and delta.

In the real world when using a discrete delta hedging method, theta and gamma do not necessarily offset each other. This results partially from the risk and randomness that an occasionally hedged straddle exhibits. In fact, the profit-and-loss (P&L) of a long straddle can be approximated as [17,33]:

$$P\&L_{t_0,T} = \sum_{i=0}^{T-t_0} \underbrace{\frac{1}{2}\Gamma_{t_i}S_{t_i}^2}_{\Gamma_{\$,ti}} \underbrace{\left[\left(\frac{\delta S}{S}\right)^2 - \sigma_{implied}^2\delta t\right]}_{\text{Volatility spread}}, \tag{13}$$

where $\sigma_{implied}$ denotes the implied volatility and δ describes the change in a variable. The first term $\Gamma_{\$,ti}$ is known as dollar gamma, and the last expression illustrates the difference between realized and implied variance, implying that a hedged ATM straddle is indeed a volatility play. However, this approach is still not a pure volatility trade due to the interaction of the dollar gamma with the volatility spread. This relationship creates a path dependency of the P&L. Noticeable, the highest P&L will be achieved when the underlying follows no clear trend and rather oscillates in relatively big movements around the strike price. This is driven by a high gamma exposure along the followed path since the straddle is most of the time relatively close to ATM. A starting trend in either directions would cut hedging profits, despite the positive variance difference. Concluding, delta hedged ATM straddles provide a way to express a view on volatility with a relatively low directional exposure.

3. Back-Testing Framework

This section describes the design of the back-testing study. First, an overview of the software and data used is provided (Section 3.1). Second, Section 3.2 introduces a method to subset index components (formation period). Third, we present our trading strategy in Section 3.3 (trading period). Following [2,34], we divide the dataset into formation-trading constellations, each shifted by approximately one month. Finally, Section 3.4 describes our return calculation method.

3.1. Data and Software

The empirical back-testing study is based on the daily option and price data of the S&P 500 and its constituents from January 2000 to December 2017. This index represents a highly liquid and broad equity market of leading U.S. companies. Hence, this dataset is suitable for examining any potential mispricing since investor scrutiny and analyst coverage are high. The stock price data, including outstanding shares, dividends, and stock split information, were retrieved from the Center for Research in Security Prices (CRSP). Information about the index composition and Standard Industrial Classification (SIC) codes were obtained from Compustat. For the options data of the S&P 500 and its members, we rely on the OptionMetrics Ivy database, which offers a comprehensive information set. From that database, all available one month options were extracted. We mention that OptionMetrics provides for single stocks only data on American options. Thus, the returns in Section 4 are probably understated. This conclusion arises from two facts. First, the constructed strategies could also be established with European options that usually trade at a discount to American ones due to the lack of the early exercise premium. Second, a dispersion strategy is typically long individual stock options, therefore resulting in higher initial costs. Nonetheless, this study provides a conservative evaluation of the attractiveness of dispersion trades. The above-mentioned data provider was accessed via Wharton Research Data Services (WRDS). The one month U.S. Dollar LIBOR, which is in the following used as a risk-free rate proxy, was directly downloaded from the Federal Reserve Economic Research database and transformed into a continuously compounded interest rate. Moreover, we use the Kenneth R. French data library to obtain all relevant risk factors.

To keep track of the changes in the index composition, a constituent matrix with appropriate stock weights is created. As the weights of the S&P 500 are not publicly available, the individual weights are reconstructed according to the market capitalization of every stock. This approach leads not to a 100% accurate representation of the index as the free-float adjustment factors, used by the index provider, are not considered. However, it provides us with a reliable proxy. The options data was cleaned by eliminating all data points with missing quotes. Furthermore, the moneyness was calculated for every option to determine ATM options.

All concepts were implemented in the general-purpose programming language Python. For some calculations and graphs, the statistical programming language R was used as a supplementary [35]. Computationally intensive calculations were outsourced to cloud computing platforms.

3.2. Formation Period

Transaction costs play a major role in trading financial securities (see [36,37]). In particular, when traded products are complex or exotic, transaction costs might be substantial. Reference [38] showed that the portfolio construction is of great importance in order to execute strategies cost efficiently in the presence of transaction costs. Therefore, portfolio building represents a material optimization potential for trading strategies. One simple way to reduce transaction fees is to trade less. In dispersion trades, the single option basket is the main trading costs driver. Therefore, it is desirable to reduce the number of traded assets, especially when the portfolio is delta hedged. However, trading less stocks as the index incorporates could result in an insufficient replication, which might not represent the desired dispersion exposure accurately.

To determine an appropriate subset of index constituents that acts as a hedge for the index position, a principal component analysis (PCA) is used. This statistical method converts a set of correlated variables into a set of linearly uncorrelated variables via an orthogonal transformation [39,40]. The main goal of this method is to find the dominant pattern of price movements, as well as stocks that incorporate this behavior most prominently. Selecting those assets leads to a portfolio that explains the majority of the index movement.

The fundamentals of the applied procedure are based on [15,16,41], but we improve the selection process by identifying stocks with the highest explanatory power. Therefore, we are in a position to get a basket of stocks that explains the index in a more accurate way. To be more specific, our method is comprised of six steps that recur every trading day:

1. Calculate the covariance matrix of all index members based on the trailing twelve month daily log returns.

2. Decompose the covariance matrix into the eigenvector and order the principal components according to their explanatory power.

3. Determine the first I principal components that cumulatively explain 90% of the variance.

4. Compute the explained variation of every index constituent through performing Steps 1 and 2 while omitting the specific index member and comparing the new explained variance of the I components to that of the full index member set.

5. Select the top N stocks with the highest explained variation.

6. Calculate the individual weights as the ratio of one index member's explained variation to the total explained variation of the selected N stocks.

To illustrate our approach in more detail, we report an example of our portfolio construction methodology for the trading day 29/11/2017 below.

1. Calculating the trailing 12 month return covariance matrix, after excluding stocks with missing data points, yields the following 410×410 matrix.

	AAPL	MSFT	AMZN	FB	...	SIG	DISCA	VIA	LEN
AAPL	0.00012	0.00004	0.00007	0.00006	...	-0.00003	0.00000	-0.00002	0.00002
MSFT	0.00004	0.00008	0.00007	0.00005	...	-0.00002	0.00000	-0.00001	0.00002
AMZN	0.00007	0.00007	0.00017	0.00009	...	-0.00004	0.00002	-0.00001	0.00003
FB	0.00006	0.00005	0.00009	0.00011	...	-0.00004	0.00003	0.00002	0.00003
⋮	⋮	⋮	⋮	⋮	⋮	...	⋮	⋮	⋮	⋮
SIG	-0.00003	-0.00002	-0.00004	-0.00004	...	0.00119	0.00010	0.00003	0.00004
DISCA	0.00000	0.00000	0.00002	0.00003	...	0.00010	0.00030	0.00017	0.00005
VIA	-0.00002	-0.00001	-0.00001	0.00002	...	0.00003	0.00017	0.00048	0.00004
LEN	0.00002	0.00002	0.00003	0.00003	...	0.00004	0.00005	0.00004	0.00020

2. Decomposing the covariance matrix from 1 into the eigenvectors results in 410 principal components. To keep this section concise, we report the selected components in Table 1 below.

3. Examining the cumulative variance of the principal components in the last column of Table 1 shows that we have to set $I = 36$ to explain 90% of the variance.

4. After repeating Steps 1 and 2 while omitting one index member at a time, we receive the new cumulative variance of the 36 components for every stock that enables us to calculate the individual explanatory power by comparing the new cumulative variance to that of the full index member set (Columns 3–5 in Table 2).

5. We select the top five stocks with the highest explained variation, which in our example are Xcel Energy Inc. (XEL), Lincoln National Corporation (LNC), CMS Energy Corporation (CMS), Bank of America Corporation (BAC), and SunTrust Banks, Inc. (STI).

6. Based on the explained variation of the top five stocks, we calculate the appropriate portfolio weights as the ratio of individually explained variation and total explained variation of the selected stocks. Eventually, we arrive in Table 2 at the reported portfolio weights.

Table 1. Total explained variance of the selected principal components.

Principal Component	% of Variance	Cumulative Variance %
1	32.01	32.01
2	17.02	49.03
3	6.32	55.35
4	5.65	61.00
5	4.74	65.73
⋮	⋮	⋮
35	0.34	89.82
36	0.33	90.16
37	0.31	90.47
38	0.30	90.77
39	0.29	91.06
40	0.28	91.34
⋮	⋮	⋮
410	0.00	100.00

Source: authors' calculations.

Table 2. Ranking of the index constituents by explanatory power and portfolio weights.

Rank	Stock Ticker	Cumulative Variance % All Constituents	Omitting Stocks	Explanatory Power %	Portfolio Weight %
1	XEL	90.1576	90.1358	0.0219	20.2518
2	LNC	90.1576	90.1359	0.0217	20.1303
3	CMS	90.1576	90.1360	0.0216	20.0108
4	BAC	90.1576	90.1361	0.0215	19.9274
5	STI	90.1576	90.1364	0.0212	19.6797
⋮	⋮	⋮	⋮	⋮	⋮
406	ULTA	90.1576	90.2146	−0.0570	0.0000
407	ADM	90.1576	90.2171	−0.0595	0.0000
408	NRG	90.1576	90.2177	−0.0601	0.0000
409	HRB	90.1576	90.2207	−0.0631	0.0000
410	EFX	90.1576	90.2333	−0.0757	0.0000

Source: authors' calculations.

3.3. Trading Period

As [42] showed that even professional traders that are normally considered as rational and sophisticated suffer from behavioral biases, our strategy is based on predefined and clear rules to alleviate any unconscious tendencies. In line with [15,16], we implement our trading strategies based on one month ATM options. The following rules specify our trading framework:

1. Whenever one month ATM options are available, a trading position is established.
2. A trading position consists always of a single stock option basket and an index leg.
3. Every position is held until expiry.

Whenever a new position is established, we invest 20% of our capital. The remaining capital stock acts as a liquidity buffer to cover obligations that may emerge from selling options. All uncommitted capital is invested at LIBOR. In total, we construct the four trading systems PCA straddle delta hedged (PSD), PCA straddle delta unhedged (PSU), largest constituents straddle delta hedged (LSD), and largest constituents straddle delta unhedged (LSU). In order to benchmark our index subsetting scheme (Section 3.2), we also apply our strategies to a naive subset of the index, consisting of the five largest constituents. As a point of reference, a simple buy-and-hold strategy on the index (MKT) is reported. Details can be found in the following lines.

- PCA straddle delta hedged (PSD): The replicating portfolio of this strategy consists of the top five stocks that are selected with the statistical approach outlined in Section 3.2. A long straddle position of the basket portfolio is established while index straddles are sold. The overall position is delta hedged on a daily basis.
- PCA straddle delta unhedged (PSU): The selection process and the trade construction are similar to PSD. However, the directional exposure remains unhedged during the lifetime of the trade. This illustrates a simpler version of PSD.
- Largest constituents straddle delta hedged (LSD): The replicating portfolio of this strategy follows a naive subsetting approach and contains the top five largest constituents of the index at trade inception. Basket straddles are bought while index straddles are shorted. The directional exposure is delta hedged on a daily basis.
- Largest constituents straddle delta unhedged (LSU): The trade construction and selection process is identical to LSD. However, the overall delta position remains unhedged, hence representing a less sophisticated approach than LSD.
- Naive buy-and-hold strategy (MKT): This approach represents a simple buy-and-hold strategy. The index is bought in January 2000 and held during the complete back-testing period. MKT is the simplest strategy in our study.

Transaction costs are inevitable when participating in financial markets. Thus, transaction fees have to be considered in evaluating trading strategies to provide a more realistic picture of profitability. Besides market impact, bid-ask spreads, and commissions, slippages are the main cost driver. Over the last few years, trading costs decreased due to electronic trading, decimalization, increased competition, and regulatory changes (see [43,44]). The retail sector also benefited from this development as brokers such as Charles Schwab first decreased and then completely eliminated fees for stocks, ETFs, and options that are listed on U.S. or Canadian exchanges [45]. However, transaction costs are hard to estimate as they depend on multiple factors such as asset class and client profile. To account for asset specific trading fees in our back-testing study, we apply 10 bps for every half turn per option, to which 2.5 bps are added if delta hedging is performed. In light of our trading strategy in a highly liquid equity market, the cost assumptions appear to be realistic.

3.4. Return Calculation

In contrast to [2,37,46], who constructed a fully invested portfolio, we base our returns on a partially invested portfolio. Our calculation is similar to the concept of return on risk-adjusted capital (RORAC). There are two reasons for choosing this method. First, short selling options incorporates extreme payoffs that can easily outstrip option premiums. As a result, investors need substantial liquidity to cover any future cash outflows to honor their obligations. Second, writing options requires a margin to enter and maintain the position. For example, the initial margin for a one month short index ATM call position at the Chicago Board Options Exchange (CBOE) amounts to 100% of the options proceeds plus 15% of the aggregated underlying index value minus the out-of-the-money amount [47].

The return of a dispersion trade is calculated as:

$$R_{t,T} = \begin{cases} \dfrac{P_{T,Stocks}}{V_{t,Stocks}} - \dfrac{P_{T,Index}}{V_{t,Index}}, & \text{if long dispersion,} \\ -\dfrac{P_{T,Stocks}}{V_{t,Stocks}} + \dfrac{P_{T,Index}}{V_{t,Index}}, & \text{if short dispersion,} \end{cases} \tag{14}$$

where V_t represents the initial costs of the individual legs:

$$V_{t,Stocks} = \sum_i^N w_i \left(C_{i,t}(K_i, T) + P_{i,t}(K_i, T) \right), \tag{15}$$

$$V_{t,Index} = C_{I,t}(K_I, T) + P_{I,t}(K_I, T). \tag{16}$$

C_t and P_t denote the prices for calls and puts for a specific time to maturity (T) and strike (K). When delta hedging is conducted, the generated P&L is added to the nominator of Equation (14) for both legs. As [18] assumed continuous hedging is impracticable in reality due to transaction costs and a lack of order execution speed, we undertake daily delta hedging at market close. To calculate the delta exposure (Δ), the Black–Scholes framework is used. $IV_j \forall j \in (t, T)$ is assumed to be the annualized one month trailing standard deviation of log returns. Any proceeds (losses) from delta hedging are invested (financed) at dollar LIBOR (r). This rate also serves as borrowing rate when cash is needed to buy shares (S). Hence, the delta P&L at T for a portfolio of N options is determined by:

$$P\&L_{\Delta,Portfolio} = \sum_{t=1}^{T}\sum_{i=1}^{N} w_i\left[(\Delta_{i,t} - \Delta_{i,t-1})S_{i,t} * e^{r(T-t)} - \Delta_{i,t-1}(S_{i,t} + D_{i,t} - S_{i,t-1})\right], \quad (17)$$

where $D_{i,t}$ denotes the present value at time t of the dividend payment of stock i.

4. Results

We follow [48] and conduct a fully-fledged performance evaluation on the strategies PSD, PSU, LSD, and LSU from January 2000 to December 2017—compared to the general market MKT. The key results for the options portfolio of the top five stocks are depicted in two panels—before and after transaction costs. First, we evaluate the performance of all trading strategies (Section 4.1), conduct a sub-period analysis (Section 4.2), and analyze the sensitivity to varying market frictions (Section 4.3). Second, Section 4.4 checks the robustness, and Section 4.5 examines the exposure to common systematic risk factors. Finally, we investigate the number of principal components and the corresponding sector exposure of our PCA based selection process (Section 5).

4.1. Strategy Performance

Table 3 shows the risk-return metrics per trade and the corresponding tradings statistics for the top five stocks per strategy from January 2000 to December 2017. We observe statistically significant returns for PSD and PSU, with Newey–West (NW) t-statistics above 2.20 before transaction costs and above 1.90 after transaction costs. A similar pattern also emerges from the economic perspective: the mean return per trade is well above zero percent for PSD (0.84 percent) and PSU (2.14 percent) after transaction costs. In contrast, LSD produces a relatively small average return of 0.30 percent per trade. It is very interesting that LSU achieves 1.28 percent, but this is not statistically significant. The naive buy-and-hold strategy MKT achieves identical results before and after transaction costs because the one-off fees are negligible. The range, i.e., the difference of maximum and minimum, is substantially lower for the delta hedged strategies PSD and LSD, which reflects the lower directional risk of those approaches. Furthermore, the standard deviation of PSU (15.23 percent) and LSU (13.53 percent) is approximately two times higher than that of PSD (6.78 percent) and LSD (7.25 percent). We follow [49] and report the historical value at risk (VaR) figures. Overall, the tail risk of the delta hedged strategies is greatly reduced, e.g., the historical VaR 5% after transaction costs for PSD is −11.13 percent compared to −20.90 percent for PSU. The decline from a historical peak, called maximum drawdown, is at a relatively low level for PSD (70.53 percent) compared to PSU (94.70 percent), LSD (82.01 percent), and LSU (85.64 percent). The hit rate, i.e., the number of trades with a positive return, varies between 52.15 percent (LSD) and 56.71 percent (PSD). Across all systems, the number of actually executed trades is 395 since none of the strategies suffers a total loss. Consequently, the average number of trades per year is approximately 22; this number is well in line with [50].

In Table 4, we report annualized risk-return measures for the strategies PSD, PSU, LSD, and LSU. The mean return after transaction costs ranges from 0.77 percent for LSD to 26.51 percent for PSU. As anticipated from Table 3, the standard deviation of both delta hedged strategies amounts to approximately 20%—half of the unhedged counterparts. Notably, the Sharpe ratio, i.e., the excess return per unit of standard deviation, of PSD clearly outperforms the benchmarks with a value of 0.40 after transaction costs. Concluding, PSD generates promising risk-return characteristics, even after transaction costs.

Table 3. Return characteristics, risk metrics, and trading statistics per trade for PCA straddle delta hedged (PSD), PCA straddle delta unhedged (PSU), largest constituents straddle delta hedged (LSD), and largest constituents straddle delta unhedged (LSU) from January 2000 until December 2017. NW denotes Newey–West standard errors and CVaR the conditional value at risk.

	Before Transaction Costs					After Transaction Costs				
	PSD	PSU	LSD	LSU	MKT	PSD	PSU	LSD	LSU	MKT
Mean return	0.0100	0.0228	0.0044	0.0140	0.0022	0.0084	0.0214	0.0030	0.0128	0.0022
t-statistic (NW)	2.2413	2.2086	0.8608	1.5083	1.2897	1.9069	2.0933	0.5809	1.3852	1.2897
Standard error (NW)	0.0044	0.0103	0.0051	0.0093	0.0017	0.0044	0.0102	0.0051	0.0093	0.0017
Minimum	−0.2560	−0.4539	−0.2399	−0.4798	−0.2506	−0.2556	−0.4529	−0.2396	−0.4781	−0.2506
Quartile 1	−0.0238	−0.0640	−0.0288	−0.0704	−0.0097	−0.0251	−0.0648	−0.0300	−0.0711	−0.0097
Median	0.0097	0.0163	0.0037	0.0201	0.0037	0.0082	0.0150	0.0022	0.0188	0.0037
Quartile 3	0.0489	0.1006	0.0374	0.0884	0.0170	0.0470	0.0988	0.0356	0.0866	0.0170
Maximum	0.3241	1.1694	0.3414	0.4270	0.1315	0.3202	1.1626	0.3373	0.4258	0.1315
Standard deviation	0.0678	0.1523	0.0730	0.1361	0.0363	0.0673	0.1515	0.0725	0.1353	0.0363
Skewness	−0.0818	1.2340	0.2528	−0.1259	−1.5218	−0.0806	1.2366	0.2546	−0.1249	−1.5218
Kurtosis	2.7042	8.9553	2.3025	0.9795	9.2676	2.7051	8.9824	2.3021	0.9806	9.2676
Historical VaR 1%	−0.1955	−0.3580	−0.1820	−0.3584	−0.1431	−0.1955	−0.3570	−0.1820	−0.3574	−0.1431
Historical CVaR 1%	−0.2166	−0.4080	−0.2133	−0.4068	−0.1788	−0.2165	−0.4069	−0.2132	−0.4056	−0.1788
Historical VaR 5%	−0.1106	−0.2091	−0.1178	−0.2052	−0.0486	−0.1113	−0.2090	−0.1184	−0.2051	−0.0486
Historical CVaR 5%	−0.1573	−0.2889	−0.1632	−0.2977	−0.1000	−0.1576	−0.2884	−0.1635	−0.2971	−0.1000
Maximum drawdown	0.6731	0.9358	0.8074	0.8534	0.4990	0.7053	0.9470	0.8201	0.8564	0.4990
Trades with return ≥ 0	0.5747	0.5519	0.5342	0.5671	0.5975	0.5671	0.5468	0.5215	0.5646	0.5975
Number of trades	395	395	395	395	1	395	395	395	395	1
Avg. trades per year	21.9444	21.9444	21.9444	21.9444	0.0556	21.9444	21.9444	21.9444	21.9444	0.0556

Source: authors' calculations.

Table 4. Annualized risk-return measures for PSD, PSU, LSD, and LSU from January 2000 until December 2017.

	Before Transaction Costs					After Transaction Costs				
	PSD	PSU	LSD	LSU	MKT	PSD	PSU	LSD	LSU	MKT
Mean return	0.1841	0.2988	0.0401	0.1049	0.0347	0.1452	0.2651	0.0077	0.0779	0.0347
Mean excess return	0.1646	0.2794	0.0206	0.0854	0.0152	0.1257	0.2456	−0.0117	0.0585	0.0152
Standard deviation	0.3192	0.7169	0.3438	0.6403	0.1710	0.3169	0.7128	0.3414	0.6367	0.1710
Downside deviation	0.2074	0.4110	0.2271	0.4264	0.1305	0.2090	0.4114	0.2287	0.4266	0.1305
Sharpe ratio	0.5157	0.3897	0.0599	0.1334	0.0890	0.3967	0.3446	−0.0344	0.0918	0.0890
Sortino ratio	2.3481	2.0620	0.4254	0.6190	0.6389	1.7935	1.7911	0.0799	0.4518	0.6389

Source: authors' calculations.

4.2. Sub-Period Analysis

Investors are concerned about the stability of the results, potential drawdowns, and the behavior in high market turmoils. Inspired by the time-varying returns of [51–53], we analyze the performance of our implemented trading strategies over the complete sample period. Figure 3 illustrates the different dispersion structures across the three different sub-periods January 2000–December 2005, January 2006–December 2011, and January 2012–December 2017. The graphs show the development of an investment of 1 USD at the beginning of each sub-period.

The first sub-period ranges from 2000 to 2005 and includes the dot-com crash, the 9/11 attacks, and the time of moderation. For PSD and LSD, 1 USD invested in January 2000 grows to more than 2.00 USD at the end of this time range; both show a steady growth without any substantial drawdowns. PSU, LSU, and MKT exhibit a similar behavior, which is clearly worse than the hedged strategies. The second sub-period ranges from 2006 to 2011 and describes the global financial crisis and its aftermath. The strategy PSD seems to be robust against any external effects since it copes with the global financial crisis in a convincing way. As expected, the unhedged trading approaches PSU and LSU show strong swings during high market turmoils. The third sub-period ranges from 2012 to 2017 and specifies the period of regeneration and comebacks. The development of all strategies does not decline even after transaction costs; profits are not being arbitraged away. Especially PSU outperforms in this time range with a cumulative return up to 300 as a consequence of too high index option premiums and high profits on single stock options, e.g., Goldman Sachs Group, Inc. and United Rentals, Inc.

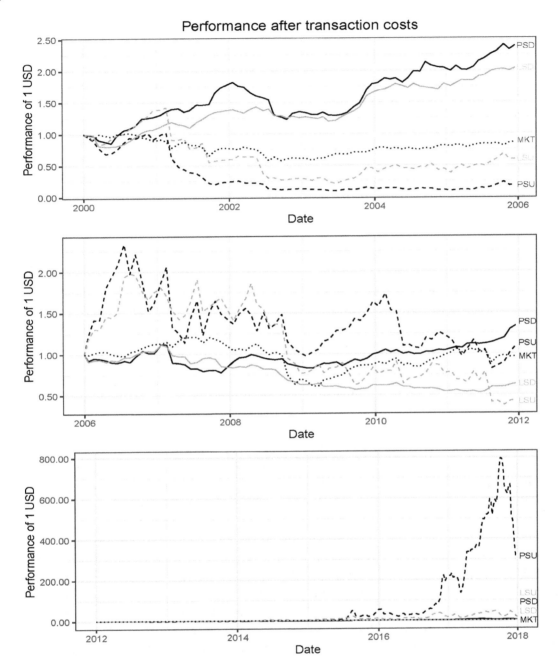

Figure 3. Development of an investment of 1 USD in PSD, PSU, LSD, and LSU after transaction costs compared to the S&P 500 (MKT). The time period is divided intro three sub-periods from January 2000–December 2005, January 2006–December 2011, and January 2012–December 2017. Source: authors' calculations.

4.3. Market Frictions

This subsection evaluates the robustness of our trading strategies in light of market frictions. Following [54], we analyze the annualized mean return and Sharpe ratio for varying transaction cost levels (see Table 5). Motivated by the literature, our back-testing study supposes transaction costs of 10 bps per straddle and 2.5 bps per stock for delta hedging. The results for 0 bps and 10 bps are identical to Table 4. Due to the same trading frequencies, all strategies are similarly affected by transaction costs; the naive buy-and-hold strategy MKT is constant (see Section 4.1). Taking annualized returns into account, we observe that the breakeven point for PSD and LSU is between 40 bps and 80 bps. As expected, PSU has a higher level where costs and returns are equal; the breakeven point is around 90 bps. The additional consideration of the risk side leads to the Sharpe ratio, with the results being similar to before. As expected, the breakeven points are reached for lower transactions costs, as the Sharpe ratio is calculated on the basis of excess returns. The thresholds vary between approximately 5 bps for LSD and 90 bps for PSU. Concluding, the delta hedged strategies PSD and PSU provide promising results in the context of risk-return measures, even for investors that are exposed to different market conditions and thus higher transaction costs.

Table 5. Annualized mean return and Sharpe ratio for PSD, PSU, LSD, and LSU from January 2000 until December 2017 for different transaction costs per trade per straddle in bps.

		Annualized Return					Sharpe Ratio				
		PSD	PSU	LSD	LSU	MKT	PSD	PSU	LSD	LSU	MKT
	0	0.1841	0.2988	0.0401	0.1049	0.0347	0.5157	0.3897	0.0599	0.1334	0.0890
	1	0.1802	0.2954	0.0368	0.1022	0.0347	0.5037	0.3851	0.0504	0.1292	0.0890
	5	0.1645	0.2818	0.0238	0.0913	0.0347	0.4560	0.3670	0.0126	0.1126	0.0890
	10	0.1452	0.2651	0.0077	0.0779	0.0347	0.3967	0.3446	−0.0344	0.0918	0.0890
	15	0.1262	0.2485	−0.0080	0.0647	0.0347	0.3380	0.3222	−0.0809	0.0712	0.0890
Transaction costs	20	0.1075	0.2321	−0.0236	0.0516	0.0347	0.2798	0.3001	−0.1271	0.0508	0.0890
	40	0.0356	0.1687	−0.0836	0.0007	0.0347	0.0521	0.2130	−0.3082	−0.0299	0.0890
	50	0.0014	0.1381	−0.1122	−0.0238	0.0347	−0.0589	0.1703	−0.3967	−0.0696	0.0890
	60	−0.0318	0.1083	−0.1400	−0.0478	0.0347	−0.1681	0.1283	−0.4839	−0.1088	0.0890
	90	−0.1252	0.0232	−0.2185	−0.1166	0.0347	−0.4852	0.0054	−0.7380	−0.2238	0.0890
	100	−0.1544	−0.0038	−0.2431	−0.1384	0.0347	−0.5876	−0.0345	−0.8203	−0.2613	0.0890

Source: authors' calculations.

4.4. Robustness Check

As stated previously, the 20 percent reinvestment rate, the top stocks option portfolio, which is traded unconditionally on correlation, and the number of five target stocks was motivated based on the existing literature (Section 3.3). Since data snooping is an important issue in many research studies, we examine the sensitivity of our PSD results with respect to variations of these hyperparameters.

In contrast to the reinvestment rate and the number of target stocks, trading based on unconditional correlation is not a hyperparameter in our framework. However, it is beneficial to examine if changes in the entry signal lead to substantial changes in our strategy performance. In Section 2.1, the concept of measuring implied costs as average implied correlation is introduced. Based on this approach, the relative mispricing between the index and the replicating basket can be quantified. Applying Equation (7) to forecasted or historical volatility yields an average expected correlation. Comparing this metric to the implied average correlation provides insights regarding the current pricing of index options. As discussed in Section 2.1, index options trade usually richer in terms of implied volatility than the replication portfolio. However, there are times at which the opposite might be the case. Following, an investors would set up a short dispersion trade: selling the basket and buying the index. A simple trading signal can be derived from average correlation levels:

$$\text{Long dispersion if } \quad \bar{\rho}_{implied} > \bar{\rho}_{historical},$$

$$\text{Short dispersion if } \quad \bar{\rho}_{implied} < \bar{\rho}_{historical}.$$

For our robustness check, we rely on historical volatility as a baseline approach. However, more advanced statistical methods could be applied to forecast volatility and determine current pricing levels (see [55–57]). Table 6 reports the annualized return of PSD for a variety of replicating portfolio sizes, reinvestment rates, and correlation based entry signals. First of all, a higher reinvestment rate leads to higher annualized mean returns; concurrently, higher risk aggravates the Sharpe ratio and the maximum drawdown. We observe several total losses for reinvestment rates of 80 percent and 100 percent, which is a result of the corresponding all-or-nothing strategy. Higher annualized returns and Sharpe ratios can generally be found at lower numbers of top stocks indicating that our selection algorithm introduced in Section 3.2 is meaningful. Regarding the correlation filter, we recognize that the strategy based on conditional correlation leads to worse results than the unconditional counterpart, e.g., the annualized mean return for the top five stocks and an investment rate of 20 percent is 9.53 percent (conditional correlation) vs. 18.41 percent (unconditional correlation). Summarizing, our initial hyperparameter setting does not hit the optimum; our selection procedure identifies the right top stocks; and considering unconditional correlation has a positive impact on the trading results.

Table 6. Annualized mean return, Sharpe ratio, and maximum drawdown before transaction costs for a varying number of top stocks, the amount of reinvestment, and the correlation filter from January 2000 until December 2017.

	Reinvestment	5%	10%	20%	40%	80%	100%
Mean return							
Top 5	Uncond.Correlation	0.07120	0.11478	0.18411	0.23003	NA	NA
	Cond.Correlation	0.05096	0.07288	0.09532	0.03780	NA	NA
Top 10	Uncond. Correlation	0.06976	0.11226	0.18090	0.23413	−0.11755	NA
	Cond. Correlation	0.04677	0.06481	0.08092	0.02113	NA	NA
Top 20	Uncond. Correlation	0.07394	0.12131	0.20171	0.28533	0.00145	−0.59641
	Cond. Correlation	0.05318	0.07825	0.11008	0.08608	NA	NA
Sharpe ratio							
Top 5	Uncond. Correlation	0.6467	0.5969	0.5157	0.3298	NA	NA
	Cond. Correlation	0.3902	0.3321	0.2361	0.0285	NA	NA
Top 10	Uncond. Correlation	0.6492	0.6004	0.5226	0.3475	−0.1109	NA
	Cond. Correlation	0.3496	0.2912	0.1976	0.0027	NA	NA
Top 20	Uncond. Correlation	0.7226	0.6774	0.6064	0.4424	−0.0150	−0.4100
	Cond. Correlation	0.4432	0.3879	0.2994	0.1101	NA	NA
Maximum drawdown							
Top 5	Uncond. Correlation	0.2146	0.4017	0.6731	0.9258	1.0000	1.0000
	Cond. Correlation	0.2520	0.4943	0.8124	0.9908	1.0000	1.0000
Top 10	Uncond. Correlation	0.2363	0.4332	0.7053	0.9447	1.0000	1.0000
	Cond. Correlation	0.2898	0.5403	0.8399	0.9920	1.0000	1.0000
Top 20	Uncond. Correlation	0.2282	0.4198	0.6885	0.9294	0.9999	1.0000
	Cond. Correlation	0.2744	0.5187	0.8232	0.9897	1.0000	1.0000

Source: authors' calculations.

4.5. Risk Factor Analysis

Table 7 evaluates the exposure of PSD and PSU after transaction costs to systematic sources of risk (see [48]). Therefore, we apply the Fama–French three factor model (FF3) and the Fama–French 5-factor model (FF5) of [58,59], and the Fama–French 3+2 factor model (FF3+2) presented by [2]. Hereby, FF3 measures the exposure to the general market, small minus big capitalization stocks (SMB), and high minus low book-to-market stocks (HML). Next, FF3+2 enlarges the first model by a momentum factor and a short-term reversal factor. Finally, FF5 extends FF3 by a factor capturing robust minus weak (RMW5) profitability and a factor capturing conservative minus aggressive (CMA5) investment behavior.

Across all three models, we observe statistically significant monthly alphas ranging between 0.74% and 0.79% for PSD and between 2.01% and 2.19% for PSU. The highest explanatory content is given for FF3+2 with adjusted R^2 of 0.0142 and 0.0118; probably, the momentum and reversal factor possess a high explanatory power. Not significant loadings for SMB5, HML5, RMW5, and CMA5 confirm our long–short portfolio we are constructing. Exposure to HML (PSD) and the reversal factor (PSU) underlies our selection and trading process (see Section 3).

Table 7. Risk factor exposure of PSD and PSU. The standard error is reported in brackets. FF3, Fama–French three factor model; SMB, small minus big capitalization stocks; HML, high minus low book-to-market stocks; RMW, robust minus weak; CMA, conservative minus aggressive.

	PSD			PSU		
	FF3	FF3+2	FF5	FF3	FF3+2	FF5
Intercept	0.0075 **	0.0079 **	0.0074 **	0.0201 **	0.0222 ***	0.0219 ***
	(0.0035)	(0.0035)	(0.0035)	(0.0078)	(0.0080)	(0.0080)
Market	0.1200	0.1316	0.1517 *	0.2128	0.4157 **	0.0560
	(0.0834)	(0.0926)	(0.0909)	(0.1894)	(0.2084)	(0.2056)
SMB	0.1626	0.1736		0.1325	0.1920	
	(0.1359)	(0.1374)		(0.3085)	(0.3092)	
HML	0.2424 **	0.2360 **		0.0117	0.0767	
	(0.1074)	(0.1146)		(0.2440)	(0.2579)	
Momentum		−0.0225			0.0711	
		(0.0893)			(0.2008)	
Reversal		−0.0656			−0.5416 **	
		(0.0968)			(0.2178)	
SMB5			0.1168			0.0847
			(0.1551)			(0.3506)
HML5			0.1383			0.3636
			(0.1396)			(0.3157)
RMW5			−0.0216			−0.2720
			(0.1815)			(0.4102)
CMA5			0.2194			−0.8783
			(0.2362)			(0.5340)
R^2	0.0256	0.0267	0.0264	0.0050	0.0243	0.0146
Adj.R^2	0.0181	0.0142	0.0139	−0.0026	0.0118	0.0019
No. obs.	395	395	395	395	395	395
RMSE	0.0672	0.0674	0.0674	0.1527	0.1516	0.1523

*** $p < 0.01$, ** $p < 0.05$, * $p < 0.1$. Source: authors' calculations.

4.6. Analysis of PCA Components and Market Exposure

Following [60], we report the Kaiser–Meyer–Olkin criterion (KMO) and Bartlett's sphericity test in Table 8 to examine the suitability of our data for a PCA analysis. Bartlett's test of sphericity, which tests the hypothesis that the correlation matrix is an identity matrix and therefore the variables are unrelated to each other and not suitable to detect any structure, is for all of our trading dates at a significance level of 1% [61]. KMO is a sampling adequacy measure that describes the proportion of variance in the variables that might be caused by shared underlying factors [62,63]. A low KMO score is driven by high partial correlation in the underlying data. The threshold for an acceptable sampling adequacy for a factor analysis is normally considered to be 0.5 [64]. However, in our context of finding the top five stocks that describe the index as closely as possible, a low KMO value is actually favorable as it indicates that strong relationships amongst the S&P 500 constituents exist that we aim to exploit with our methodology. As expected, our KMO values are on almost all trading days below the threshold with an average and median of 0.2833 and 0.2619, respectively. There are two determinants that explain the low KMO values in our study and support our approach. (i) Stocks are often dependent on the same risk factors, one of the most prominent factors being the market (for more, see [65,66]), and therefore exhibit rather high partial correlations. (ii) On every trading day, we analyze around 450 S&P 500 index members, which results in 101,250 different partial correlations. Due to the substantial number of combinations, you will find structure and high partial correlations in the data.

Table 8. Kaiser–Meyer–Olkin (KMO) criterion and Bartlett's sphericity test results. The KMO values and *p*-values of Bartlett's test are segmented into six and three buckets, respectively.

| | Kaiser-Meyer-Olkin Criterion | | | | | | Bartlett's Sphericity Test | | |
| | KMO Value | | | | | | *p*-Value | | |
Segment	0–0.1	0.1–0.2	0.2–0.3	0.3–0.5	≥ 0.5	Total	< 1%	≥ 1%	Total
Count	7	84	148	138	18	395	395	0	395
Average	0.0895	0.1600	0.2445	0.3725	0.5701	0.2833	0.0000	NA	0.0000
Median	0.0878	0.1668	0.2431	0.3530	0.5502	0.2619	0.0000	NA	0.0000

Source: authors' calculations.

Figure 4 reports the number of required principal components to explain 90 percent of the S&P 500 constituents' return variation and the standardized S&P 500 index. Overall, we observe synchronous developments of both time series, i.e., if one variable increases, the other increases, and vice versa. Specifically, the number of PCA components ranges between 15 and 45 from 2000 until 2007. The value decreases to approximately five with the beginning of the financial crisis in 2008. This fact is not surprising since downsides of the S&P 500 lead to a higher pair-wise correlation of the stock constituents. Consequently, a lower number of shares is in a position to describe 90 percent of stock price variations. After 2011, the general market possesses a positive trend without any strong swings. Thus, the number of PCA components increases to approximately 20.

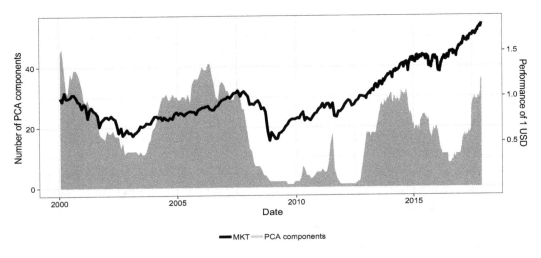

Figure 4. Number of required principal components to explain 90% of S&P 500 constituents return variation and S&P 500 index performance (MKT) from January 2000–December 2017. Source: authors' calculations.

Last, but not least, Figure 5 shows the yearly sector exposure based on our PCA selection process from January 2000 to December 2017. In line with the Standard Industrial Classification, all companies are categorized into the following nine economic sectors: "Mining", "Manufacturing", "Wholesale Trade", "Finance, Insurance, Real Estate", "Construction", "Transportation and Public Utilities", "Real Trade", "Services". Each point on the horizontal axis refers to the sectors that are used in the year after to the respective point. First of all, we observe that the sum of positive sector exposures increases in times of high market turmoil. Especially, the cumulative value exceeds three in 2013 because of a high exposure in "Finance, Insurance, Real Estate", especially for Bank of America Corporation and Goldman Sachs Group, Inc. Furthermore, the exposure of each sector varies over time, i.e., industry branches are preferred and avoided in times of bull and bear markets. As such, the percentage of financial stocks increases in 2009 and 2013, the peak of the global financial and European debt crisis.

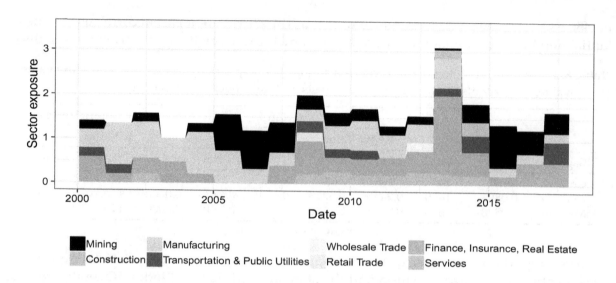

Figure 5. Yearly sector exposure based on the PCA selection process from January 2000–December 2017. Sector short positions are for illustrative purposes not included. Source: authors' calculations.

5. Conclusions and Policy Recommendations

In this manuscript, we developed a dispersion trading strategy based on a statistical stock selection process and applied our approach to the S&P 500 index and its constituents from January 2000 to December 2017. We contributed to the existing literature in four ways. First, we developed an index subsetting procedure that considers the individual index explanatory power of stocks in the weighting scheme. Therefore, we are in a position to build a replicating option basket with as little as five securities. Second, the large-scale empirical study provides a reliable back-testing for our dispersion trades. Hence, the profitability and robustness of those relative value trades can be examined across a variety of market conditions. Third, we analyzed the added value of our strategies by benchmarking them against a naive index subsetting approach and a simple buy-and-hold strategy. The trading frameworks that employ the PCA selection process outperformed its peers with an annualized mean return of 14.52 and 26.51 percent for PSD and PSU, respectively. The fourth contribution focuses on the conducted deep dive analysis of our selection process, i.e., sector exposure and number of required principal components over time, and the robustness checks. We showed that our trading systems possess superior risk-return characteristics compared to the benchmarking dispersion strategies.

Our study reveals two main policy recommendations. First of all, our framework shows that advanced statistical methods can be utilized to determine a portfolio replicating basket and could therefore be used for sophisticated risk management. Regulatory market risk assessments of financial institutions often rely on crude approaches that stress bank's capital requirements disproportionately to the underlying risk. However, regulators should explore the possibility of employing more advanced statistical models in their risk assessments, such as considering PCA built replicating baskets to hedge index exposures, to adequately reflect risk. Finally, investors should be aware that a principal component analysis can be used to cost-efficiently set up dispersion trades, and they should use their comprehensive datasets to improve the stock selection process further.

For future research endeavors, we identify the following three areas. First, the back-testing framework should be applied to other indices and geographical areas, i.e., price weighted equity markets and emerging economies, to shed light on any idiosyncrasies related to geographical or index construction differences. Second, efforts could be undertaken to improve the correlation filter from Section 4.4, so that profitable short dispersion opportunities can be spotted more accurately. Third, financial product innovations in a dispersion context should be subject to future studies, particularly the third generation of volatility derivatives such as variance, correlation, and gamma swaps.

Author Contributions: L.S. conceived of the research method. The experiments are designed and performed by L.S. The analyses were conducted and reviewed by L.S. and J.S. The paper was initially drafted and revised by L.S. and J.S. It was refined and finalized by L.S. and J.S. All authors read and agreed to the published version of the manuscript.

Acknowledgments: We are further grateful to four anonymous referees for many helpful discussions and suggestions on this topic.

References

1. Pole, A. *Statistical Arbitrage: Algorithmic Trading Insights and Techniques*; John Wiley & Sons: Hoboken, NJ, USA, 2011.

2. Gatev, E.; Goetzmann, W.N.; Rouwenhorst, K.G. Pairs trading: Performance of a relative-value arbitrage rule. *Rev. Financ. Stud.* **2006**, *19*, 797–827. [CrossRef]

3. Do, B.; Faff, R. Does simple pairs trading still work? *Financ. Anal. J.* **2010**, *66*, 83–95. [CrossRef]

4. Ramos-Requena, J.; Trinidad-Segovia, J.; Sánchez-Granero, M. Introducing Hurst exponent in pair trading. *Phys. Stat. Mech. Its Appl.* **2017**, *488*, 39–45. [CrossRef]

5. Ramos-Requena, J.P.; Trinidad-Segovia, J.E.; Sánchez-Granero, M.Á. Some notes on the formation of a pair in pairs trading. *Mathematics* **2020**, *8*, 348. [CrossRef]

6. Sánchez-Granero, M.; Balladares, K.; Ramos-Requena, J.; Trinidad-Segovia, J. Testing the efficient market hypothesis in Latin American stock markets. *Phys. Stat. Mech. Its Appl.* **2020**, *540*, 123082. [CrossRef]

7. Bennett, C. *Trading Volatility: Trading Volatility, Correlation, Term Structure and Skew*; CreateSpace: Charleston, SC, USA, 2014.

8. Nasekin, S.; Härdle, W.K. Model-driven statistical arbitrage on LETF option markets. *Quant. Financ.* **2019**, *19*, 1817–1837. [CrossRef]

9. Glasserman, P.; He, P. Buy rough, sell smooth. *Quant. Financ.* **2020**, *20*, 363–378. [CrossRef]

10. Gangahar, A. Smart Money on Dispersion. Financial Times. 2006. Available online: https://www.ft.com/content/a786ce1e-3140-11db-b953-0000779e2340 (accessed on 16 August 2020)

11. Sculptor Capital Management Inc. Sculptor Capital Management Inc. website. 2020. Available online: https://www.sculptor.com/ (accessed on 16 August 2020)

12. Alloway, T. A $12bn Dispersion Trade. Financial Times. 2011. Available online: https://ftalphaville.ft.com/2011/06/17/597511/a-12bn-dispersion-trade/ (accessed on 16 August 2020)

13. Marshall, C.M. Dispersion trading: Empirical evidence from U.S. options markets. *Glob. Financ. J.* **2009**, *20*, 289–301. [CrossRef]

14. Maze, S. Dispersion trading in south africa: An analysis of profitability and a strategy comparison. *SSRN Electron. J.* **2012**. . [CrossRef]

15. Ferrari, P.; Poy, G.; Abate, G. Dispersion trading: An empirical analysis on the S&P 100 options. *Invest. Manag. Financ. Innov.* **2019**, *16*, 178–188.

16. Deng, Q. Volatility dispersion trading. *SSRN Electron. J.* **2008**. . [CrossRef]

17. Wilmott, P. *Paul Wilmott Introduces Quantitative Finance*, 2nd ed.; John Wiley: Chichester, UK, 2008.

18. Black, F.; Scholes, M. The pricing of options and corporate liabilities. *J. Political Econ.* **1973**, *81*, 637–654. [CrossRef]

19. Jiang, X. Return dispersion and expected returns. *Financ. Mark. Portf. Manag.* **2010**, *24*, 107–135. [CrossRef]

20. Chichernea, S.C.; Holder, A.D.; Petkevich, A. Does return dispersion explain the accrual and investment anomalies? *J. Account. Econ.* **2015**, *60*, 133–148. [CrossRef]

21. Andersen, T.G.; Bollerslev, T. Answering the skeptics: Yes, standard volatility models do provide accurate forecasts. *Int. Econ. Rev.* **1998**, *39*, 885. [CrossRef]

22. Andersen, T.G.; Bollerslev, T.; Diebold, F.X.; Labys, P. The distribution of realized exchange rate volatility. *J. Am. Stat. Assoc.* **2001**, *96*, 42–55. [CrossRef]

23. Barndorff-Nielsen, O.E.; Shephard, N. Estimating quadratic variation using realized variance. *J. Appl. Econom.* **2002**, *17*, 457–477. [CrossRef]

24. Markowitz, H. Portfolio selection. *J. Financ.* **1952**, *7*, 77.

25. Driessen, J.; Maenhout, P.J.; Vilkov, G. Option-implied correlations and the price of correlation risk. *SSRN Electron. J.* **2013**. [CrossRef]

26. Faria, G.; Kosowski, R.; Wang, T. The correlation risk premium: International evidence. *SSRN Electron. J.* **2018**. [CrossRef]

27. Bollen, N.P.B.; Whaley, R.E. Does net buying pressure affect the shape of implied volatility functions? *J. Financ.* **2004**, *59*, 711–753. [CrossRef]

28. Shiu, Y.M.; Pan, G.G.; Lin, S.H.; Wu, T.C. Impact of net buying pressure on changes in implied volatility: before and after the onset of the subprime crisis. *J. Deriv.* **2010**, *17*, 54–66. [CrossRef]

29. Ruan, X.; Zhang, J.E. The economics of the financial market for volatility trading. *J. Financ. Mark.* **2020**, 100556. [CrossRef]

30. Bakshi, G.; Kapadia, N. Delta-hedged gains and the negative market volatility risk premium. *Rev. Financ. Stud.* **2003**, *16*, 527–566. [CrossRef]

31. Ilmanen, A. Do financial markets reward buying or selling insurance and lottery tickets? *Financ. Anal. J.* **2012**, *68*, 26–36. [CrossRef]

32. Gatheral, J. *The Volatility Surface: A Practitioner's Guide*; John Wiley & Sons, Inc.: Hoboken, NJ, USA, 2006.

33. Crépey, S. Delta-hedging vega risk? *Quant. Financ.* **2004**, *4*, 559–579. [CrossRef]

34. Jegadeesh, N.; Titman, S. Returns to buying winners and selling losers: Implications for stock market efficiency. *J. Financ.* **1993**, *48*, 65–91. [CrossRef]

35. R Core Team. *Stats: A Language and Environment for Statistical Computing*; R Core Team: Vienna, Austria, 2019.

36. Do, B.; Faff, R. Are pairs trading profits robust to trading costs? *J. Financ. Res.* **2012**, *35*, 261–287. [CrossRef]

37. Stübinger, J.; Schneider, L. Statistical arbitrage with mean-reverting overnight price gaps on high-frequency data of the S&P 500. *J. Risk Financ. Manag.* **2019**, *12*, 51.

38. Korajczyk, R.A.; Sadka, R. Are momentum profits robust to trading costs? *J. Financ.* **2004**, *59*, 1039–1082. [CrossRef]

39. Wold, S.; Esbensen, K.; Geladi, P. Principal component analysis. *Chemom. Intell. Lab. Syst.* **1987**, *2*, 37–52. [CrossRef]

40. Abdi, H.; Williams, L.J. Principal component analysis. *Wiley Interdiscip. Rev. Comput. Stat.* **2010**, *2*, 433–459. [CrossRef]

41. Su, X. Hedging Basket Options by Using A Subset of Underlying Assets (Working Paper). 2006. Available online: https://www.econstor.eu/bitstream/10419/22959/1/bgse14_2006.pdf (accessed on 16 August 2020).

42. von Beschwitz, B.; Massa, M. Biased short: Short sellers' disposition effect and limits to arbitrage. *J. Financ. Mark.* **2020**, *49*, 100512. [CrossRef]

43. Voya Investment Management. The Impact of Equity Market Fragmentation and Dark Pools on Trading and Alpha Generation. 2016. Available online: https://investments.voya.com (accessed on 16 August 2020).

44. Frazzini, A.; Israel, R.; Moskowitz, T.J. Trading costs. *SSRN Electron. J.* **2018**. [CrossRef]

45. Henderson, R. Schwab Opens New front in Trading War by Slashing Rates to Zero. Financial Times. 2019. Available online: https://www.ft.com/content/cf644610-e45a-11e9-9743-db5a370481bc (accessed on 16 August 2020).

46. Avellaneda, M.; Lee, J.H. Statistical arbitrage in the US equities market. *Quant. Financ.* **2010**, *10*, 761–782. [CrossRef]

47. Cboe Global Markets, I. Chicago Board Options Exchange Margin Manual. 2000. Available online: https://www.cboe.com/learncenter/pdf/margin2-00.pdf (accessed on 16 August 2020).

48. Stübinger, J.; Endres, S. Pairs trading with a mean-reverting jump-diffusion model on high-frequency data. *Quant. Financ.* **2018**, *18*, 1735–1751. [CrossRef]

49. Mina, J.; Xiao, J.Y. Return to RiskMetrics: The evolution of a standard. *Riskmetrics Group* **2001**, *1*, 1–11.

50. Stübinger, J.; Mangold, B.; Krauss, C. Statistical arbitrage with vine copulas. *Quant. Financ.* **2018**, *18*, 1831–1849. [CrossRef]

51. Liu, B.; Chang, L.B.; Geman, H. Intraday pairs trading strategies on high frequency data: The case of oil companies. *Quant. Financ.* **2017**, *17*, 87–100. [CrossRef]

52. Knoll, J.; Stübinger, J.; Grottke, M. Exploiting social media with higher-order factorization machines: Statistical arbitrage on high-frequency data of the S&P 500. *Quant. Financ.* **2019**, *19*, 571–585.

53. Stübinger, J. Statistical arbitrage with optimal causal paths on high-frequency data of the S&P 500. *Quant. Financ.* **2019**, *19*, 921–935.

54. Endres, S.; Stübinger, J. Regime-switching modeling of high-frequency stock returns with Lévy jumps. *Quant. Financ.* **2019**, *19*, 1727–1740. [CrossRef]

55. Degiannakis, S.; Filis, G.; Hassani, H. Forecasting global stock market implied volatility indices. *J. Empir. Financ.* **2018**, *46*, 111–129. [CrossRef]

56. Fang, T.; Lee, T.H.; Su, Z. Predicting the long-term stock market volatility: A GARCH-MIDAS model with variable selection. *J. Empir. Financ.* **2020**, *58*, 36–49. [CrossRef]

57. Naimy, V.; Montero, J.M.; El Khoury, R.; Maalouf, N. Market volatility of the three most powerful military countries during their intervention in the Syrian War. *Mathematics* **2020**, *8*, 834. [CrossRef]

58. Fama, E.F.; French, K.R. Multifactor explanations of asset pricing anomalies. *J. Financ.* **1996**, *51*, 55–84. [CrossRef]

59. Fama, E.F.; French, K.R. A five-factor asset pricing model. *J. Financ. Econ.* **2015**, *116*, 1–22. [CrossRef]

60. Yoshino, N.; Taghizadeh-Hesary, F. Analysis of credit ratings for small and medium-sized enterprises: Evidence from Asia. *Asian Dev. Rev.* **2015**, *32*, 18–37. [CrossRef]

61. Bartlett, M.S. The effect of standardization on a χ^2 approximation in factor analysis. *Biometrika* **1951**, *38*, 337–344. [CrossRef]

62. Kaiser, H.F. A second generation little jiffy. *Psychometrika* **1970**, *35*, 401–415. [CrossRef]

63. Kaiser, H. An index of factorial simplicity. *Psychometrika* **1974**, *39*, 31–36. [CrossRef]

64. Kaiser, H.F.; Rice, J. Little jiffy, Mark Iv. *Educ. Psychol. Meas.* **1974**, *34*, 111–117. [CrossRef]

65. Sharpe, W.F. Capital asset prices: A theory of market equilibrium under conditions of risk. *J. Financ.* **1964**, *19*, 425–442.

66. Lintner, J. The valuation of risk assets and the selection of risky investments in stock portfolios and capital budgets. *Rev. Econ. Stat.* **1965**, *47*, 13–37. [CrossRef]

Permissions

The contributors of this book come from diverse backgrounds, making this book a truly international effort. This book will bring forth new frontiers with its revolutionizing research information and detailed analysis of the nascent developments around the world.

We would like to thank all the contributing authors for lending their expertise to make the book truly unique. They have played a crucial role in the development of this book. Without their invaluable contributions this book wouldn't have been possible. They have made vital efforts to compile up to date information on the varied aspects of this subject to make this book a valuable addition to the collection of many professionals and students.

This book was conceptualized with the vision of imparting up-to-date information and advanced data in this field. To ensure the same, a matchless editorial board was set up. Every individual on the board went through rigorous rounds of assessment to prove their worth. After which they invested a large part of their time researching and compiling the most relevant data for our readers.

The editorial board has been involved in producing this book since its inception. They have spent rigorous hours researching and exploring the diverse topics which have resulted in the successful publishing of this book. They have passed on their knowledge of decades through this book. To expedite this challenging task, the publisher supported the team at every step. A small team of assistant editors was also appointed to further simplify the editing procedure and attain best results for the readers.

Apart from the editorial board, the designing team has also invested a significant amount of their time in understanding the subject and creating the most relevant covers. They scrutinized every image to scout for the most suitable representation of the subject and create an appropriate cover for the book.

The publishing team has been an ardent support to the editorial, designing and production team. Their endless efforts to recruit the best for this project, has resulted in the accomplishment of this book. They are a veteran in the field of academics and their pool of knowledge is as vast as their experience in printing. Their expertise and guidance has proved useful at every step. Their uncompromising quality standards have made this book an exceptional effort. Their encouragement from time to time has been an inspiration for everyone.

The publisher and the editorial board hope that this book will prove to be a valuable piece of knowledge for researchers, students, practitioners and scholars across the globe.

List of Contributors

Marc Pierre Henrard
muRisQ Advisory, 8B-1210 Brussels, Belgium
University College London, London WC1E 6BT, UK

Francesco Rundo
STMicroelectronics Srl-ADG Central R&D, 95121 Catania, Italy

Francesca Trenta and Sebastiano Battiato
IPLAB — Department of Mathematics and Computer Science, University of Catania, 95121 Catania, Italy

Agatino Luigi di Stallo
GIURIMATICA Lab, Department of Applied Mathematics and LawTech, 97100 Ragusa, Italy

Jong-Min Kim
Statistics Discipline, University of Minnesota at Morris, Morris, MN 56267, USA

Seong-Tae Kim
Department of Mathematics, North Carolina A&T State University, Greensboro, NC 27411, USA

Sangjin Kim
Department of Management and Information Systems, Dong-A University, Busan 49236, Korea

Jukka Isohätälä
Institute of Operations Research and Analytics, National University of Singapore, 3 Research Link, Innovation 4.0 04-01, Singapore 117602, Singapore

Alistair Milne
School of Business and Economics, Loughborough University, Epinal Way, Loughborough LE11 3TU, UK

Donald Robertson
Faculty of Economics, University of Cambridge, Cambridge CB3 9DD, UK

José Pedro Ramos-Requena and Juan Evangelista Trinidad-Segovia
Department of Economics and Business, University of Almería, Ctra. Sacramento s/n, La Cañada de San Urbano, 04120 Almería, Spain

Miguel Ángel Sánchez-Granero
Department of Matematics, University of Almería, Ctra. Sacramento s/n, La Cañada de San Urbano, 04120 Almería, Spain

Román Salmerón Gómez and Catalina García García
Department of Quantitative Methods for Economics and Business, University of Granada, 18010 Granada, Spain

Marta Bengoa
Colin Powell School, City University of New York (CUNY-CCNY), New York, NY 10031, USA
SARChI College of Business and Economics, University of Johannesburg South Africa, Senior Fellow at CIRANO, Montreal, QC H2Y1C6, Canada

Blanca Sanchez-Robles
Department of Economic Analysis at UNED University, 28040 Madrid, Spain

Yochanan Shachmurove
The City College and Graduate Center of the City University of New York (CUNY-CCNY), New York, NY 10031, USA
Faculty of Management at The University of Warsaw, 00-927Warsaw, Poland

Ainara Rodríguez Sánchez
Department of Economic Theory and History, University of Granada, 18010 Granada, Spain

José García Pérez
Department of Economy and Company, University of Almería, 04120 Almería, Spain

Prosper Lamothe-Fernández
Department of Financing and Commercial Research, UDI of Financing, Calle Francisco Tomás y Valiente, 5, Universidad Autónoma de Madrid, 28049 Madrid, Spain

David Alaminos
Department of Economic Theory and Economic History, Campus El Ejido s/n, University of Malaga, 29071 Malaga, Spain

Prosper Lamothe-López
Rho Finanzas Partner, Calle de Zorrilla, 21, 28014 Madrid, Spain

Manuel A. Fernández-Gámez
Department of Finance and Accounting, Campus El Ejido s/n, University of Malaga, 29071 Malaga, Spain

Viviane Naimy and Rim El Khoury
Faculty of Business Administration and Economics, Notre Dame University—Louaize, Zouk Mikayel, Zouk Mosbeh 72, Lebanon

José-María Montero
Department of Political Economy and Public Finance, Economic and Business Statistics, and Economic Policy, Faculty of Law and Social Sciences, University of Castilla-La Mancha, 45071 Toledo, Spain

Nisrine Maalouf
Financial Risk Management—Faculty of Business Administration and Economics, Notre Dame University—Louaize, Zouk Mikayel, Zouk Mosbeh 72, Lebanon

Lucas Schneider and Johannes Stübinger
Department of Statistics and Econometrics, University of Erlangen-Nürnberg, Lange Gasse 20, 90403 Nürnberg, Germany

Index

A

Abbreviations, 14, 137

Analogy, 52

Anatomy, 145

Autoregressive Integrated Moving Average, 16-18, 30, 177

B

Bankruptcy, 52, 62, 214

Brownian Motion, 82, 85, 211

C

Cancer, 35

Capital Markets, 96-97

Cash Flow, 5, 9, 51-52, 54, 56, 58, 66, 68, 75

Chemotherapy, 35

Clauses, 118-119, 127, 135, 137-138

Coefficient of Variation, 103, 107, 110, 113, 161-162, 166

Coefficients of Variation, 103, 111-112, 158, 162, 164, 169

Composition, 5-9, 12, 216-217

Computational Intelligence, 33-34

Computational Linguistics, 35

Conceptualization, 32, 91, 113, 136, 169, 187, 200

Confidence Interval, 167-168

Conflict Resolution, 120

Convergence, 20

Copulas, 38, 43, 230

Cryptography, 176-177

G

Gross Domestic Product, 117, 126, 137

H

Hash Function, 181

Hedge Funds, 97, 210, 214

Heterogeneity, 117-118, 124-125, 128, 132

Hurst Exponent, 82-83, 85-90, 92-97, 229

I

Identity Matrix, 149-150, 226

Inflation, 99-102, 104, 113-114, 148-151, 160, 168, 175, 209

Information Systems, 34, 36

Information Technology, 34

Integer, 77

Inventory, 53, 80-81

Investment, 28, 36-37, 40, 51-55, 57-58, 60, 62, 67-68, 71, 75, 80-82, 96-97, 116-120, 122-123, 126-127, 131-133, 135-138, 140-141, 145-147, 186, 222-223, 225, 229-230

L

Labor Costs, 122, 131

Labor Markets, 131

Law Enforcement, 141

Legal Framework, 5

Liabilities, 53, 229

Linear Equations, 77

Linear Regression, 19, 23, 85-86, 99, 101, 108, 111, 113-115, 174-175

Long Short-term Memory, 20, 26, 30, 33, 177

Lung Cancer, 35

M

Machine Learning, 16-17, 19, 27, 29-30, 33-34, 186-188

Marginal Product, 140

Market Analysis, 96

Market Equilibrium, 231

Market Price, 37, 49, 82-83

Monetary Policy, 9, 12

Money Markets, 54

Monte Carlo Simulation, 189, 198

Multiple Periods, 53

Multivariate Analysis, 192

N

Natural Language Processing, 29

Net Profit, 215

Non-profit Organization, 30

Non-small Cell Lung Cancer, 35

Nucleotides, 97

P

Pattern Recognition, 19, 33, 35

Perturbation, 159, 165

Physical Capital, 55

Policy Analysis, 145

Policy Decisions, 12

Portfolio Construction, 27, 217

Principal Component Analysis, 149, 210, 217, 228, 230

Probability, 14, 63-67, 133, 166, 169, 174-175, 180, 194

Production Function, 55

Prognosis, 177
Purchasing Power, 128, 131, 177
Python, 217

R
Recurrent Neural Network, 21, 30, 34, 177, 187
Regeneration, 222
Regression Analysis, 26, 114
Reinforcement Learning, 17, 27-28, 30, 32, 35
Resolution, 120, 138
Risk Factor, 192, 211, 225-226

S
Scale Economies, 119

Signal Processing, 35
Social Media, 27, 230
Stock Market, 17-20, 23-24, 27-28, 30, 32-36, 46, 49, 83, 97, 191, 195, 199, 208-209, 230-231
Stock Prices, 18, 21, 26, 31, 34, 82

T
Time Series Analysis, 33
Total Assets, 210
Trade-offs, 136

V
Variables, 37-38, 40-41, 52, 54-55, 61, 71, 84, 99-100, 102-104, 106-109, 111-114, 120, 122, 124-126, 128-129, 131-133, 139, 141, 144, 148-152, 155, 158, 160-163, 168-169, 173-174, 176-178, 180-182, 184, 186, 193, 217, 226

Printed in the USA
CPSIA information can be obtained
at www.ICGtesting.com
JSHW051625061123
51533JS00005B/112